ra Hearts

Jun Mochizuki

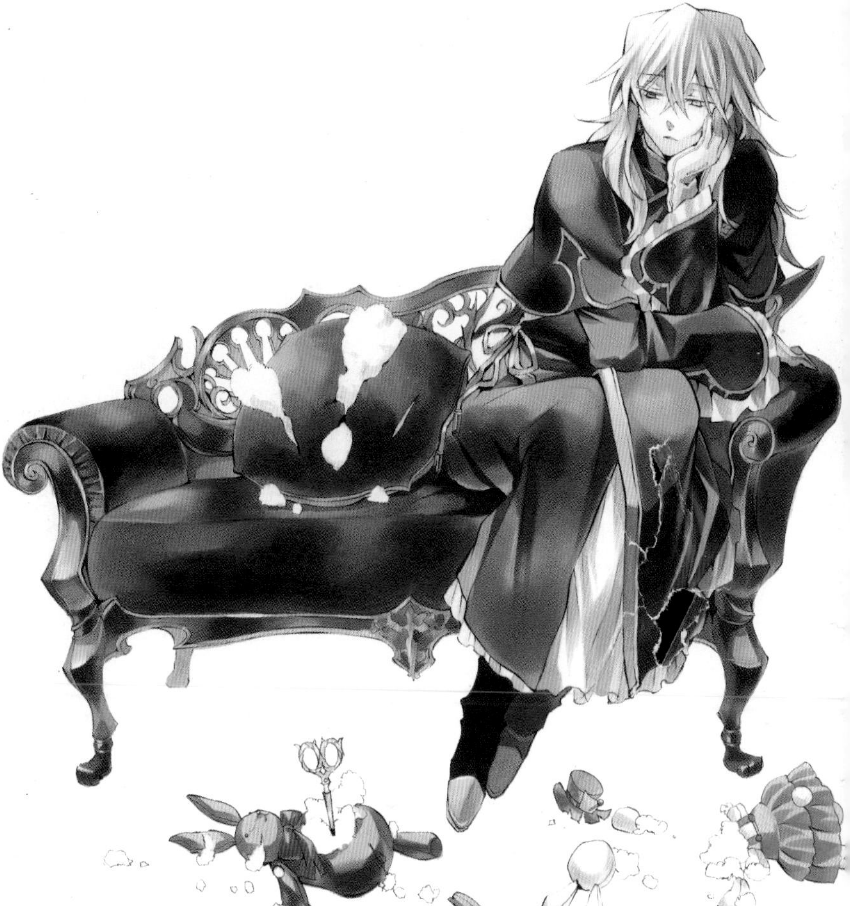

CONTENTS

Retrace : XIX
Detestably
3

Retrace : XX
Who killed poor Alice?
39

Retrace : XXI
Discord
81

Retrace : XXII
His name is···
129

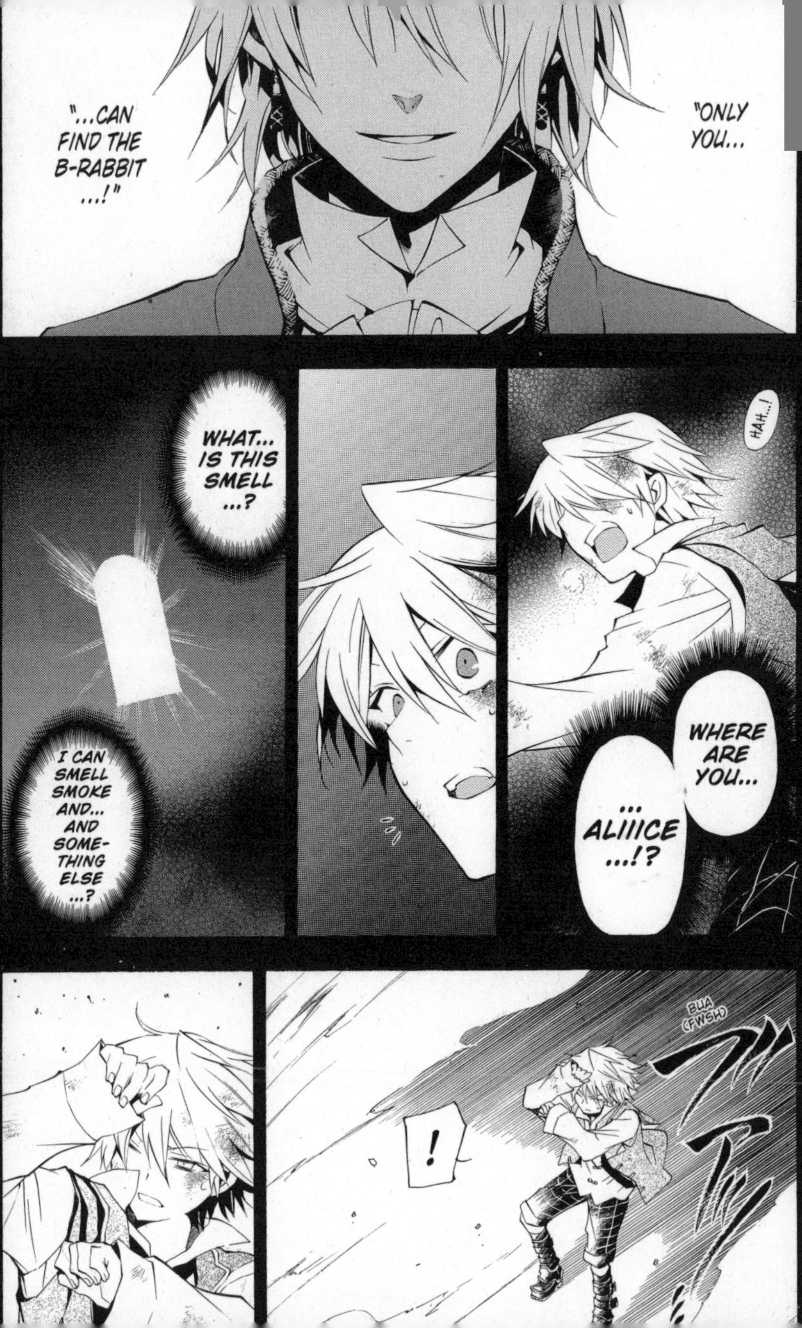
"ONLY YOU...
"...CAN FIND THE B-RABBIT ...!"
HAH...!
WHERE ARE YOU...
... ALIIICE ...!?
WHAT... IS THIS SMELL ...?
I CAN SMELL SMOKE AND... AND SOME-THING ELSE ...?
BUA (FWSH)
!

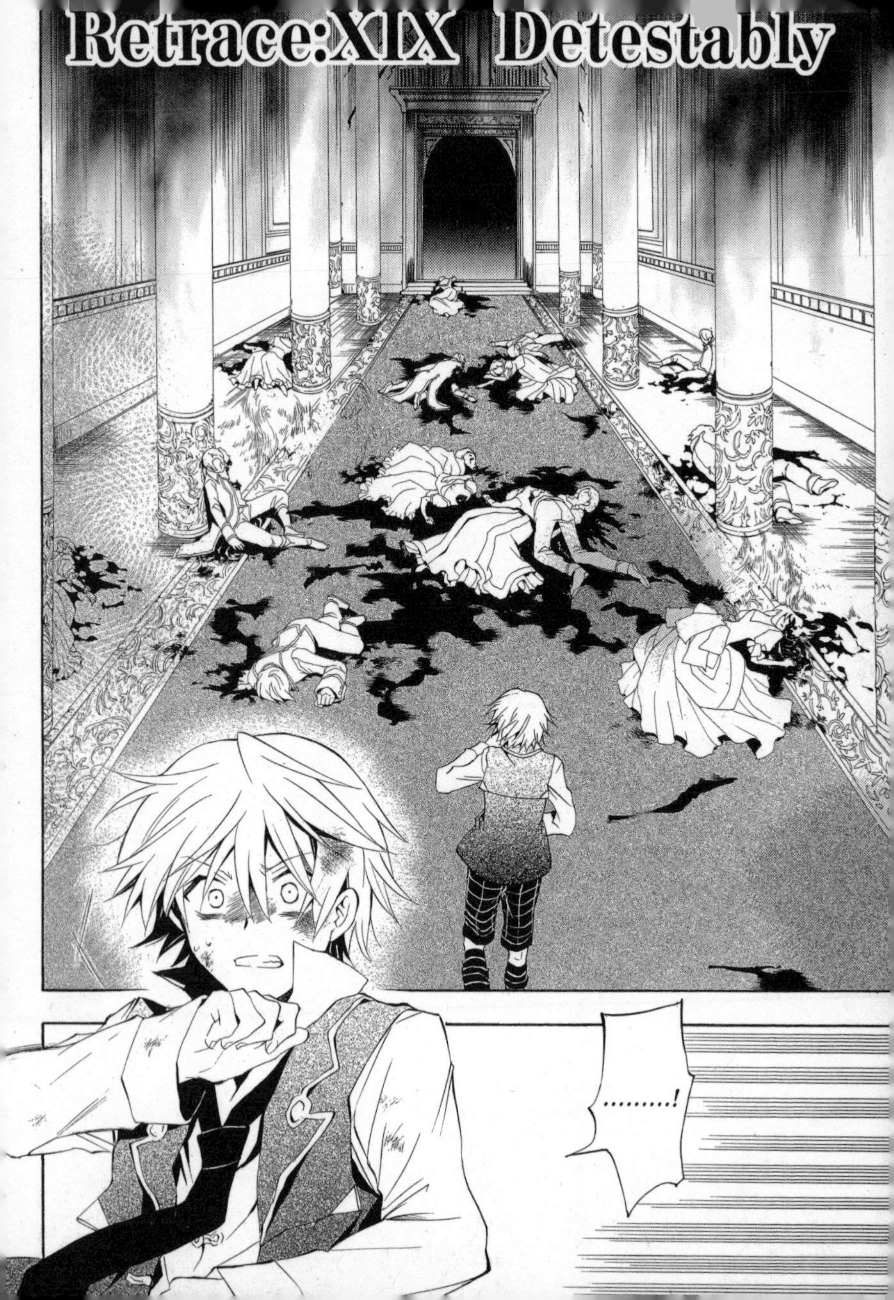
Retrace:XIX Detestably
..........!

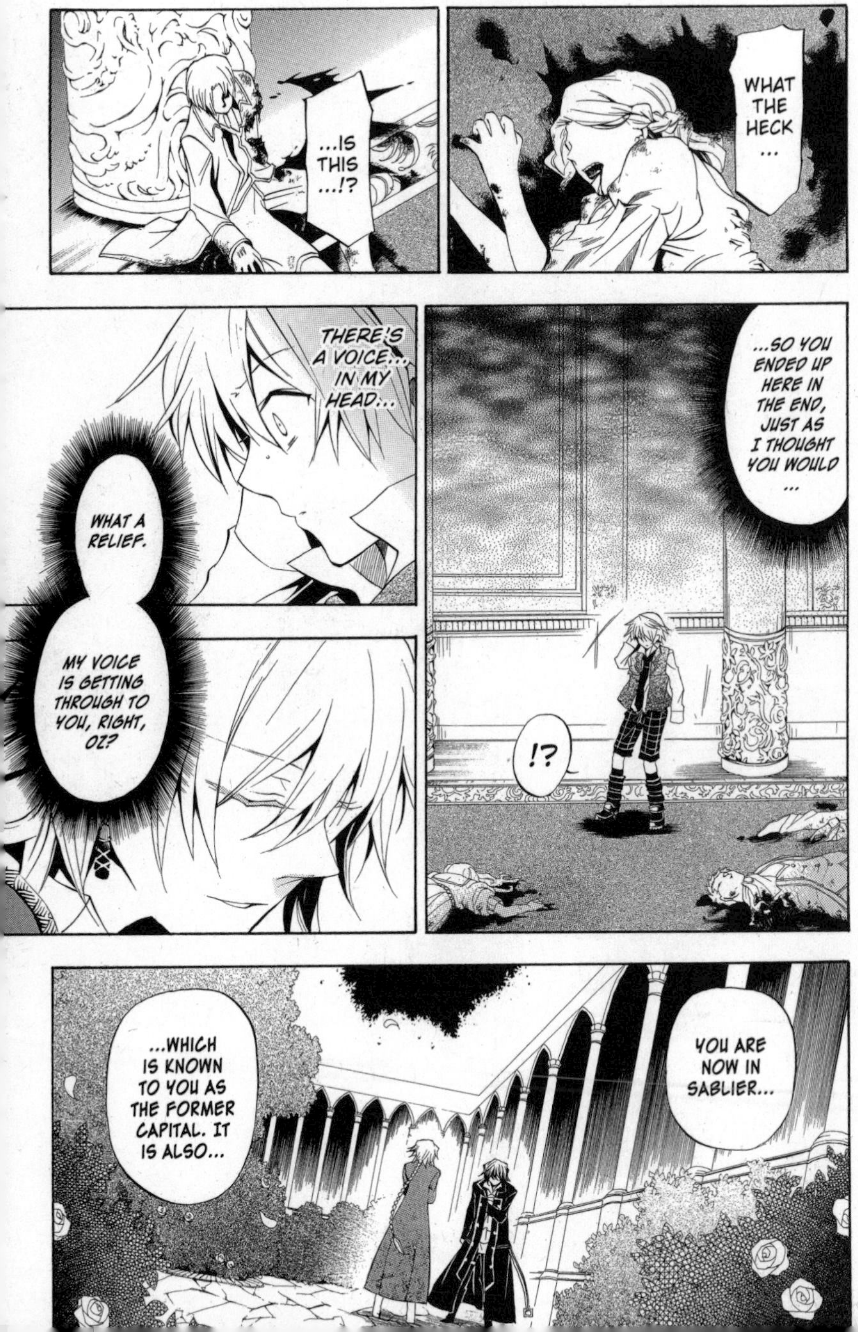
WHAT THE HECK ...
...IS THIS ...!?
...SO YOU ENDED UP HERE IN THE END, JUST AS I THOUGHT YOU WOULD ...
!?
THERE'S A VOICE... IN MY HEAD...
WHAT A RELIEF.
MY VOICE IS GETTING THROUGH TO YOU, RIGHT, OZ?
YOU ARE NOW IN SABLIER...
...WHICH IS KNOWN TO YOU AS THE FORMER CAPITAL. IT IS ALSO...

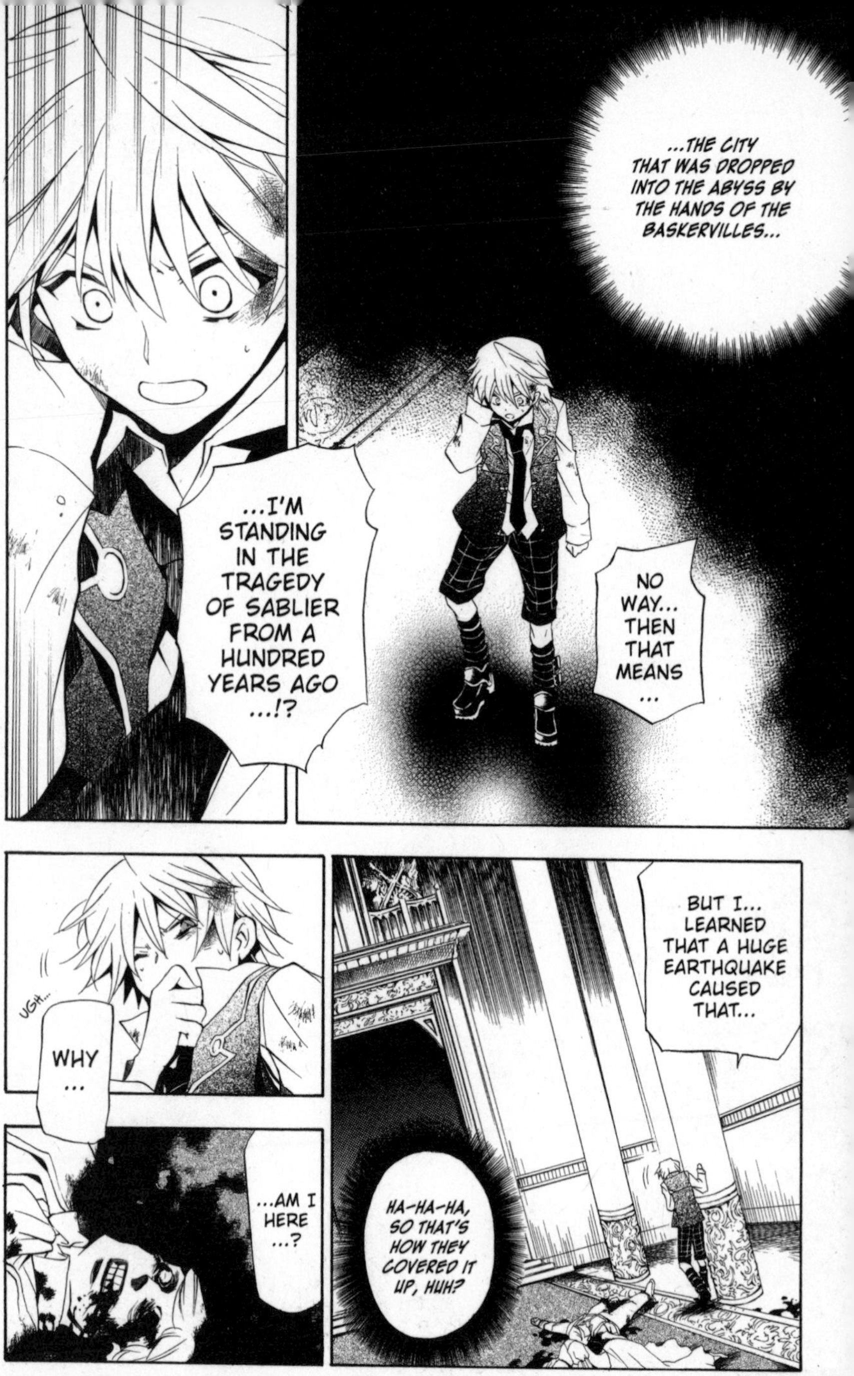
...THE CITY THAT WAS DROPPED INTO THE ABYSS BY THE HANDS OF THE BASKERVILLES...
NO WAY... THEN THAT MEANS...
...I'M STANDING IN THE TRAGEDY OF SABLIER FROM A HUNDRED YEARS AGO ...!?
BUT I... LEARNED THAT A HUGE EARTHQUAKE CAUSED THAT...
HA-HA-HA, SO THAT'S HOW THEY COVERED IT UP, HUH?
UGH...
WHY...
...AM I HERE ...?

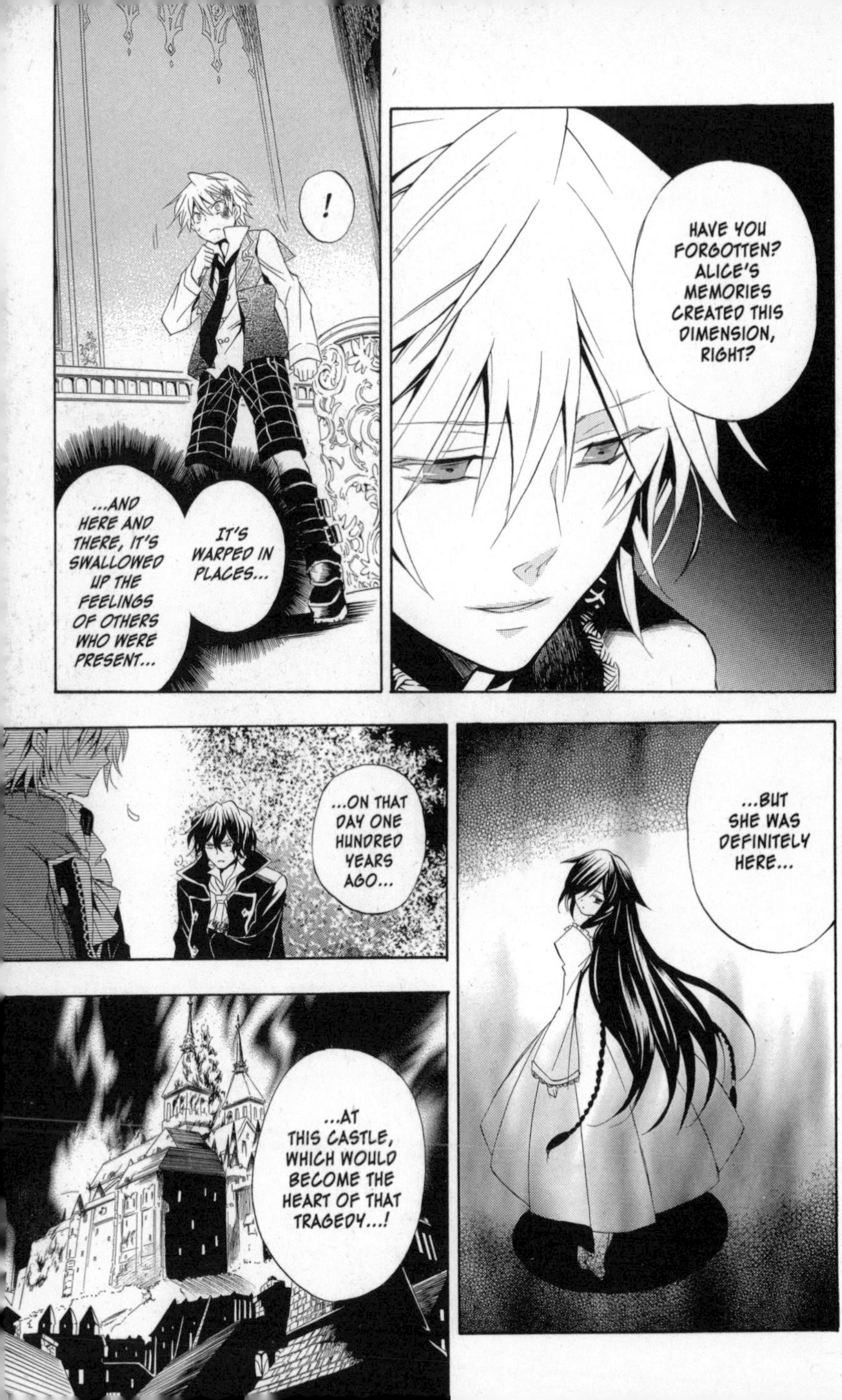
HAVE YOU FORGOTTEN? ALICE'S MEMORIES CREATED THIS DIMENSION, RIGHT?
!
IT'S WARPED IN PLACES...
...AND HERE AND THERE, IT'S SWALLOWED UP THE FEELINGS OF OTHERS WHO WERE PRESENT...
...BUT SHE WAS DEFINITELY HERE...
...ON THAT DAY ONE HUNDRED YEARS AGO...
...AT THIS CASTLE, WHICH WOULD BECOME THE HEART OF THAT TRAGEDY...!

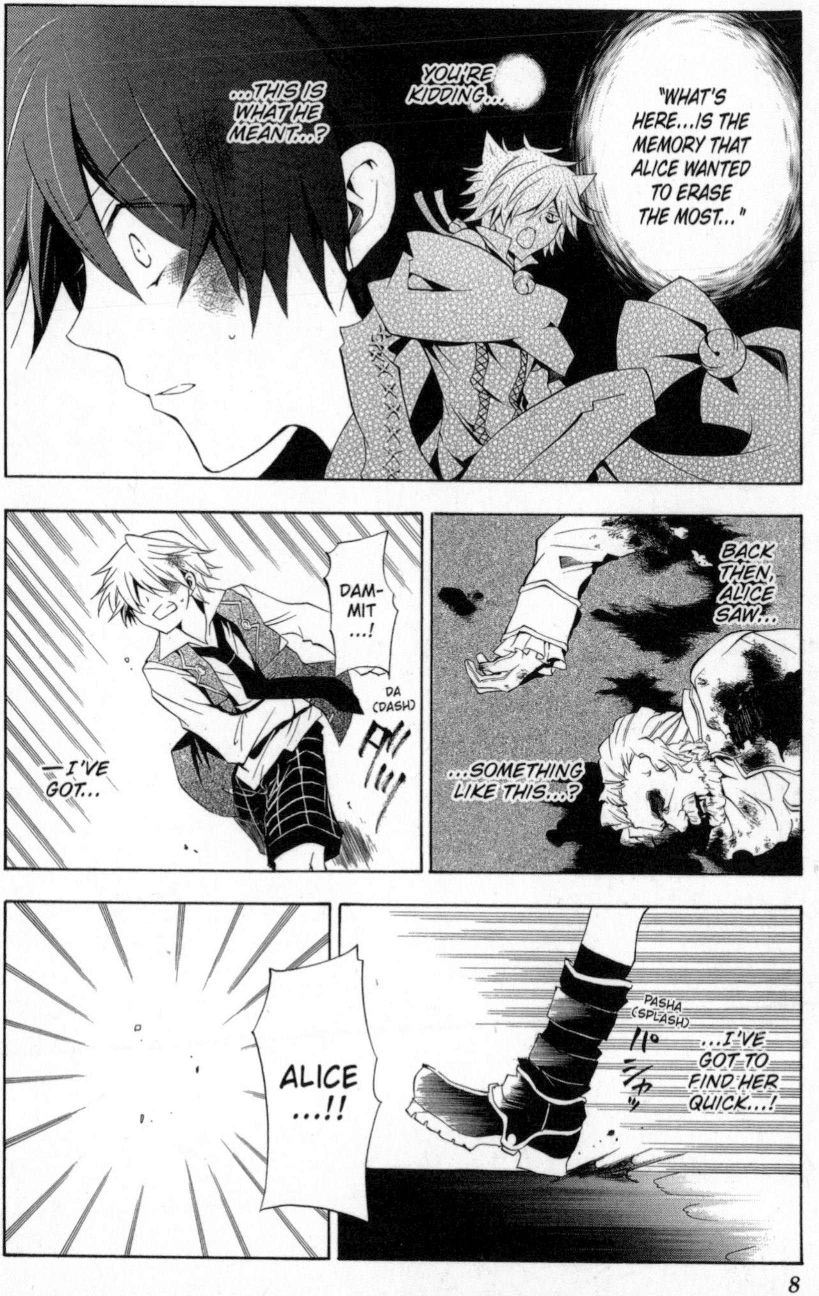
"WHAT'S HERE...IS THE MEMORY THAT ALICE WANTED TO ERASE THE MOST..."
YOU'RE KIDDING...
...THIS IS WHAT HE MEANT...?
BACK THEN, ALICE SAW...
...SOMETHING LIKE THIS...?
DAM-MIT ...!
DA (DASH)
—I'VE GOT...
PASHA (SPLASH)
...I'VE GOT TO FIND HER QUICK...!
ALICE ...!!

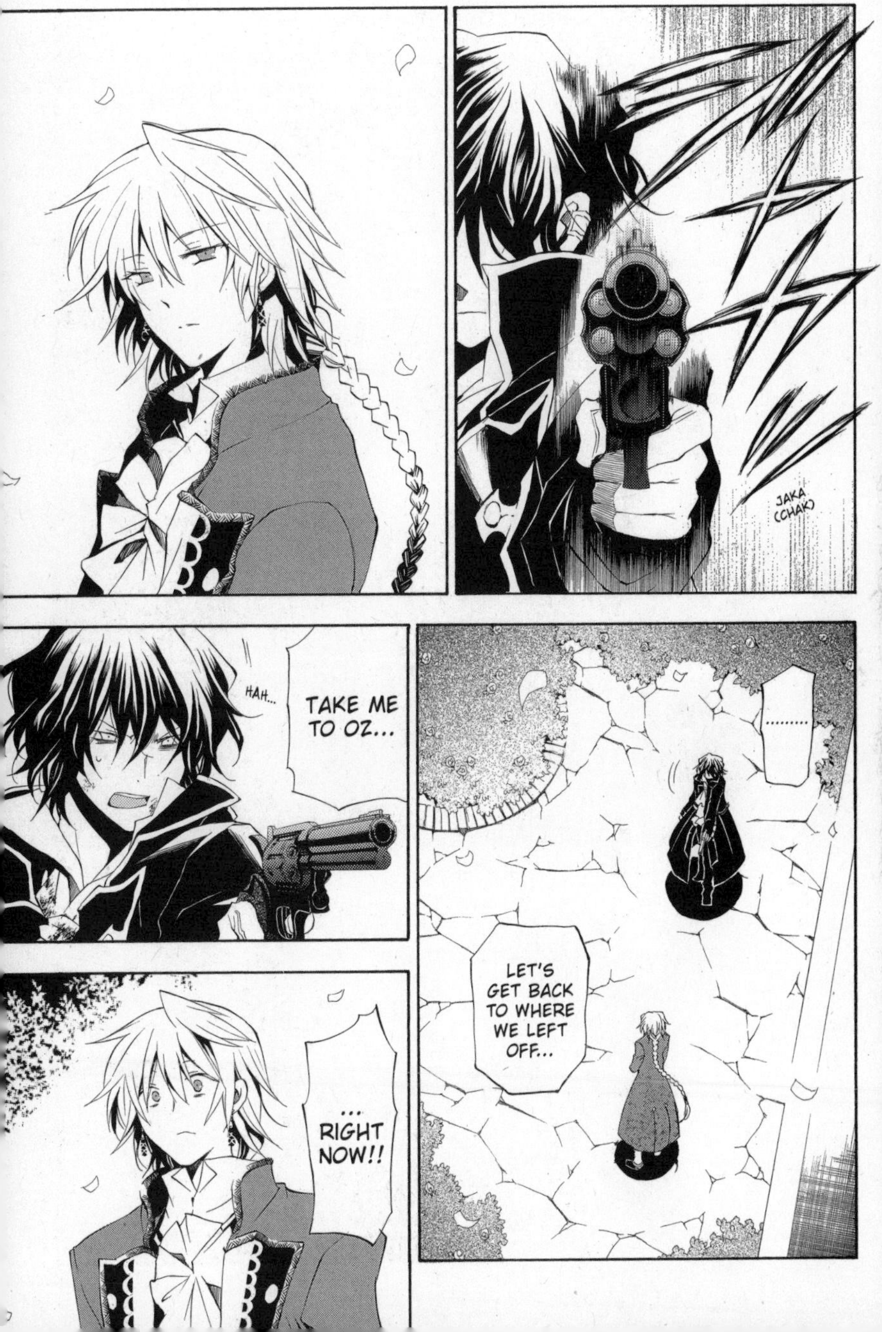
JAKA (CHAK)
....
LET'S GET BACK TO WHERE WE LEFT OFF...
HAH...
TAKE ME TO OZ...
... RIGHT NOW!!

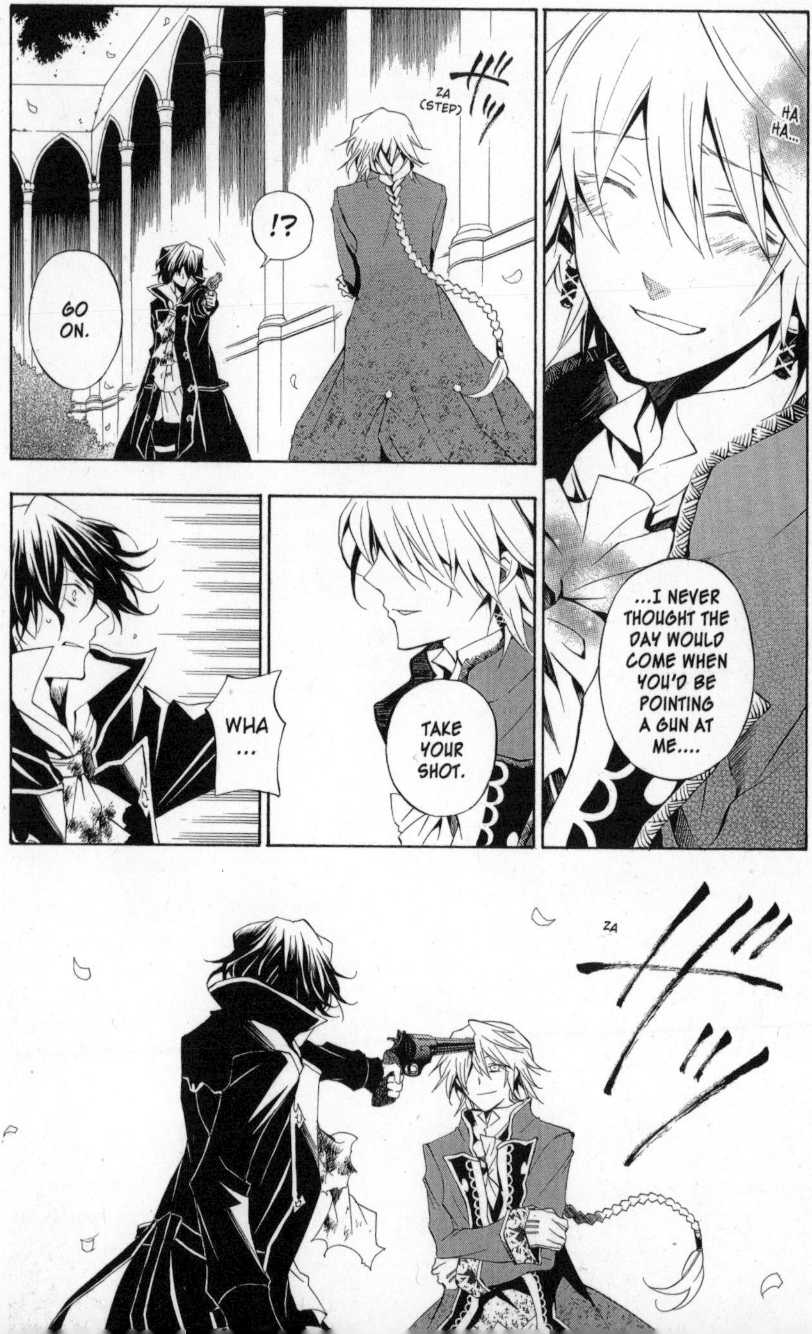
HA HA...
...I NEVER THOUGHT THE DAY WOULD COME WHEN YOU'D BE POINTING A GUN AT ME....
ZA (STEP)
!?
GO ON.
TAKE YOUR SHOT.
WHA ...
ZA

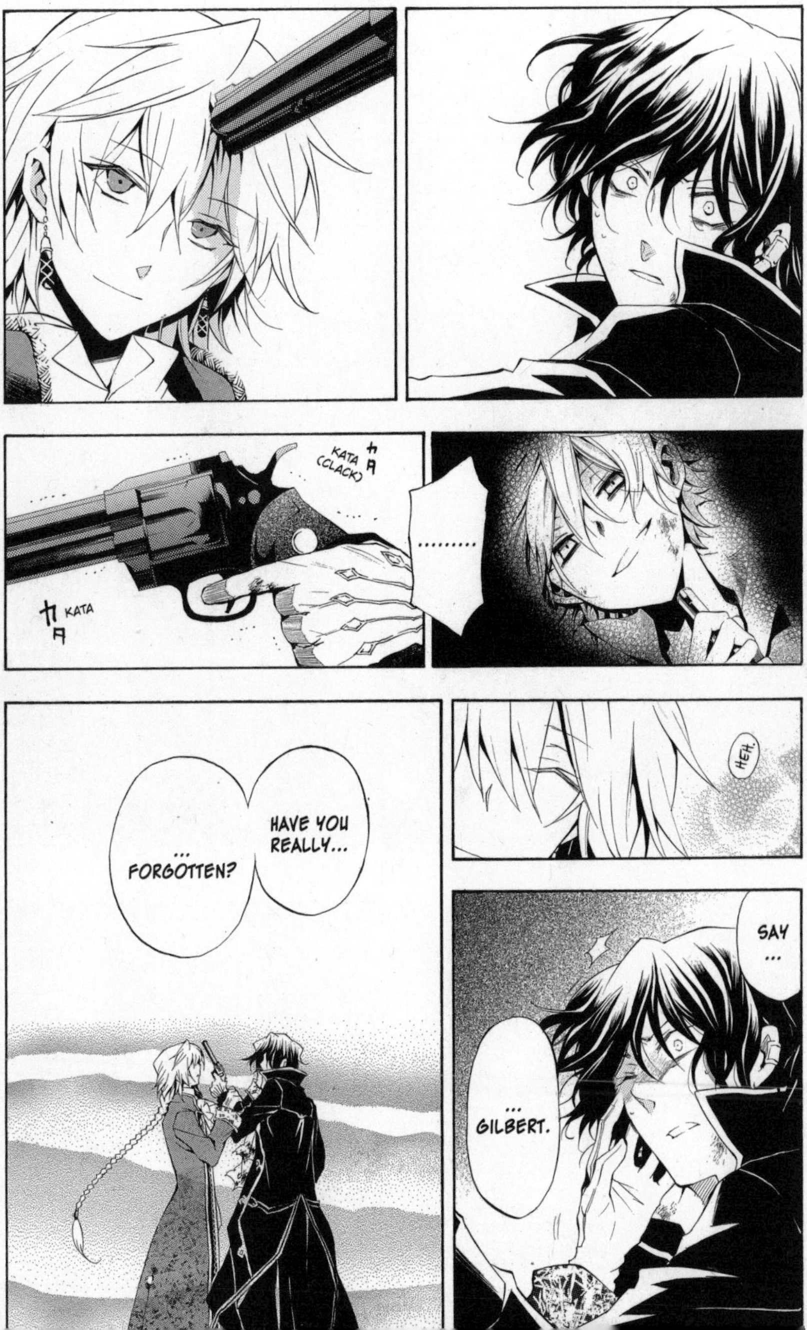
....
カタ
KATA (CLACK)
カタ
KATA
HEH.
SAY ...
... GILBERT.
HAVE YOU REALLY...
... FORGOTTEN?

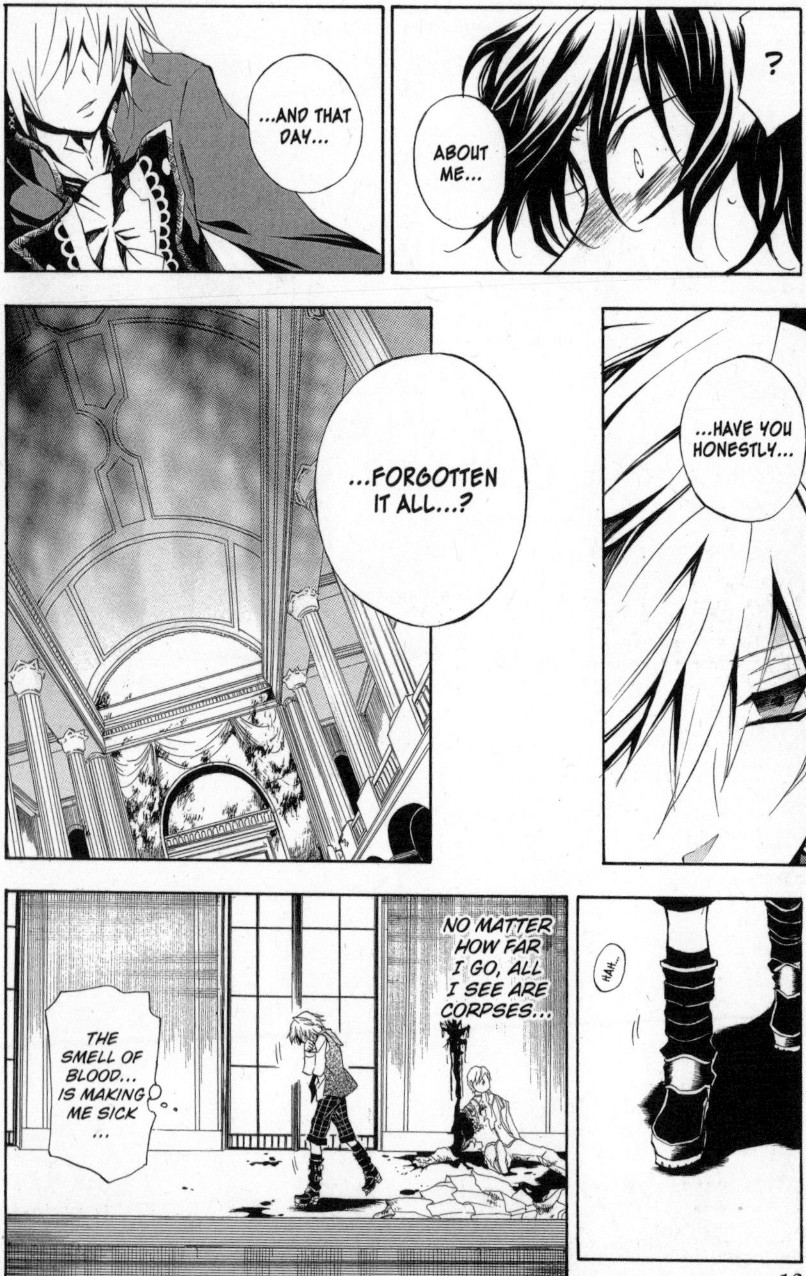
?
ABOUT ME...
...AND THAT DAY...
...HAVE YOU HONESTLY...
...FORGOTTEN IT ALL...?
HAH...
NO MATTER HOW FAR I GO, ALL I SEE ARE CORPSES...
THE SMELL OF BLOOD... IS MAKING ME SICK ...

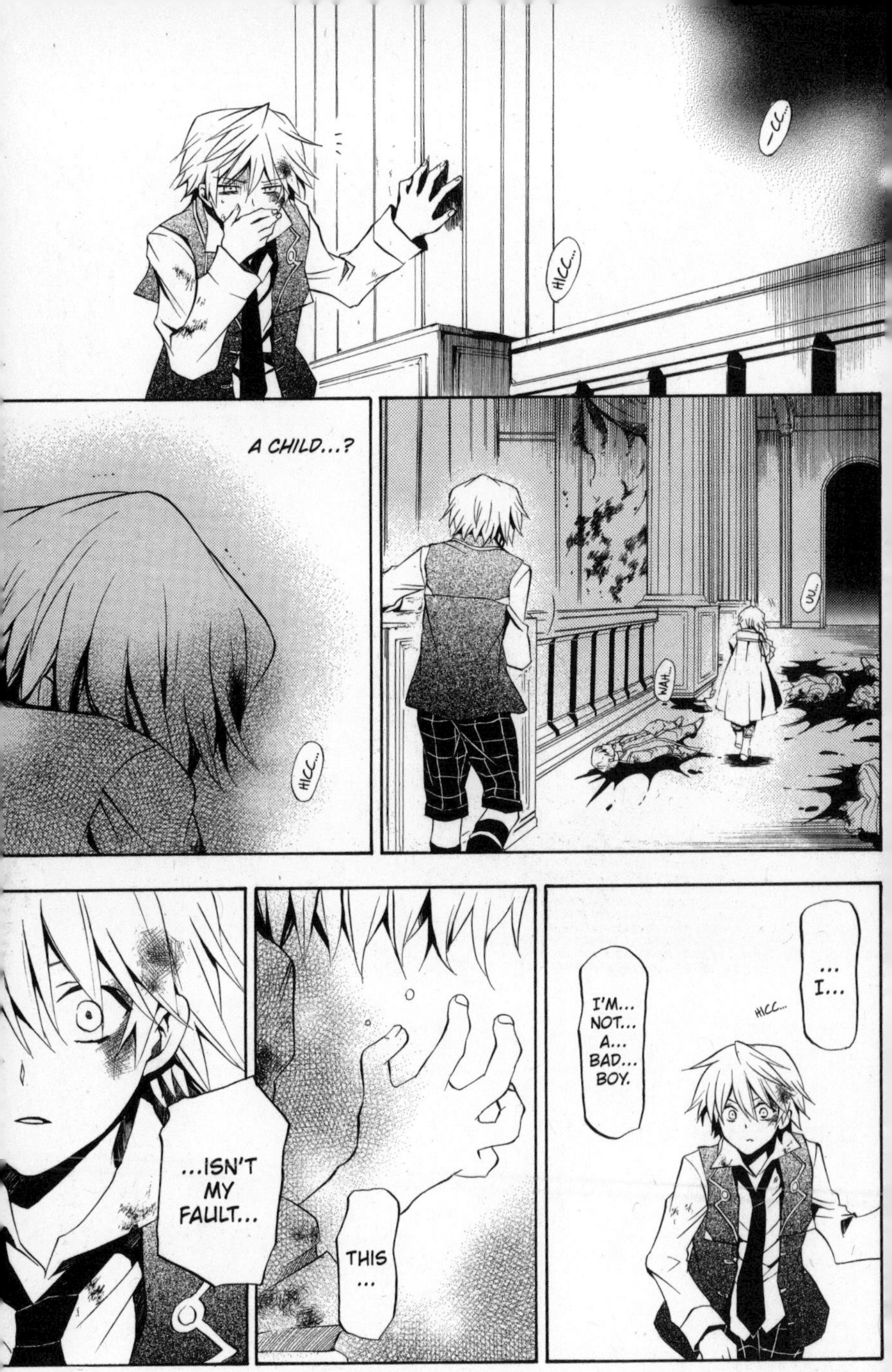

—UU...
HICC...
UU...
WAH...
A CHILD...?
HICC...
... I...
HICC...
I'M... NOT... A... BAD... BOY.
THIS ...
...ISN'T MY FAULT...

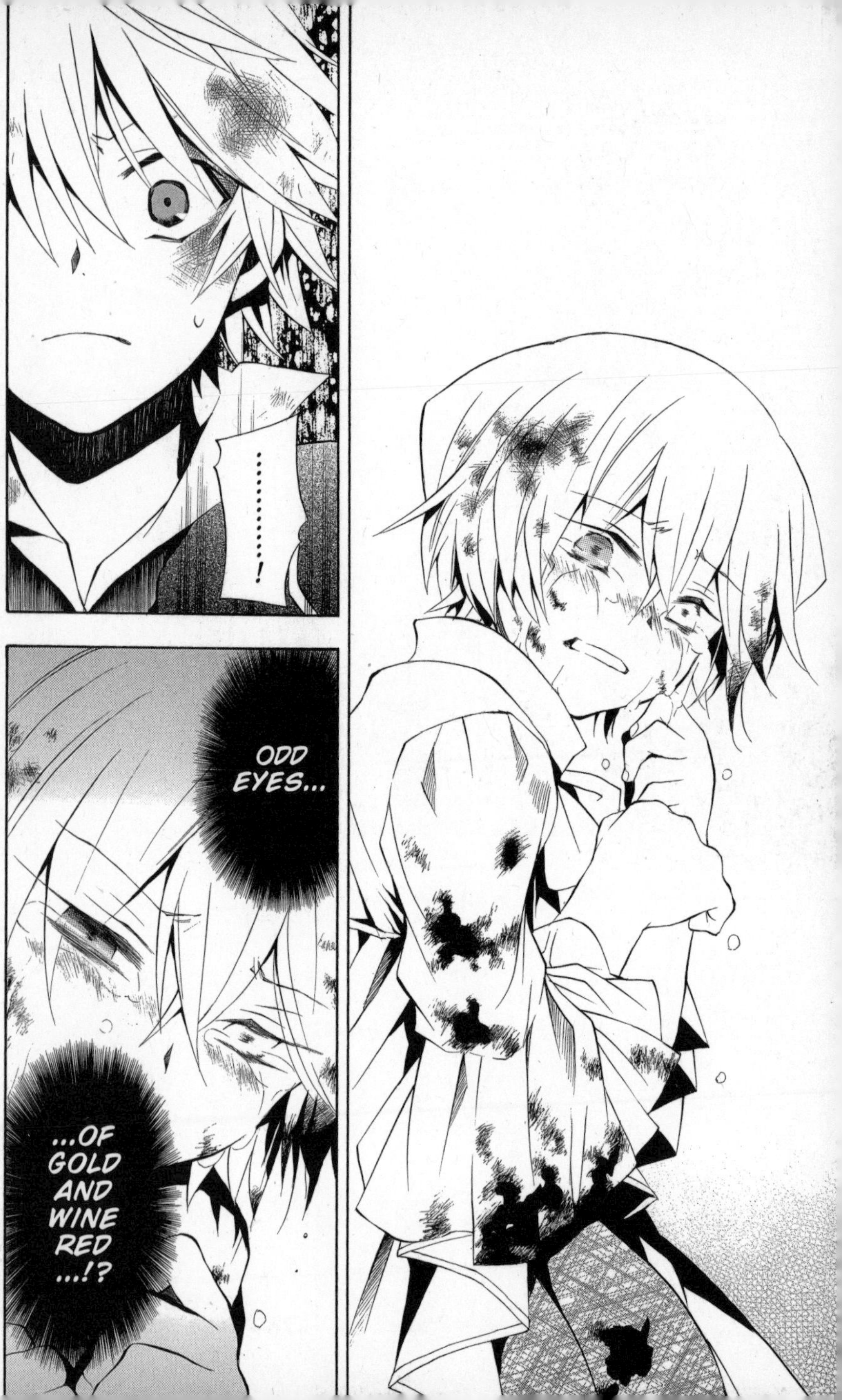
……!
ODD EYES...
...OF GOLD AND WINE RED ...!?

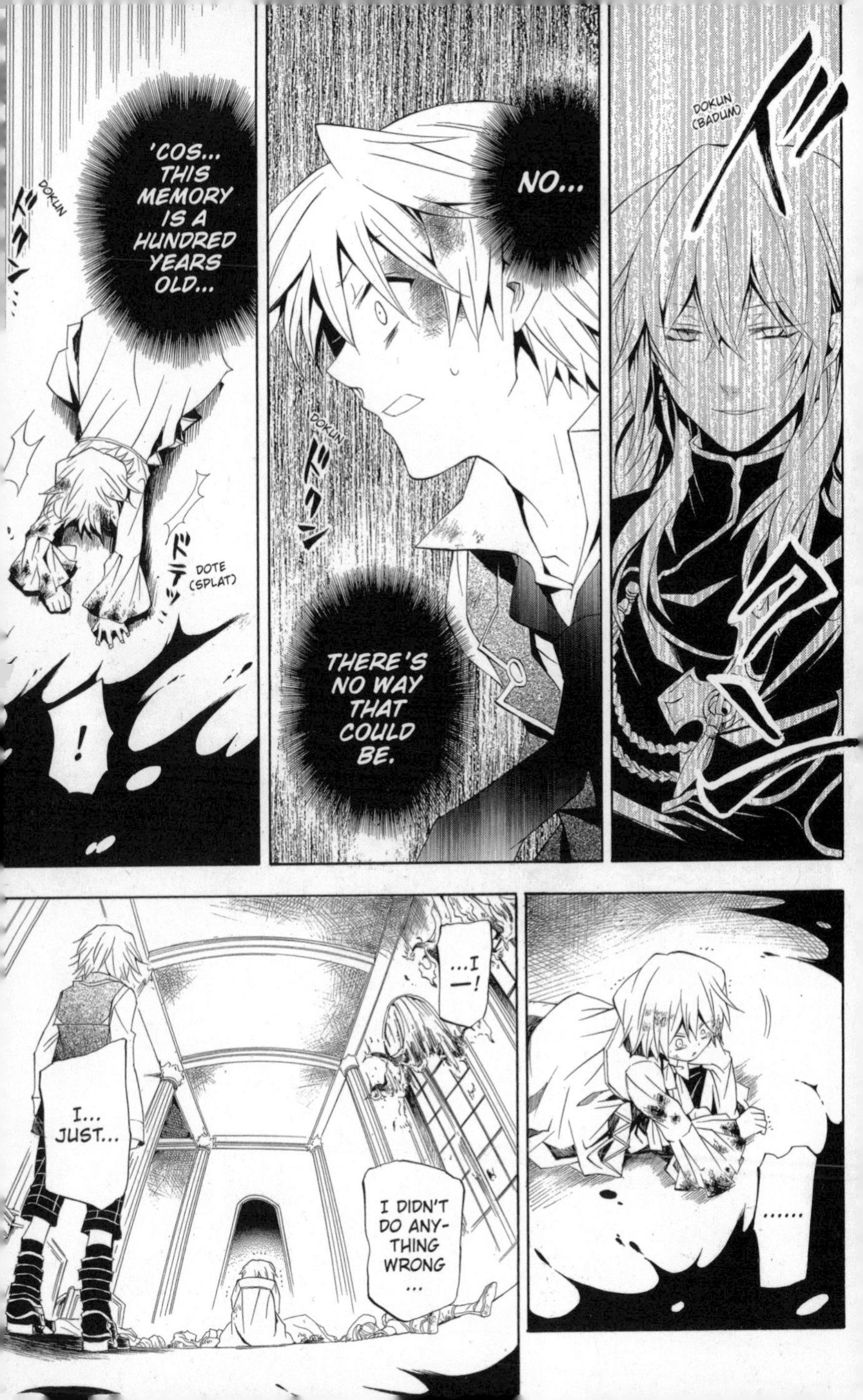

DOKUN (BADUM)
NO...
DOKUN
THERE'S NO WAY THAT COULD BE.
'COS... THIS MEMORY IS A HUNDRED YEARS OLD...
DOKUN
DOTE (SPLAT)
!
......
...I —!
I DIDN'T DO ANY-THING WRONG ...
I... JUST...

...JUST
—!

FOR GIL
—!!

...REALLY
VINCENT
...?

THEN...
HE'S...

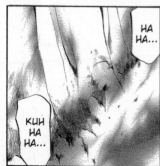

HA
HA...

KUH
HA
HA...

....

...
KUH.

...
HA.

16

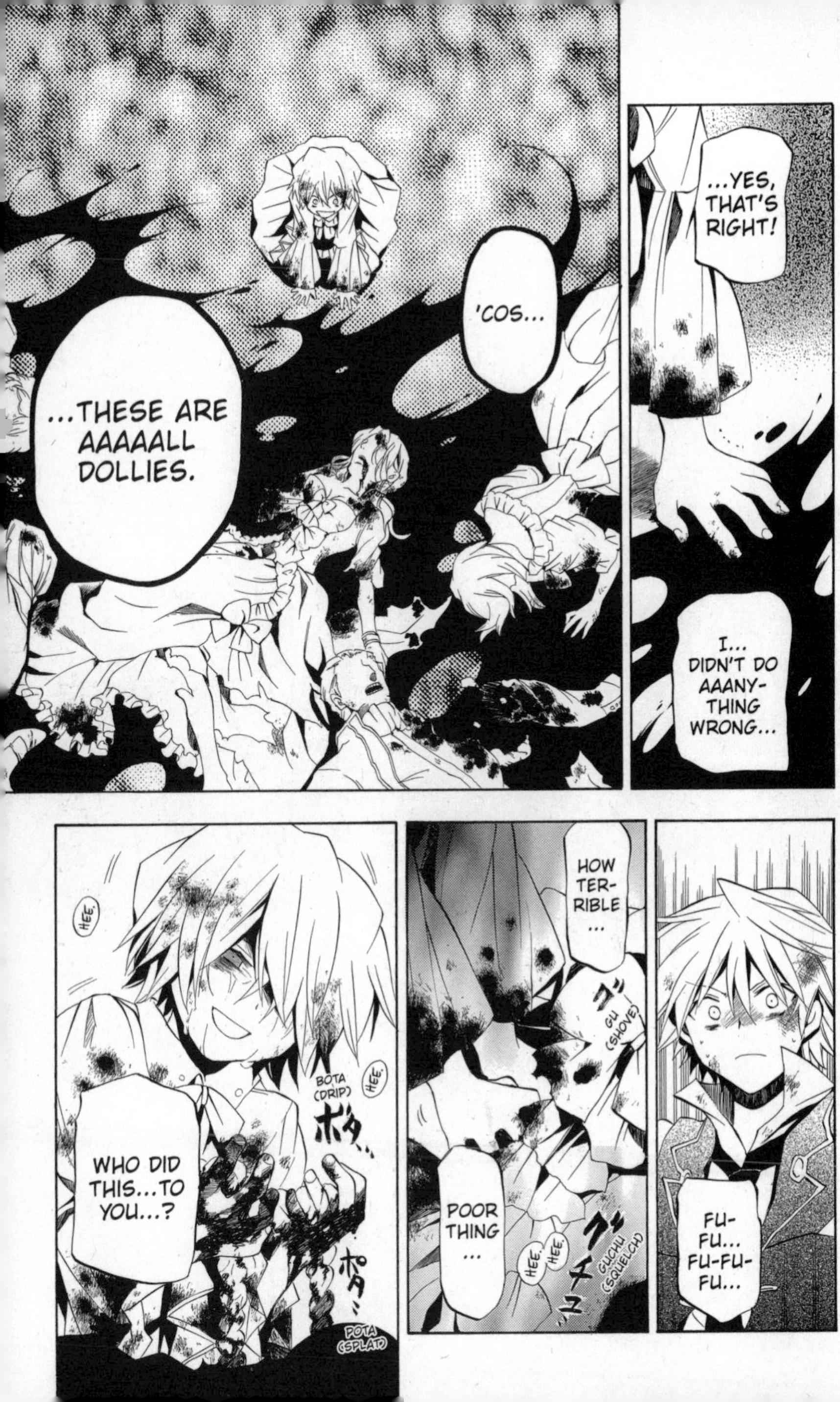
...YES, THAT'S RIGHT!
I... DIDN'T DO AAANY-THING WRONG...
'COS...
...THESE ARE AAAAALL DOLLIES.
FU-FU... FU-FU-FU...
HOW TER-RIBLE...
GU (SHOVE)
POOR THING...
HEE. HEE.
GUCHU (SQUELCH)
HEE.
BOTA (DRIP)
HEE.
WHO DID THIS...TO YOU...?
POTA (SPLAT)

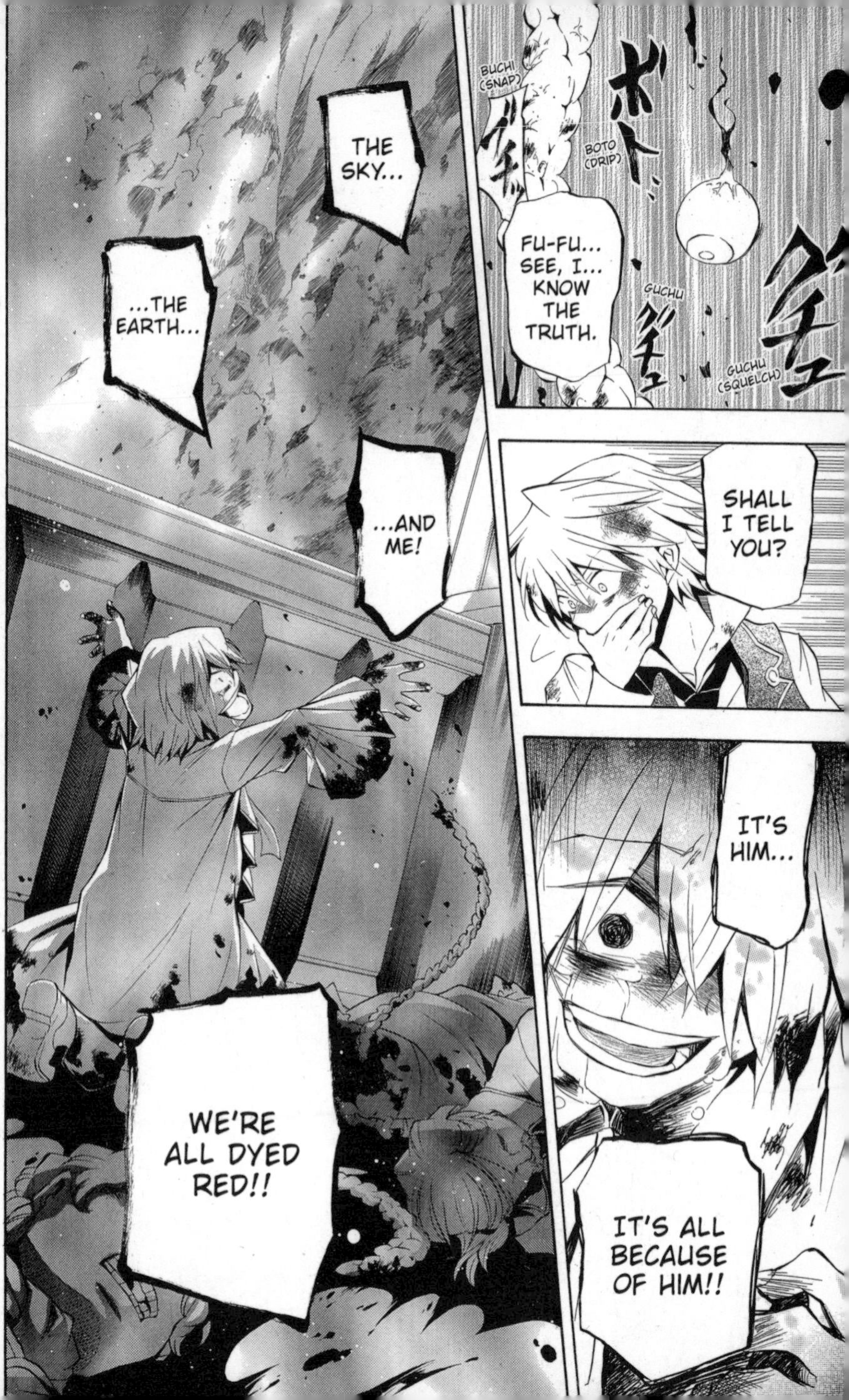
BUCHI (SNAP)
BOTO (DRIP)
GUCHU
GUCHU (SQUELCH)
FU-FU... SEE, I... KNOW THE TRUTH.
SHALL I TELL YOU?
IT'S HIM...
IT'S ALL BECAUSE OF HIM!!
THE SKY...
...THE EARTH...
...AND ME!
WE'RE ALL DYED RED!!

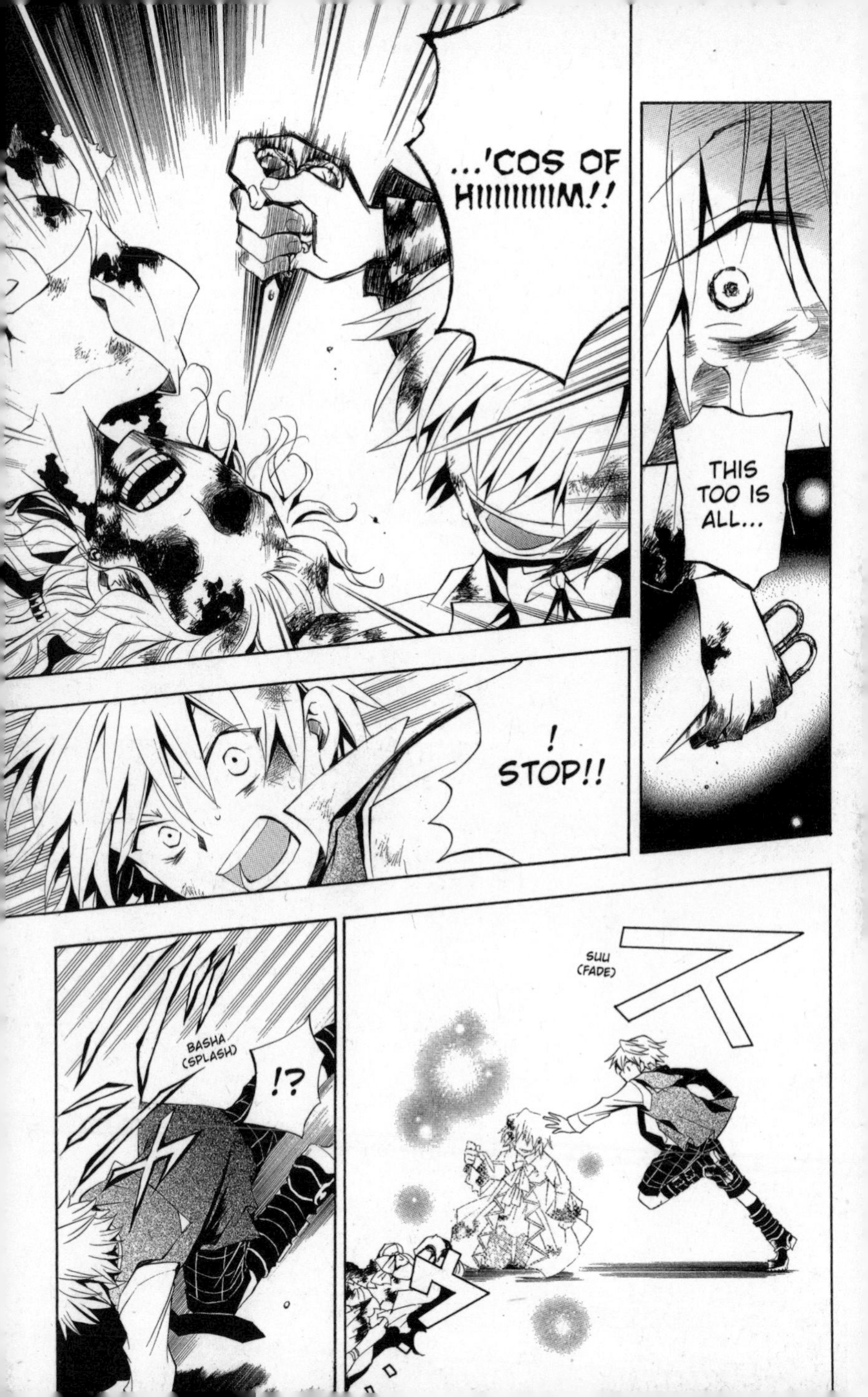
THIS TOO IS ALL...
...'COS OF HIIIIIIIIIM!!
!
STOP!!
SUU (FADE)
BASHA (SPLASH)
!?

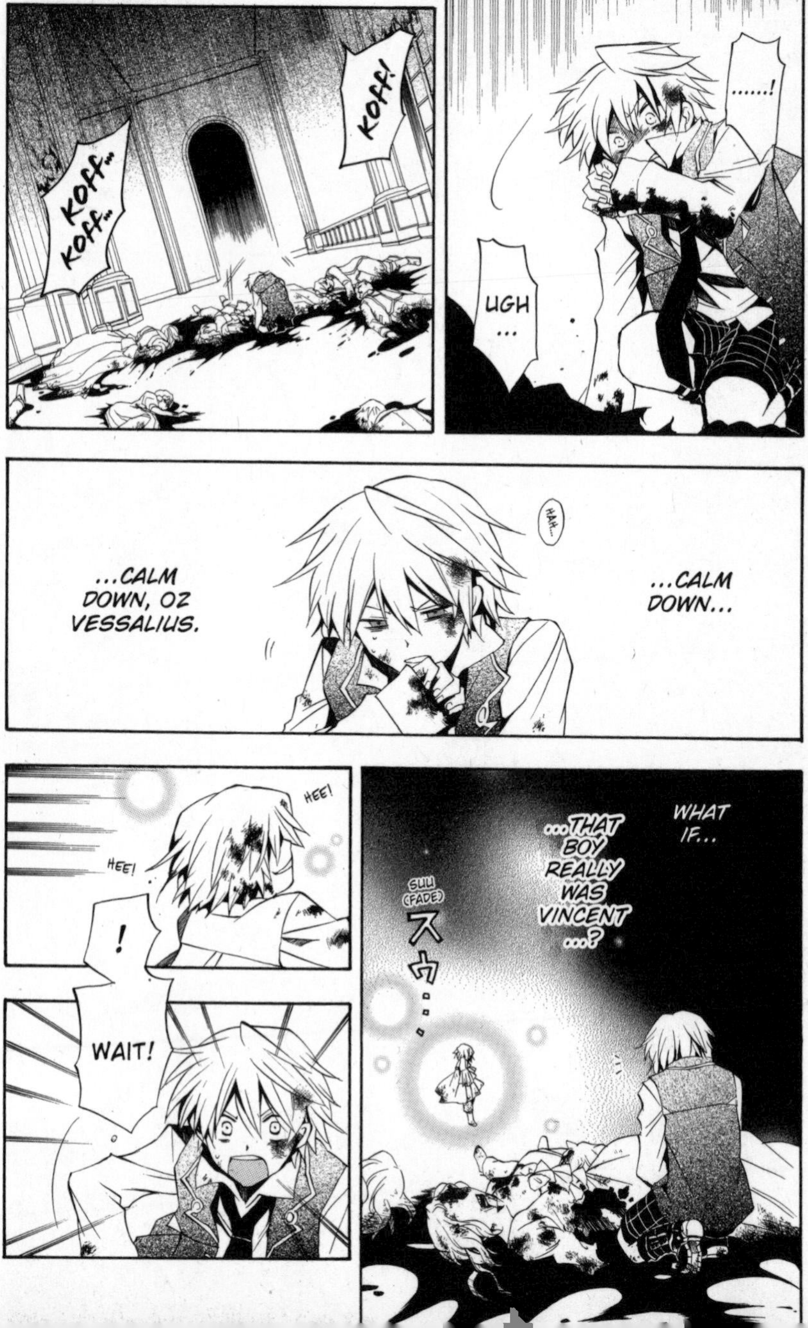
......!
UGH ...
KOFF!
KOFF... KOFF...
HAH...
...CALM DOWN...
...CALM DOWN, OZ VESSALIUS.
WHAT IF...
...THAT BOY REALLY WAS VINCENT ...?
SUU (FADE)
スゥ...
HEE!
HEE!
!
WAIT!

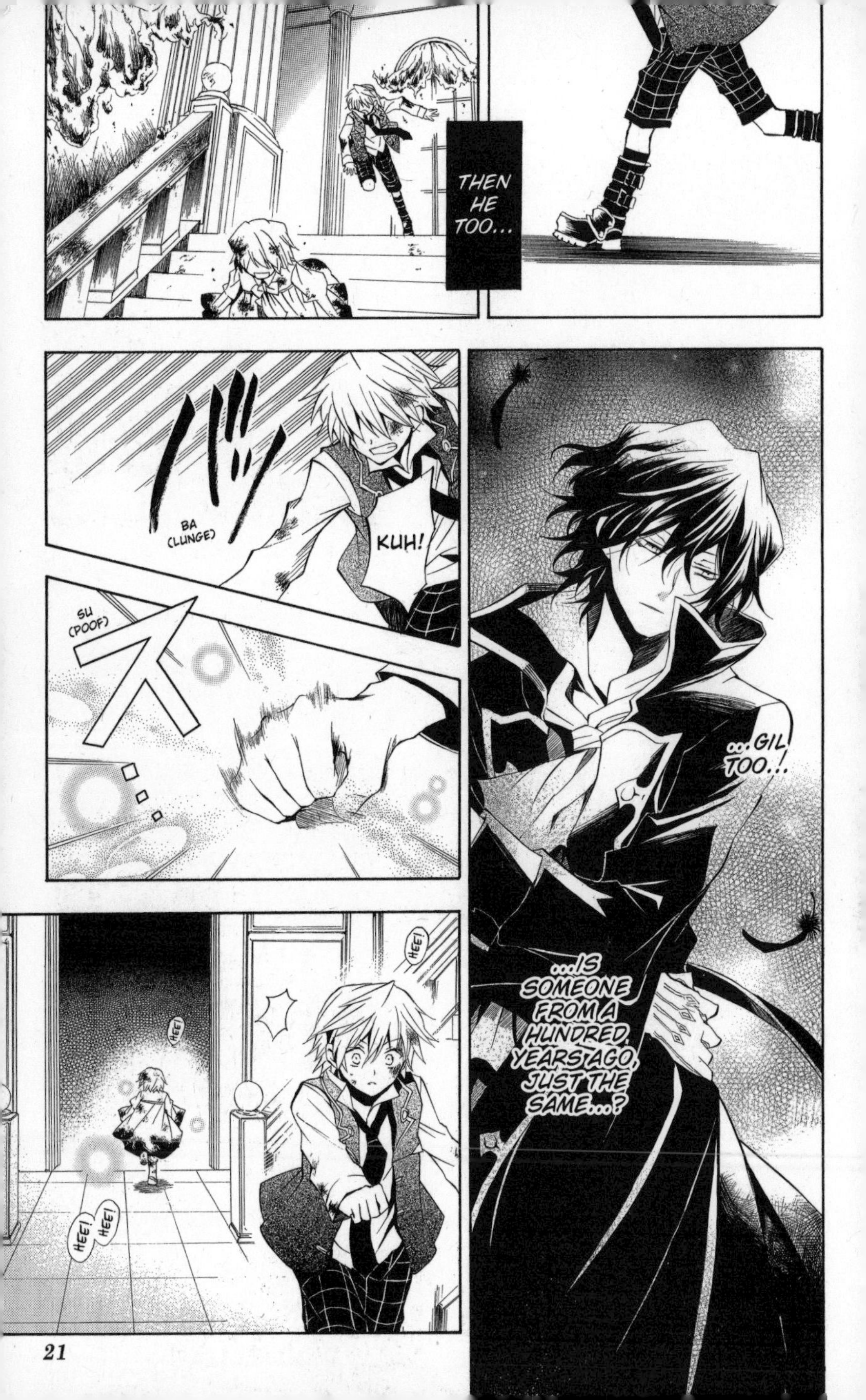
THEN HE TOO...
...GIL TOO...
...IS SOMEONE FROM A HUNDRED YEARS AGO, JUST THE SAME...?
BA (LUNGE)
KUH!
SU (POOF)
HEE!
HEE!
HEE! HEE!

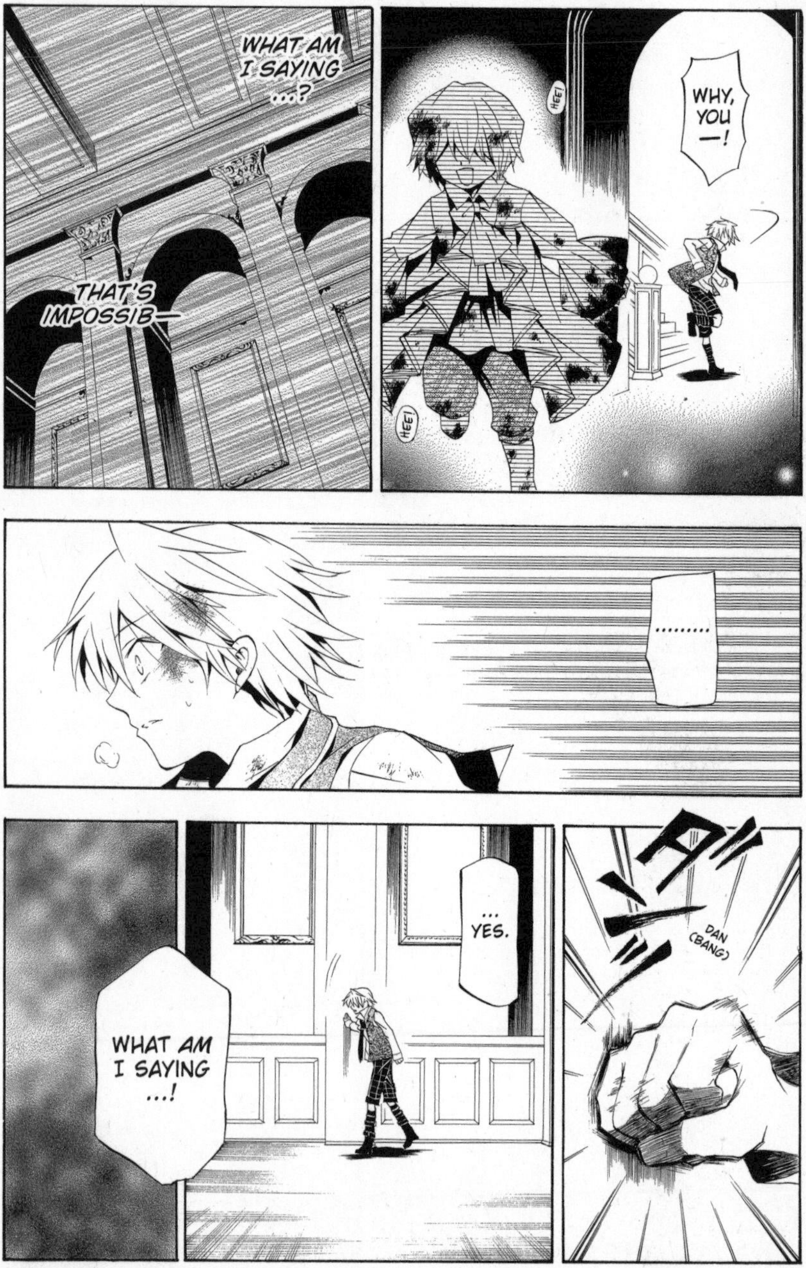
WHY, YOU—!
HEE!
HEE!
WHAT AM I SAYING ...?
THAT'S IMPOSSIB—
....
DAN (BANG)
... YES.
WHAT AM I SAYING ...!

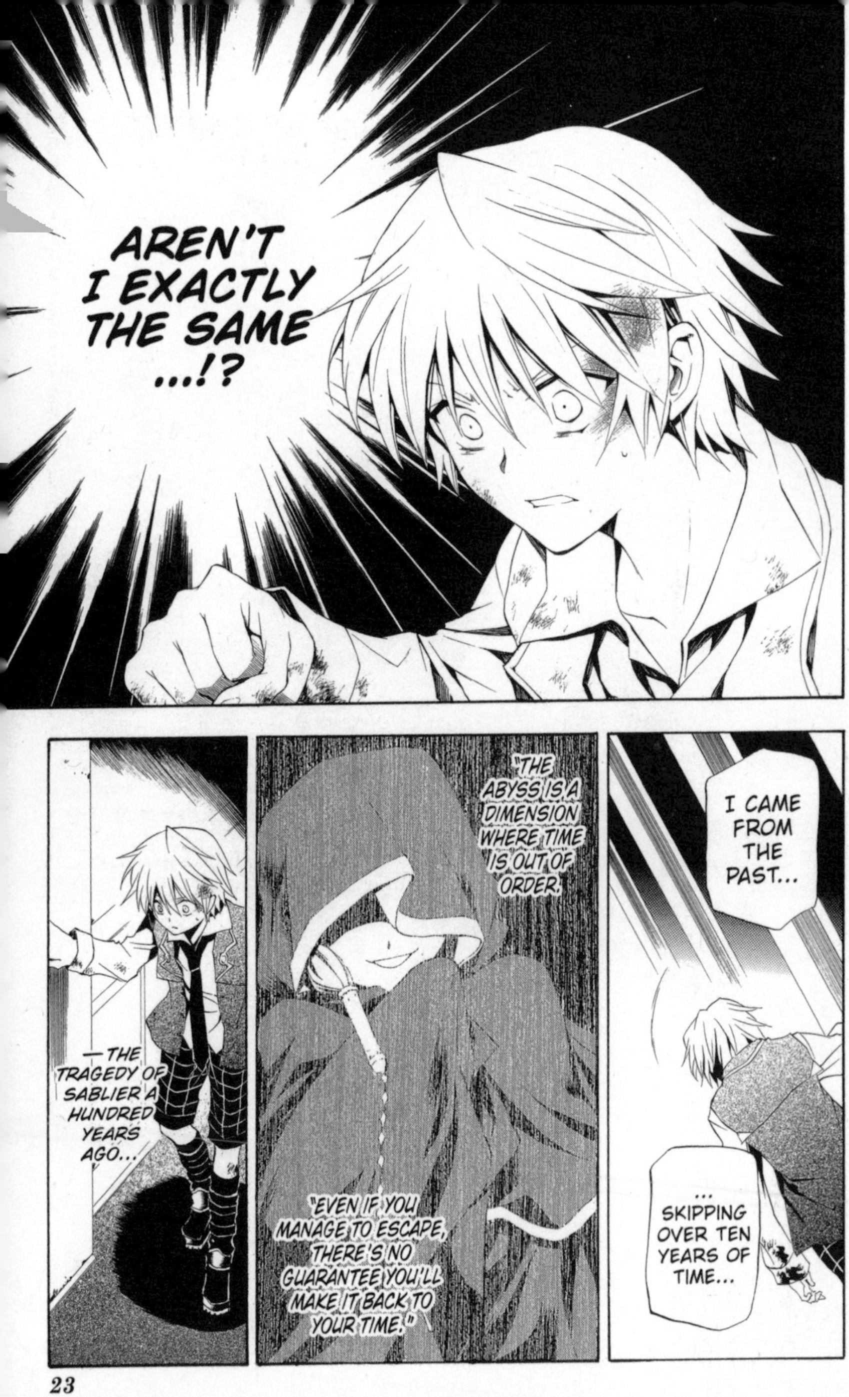
AREN'T I EXACTLY THE SAME ...!?
I CAME FROM THE PAST...
... SKIPPING OVER TEN YEARS OF TIME...
"THE ABYSS IS A DIMENSION WHERE TIME IS OUT OF ORDER.
"EVEN IF YOU MANAGE TO ESCAPE, THERE'S NO GUARANTEE YOU'LL MAKE IT BACK TO YOUR TIME."
—THE TRAGEDY OF SABLIER A HUNDRED YEARS AGO...

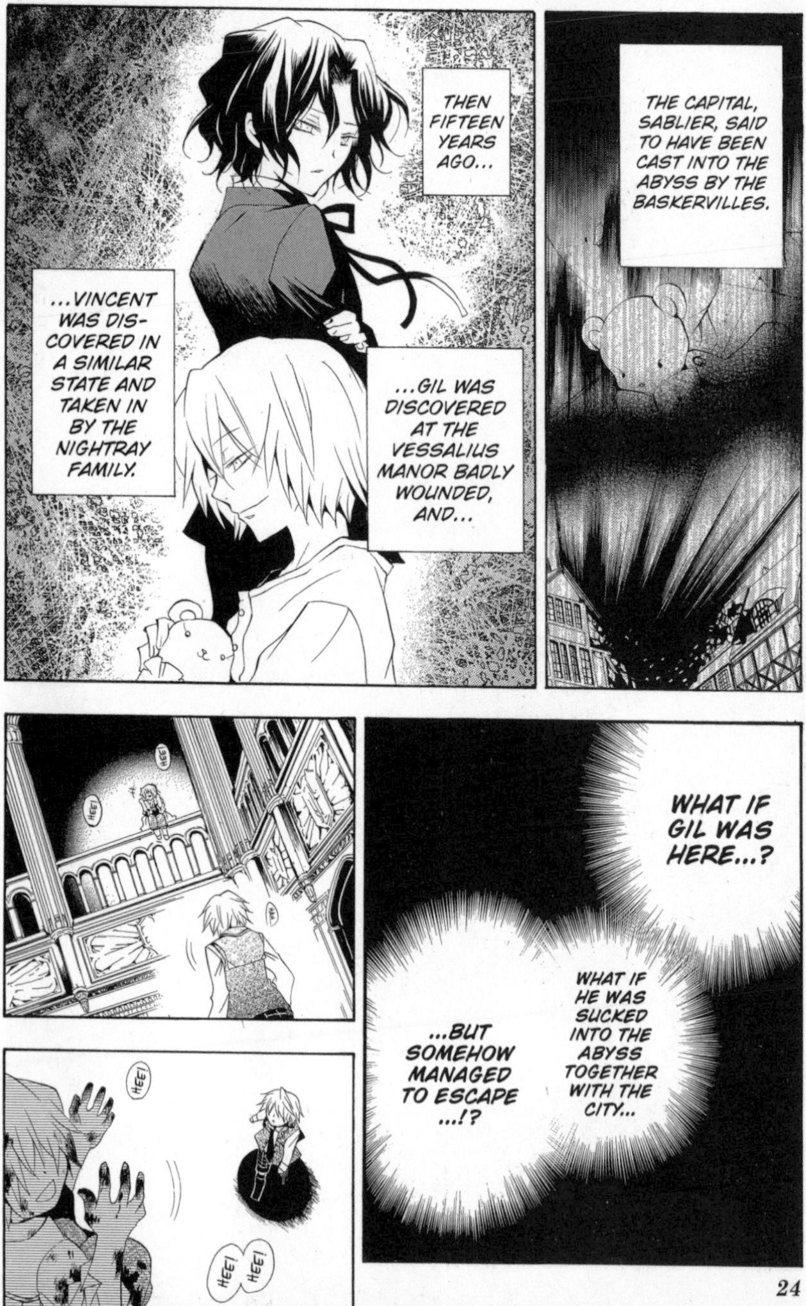
THE CAPITAL, SABLIER, SAID TO HAVE BEEN CAST INTO THE ABYSS BY THE BASKERVILLES.
THEN FIFTEEN YEARS AGO...
...GIL WAS DISCOVERED AT THE VESSALIUS MANOR BADLY WOUNDED, AND...
...VINCENT WAS DIS-COVERED IN A SIMILAR STATE AND TAKEN IN BY THE NIGHTRAY FAMILY.
WHAT IF GIL WAS HERE...?
WHAT IF HE WAS SUCKED INTO THE ABYSS TOGETHER WITH THE CITY...
...BUT SOMEHOW MANAGED TO ESCAPE ...!?
HEE!
HEE!
HEE!
HEE!
HEE!

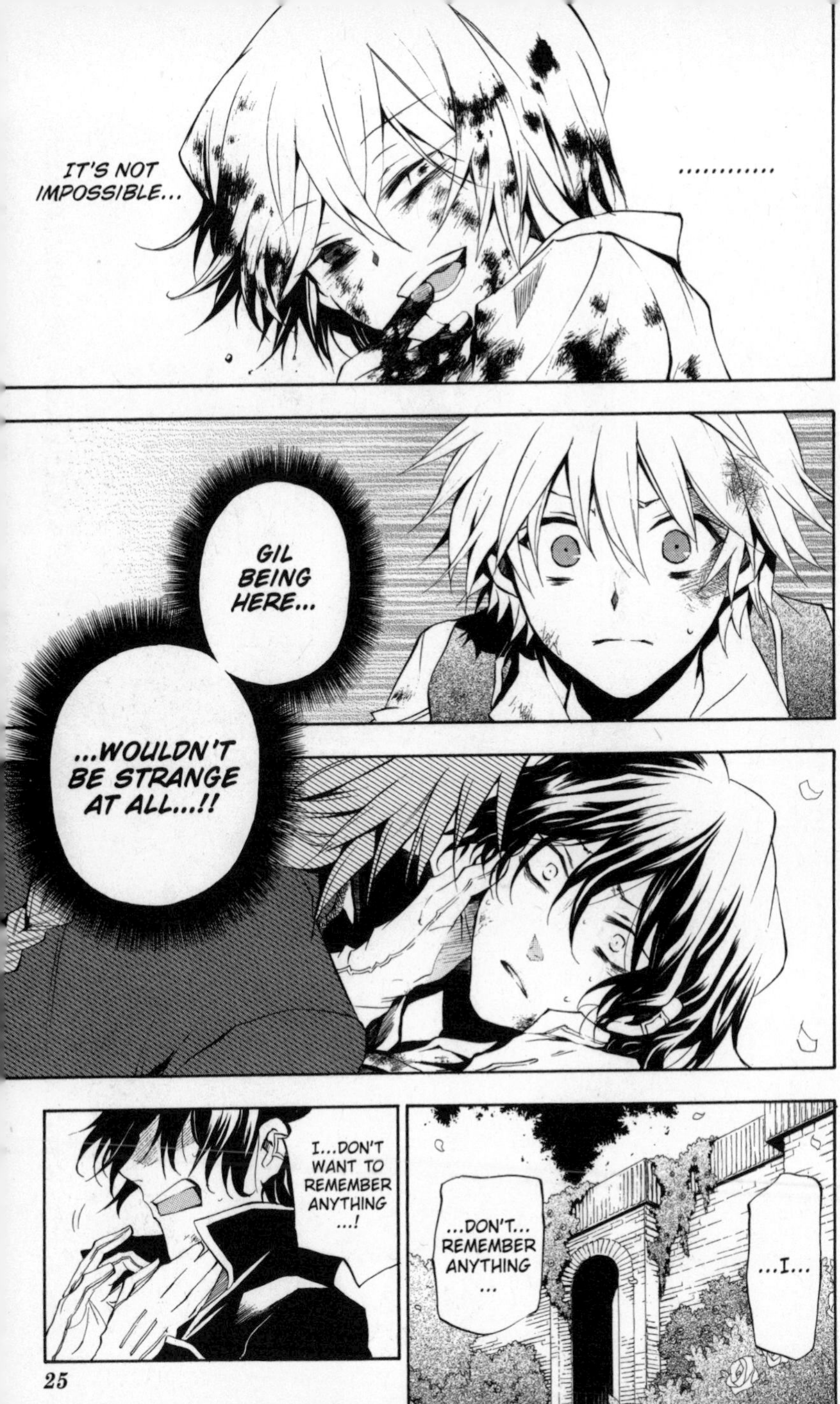
....
IT'S NOT IMPOSSIBLE...
GIL BEING HERE...
...WOULDN'T BE STRANGE AT ALL...!!
...I...
...DON'T... REMEMBER ANYTHING ...
I...DON'T WANT TO REMEMBER ANYTHING ...!

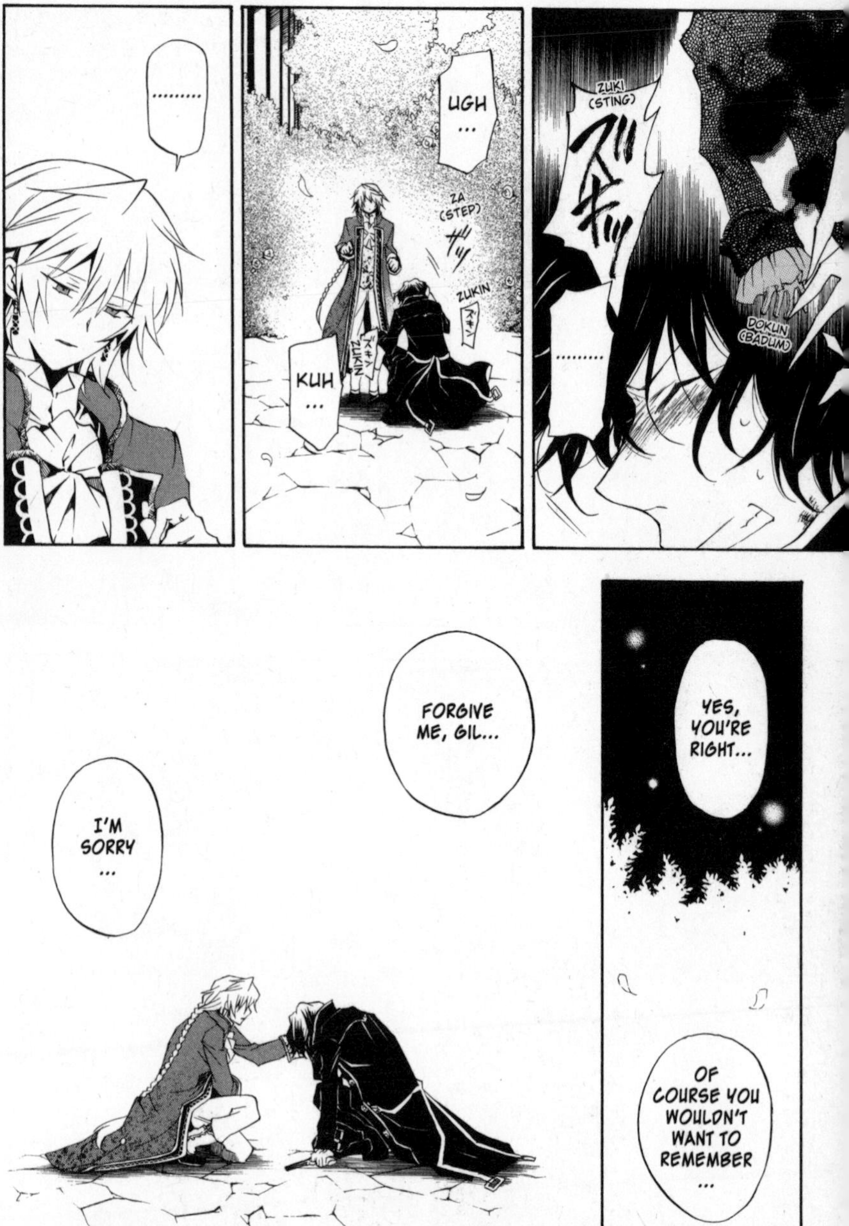
ZUKI (STING)
ズキッ
....
DOKUN (BADUM)
UGH ...
ZA (STEP)
ザッ
ZUKIN
ズキン
ズキン ZUKIN
KUH ...
....
YES, YOU'RE RIGHT...
OF COURSE YOU WOULDN'T WANT TO REMEMBER ...
FORGIVE ME, GIL...
I'M SORRY ...

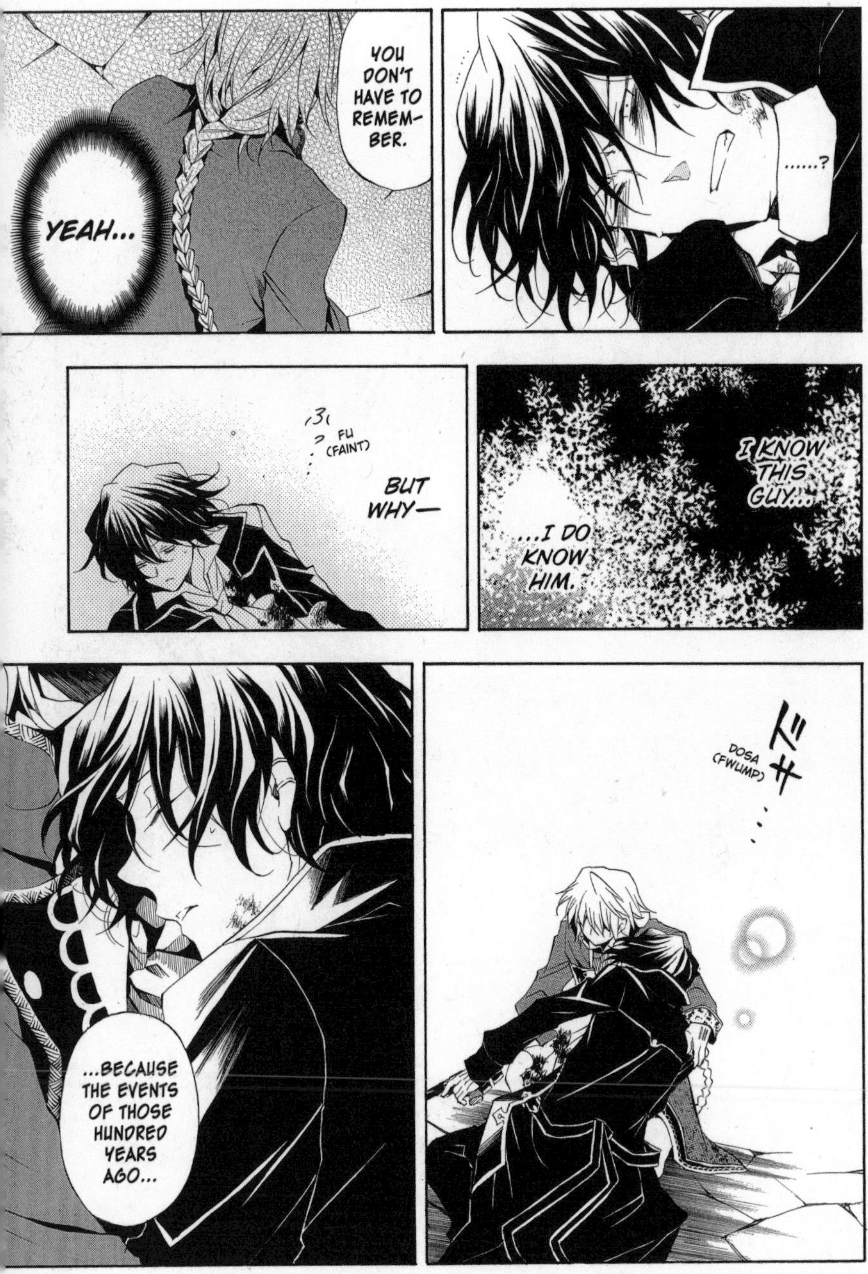
......?
YOU DON'T HAVE TO REMEMBER.
YEAH...
I KNOW THIS GUY...
...I DO KNOW HIM.
FU (FAINT)
BUT WHY—
DOSA (FWUMP)
...BECAUSE THE EVENTS OF THOSE HUNDRED YEARS AGO...

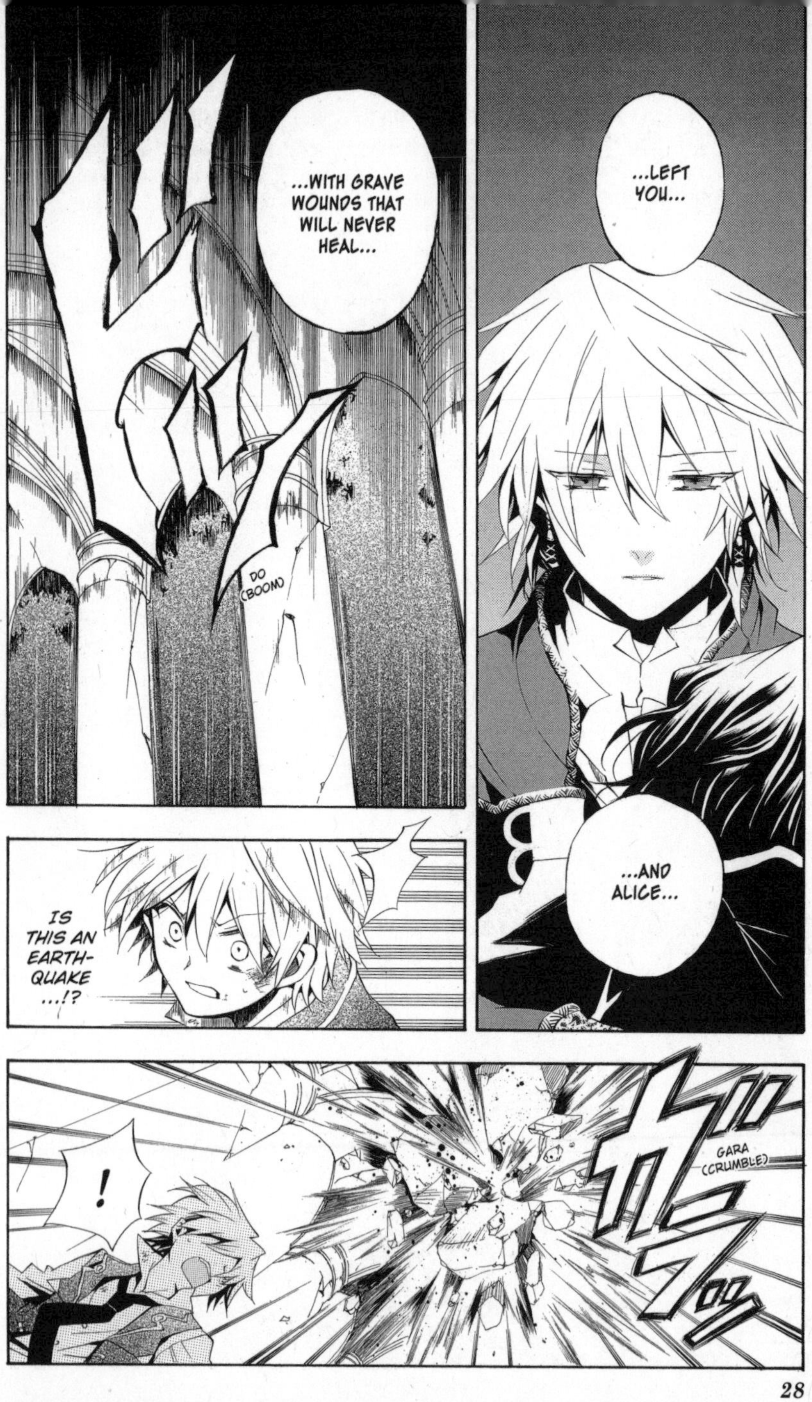
...LEFT YOU...
...AND ALICE...
...WITH GRAVE WOUNDS THAT WILL NEVER HEAL...
DO (BOOM)
IS THIS AN EARTHQUAKE ...!?
GARA (CRUMBLE)
!

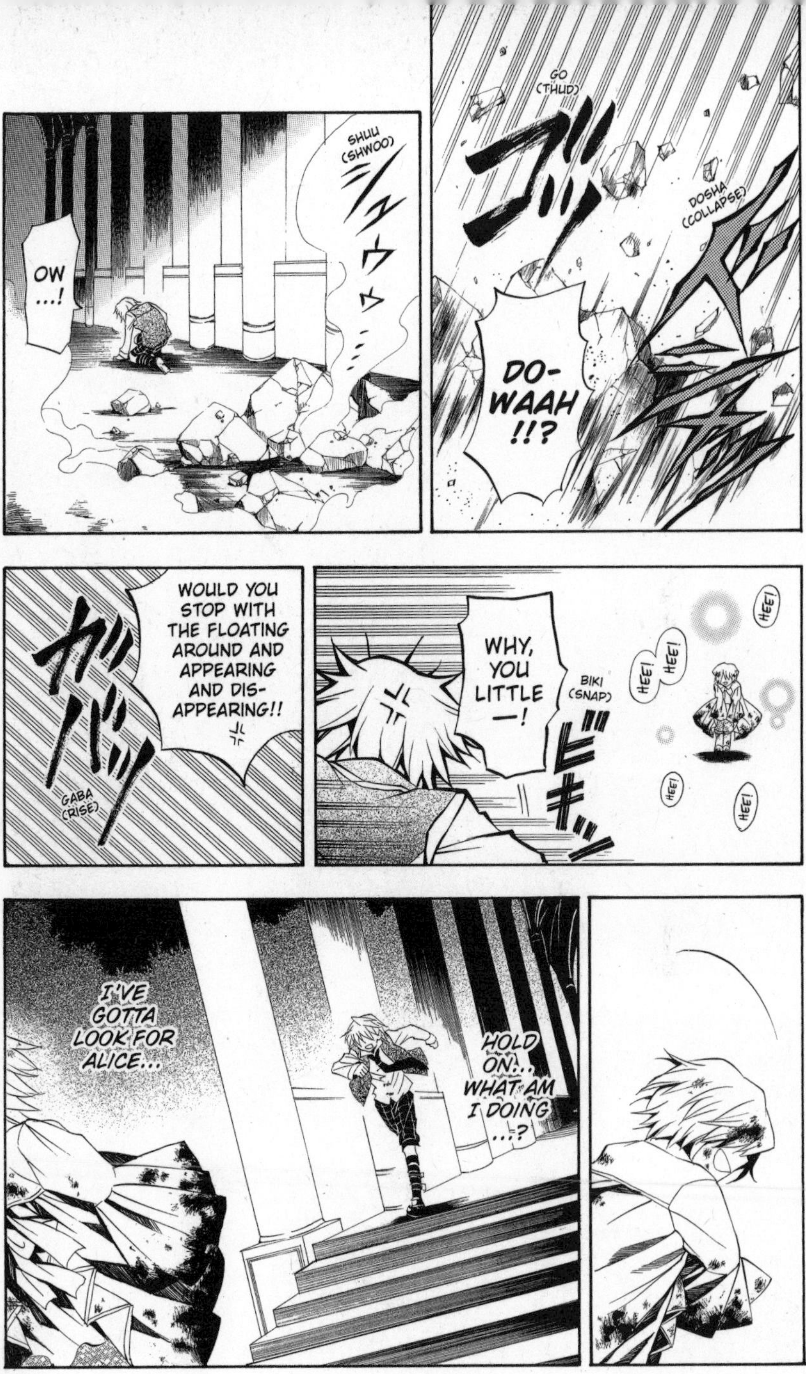
GO (THUD)
DOSHA (COLLAPSE)
DO-WAAH!!?
SHUU (SHWOO)
OW ...!
HEE!
HEE!
HEE!
HEE!
HEE!
BIKI (SNAP)
WHY, YOU LITTLE—!
WOULD YOU STOP WITH THE FLOATING AROUND AND APPEARING AND DIS-APPEARING!!
GABA (RISE)
HOLD ON... WHAT AM I DOING ...?
I'VE GOTTA LOOK FOR ALICE...

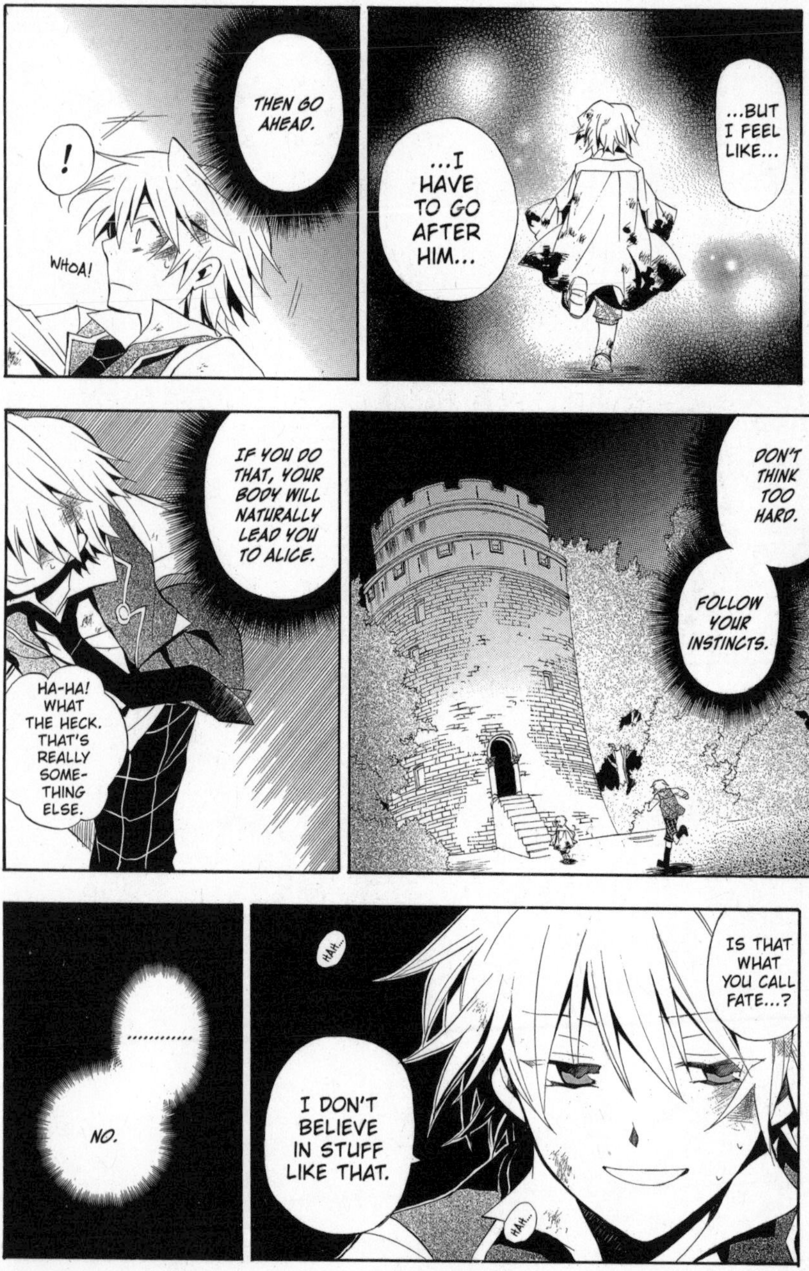
...BUT I FEEL LIKE...
...I HAVE TO GO AFTER HIM...
THEN GO AHEAD.
!
WHOA!
DON'T THINK TOO HARD.
FOLLOW YOUR INSTINCTS.
IF YOU DO THAT, YOUR BODY WILL NATURALLY LEAD YOU TO ALICE.
HA-HA! WHAT THE HECK. THAT'S REALLY SOME-THING ELSE.
HAH...
IS THAT WHAT YOU CALL FATE...?
I DON'T BELIEVE IN STUFF LIKE THAT.
HAH...
....
NO.

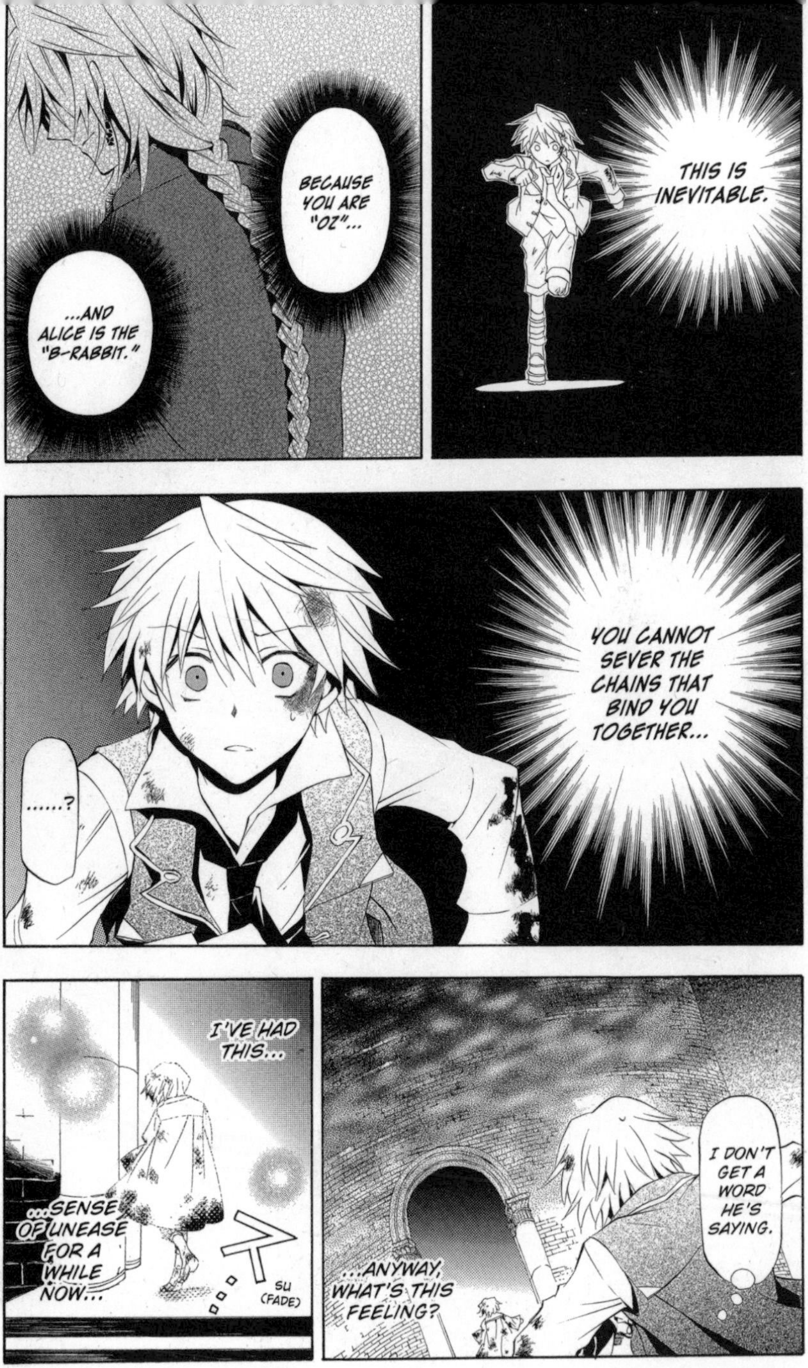
THIS IS INEVITABLE.
BECAUSE YOU ARE "OZ"...
...AND ALICE IS THE "B-RABBIT."
YOU CANNOT SEVER THE CHAINS THAT BIND YOU TOGETHER...
......?
I DON'T GET A WORD HE'S SAYING.
...ANYWAY, WHAT'S THIS FEELING?
I'VE HAD THIS...
...SENSE OF UNEASE FOR A WHILE NOW...
SU (FADE)

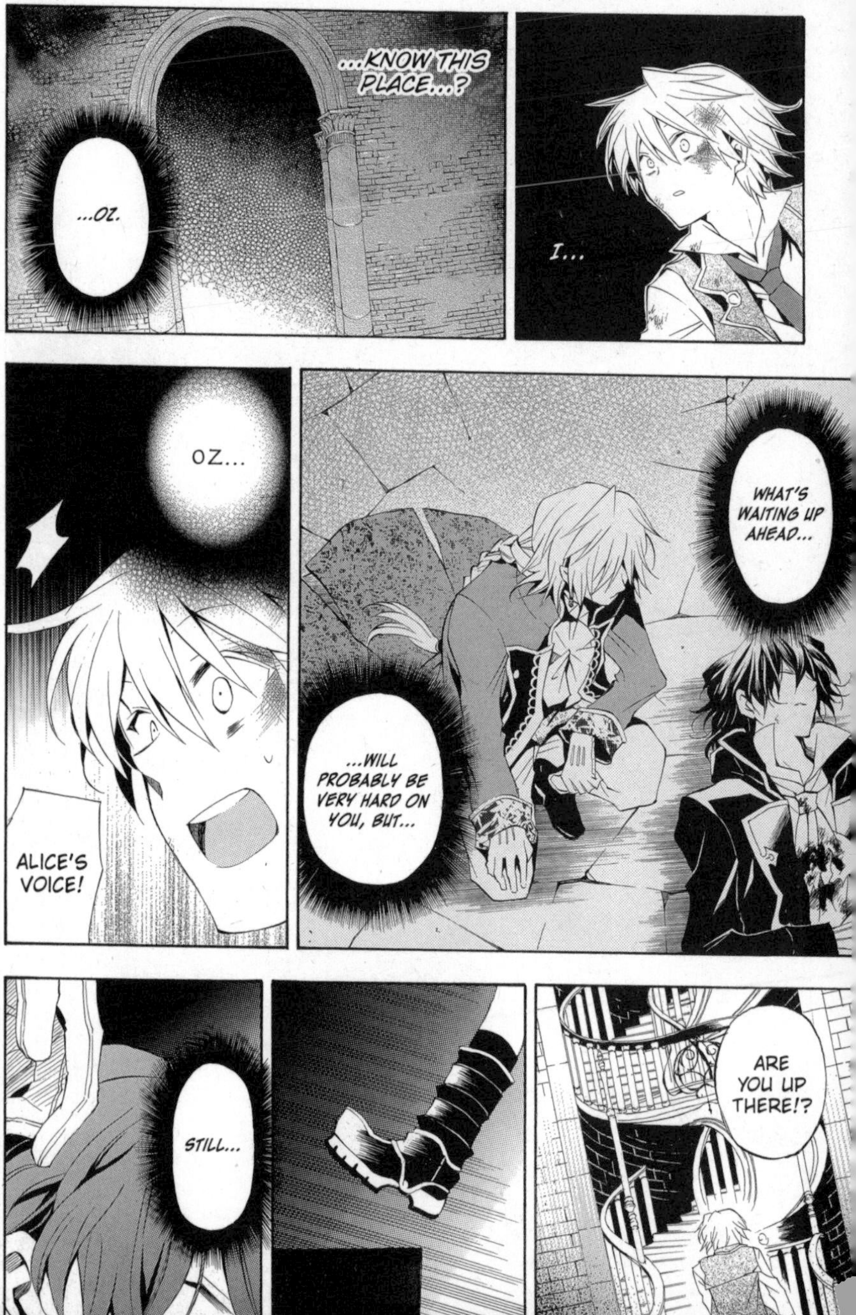
I...
...KNOW THIS PLACE...?
...OZ.
WHAT'S WAITING UP AHEAD...
...WILL PROBABLY BE VERY HARD ON YOU, BUT...
OZ...
ALICE'S VOICE!
ARE YOU UP THERE!?
STILL...

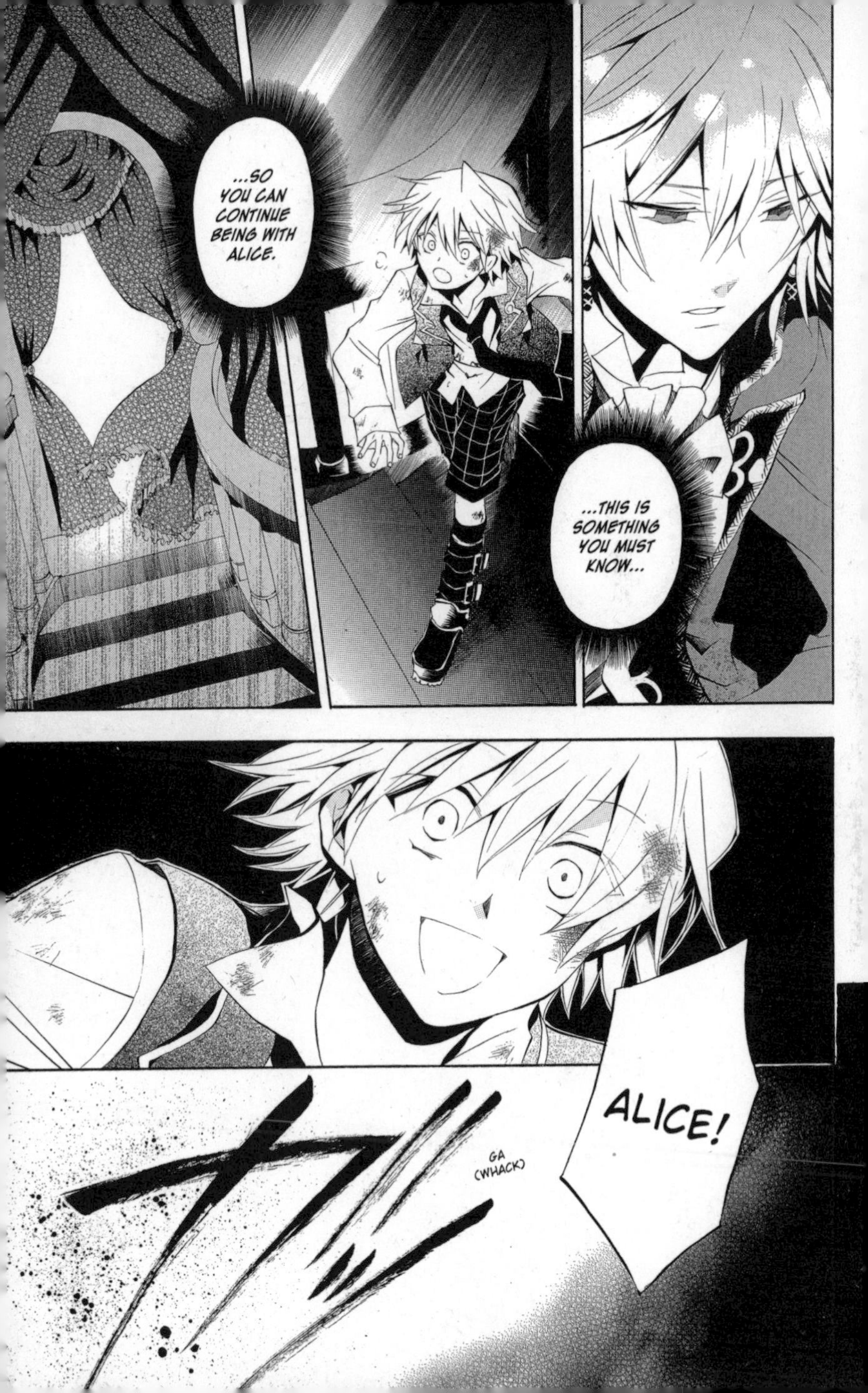
...THIS IS SOMETHING YOU MUST KNOW...
...SO YOU CAN CONTINUE BEING WITH ALICE.
ALICE!
GA (WHACK)

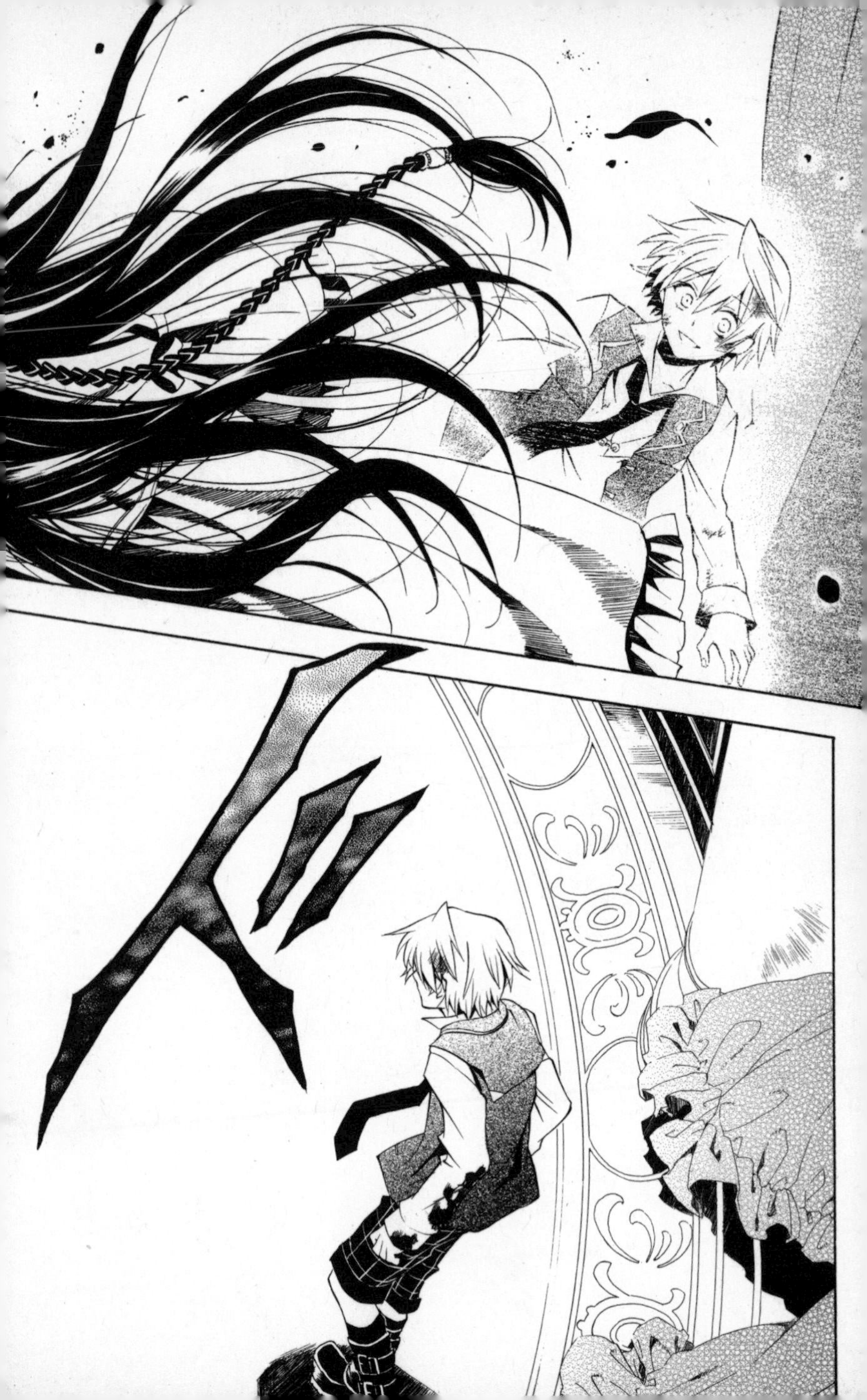
ド

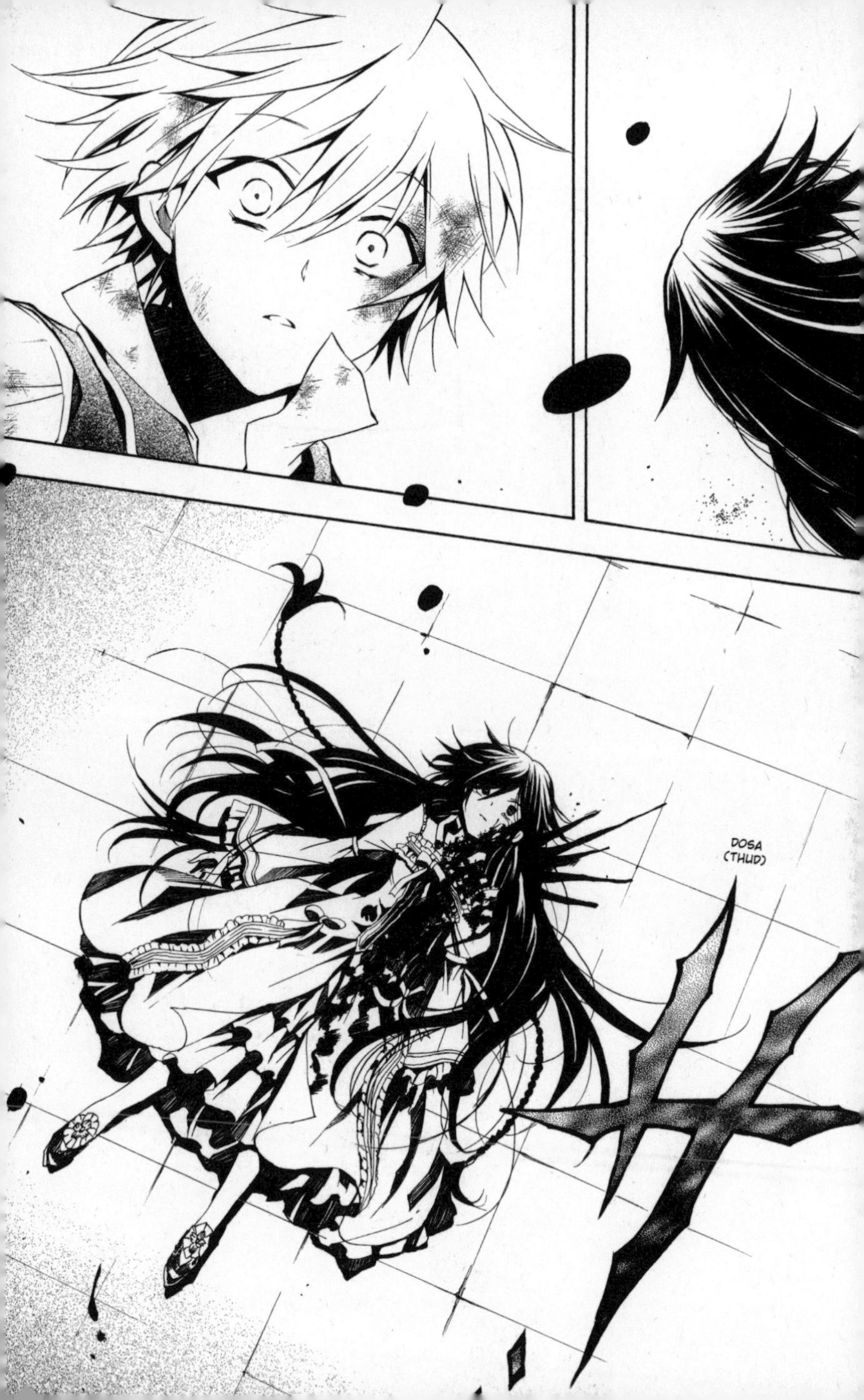
DOSA
(THUD)

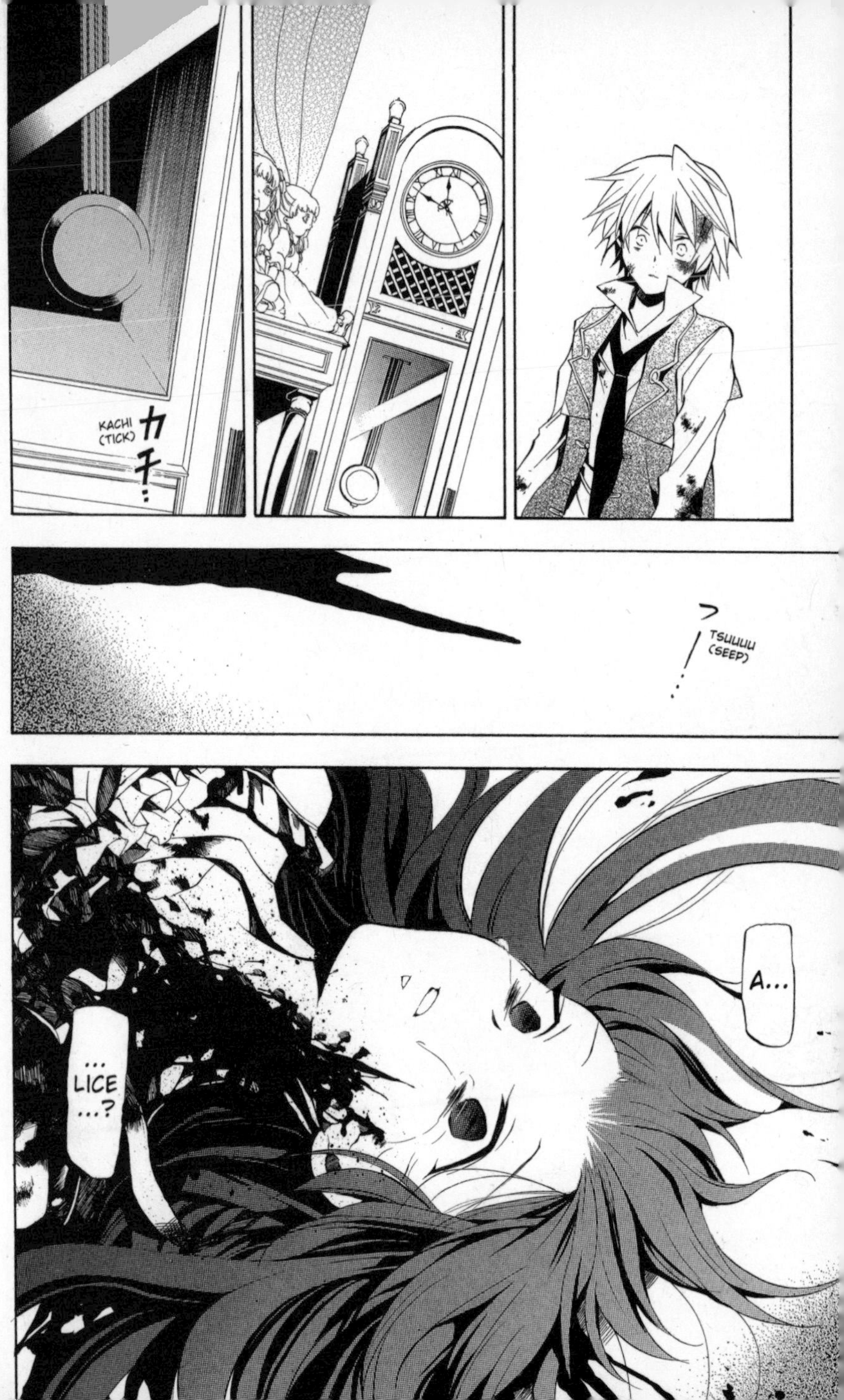
KACHI (TICK)
カチ…
TSUUUU (SEEP)
A...
...LICE ...?

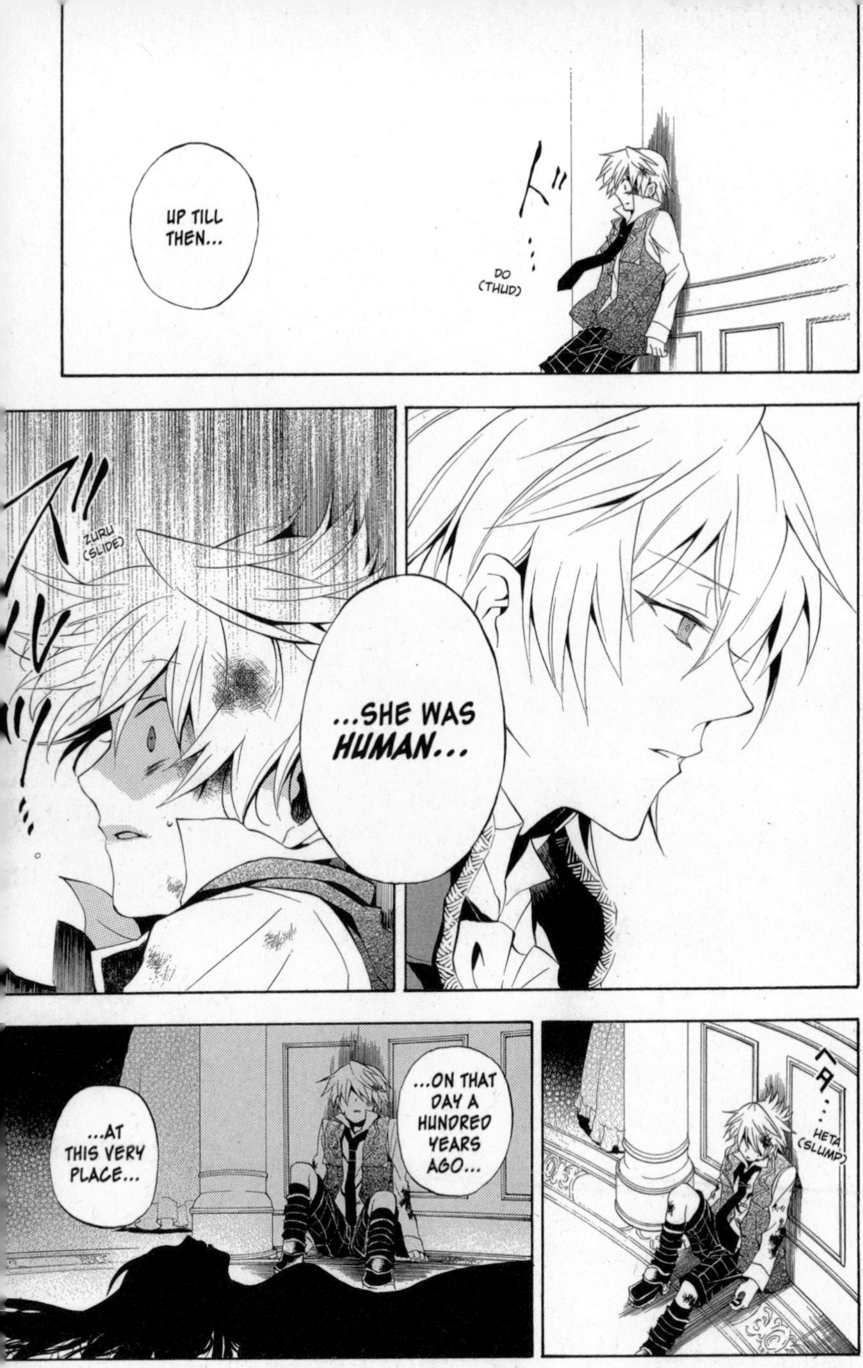
DO (THUD)
UP TILL THEN...
...SHE WAS *HUMAN*...
ZURU (SLIDE)
HETA (SLUMP)
...ON THAT DAY A HUNDRED YEARS AGO...
...AT THIS VERY PLACE...

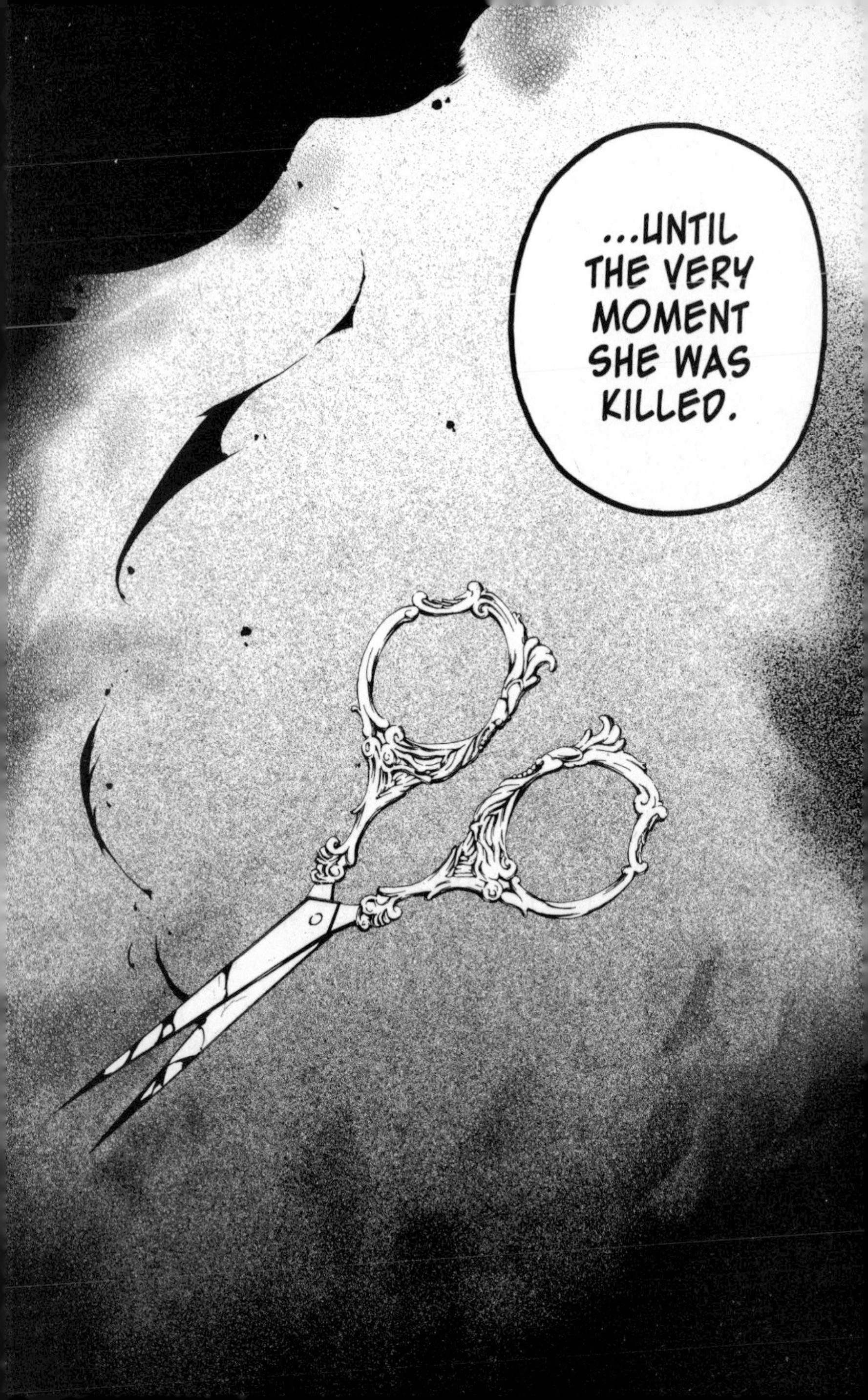
...UNTIL THE VERY MOMENT SHE WAS KILLED.

Retrace:XX
Who killed poor Alice?

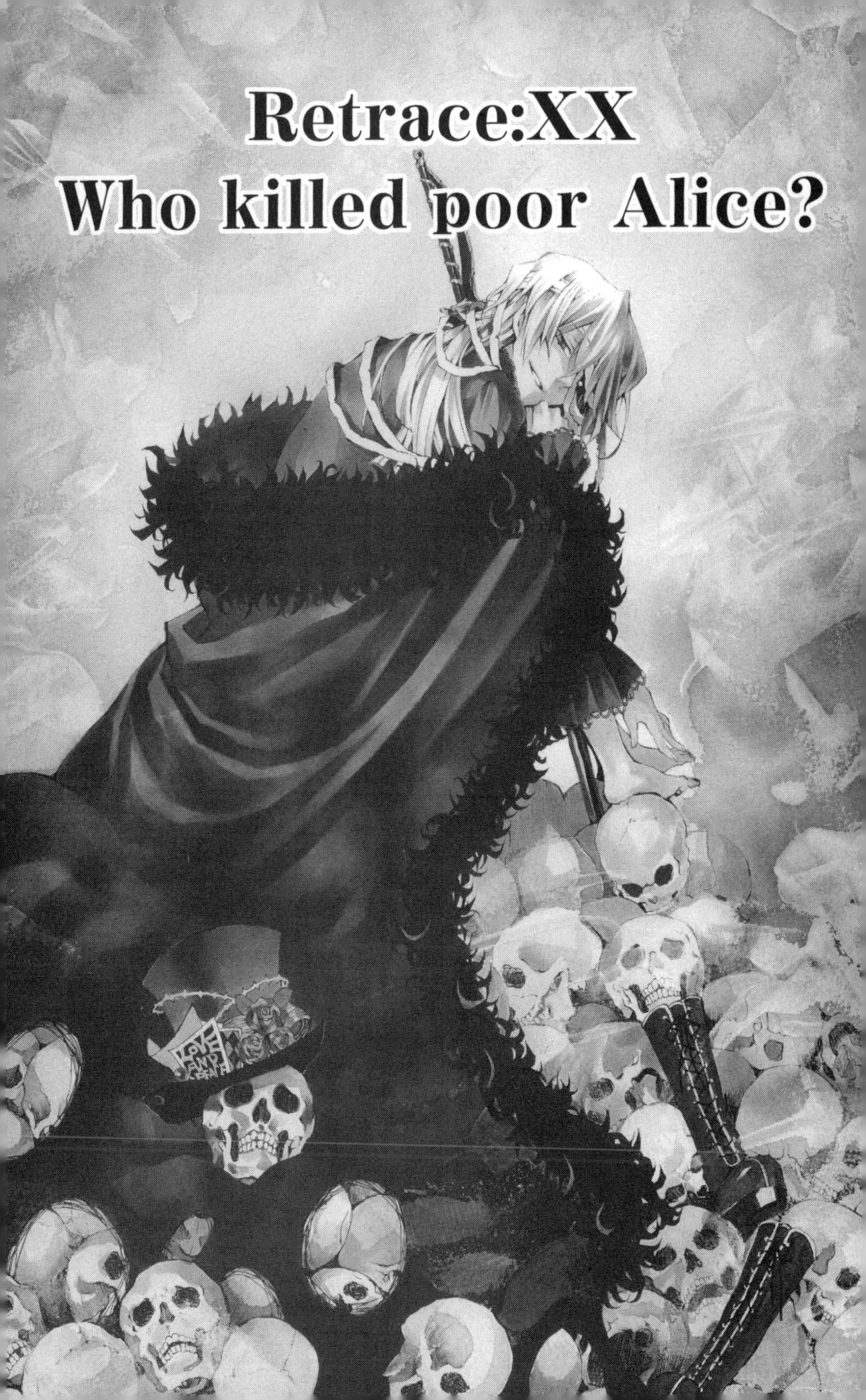

BONUS: TEN YEARS OF MISTER HATTER AND MASTER GILBERT, PART ONE

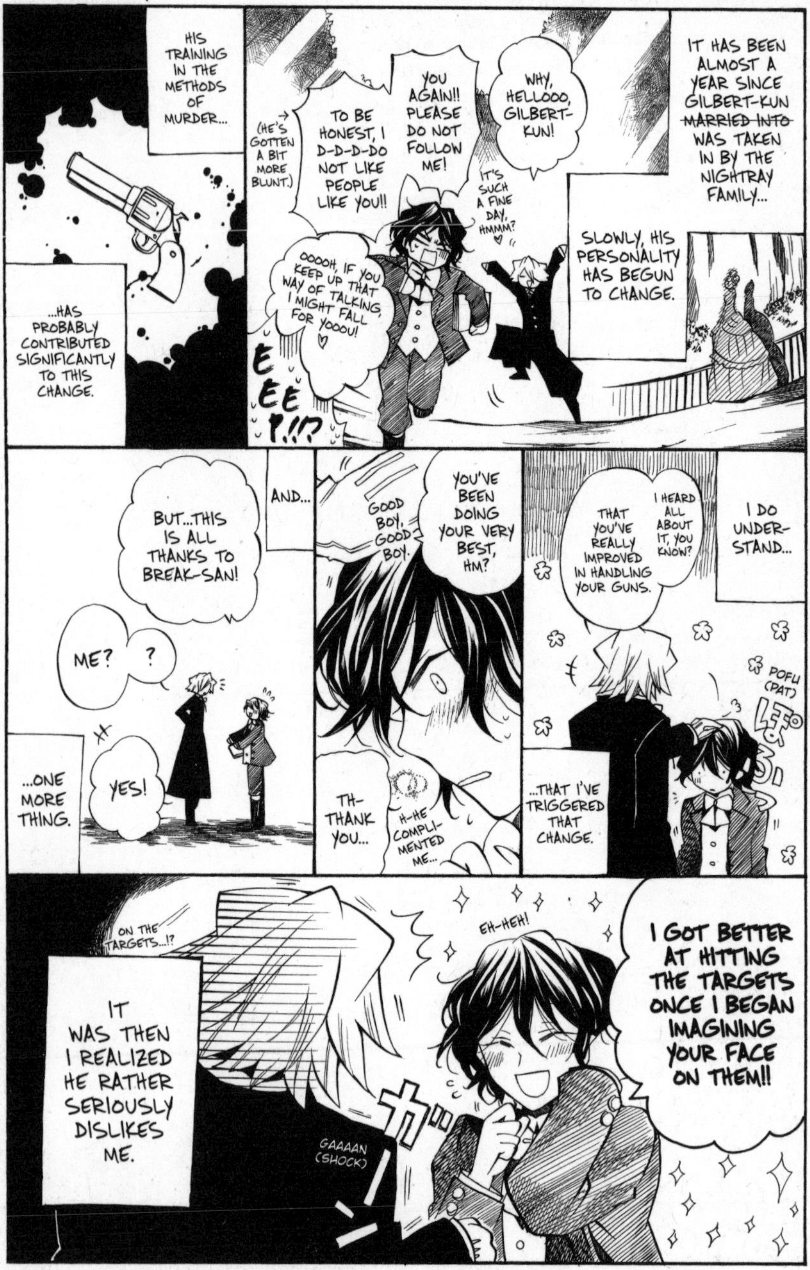
IT HAS BEEN ALMOST A YEAR SINCE GILBERT-KUN ~~MARRIED INTO~~ WAS TAKEN IN BY THE NIGHTRAY FAMILY...
SLOWLY, HIS PERSONALITY HAS BEGUN TO CHANGE.
WHY, HELLOOO, GILBERT-KUN!
IT'S SUCH A FINE DAY, HMMM?
YOU AGAIN!! PLEASE DO NOT FOLLOW ME!
TO BE HONEST, I D-D-D-DO NOT LIKE PEOPLE LIKE YOU!!
(HE'S GOTTEN A BIT MORE BLUNT.)
OOOOH, IF YOU KEEP UP THAT WAY OF TALKING, I MIGHT FALL FOR YOOOU!
EEE?!!?
HIS TRAINING IN THE METHODS OF MURDER...
...HAS PROBABLY CONTRIBUTED SIGNIFICANTLY TO THIS CHANGE.
I DO UNDERSTAND...
I HEARD ALL ABOUT IT, YOU KNOW?
THAT YOU'VE REALLY IMPROVED IN HANDLING YOUR GUNS.
POFU (PAT)
...THAT I'VE TRIGGERED THAT CHANGE.
YOU'VE BEEN DOING YOUR VERY BEST, HM?
GOOD BOY, GOOD BOY.
TH-THANK YOU...
H-HE COMPLIMENTED ME...
AND...
BUT...THIS IS ALL THANKS TO BREAK-SAN!
ME? ?
...ONE MORE THING.
YES!
I GOT BETTER AT HITTING THE TARGETS ONCE I BEGAN IMAGINING YOUR FACE ON THEM!!
EH-HEH!
ON THE TARGETS...!?
GAAAAN (SHOCK)
IT WAS THEN I REALIZED HE RATHER SERIOUSLY DISLIKES ME.

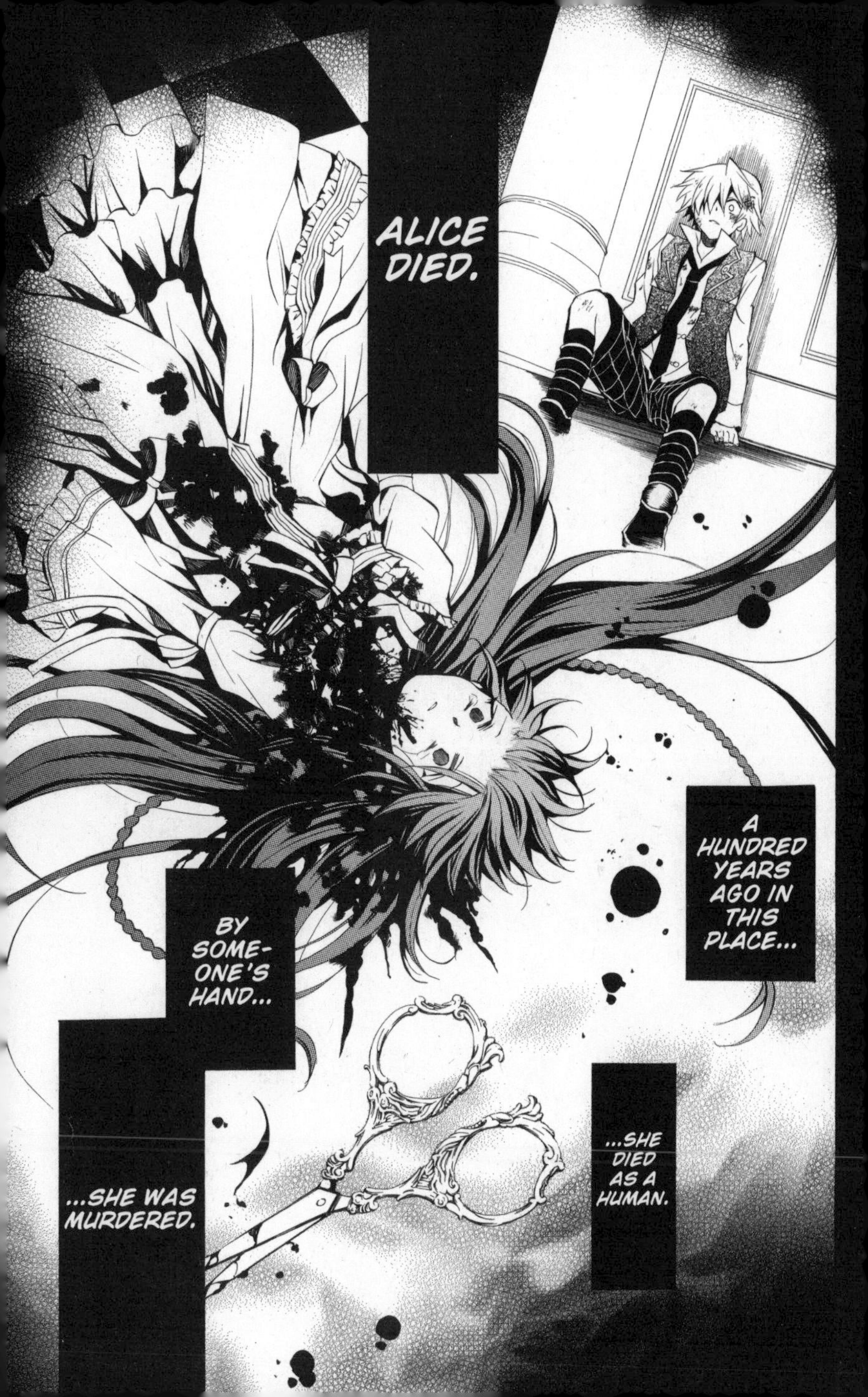
ALICE DIED.
A HUNDRED YEARS AGO IN THIS PLACE...
BY SOME-ONE'S HAND...
...SHE DIED AS A HUMAN.
...SHE WAS MURDERED.

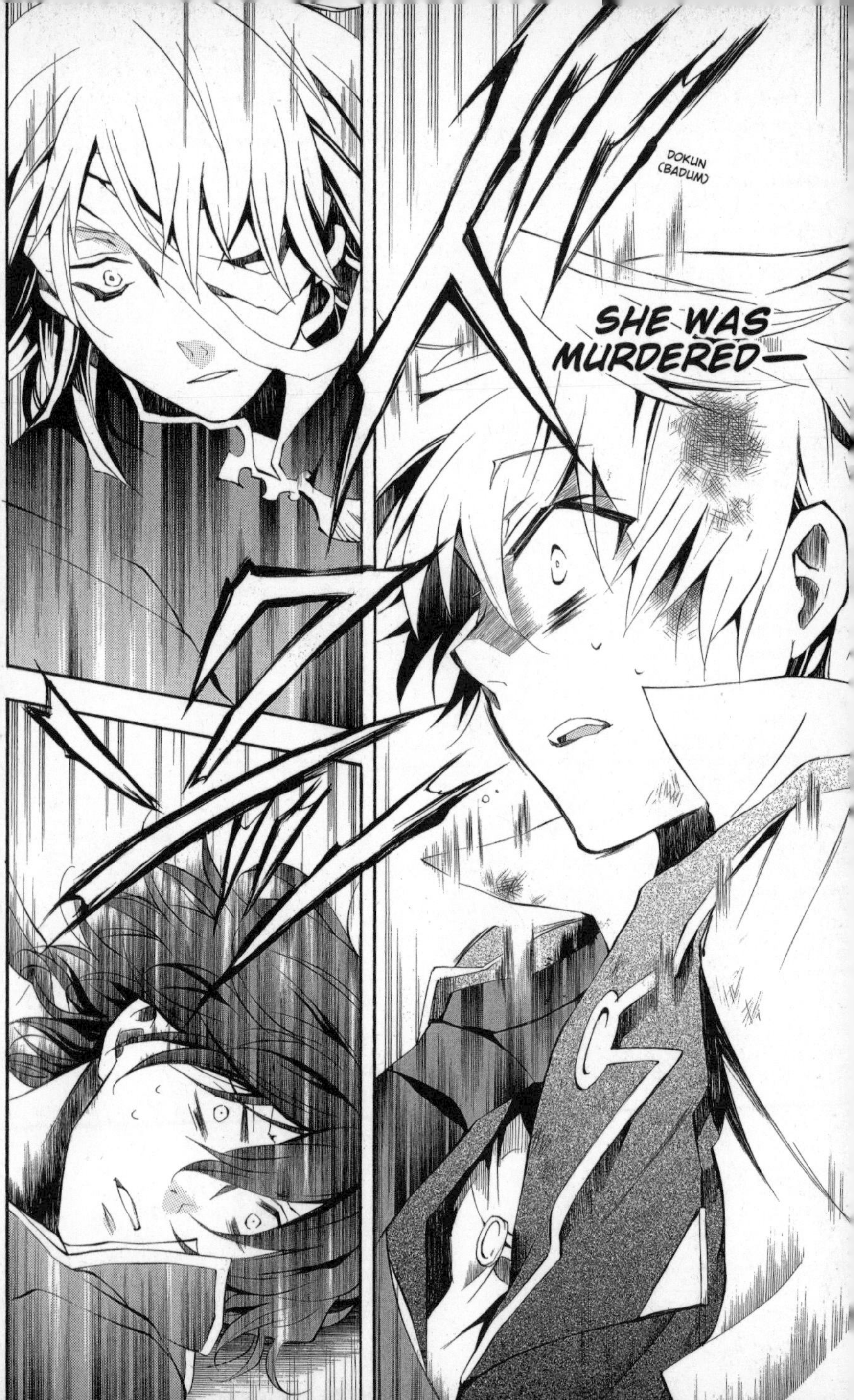
DOKUN (BADUM)
SHE WAS MURDERED—

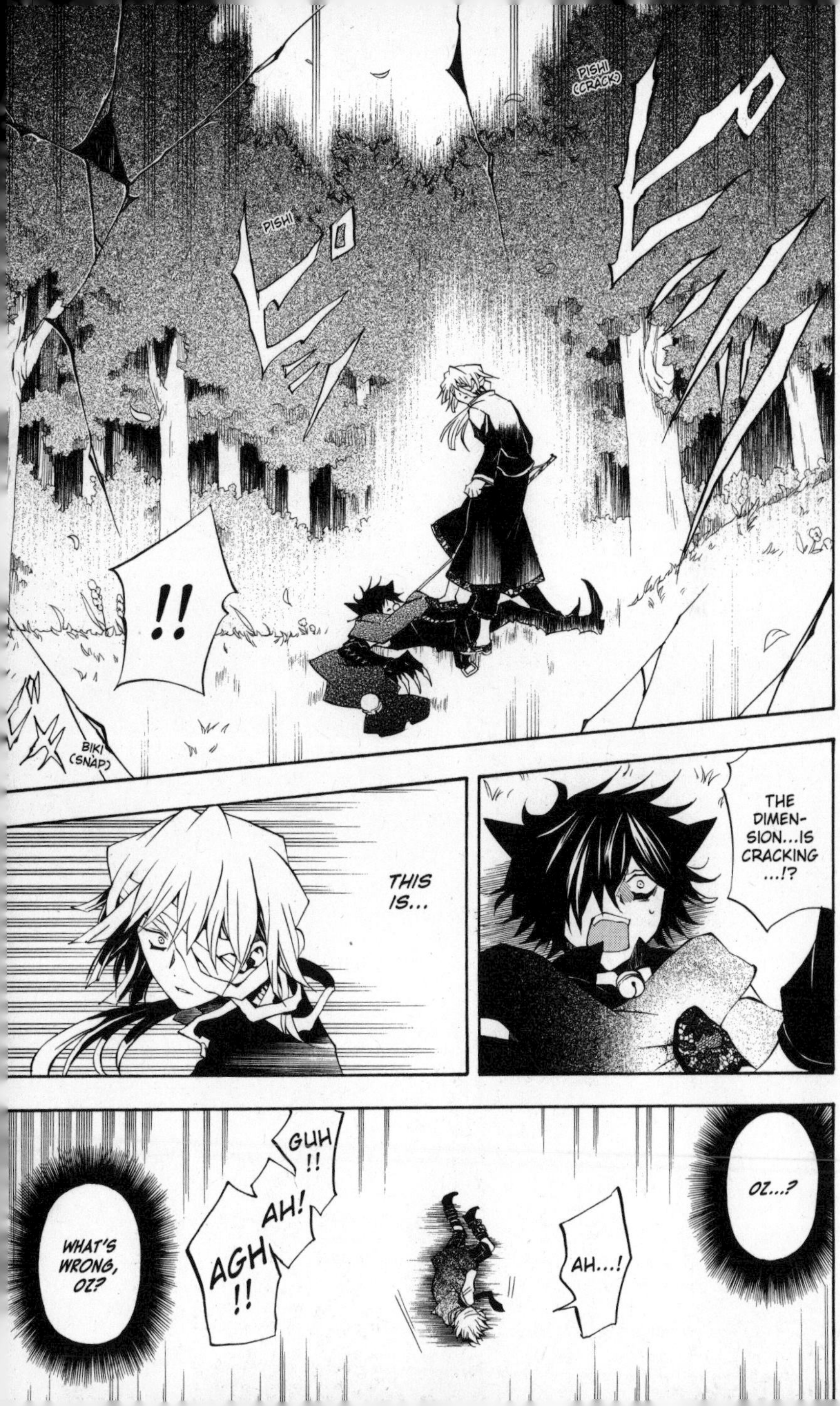
PISHI (CRACK)
PISHI
!!
BIKI (SNAP)
THE DIMENSION...IS CRACKING ...!?
THIS IS...
OZ...?
AH...!
GUH !!
AH!
AGH !!
WHAT'S WRONG, OZ?

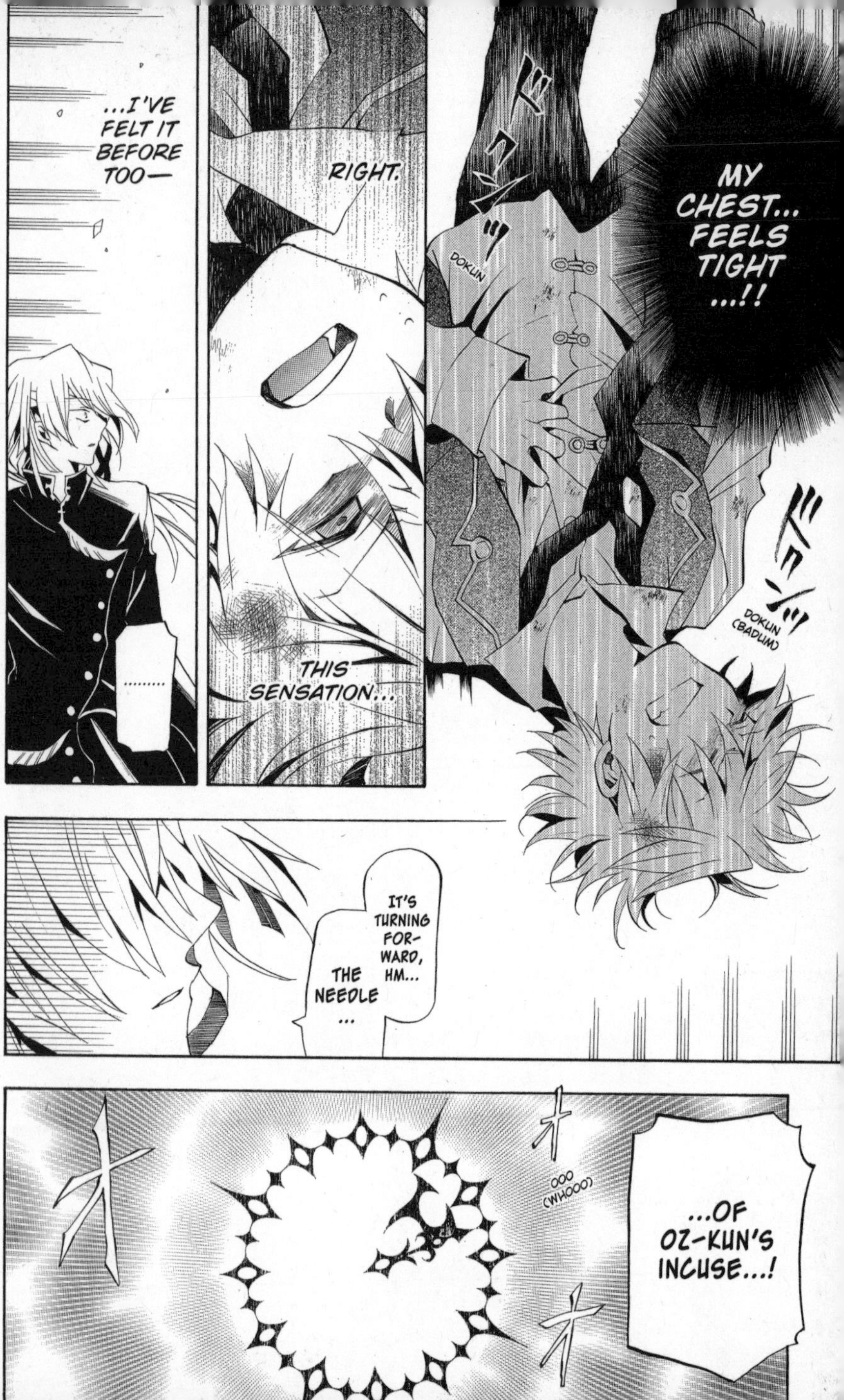
MY CHEST... FEELS TIGHT ...!!
DOKUN
DOKUN (BADUM)
RIGHT.
THIS SENSATION...
...I'VE FELT IT BEFORE TOO—
....
IT'S TURNING FORWARD, HM...
THE NEEDLE ...
...OF OZ-KUN'S INCUSE...!
OOO (WHOOO)

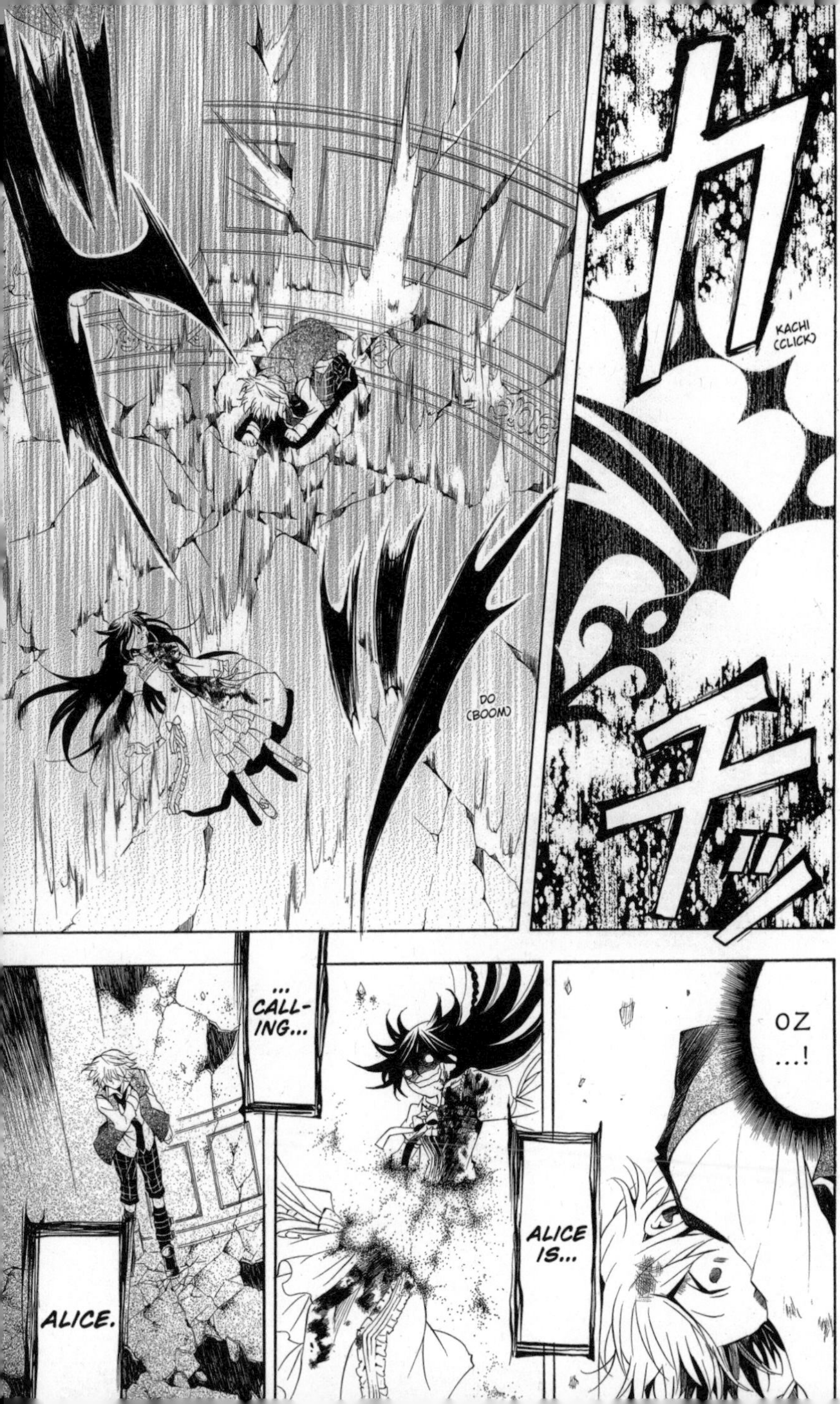
カチッ
KACHI (CLICK)
DO (BOOM)
OZ ...!
ALICE IS...
... CALLING...
ALICE.

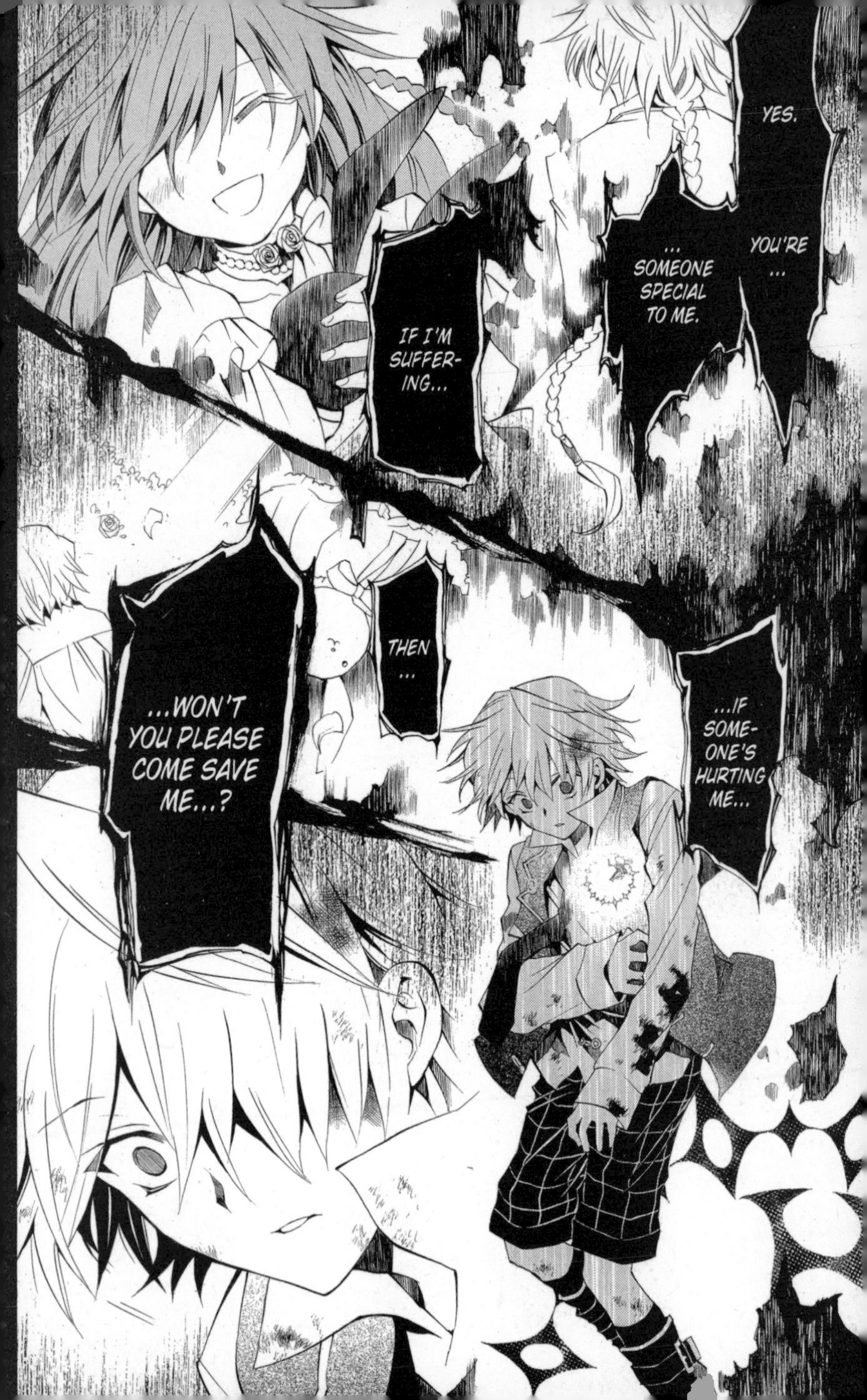
YES.
YOU'RE ...
... SOMEONE SPECIAL TO ME.
IF I'M SUFFER-ING...
...IF SOME-ONE'S HURTING ME...
THEN ...
...WON'T YOU PLEASE COME SAVE ME...?

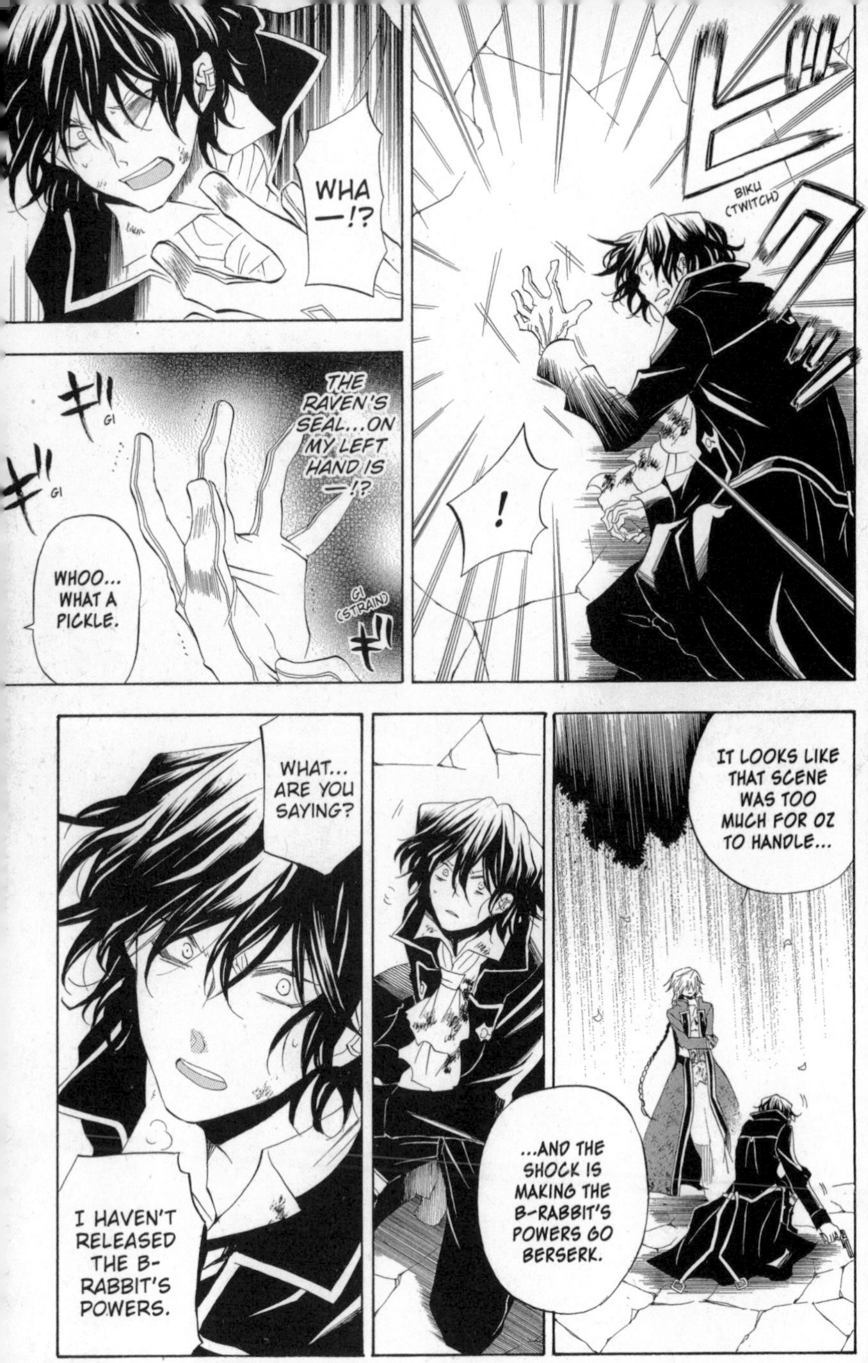
BIKU (TWITCH)
!
WHA—!?
THE RAVEN'S SEAL...ON MY LEFT HAND IS—!?
GI (STRAIN)
GI
GI
WHOO... WHAT A PICKLE.
IT LOOKS LIKE THAT SCENE WAS TOO MUCH FOR OZ TO HANDLE...
...AND THE SHOCK IS MAKING THE B-RABBIT'S POWERS GO BERSERK.
WHAT... ARE YOU SAYING?
I HAVEN'T RELEASED THE B-RABBIT'S POWERS.

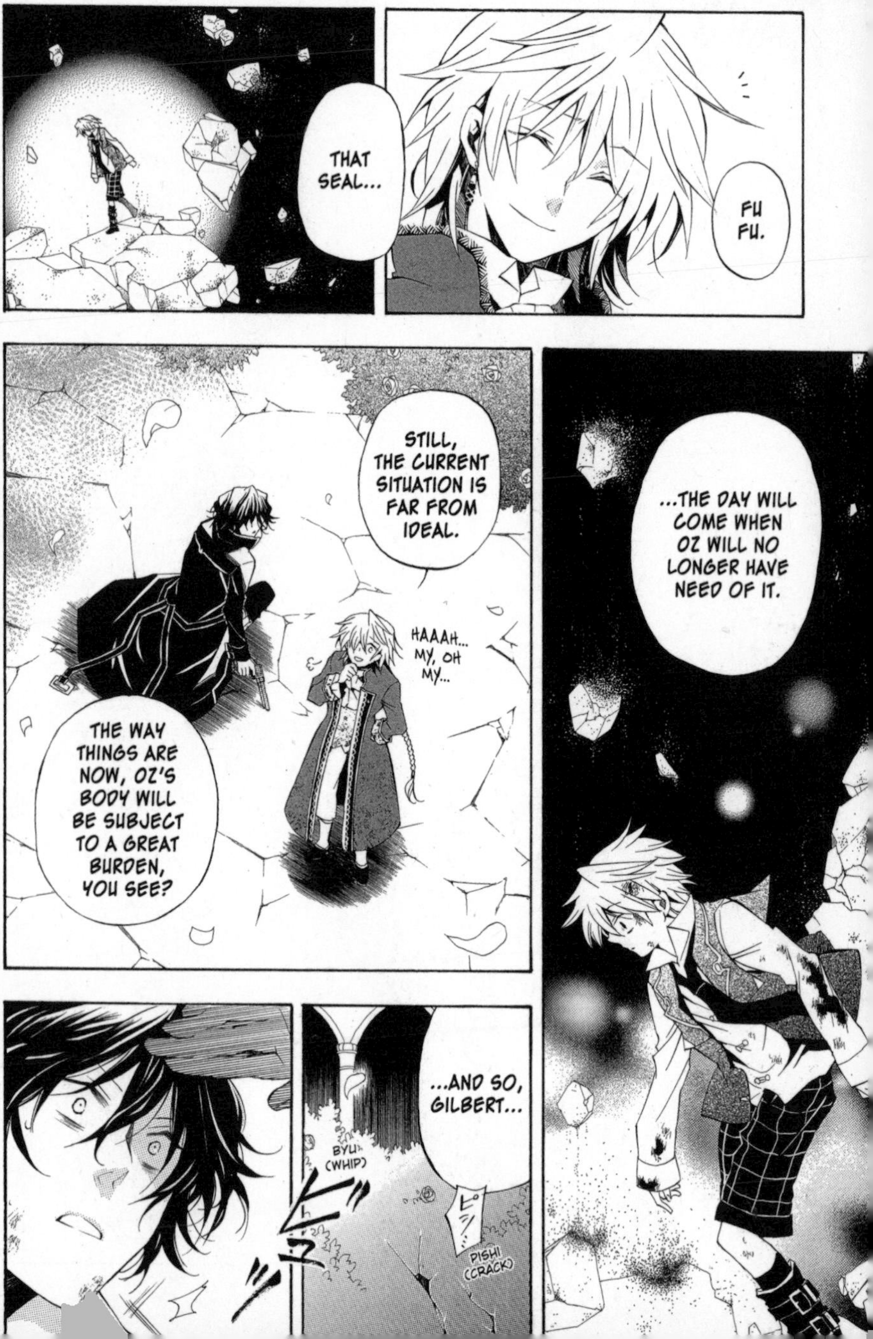
FU FU.
THAT SEAL...
...THE DAY WILL COME WHEN OZ WILL NO LONGER HAVE NEED OF IT.
STILL, THE CURRENT SITUATION IS FAR FROM IDEAL.
HAAAH... MY, OH MY...
THE WAY THINGS ARE NOW, OZ'S BODY WILL BE SUBJECT TO A GREAT BURDEN, YOU SEE?
...AND SO, GILBERT...
BYU (WHIP)
PISHI (CRACK)

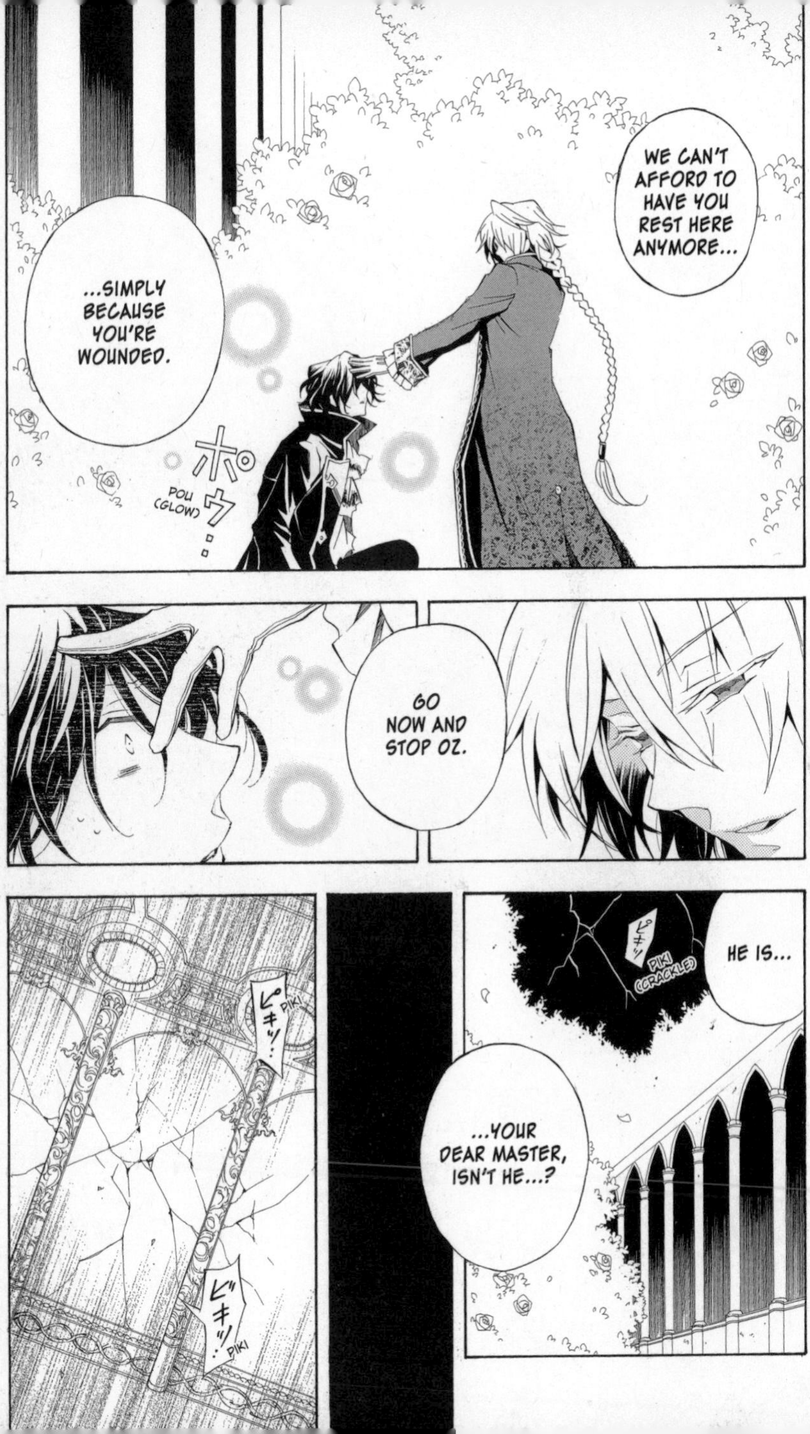
WE CAN'T AFFORD TO HAVE YOU REST HERE ANYMORE...
...SIMPLY BECAUSE YOU'RE WOUNDED.
ポウ
POU (GLOW)
GO NOW AND STOP OZ.
ピキッ
PIKI (CRACKLE)
HE IS...
...YOUR DEAR MASTER, ISN'T HE...?
ピキッ
PIKI
ピキッ
PIKI

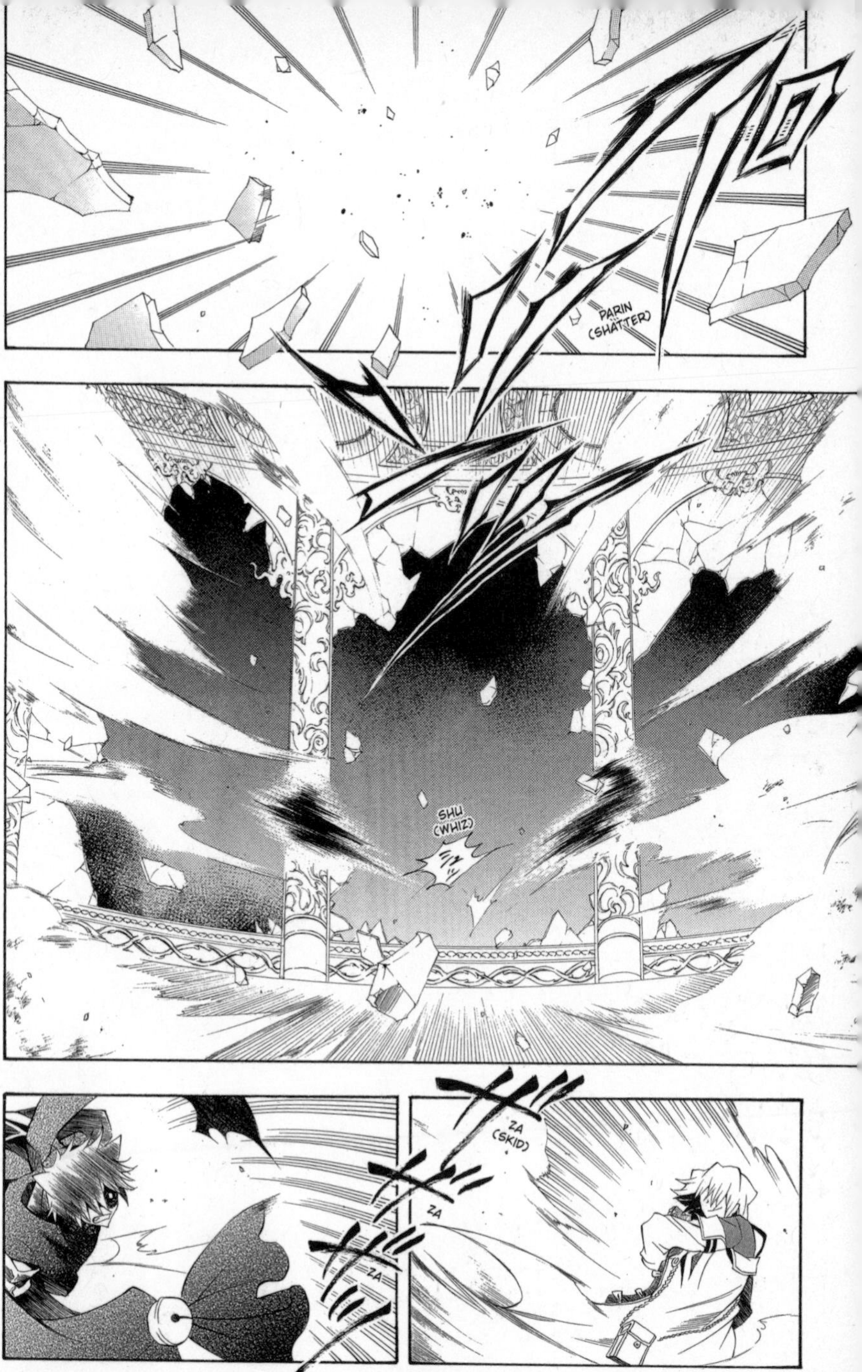
PARIN (SHATTER)
SHU (WHIZ)
ZA (SKID)
ZA
ZA

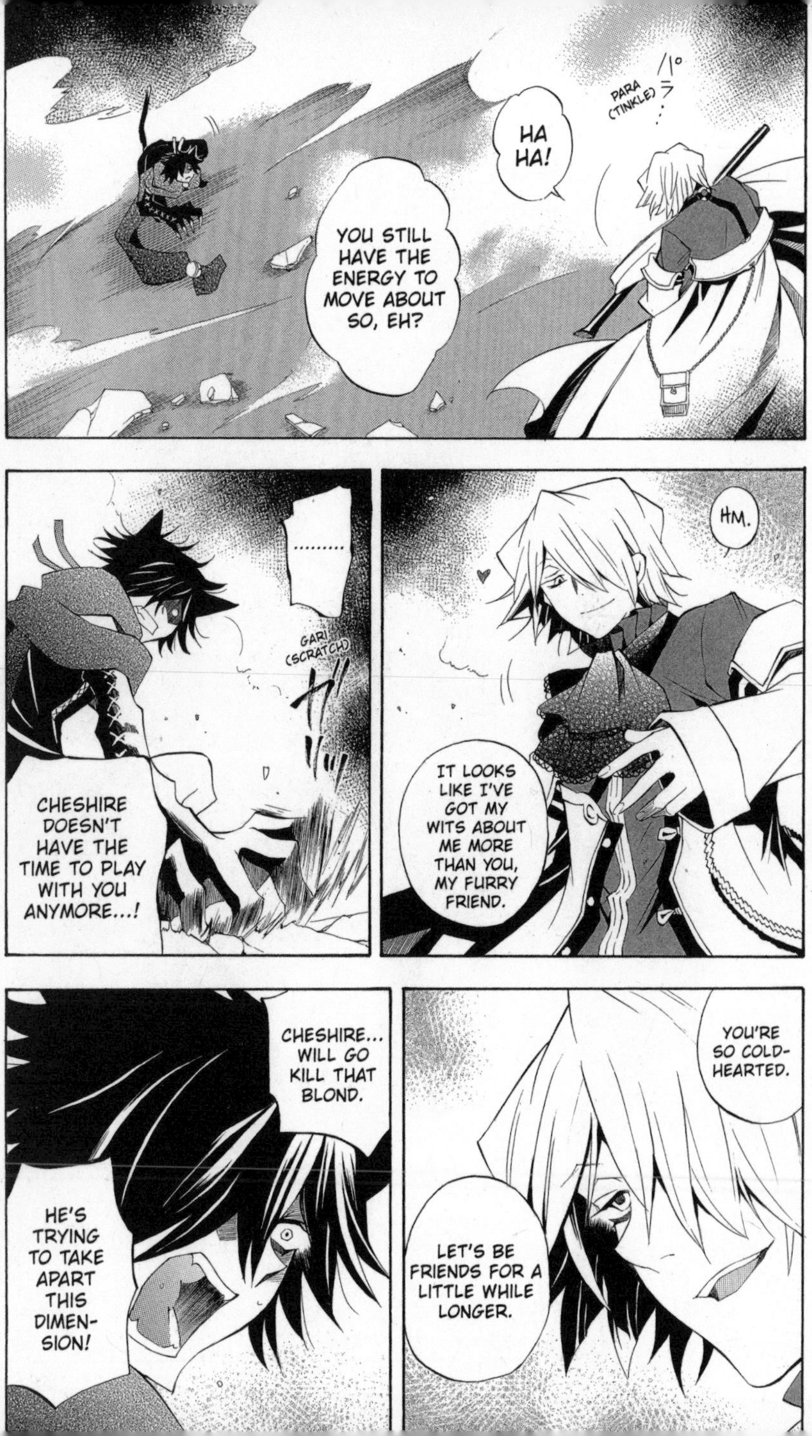
PARA (TINKLE)
HA HA!
YOU STILL HAVE THE ENERGY TO MOVE ABOUT SO, EH?
HM.
IT LOOKS LIKE I'VE GOT MY WITS ABOUT ME MORE THAN YOU, MY FURRY FRIEND.
....
GARI (SCRATCH)
CHESHIRE DOESN'T HAVE THE TIME TO PLAY WITH YOU ANYMORE...!
YOU'RE SO COLD-HEARTED.
LET'S BE FRIENDS FOR A LITTLE WHILE LONGER.
CHESHIRE... WILL GO KILL THAT BLOND.
HE'S TRYING TO TAKE APART THIS DIMEN-SION!

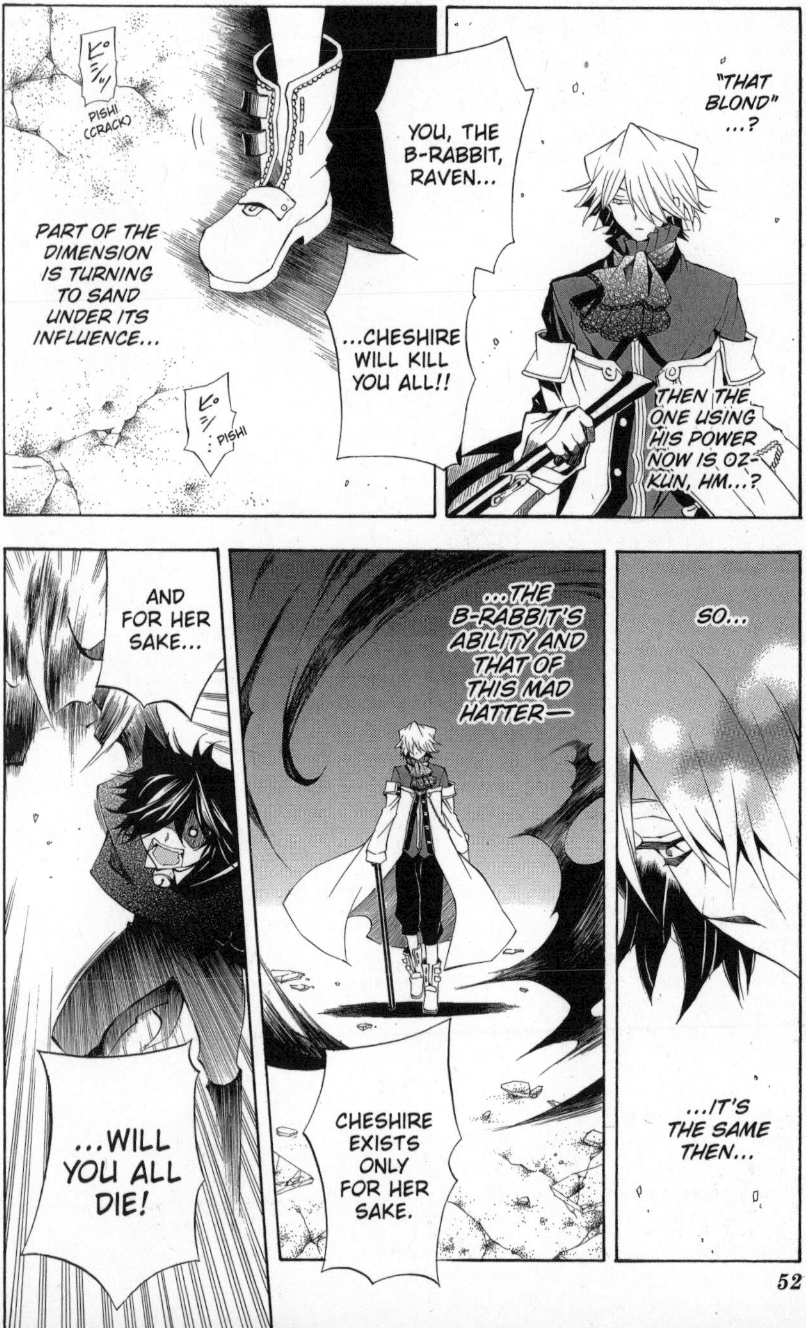
"THAT BLOND" ...?
THEN THE ONE USING HIS POWER NOW IS OZ-KUN, HM...?
YOU, THE B-RABBIT, RAVEN...
...CHESHIRE WILL KILL YOU ALL!!
ピシッ
PISHI (CRACK)
PART OF THE DIMENSION IS TURNING TO SAND UNDER ITS INFLUENCE...
ピシ
PISHI
SO...
...IT'S THE SAME THEN...
...THE B-RABBIT'S ABILITY AND THAT OF THIS MAD HATTER—
CHESHIRE EXISTS ONLY FOR HER SAKE.
AND FOR HER SAKE...
...WILL YOU ALL DIE!

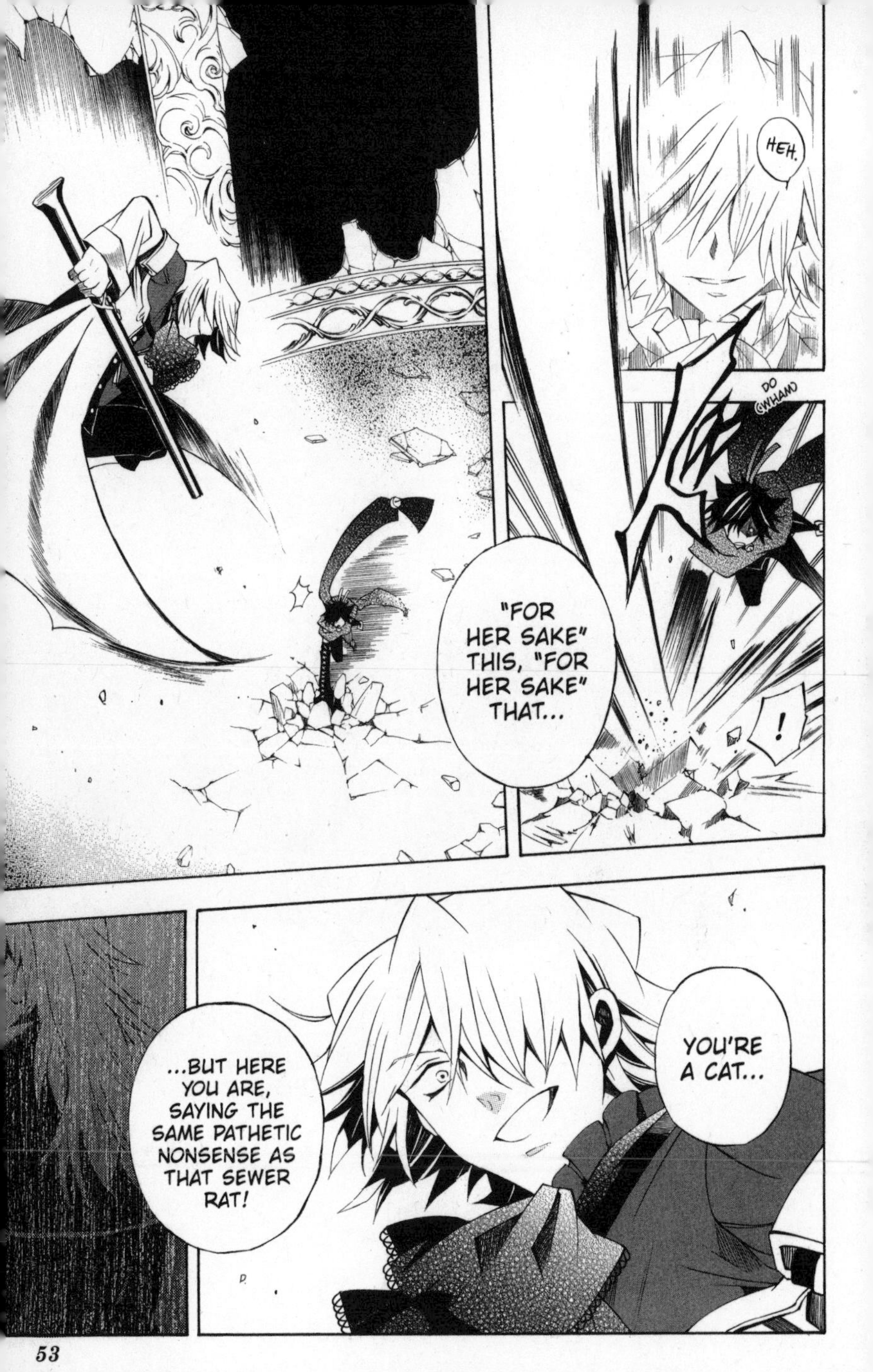
HEH.
DO (WHAM)
!
"FOR HER SAKE" THIS, "FOR HER SAKE" THAT...
YOU'RE A CAT...
...BUT HERE YOU ARE, SAYING THE SAME PATHETIC NONSENSE AS THAT SEWER RAT!

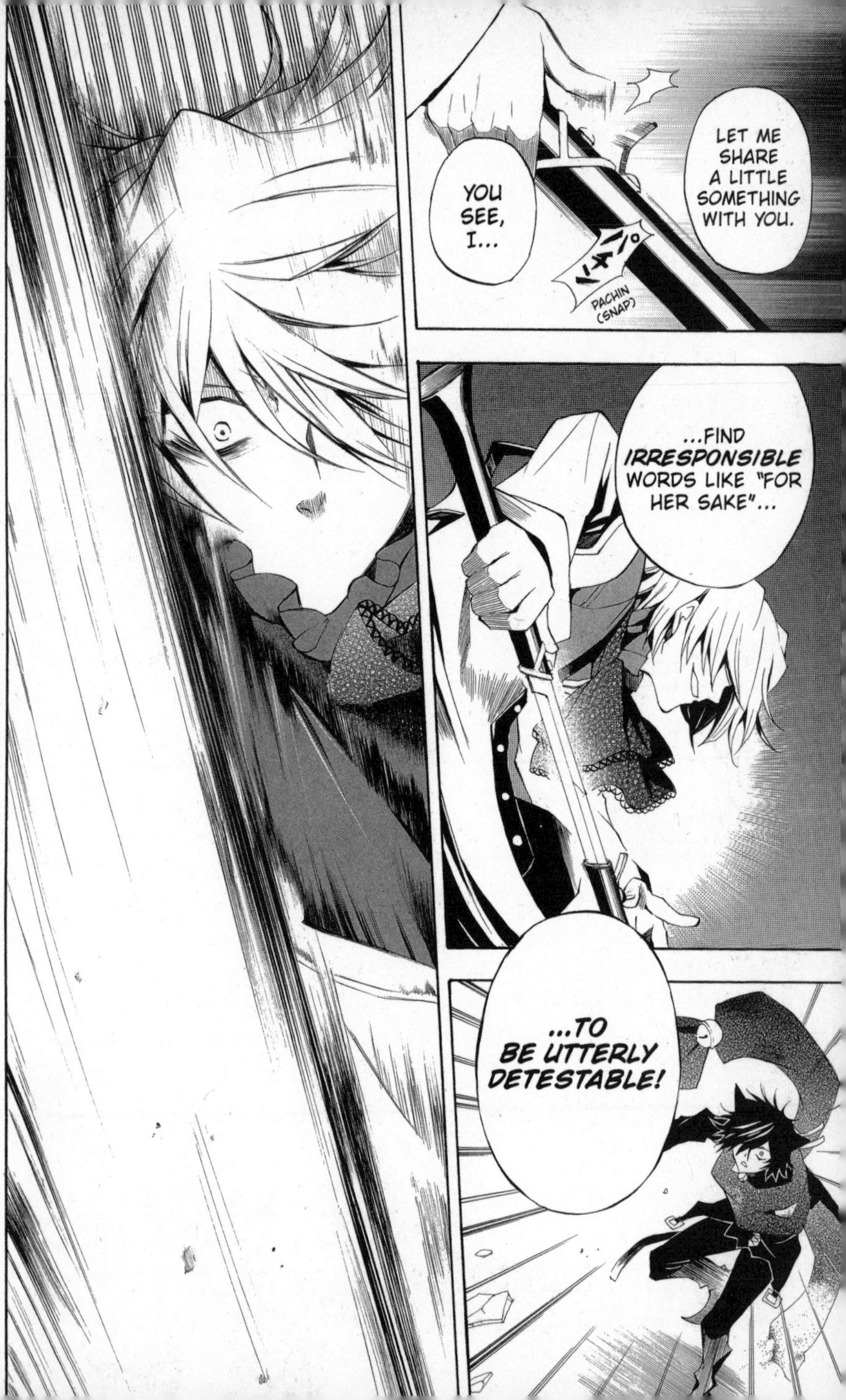
LET ME SHARE A LITTLE SOMETHING WITH YOU.
YOU SEE, I...
PACHIN (SNAP)
...FIND IRRESPONSIBLE WORDS LIKE "FOR HER SAKE"...
...TO BE UTTERLY DETESTABLE!

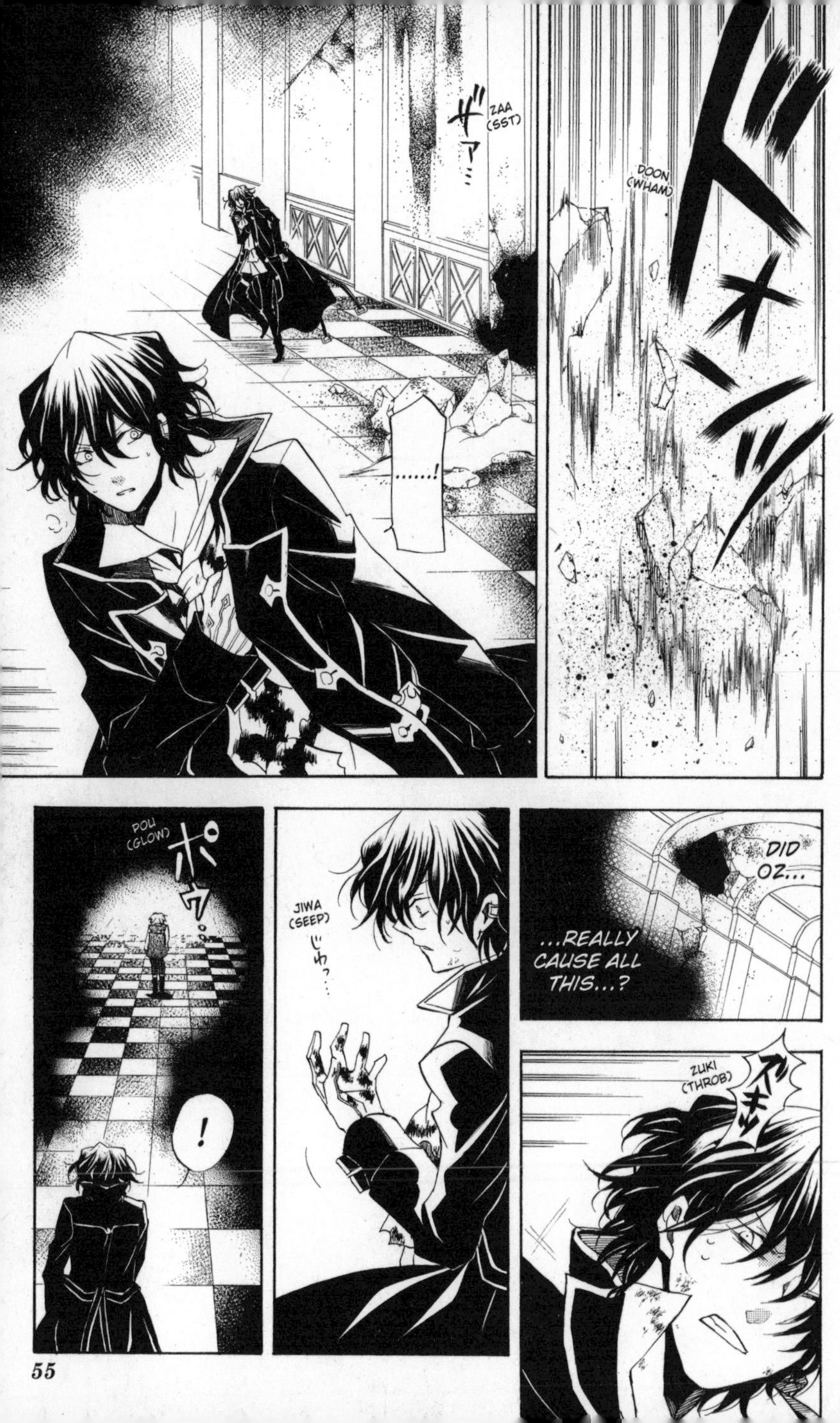
DOON (WHAM)
ZAA (SST)
......!
DID OZ...
...REALLY CAUSE ALL THIS...?
ZUKI (THROB)
JIWA (SEEP)
POU (GLOW)
!

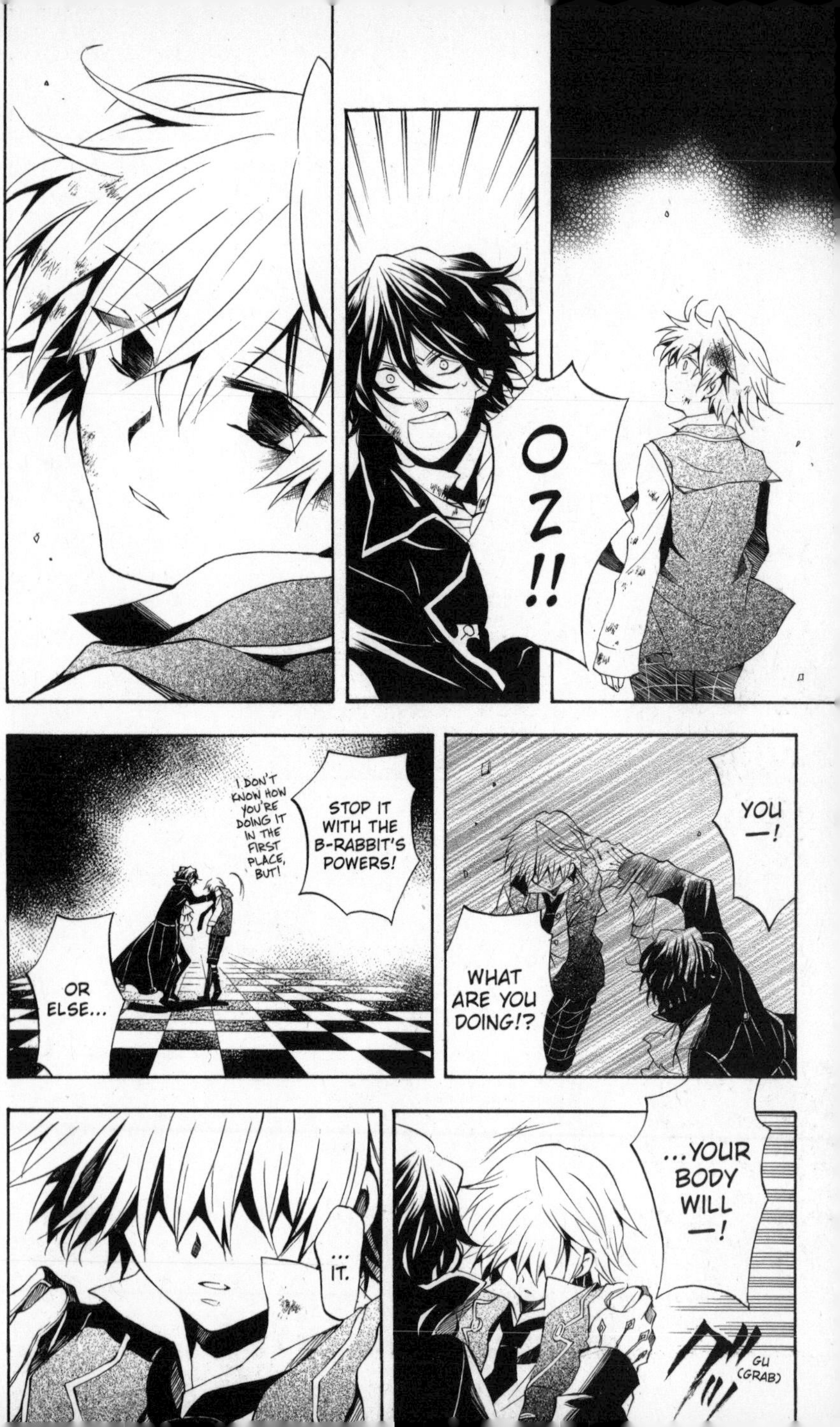
OZ!!
YOU—!
WHAT ARE YOU DOING!?
STOP IT WITH THE B-RABBIT'S POWERS!
I DON'T KNOW HOW YOU'RE DOING IT IN THE FIRST PLACE, BUT!
OR ELSE...
...YOUR BODY WILL—!
GU (GRAB)
... IT.

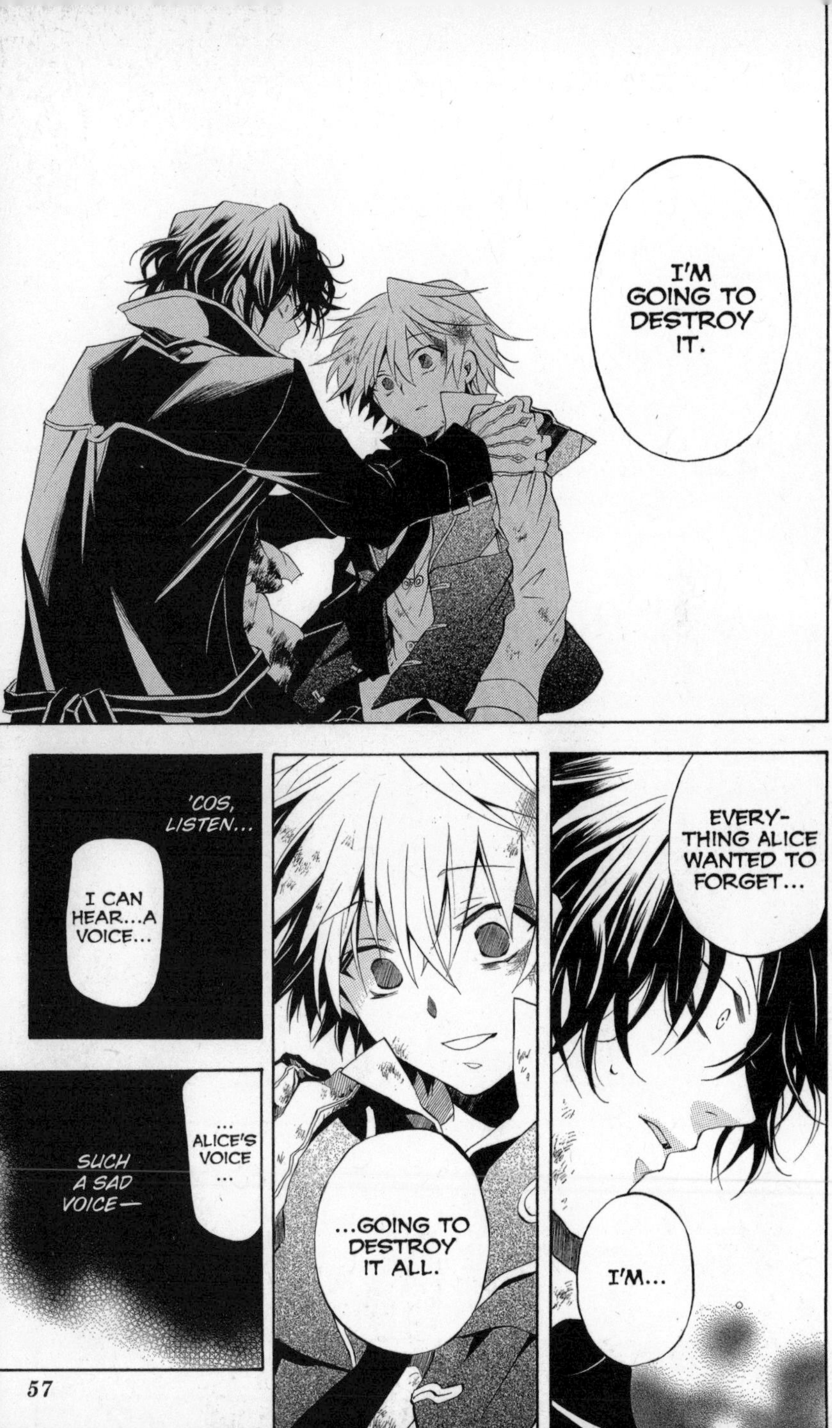
I'M GOING TO DESTROY IT.
EVERY-THING ALICE WANTED TO FORGET...
I'M...
...GOING TO DESTROY IT ALL.
'COS, LISTEN...
I CAN HEAR...A VOICE...
...ALICE'S VOICE...
SUCH A SAD VOICE—

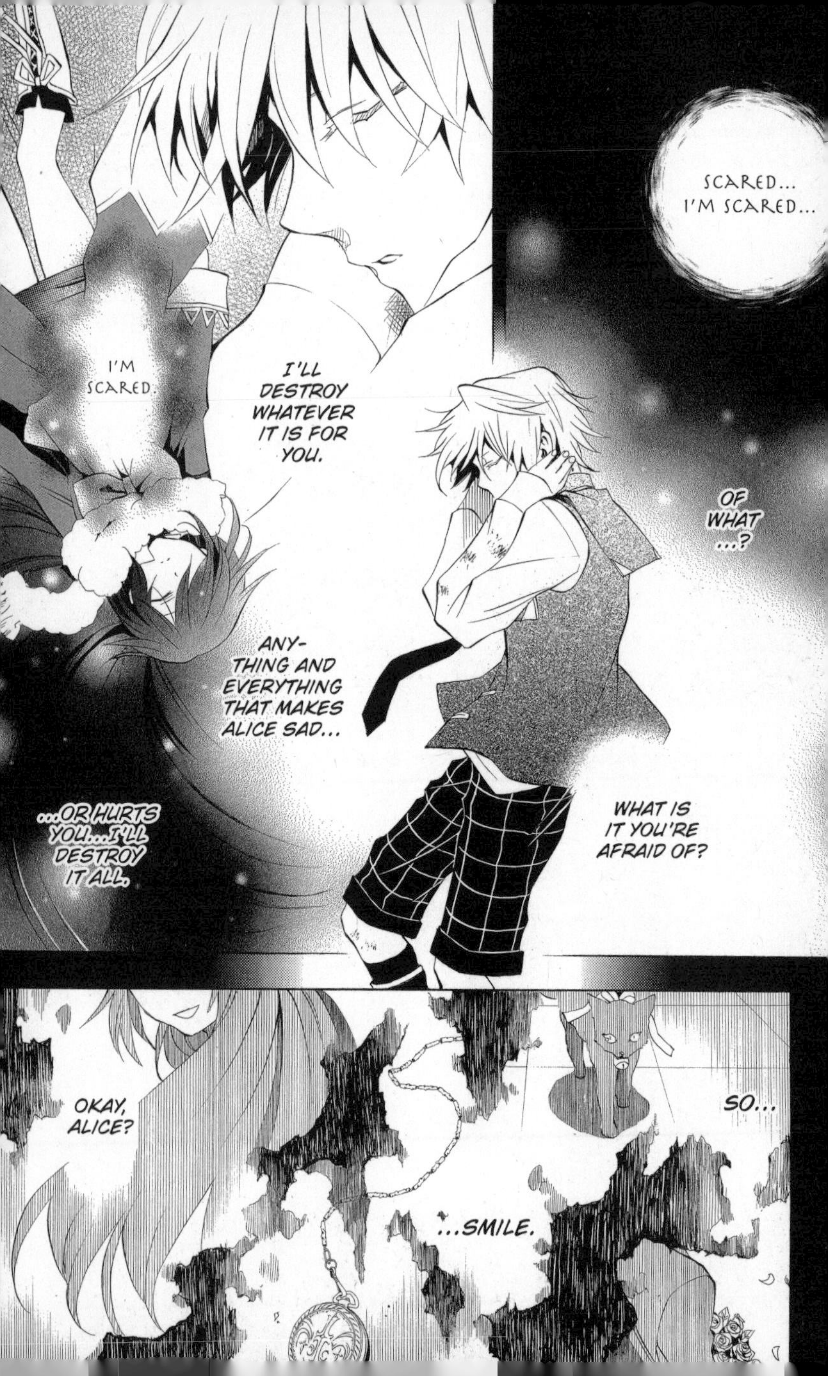
SCARED... I'M SCARED...
OF WHAT...?
WHAT IS IT YOU'RE AFRAID OF?
I'M SCARED.
I'LL DESTROY WHATEVER IT IS FOR YOU.
ANY-THING AND EVERYTHING THAT MAKES ALICE SAD...
...OR HURTS YOU... I'LL DESTROY IT ALL.
SO...
...SMILE.
OKAY, ALICE?

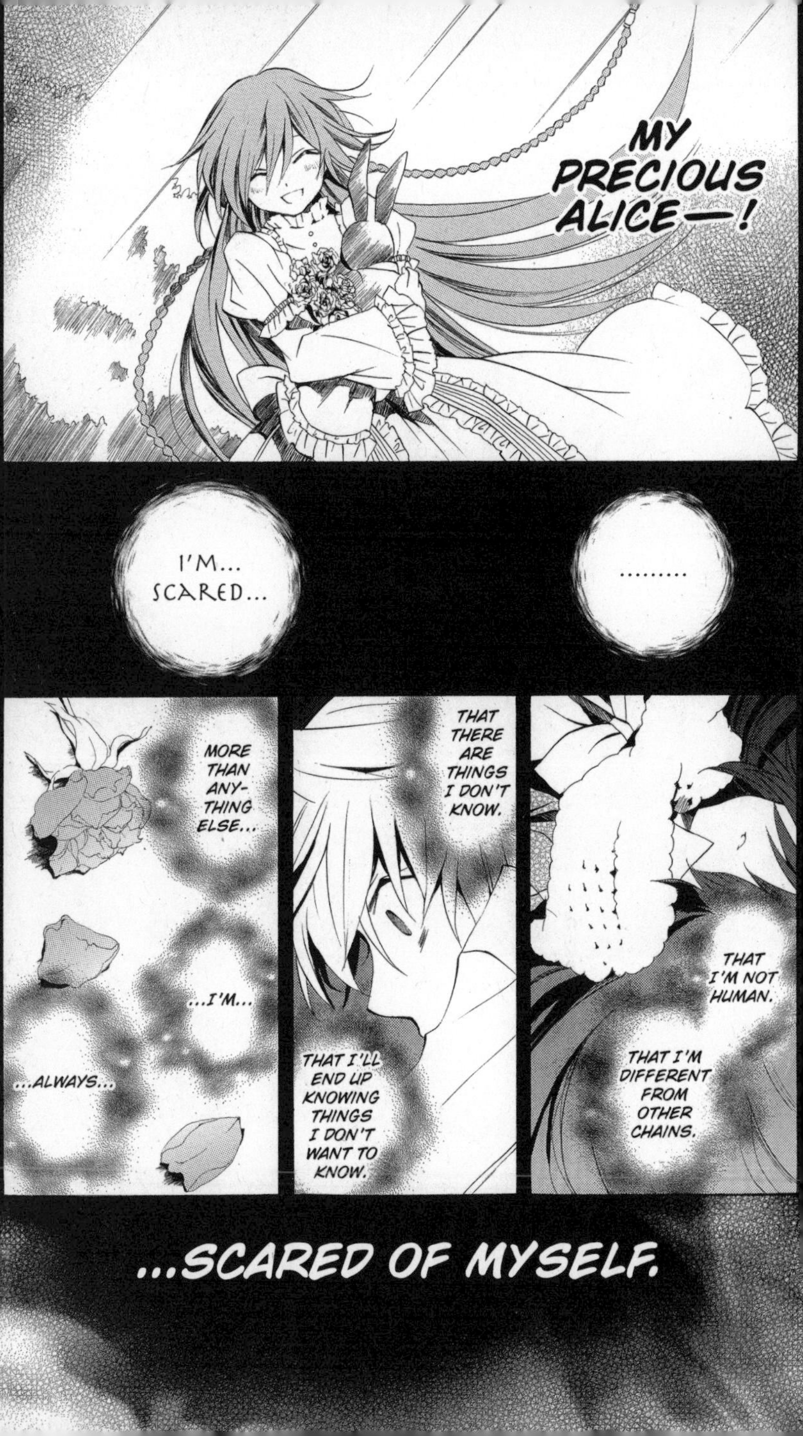
MY PRECIOUS ALICE—!
....
I'M... SCARED...
THAT I'M NOT HUMAN.
THAT I'M DIFFERENT FROM OTHER CHAINS.
THAT THERE ARE THINGS I DON'T KNOW.
THAT I'LL END UP KNOWING THINGS I DON'T WANT TO KNOW.
MORE THAN ANY-THING ELSE...
...I'M...
...ALWAYS...
...SCARED OF MYSELF.

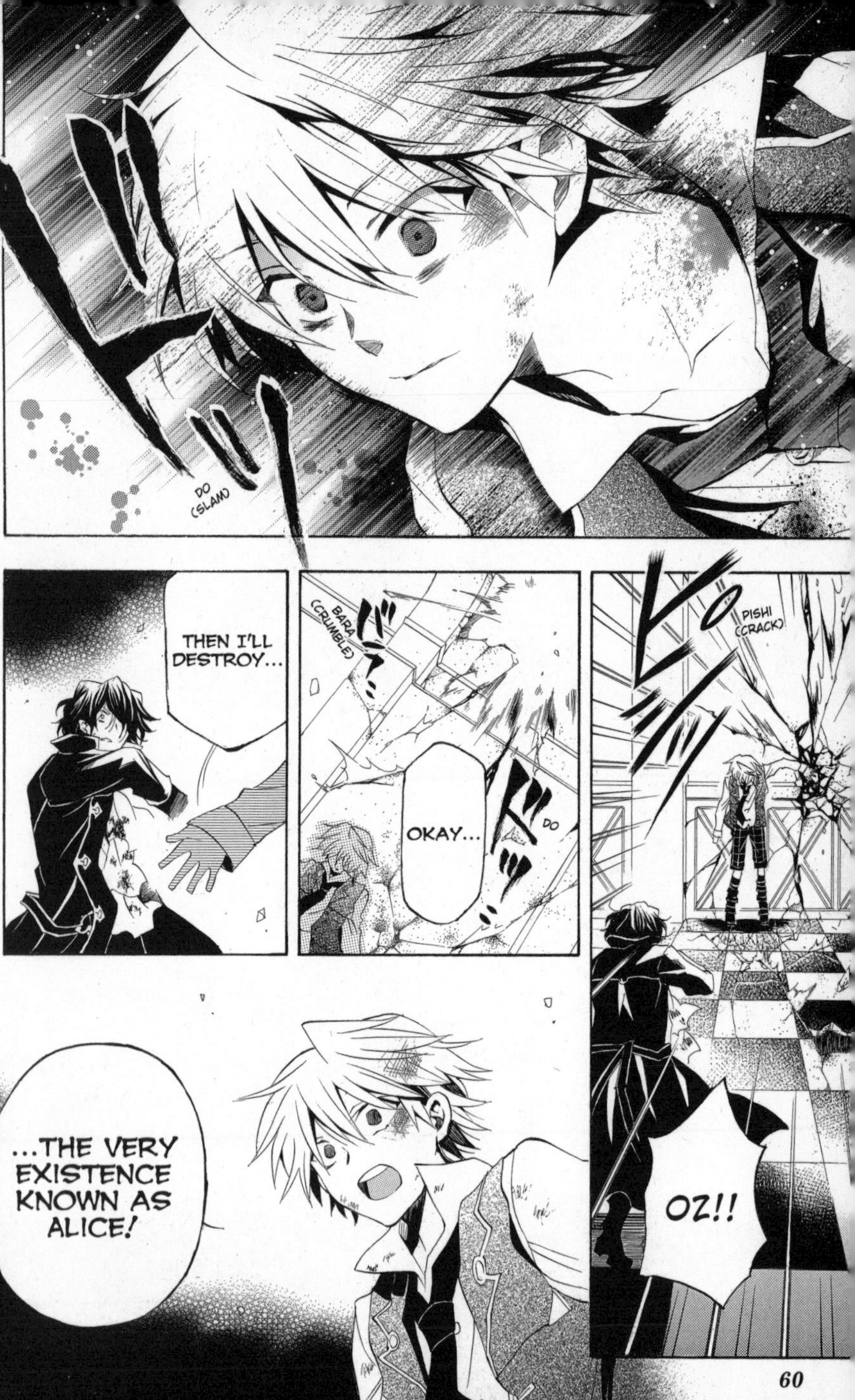
DO
(SLAM)
PISHI
(CRACK)
OZ!!
BARA
(CRUMBLE)
OKAY...
DO
THEN I'LL DESTROY...
...THE VERY EXISTENCE KNOWN AS ALICE!

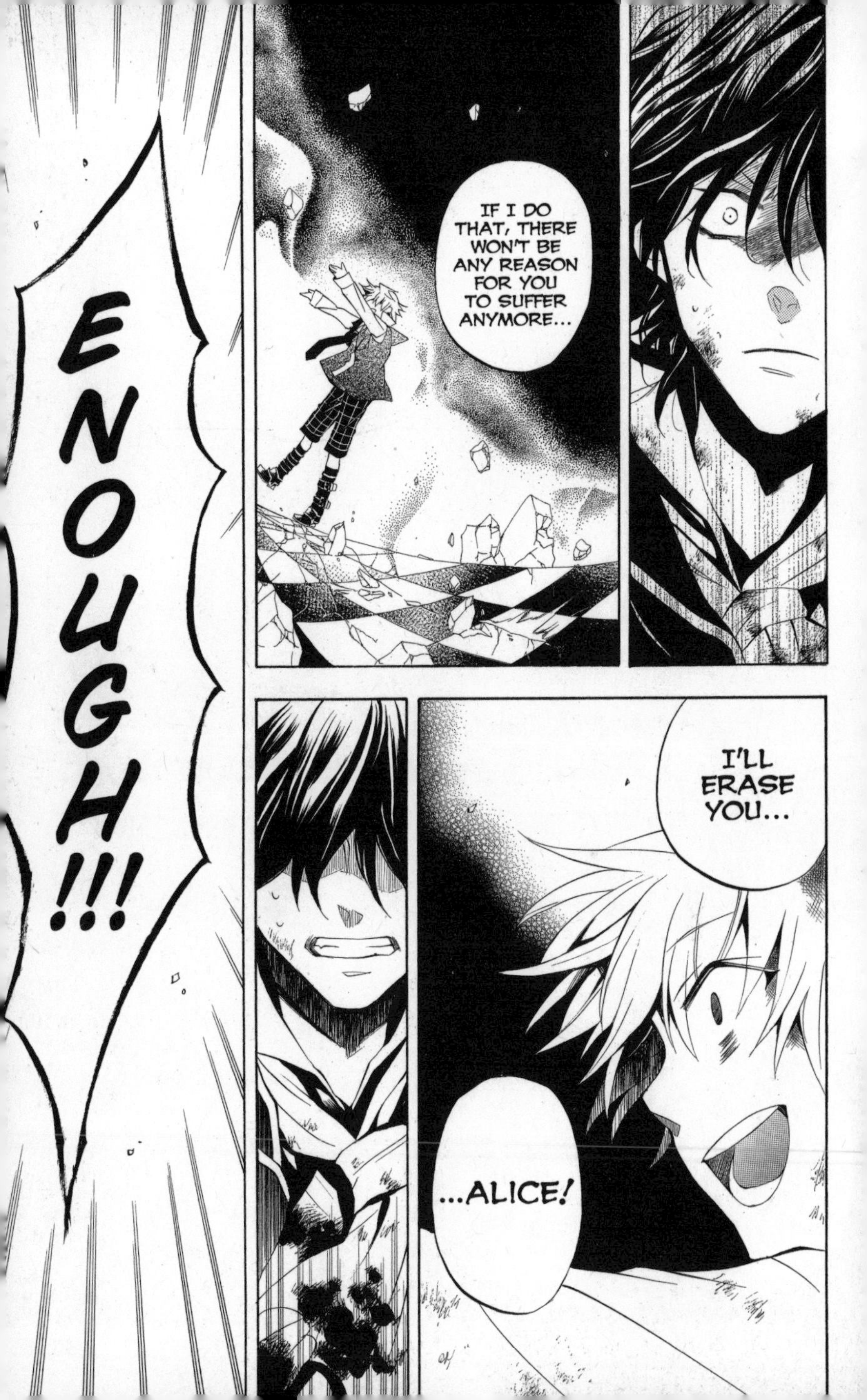
IF I DO THAT, THERE WON'T BE ANY REASON FOR YOU TO SUFFER ANYMORE...
I'LL ERASE YOU...
...ALICE!
ENOUGH!!!

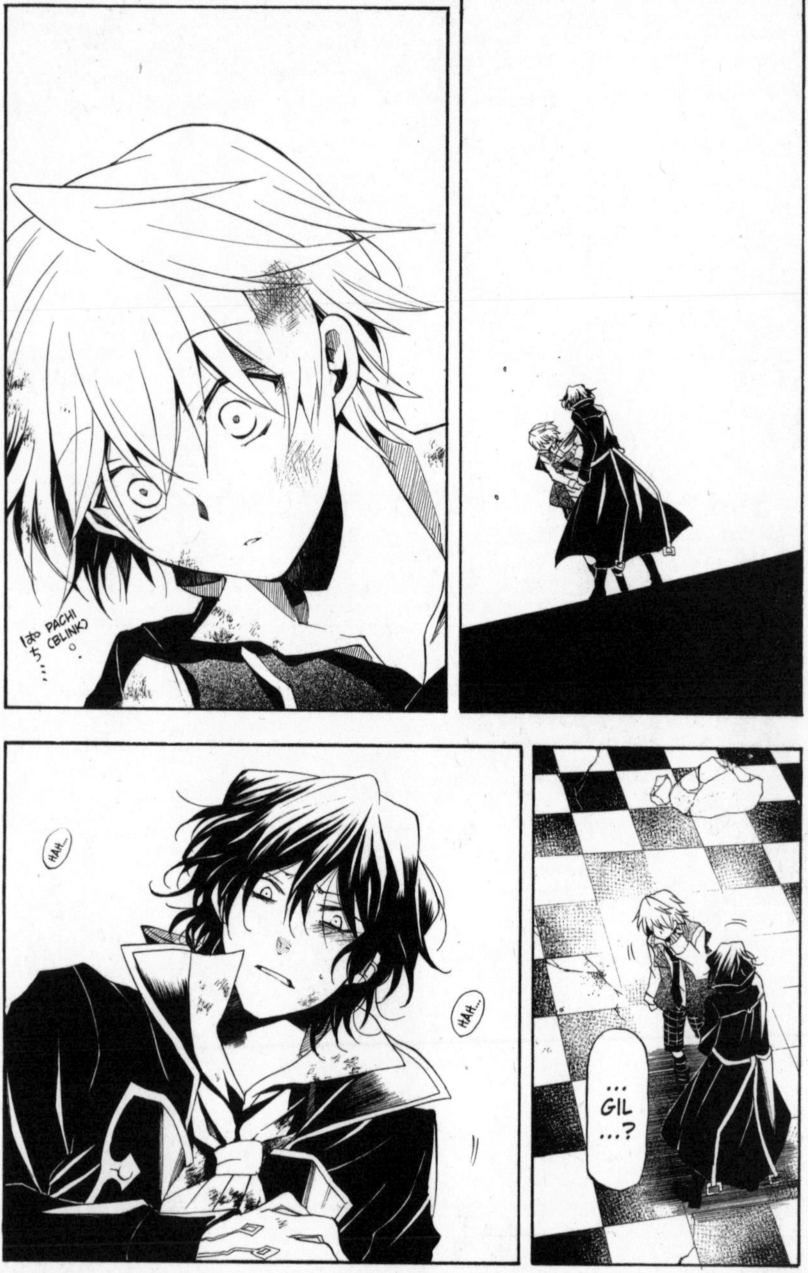
ぱち…
PACHI (BLINK)
...GIL ...?
HAH...
HAH...

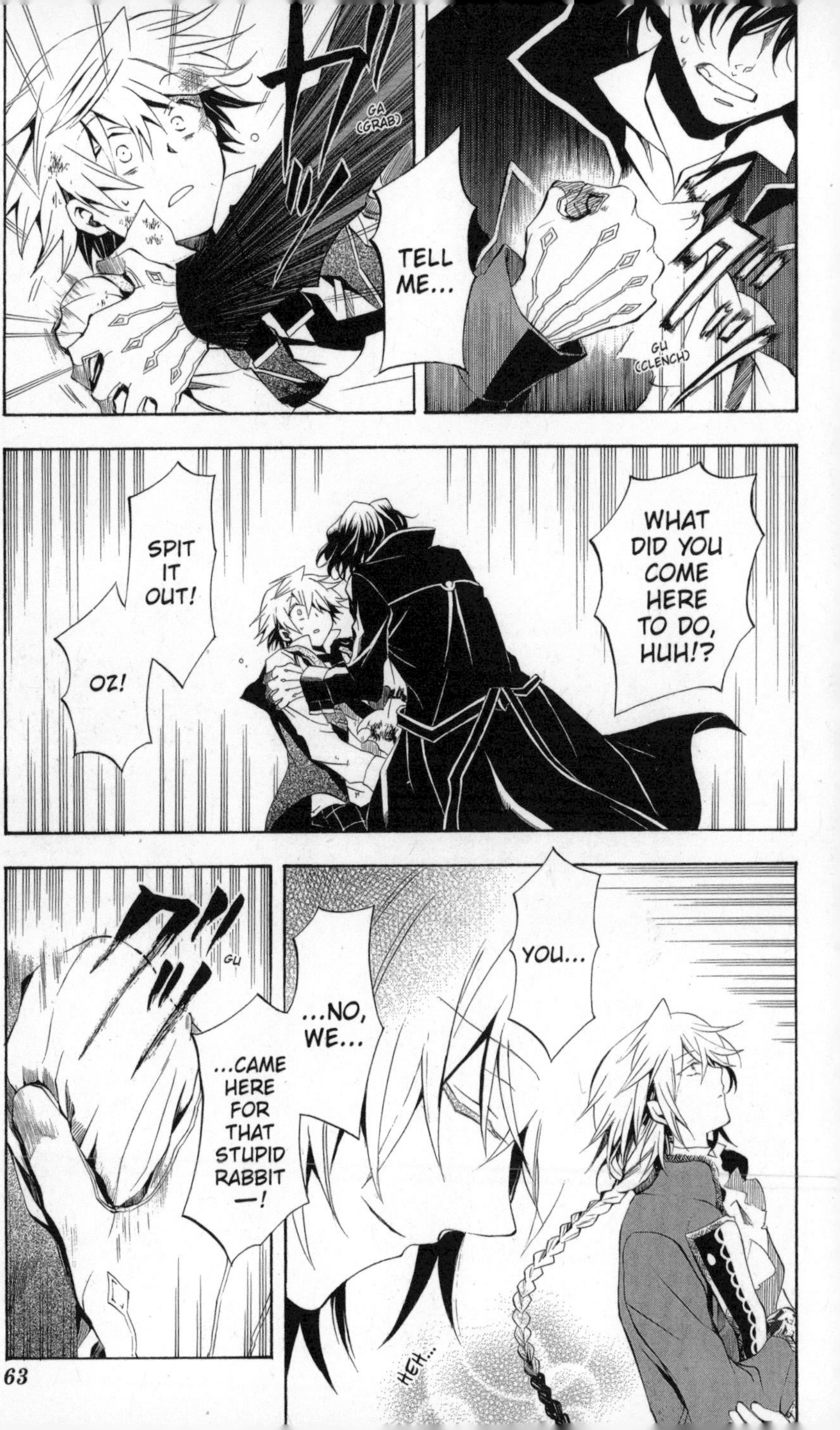
GU (CLENCH)
TELL ME...
GA (GRAB)
WHAT DID YOU COME HERE TO DO, HUH!?
SPIT IT OUT!
OZ!
YOU...
...NO, WE...
HEH...
GU
...CAME HERE FOR THAT STUPID RABBIT—!

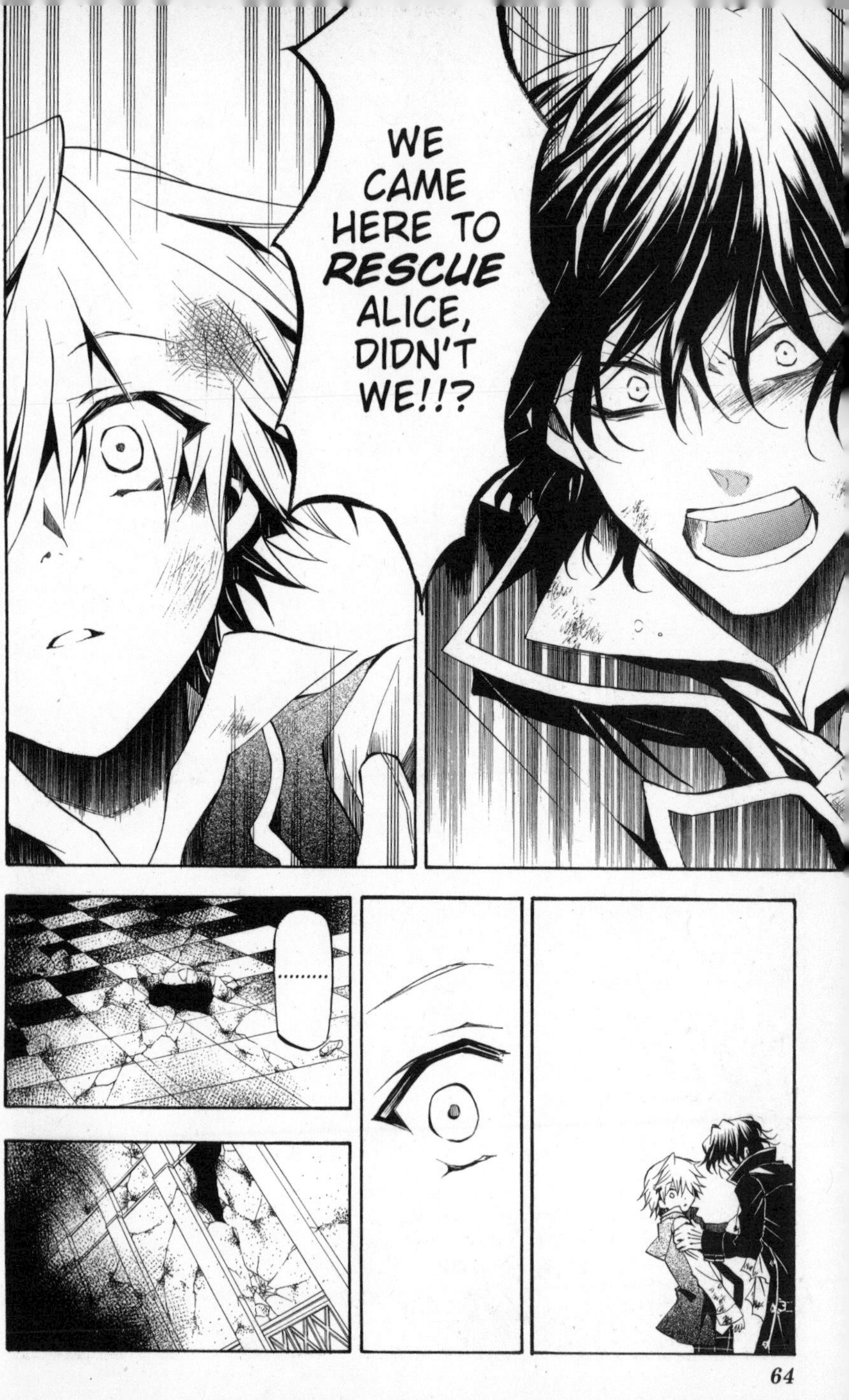
WE CAME HERE TO *RESCUE* ALICE, DIDN'T WE!!?
....

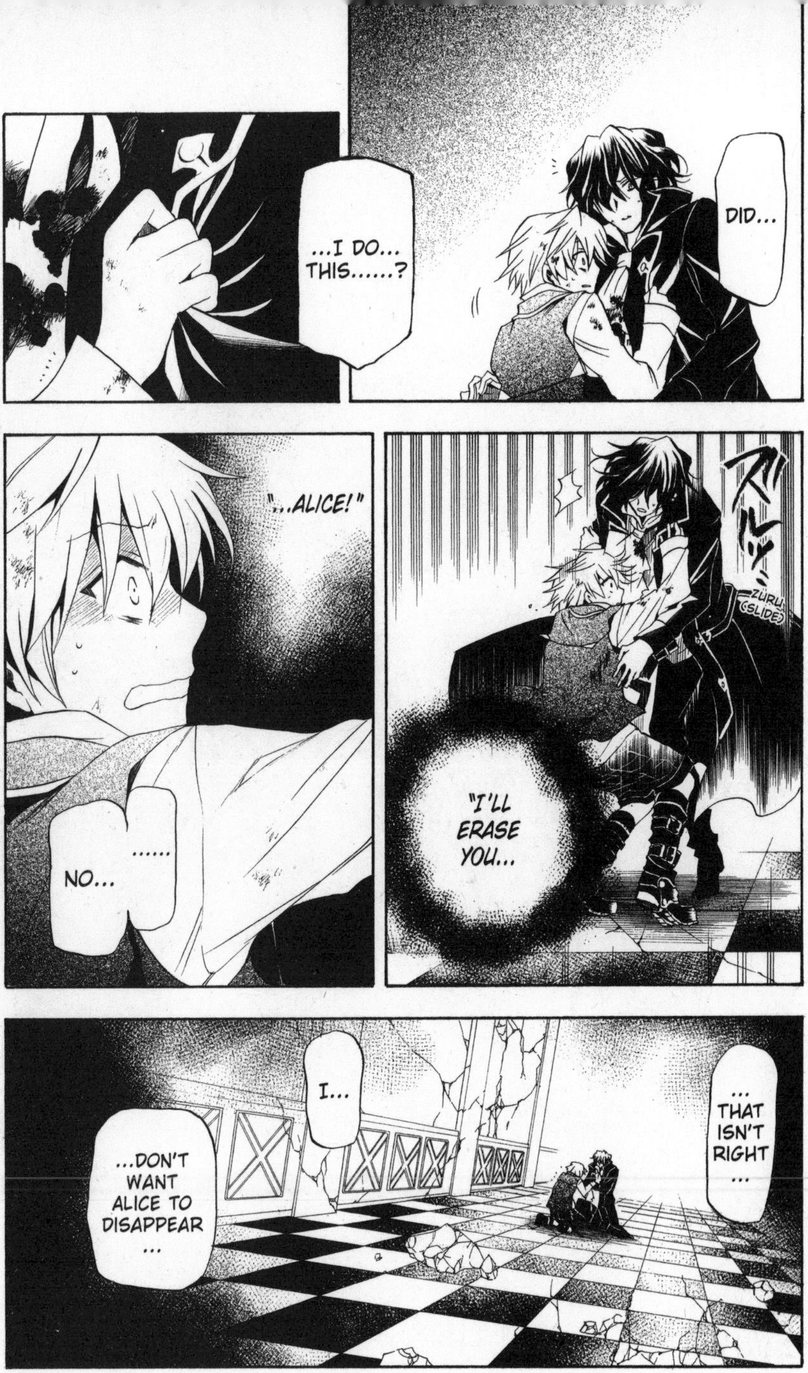
DID...
...I DO... THIS......?
ズルッ
ZURU! (SLIDE)
"I'LL ERASE YOU...
"...ALICE!"
......
NO...
...THAT ISN'T RIGHT...
I...
...DON'T WANT ALICE TO DISAPPEAR...

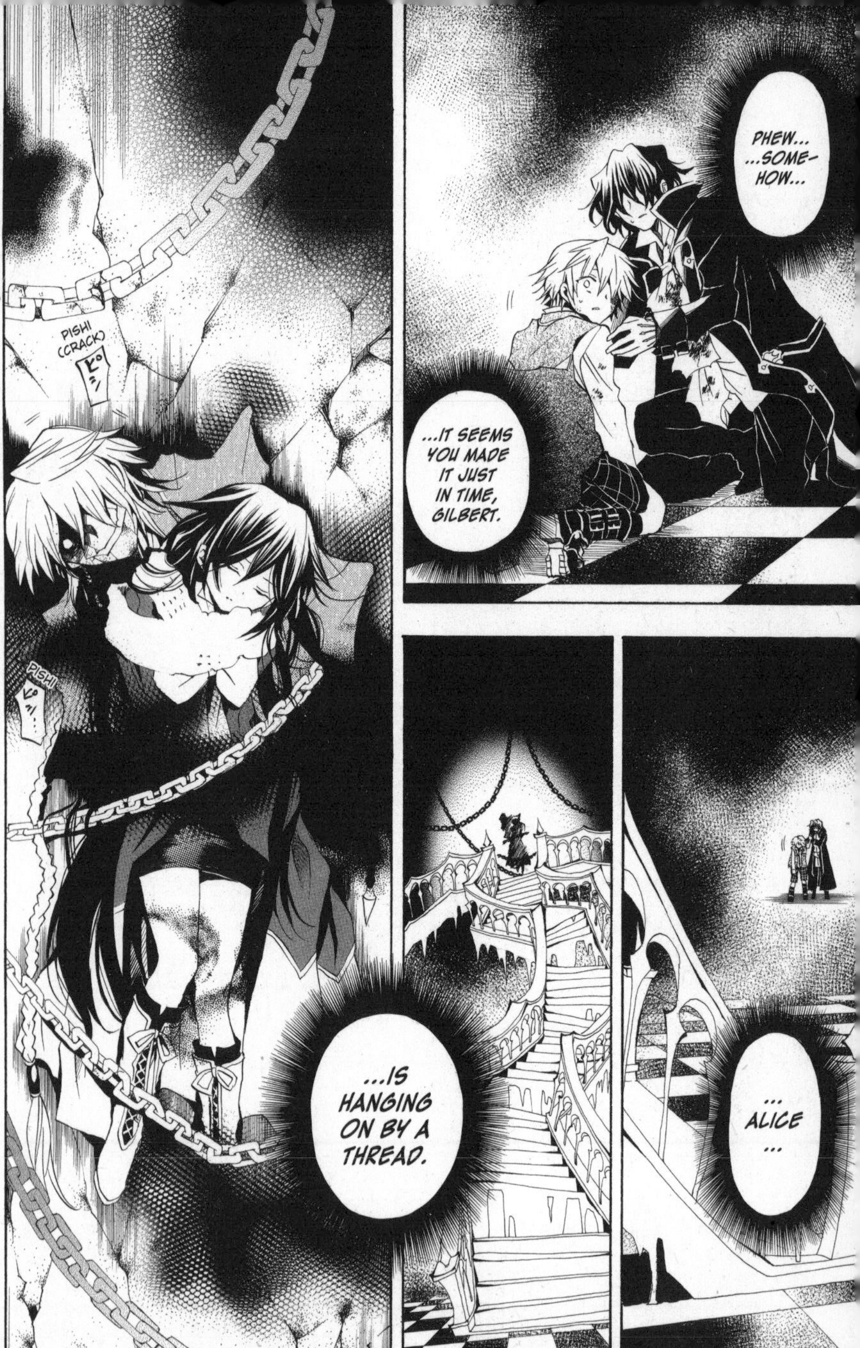
PHEW... ...SOME-HOW...
...IT SEEMS YOU MADE IT JUST IN TIME, GILBERT.
... ALICE ...
...IS HANGING ON BY A THREAD.
PISHI (CRACK)
PISHI

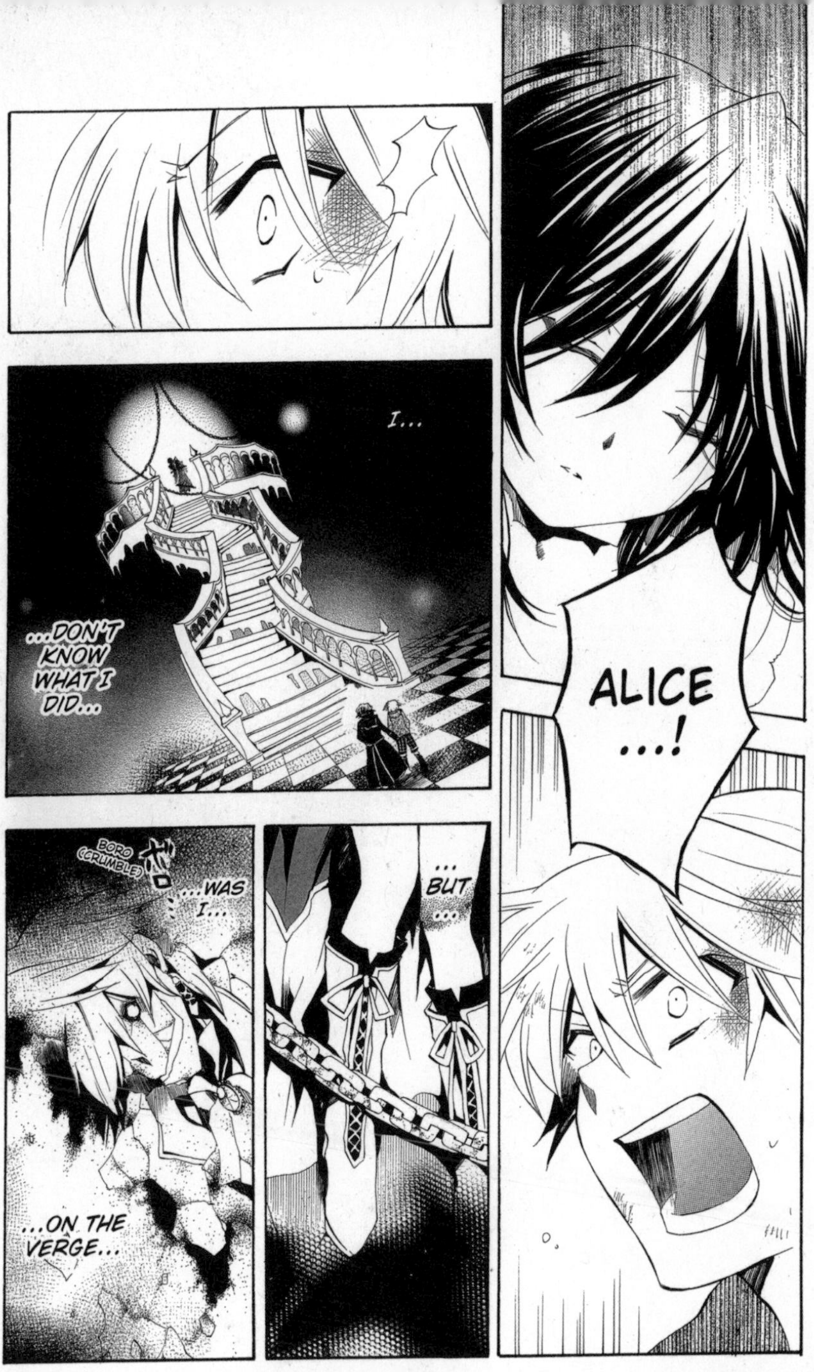
ALICE ...!
I...
...DON'T KNOW WHAT I DID...
... BUT ...
BORO (CRUMBLE)
...WAS I...
...ON THE VERGE...

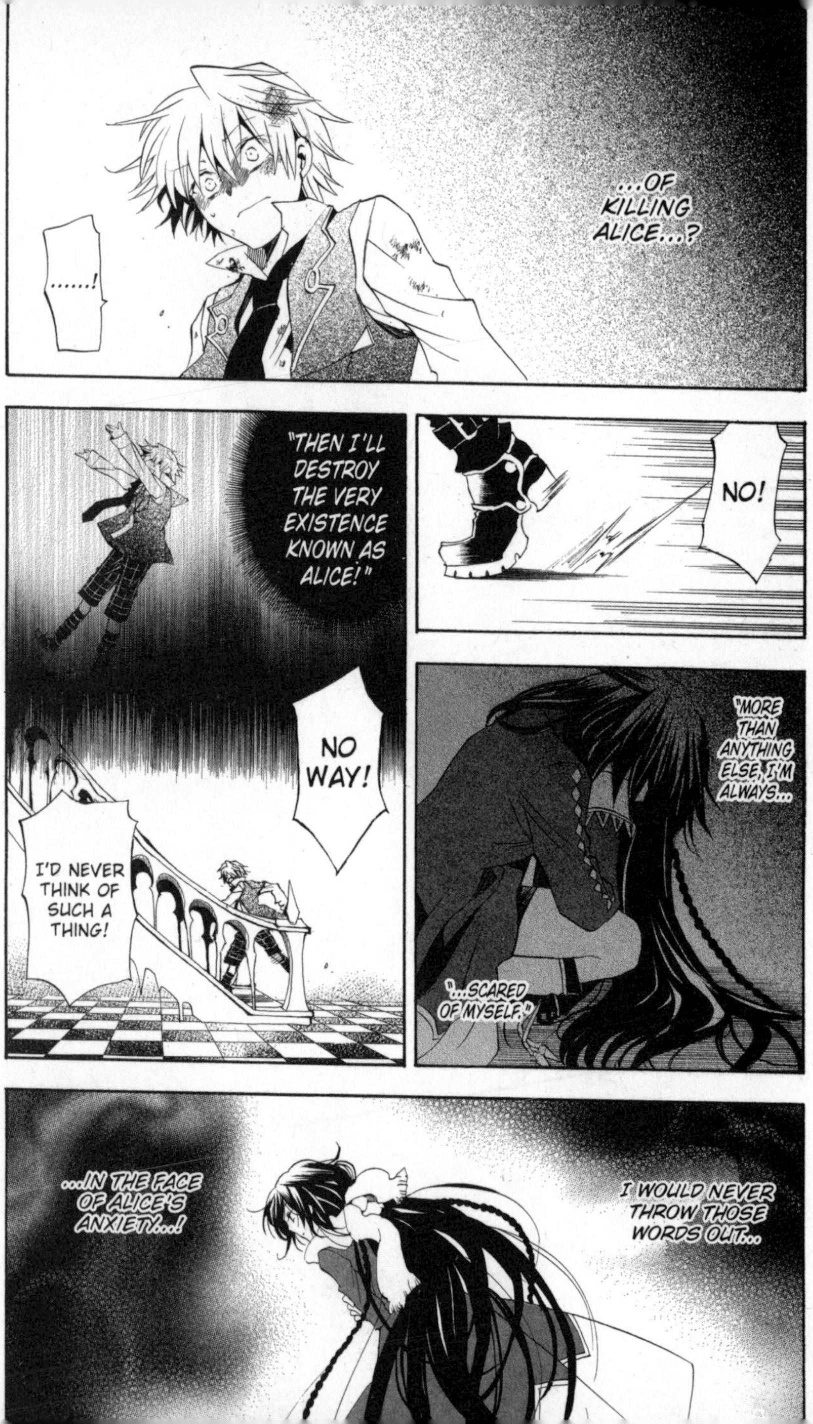
...OF KILLING ALICE...?
......!
NO!
"MORE THAN ANYTHING ELSE, I'M ALWAYS...
"...SCARED OF MYSELF."
"THEN I'LL DESTROY THE VERY EXISTENCE KNOWN AS ALICE!"
NO WAY!
I'D NEVER THINK OF SUCH A THING!
I WOULD NEVER THROW THOSE WORDS OUT...
...IN THE FACE OF ALICE'S ANXIETY...!

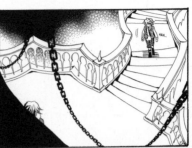

I DON'T KNOW WHAT YOU WERE LIKE WHEN YOU WERE HUMAN.

ALICE ...

...I DO KNOW WHAT ALICE IS LIKE NOW!

BUT...

....

WHO'S THERE ...?

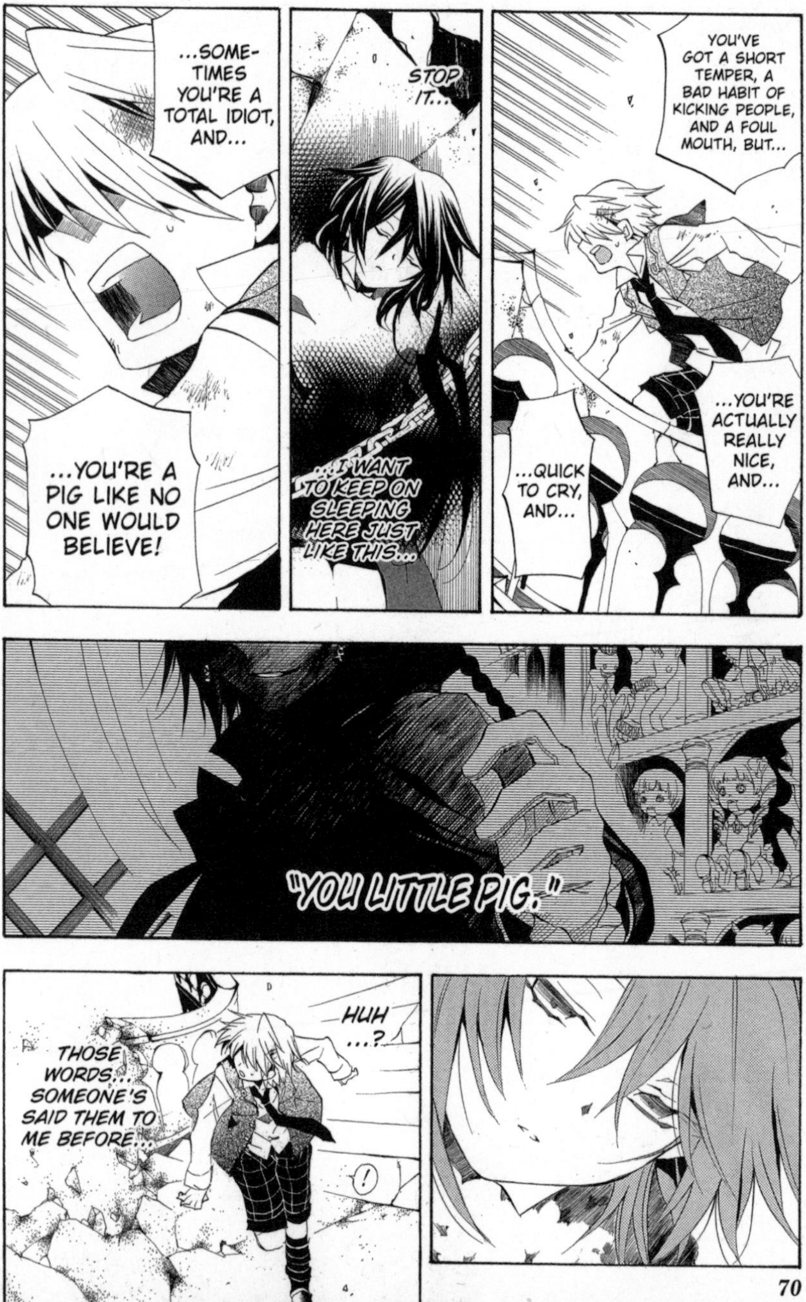
YOU'VE GOT A SHORT TEMPER, A BAD HABIT OF KICKING PEOPLE, AND A FOUL MOUTH, BUT...
...YOU'RE ACTUALLY REALLY NICE, AND...
...QUICK TO CRY, AND...
STOP IT...
...I WANT TO KEEP ON SLEEPING HERE JUST LIKE THIS...
...SOME-TIMES YOU'RE A TOTAL IDIOT, AND...
...YOU'RE A PIG LIKE NO ONE WOULD BELIEVE!
"YOU LITTLE PIG."
HUH ...?
THOSE WORDS... SOMEONE'S SAID THEM TO ME BEFORE...
!

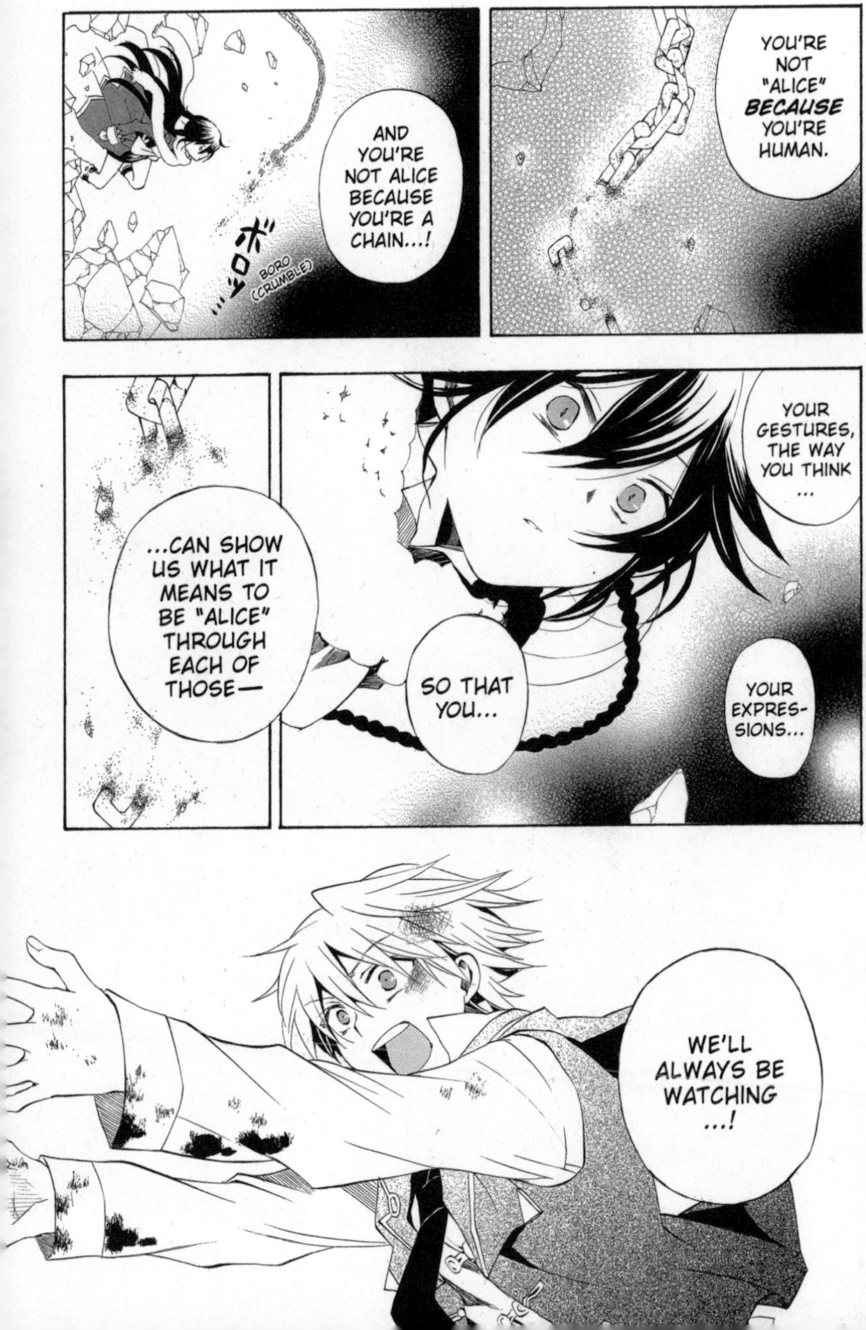
YOU'RE NOT "ALICE" ***BECAUSE*** YOU'RE HUMAN.
AND YOU'RE NOT ALICE BECAUSE YOU'RE A CHAIN...!
ボロッ...
BORO (CRUMBLE)
YOUR GESTURES, THE WAY YOU THINK...
YOUR EXPRES-SIONS...
SO THAT YOU...
...CAN SHOW US WHAT IT MEANS TO BE "ALICE" THROUGH EACH OF THOSE—
WE'LL ALWAYS BE WATCHING...!

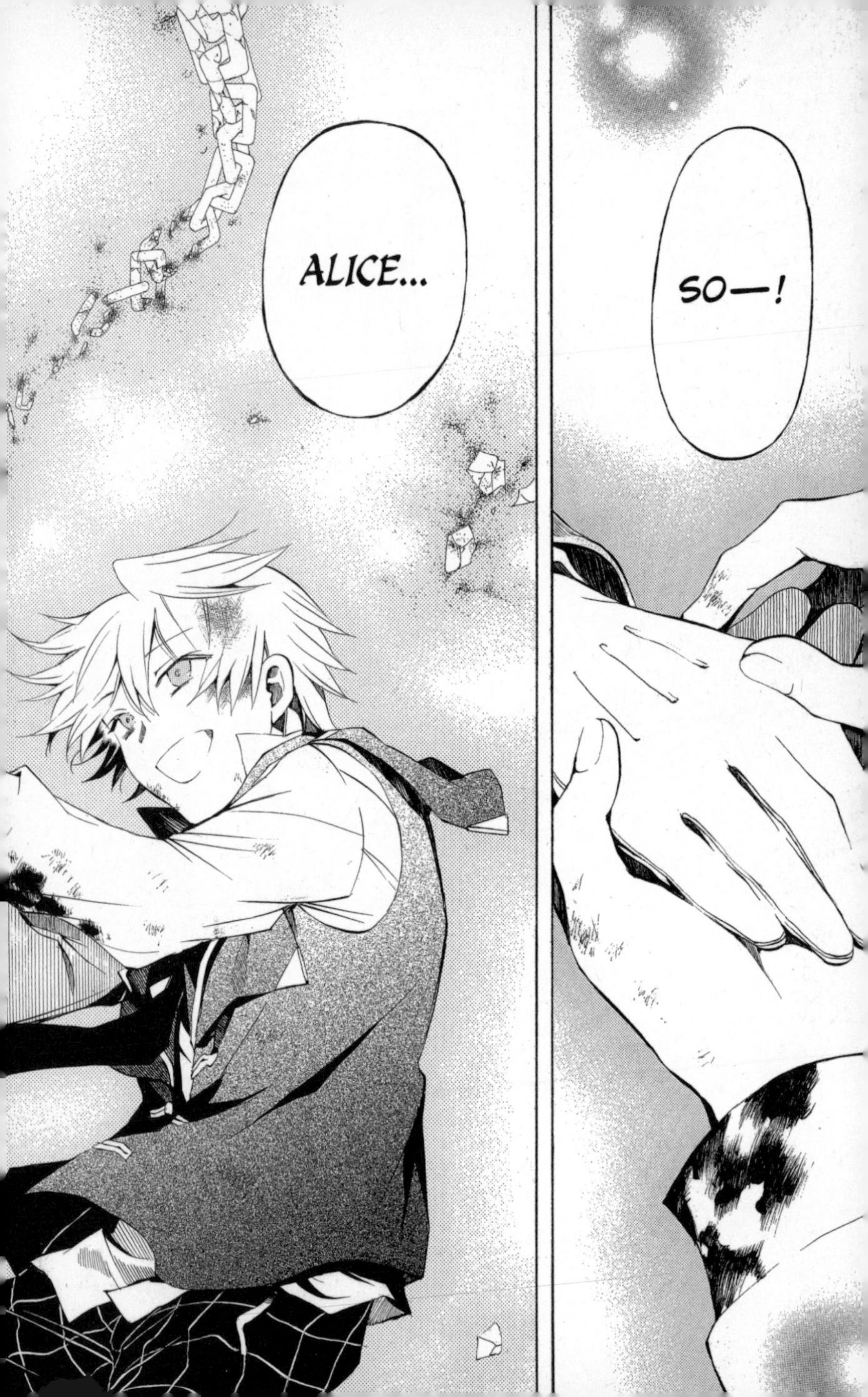
SO—!
ALICE...

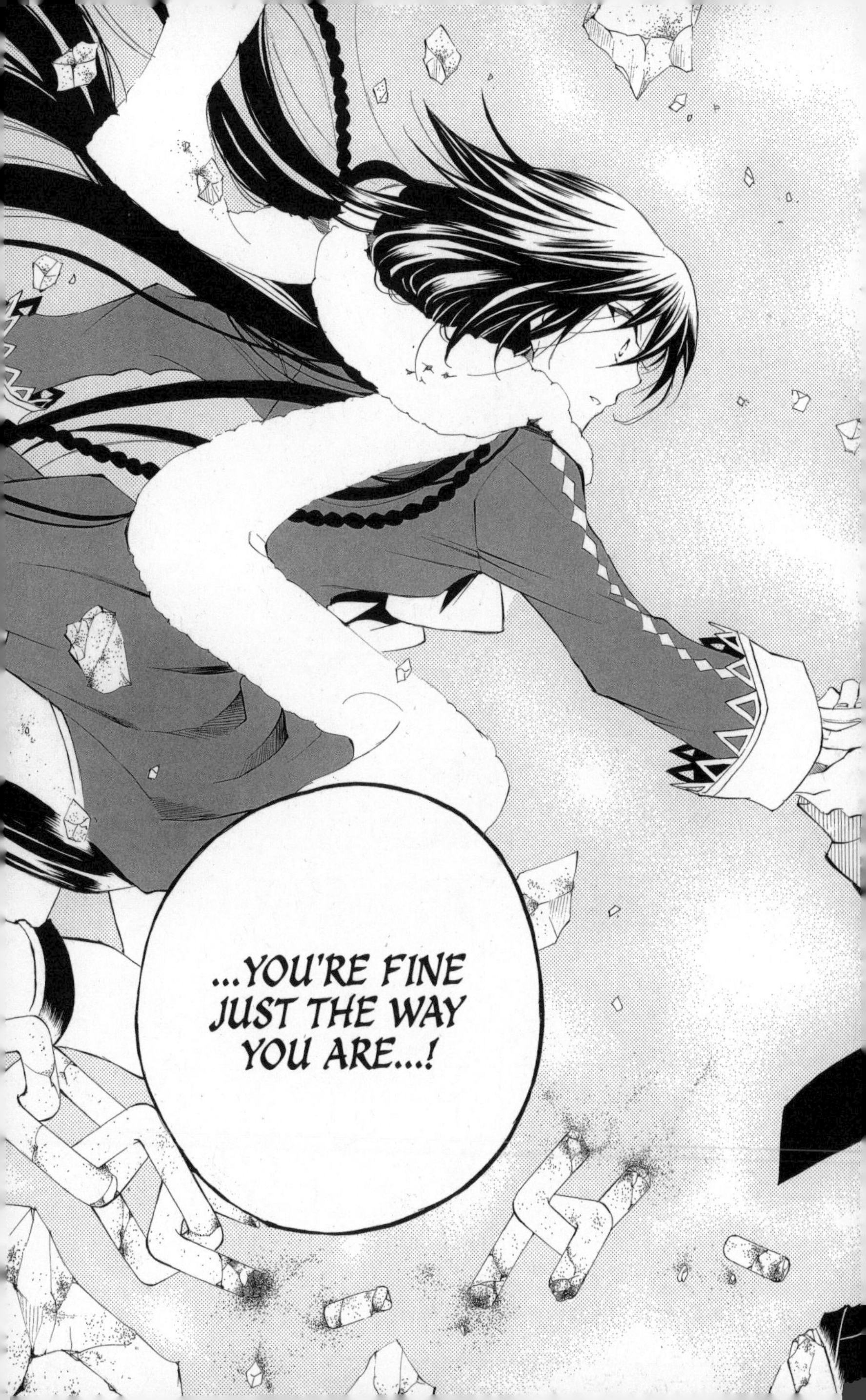
...YOU'RE FINE JUST THE WAY YOU ARE...!

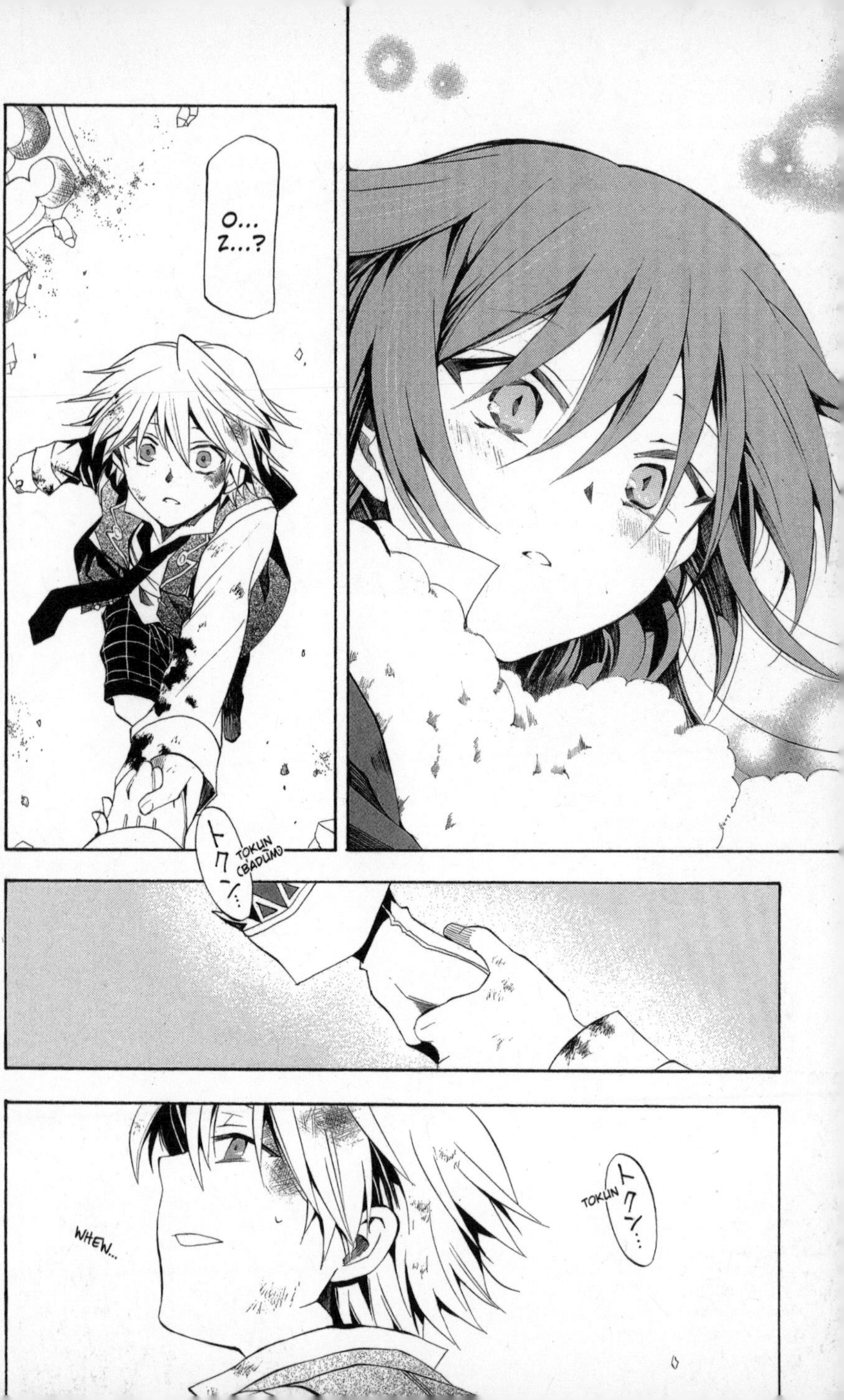
O...
Z...?
トクン…
TOKUN (BADUMP)
トクン…
TOKUN
WHEW...

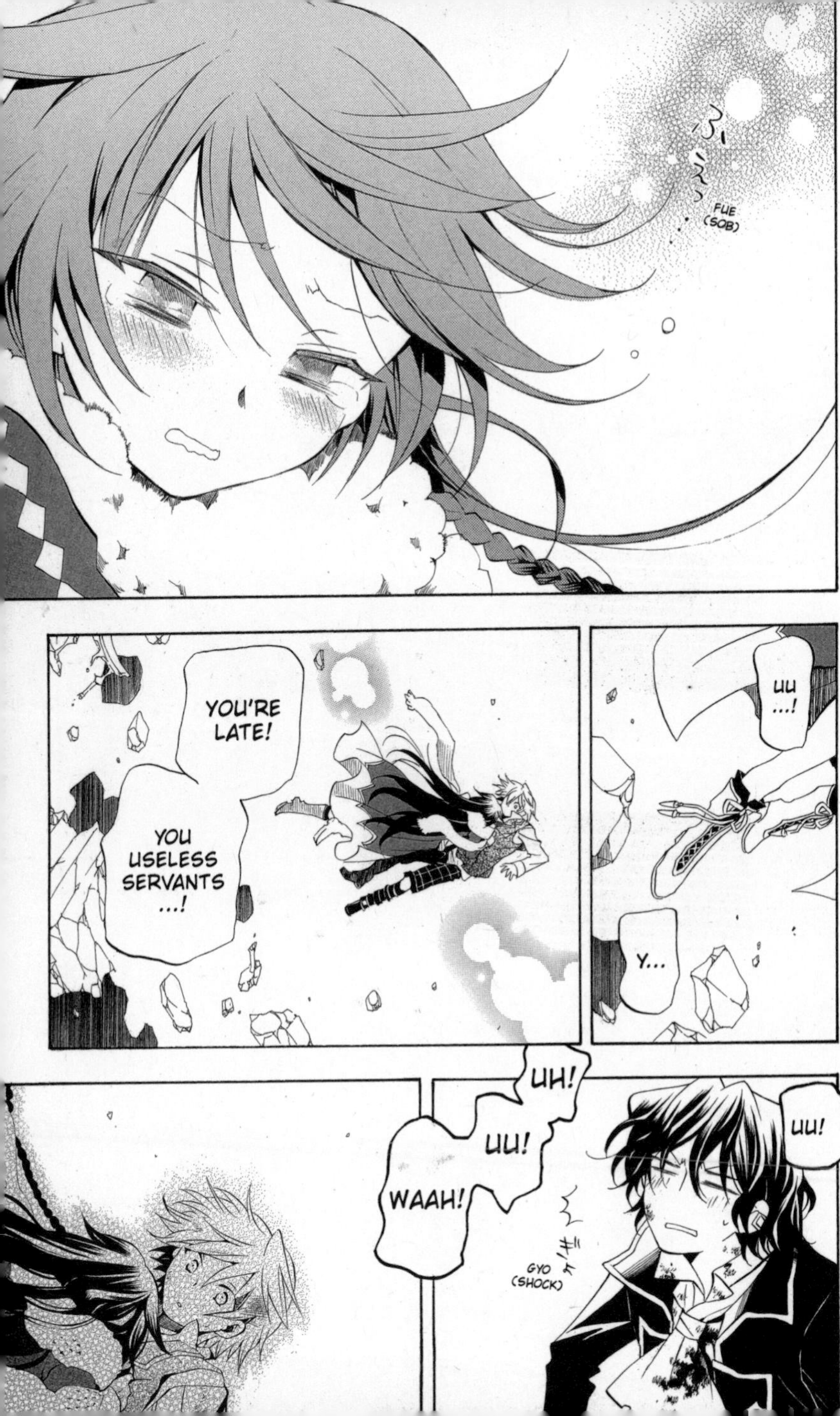

ふぇっ
FUE
(SOB)
UU ...!
Y...
YOU'RE LATE!
YOU USELESS SERVANTS ...!
UU!
ぎょ
GYO
(SHOCK)
UH!
UU!
WAAH!

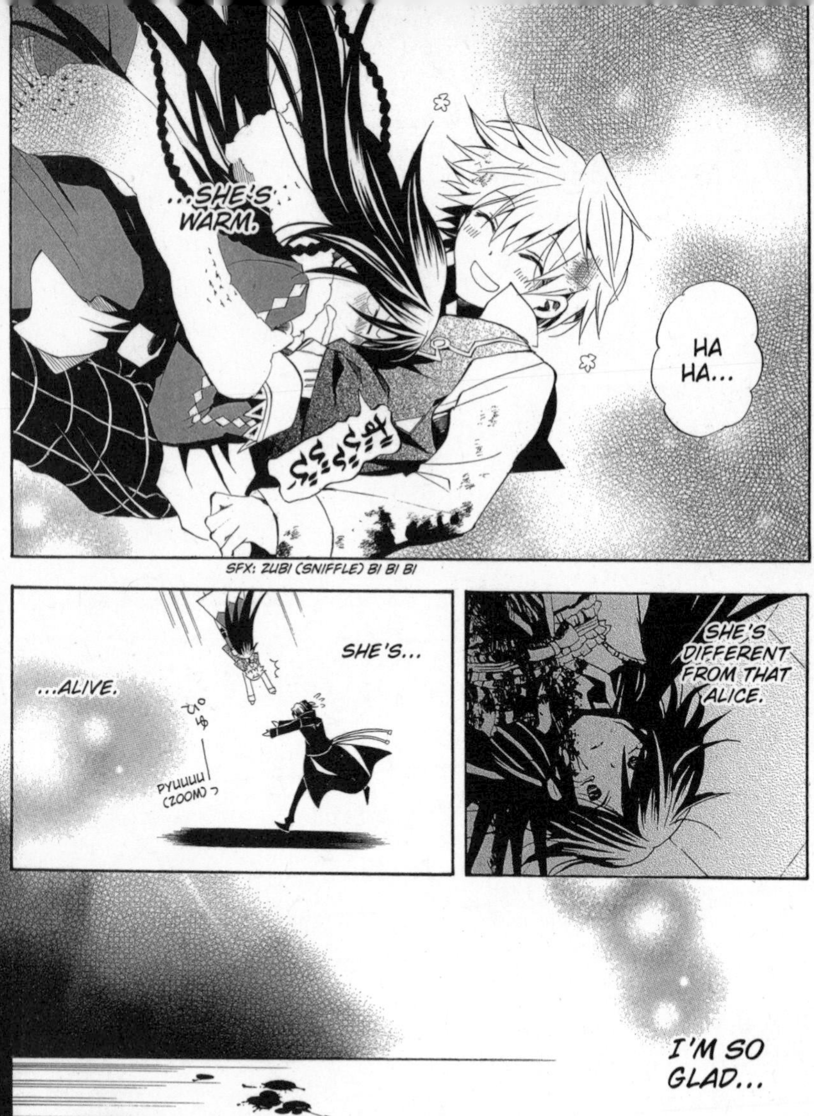
HA HA...
...SHE'S WARM.
SFX: ZUBI (SNIFFLE) BI BI BI
SHE'S DIFFERENT FROM THAT ALICE.
SHE'S...
...ALIVE.
PYUUUUU (ZOOM)
I'M SO GLAD...
BOTA (DRIP)
BOTA
BOTA

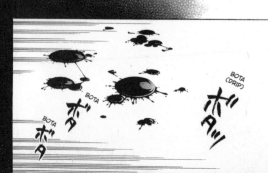

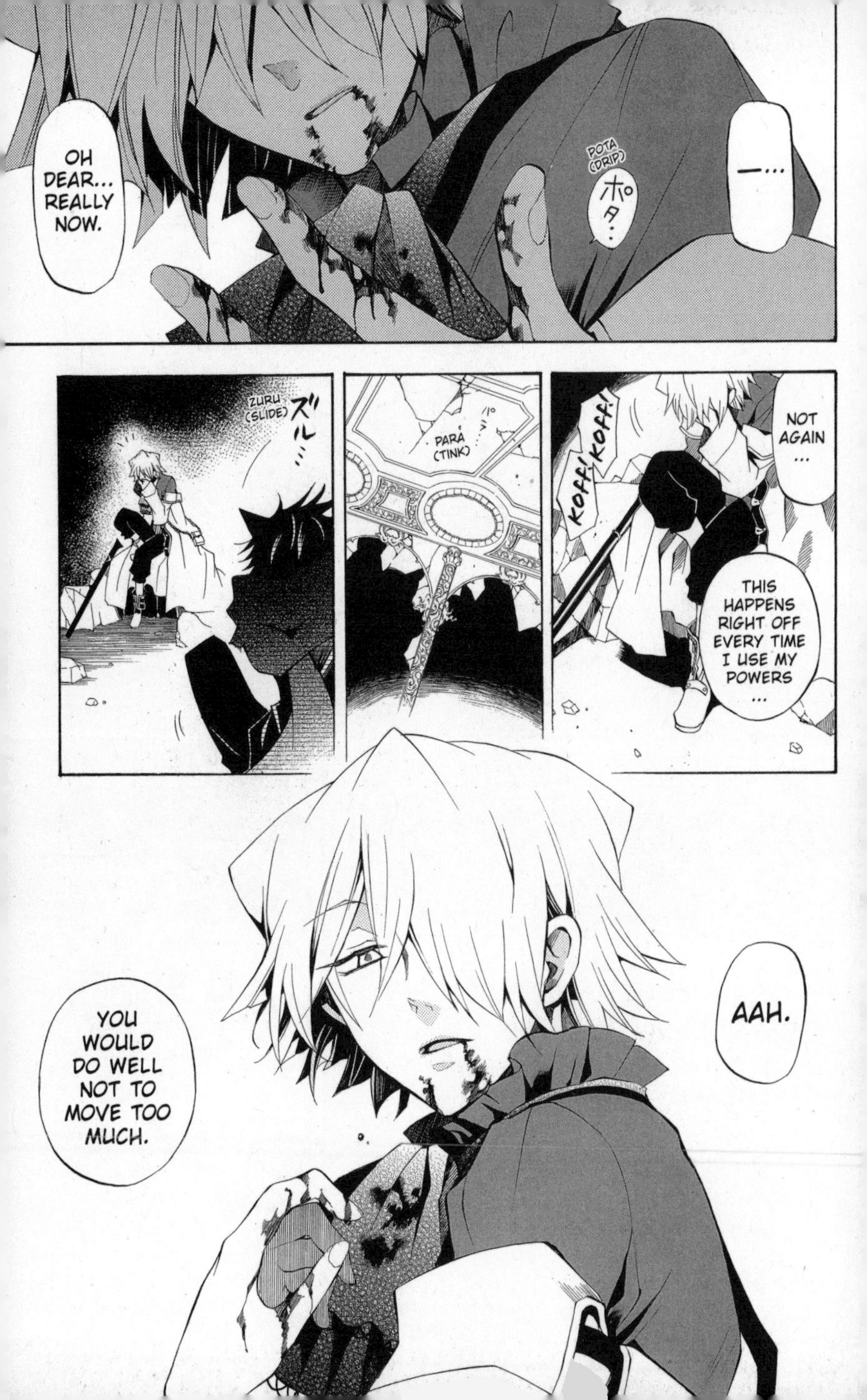
—...
POTA (DRIP)
ポタ..
OH DEAR... REALLY NOW.
NOT AGAIN ...
KOFF! KOFF!
THIS HAPPENS RIGHT OFF EVERY TIME I USE MY POWERS ...
パラ...
PARA (TINK)
ZURU (SLIDE)
ズル::
AAH.
YOU WOULD DO WELL NOT TO MOVE TOO MUCH.

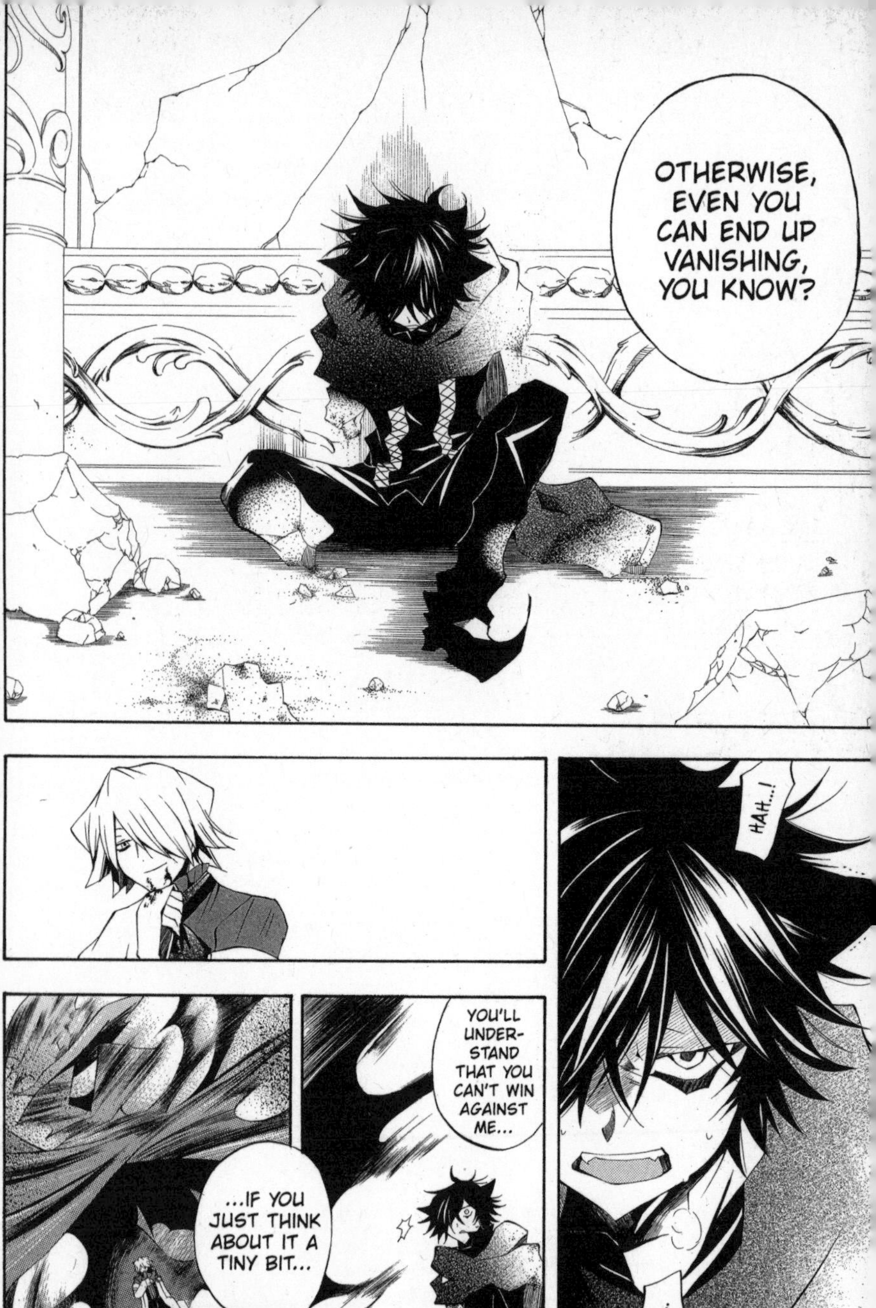
OTHERWISE, EVEN YOU CAN END UP VANISHING, YOU KNOW?
HAH...!
HAH...
YOU'LL UNDER-STAND THAT YOU CAN'T WIN AGAINST ME...
...IF YOU JUST THINK ABOUT IT A TINY BIT...

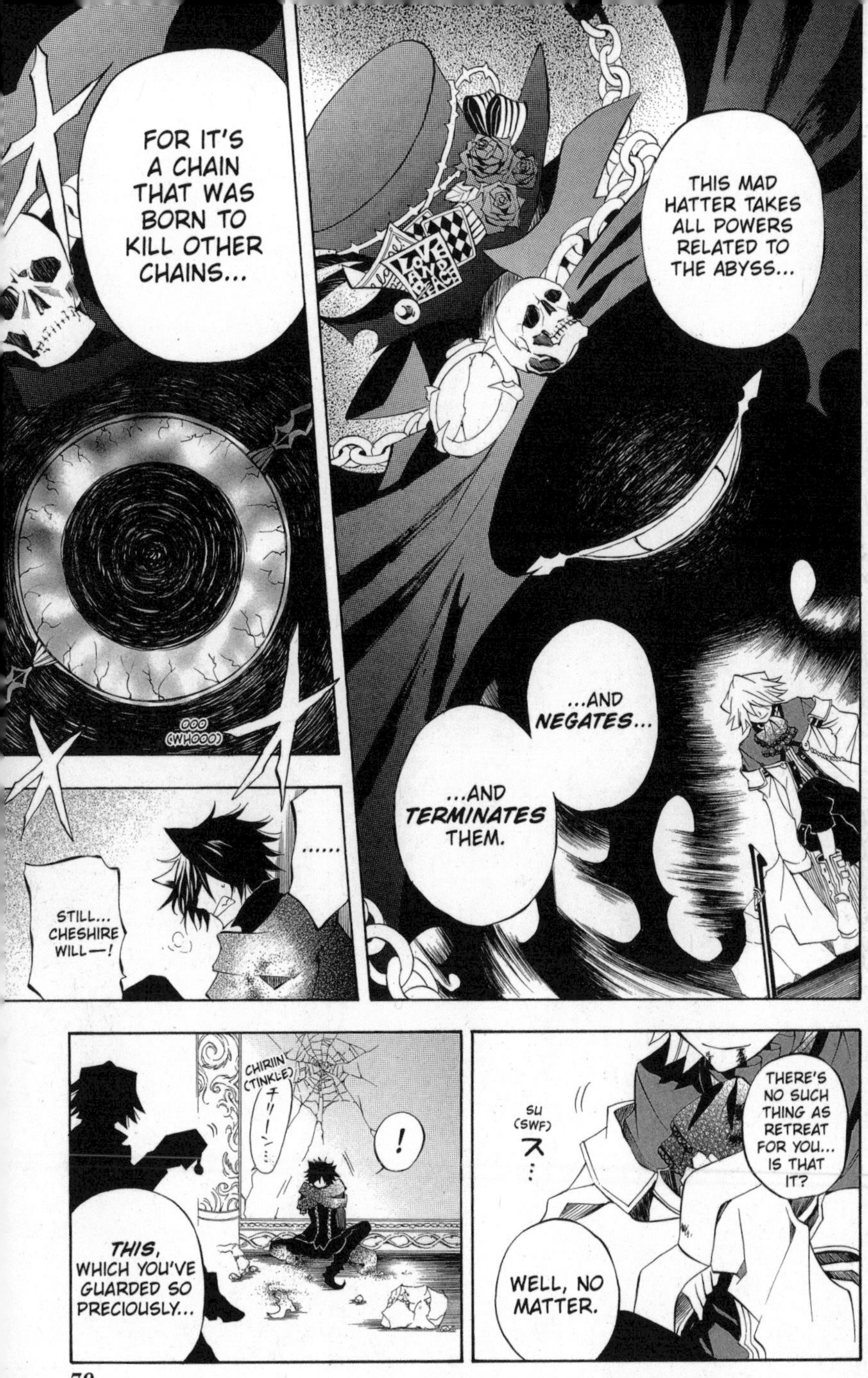

THIS MAD HATTER TAKES ALL POWERS RELATED TO THE ABYSS...
...AND *NEGATES*...
...AND *TERMINATES* THEM.
FOR IT'S A CHAIN THAT WAS BORN TO KILL OTHER CHAINS...
OOO (WHOOO)
......
STILL... CHESHIRE WILL—!
SU (SWF)
ス...
THERE'S NO SUCH THING AS RETREAT FOR YOU... IS THAT IT?
WELL, NO MATTER.
CHIRIIN (TINKLE)
チリーン...
!
THIS, WHICH YOU'VE GUARDED SO PRECIOUSLY...

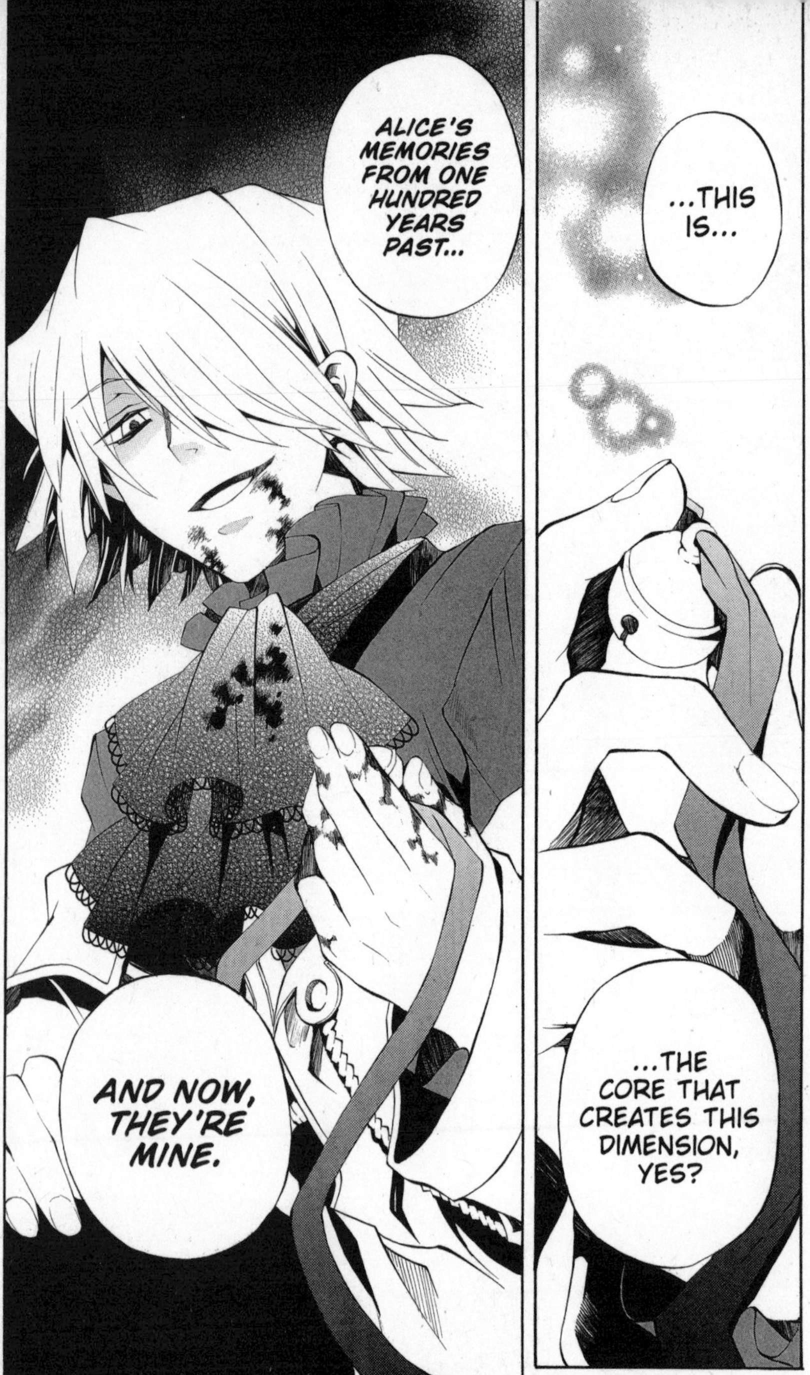
...THIS IS...
...THE CORE THAT CREATES THIS DIMENSION, YES?
ALICE'S MEMORIES FROM ONE HUNDRED YEARS PAST...
AND NOW, THEY'RE MINE.

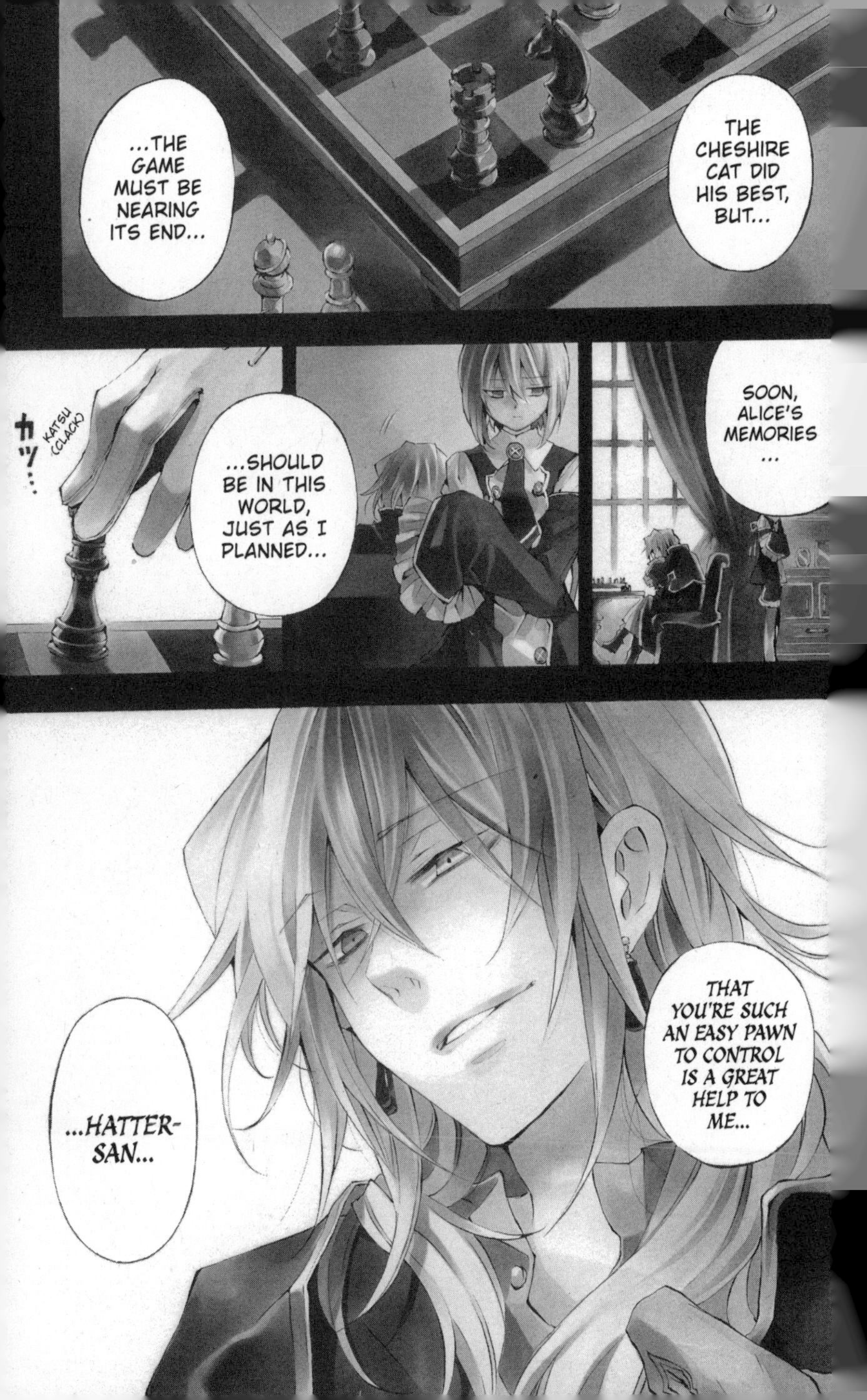
THE CHESHIRE CAT DID HIS BEST, BUT...
...THE GAME MUST BE NEARING ITS END...
SOON, ALICE'S MEMORIES ...
...SHOULD BE IN THIS WORLD, JUST AS I PLANNED...
カッ…
KATSU (CLACK)
THAT YOU'RE SUCH AN EASY PAWN TO CONTROL IS A GREAT HELP TO ME...
...HATTER-SAN...

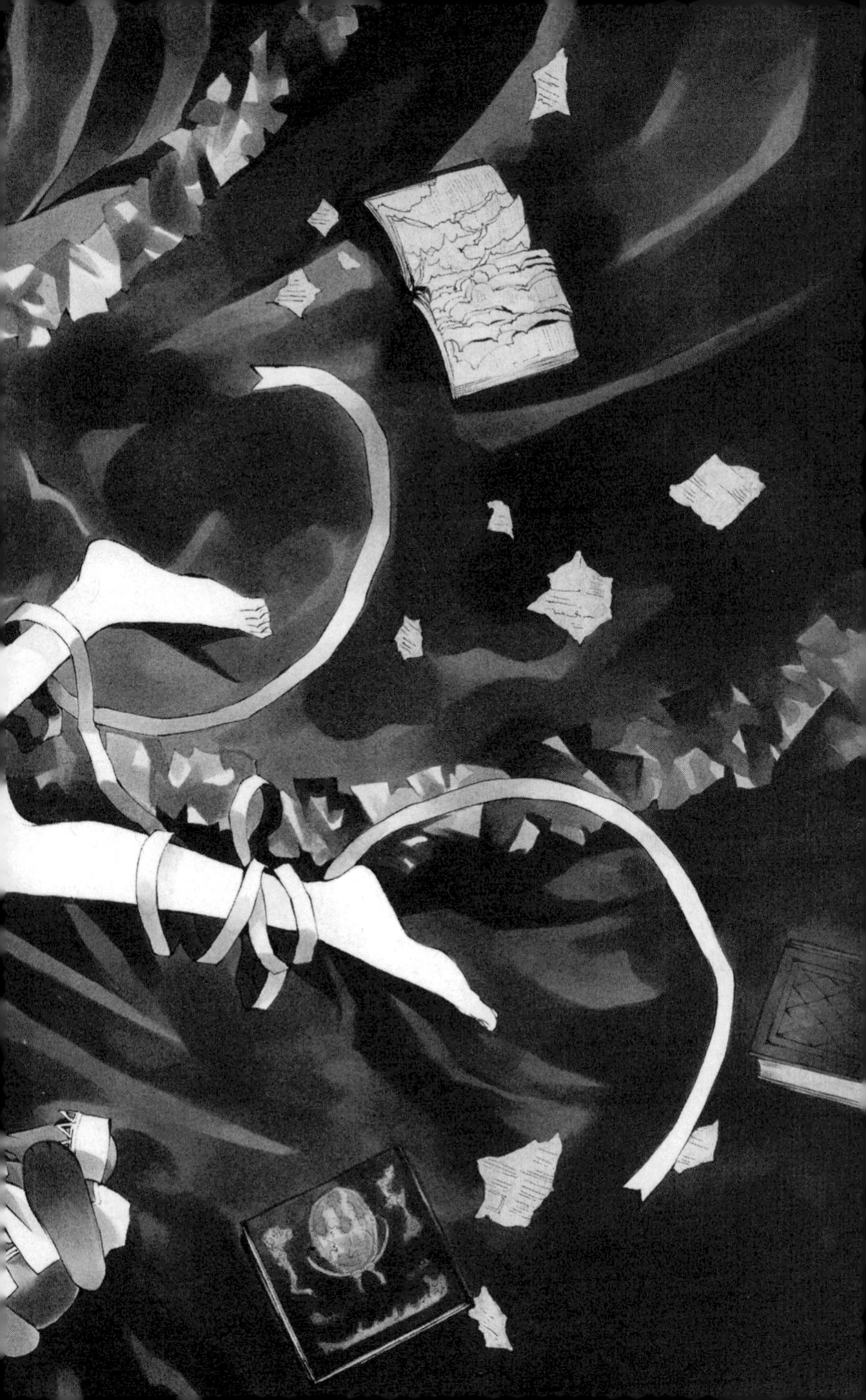

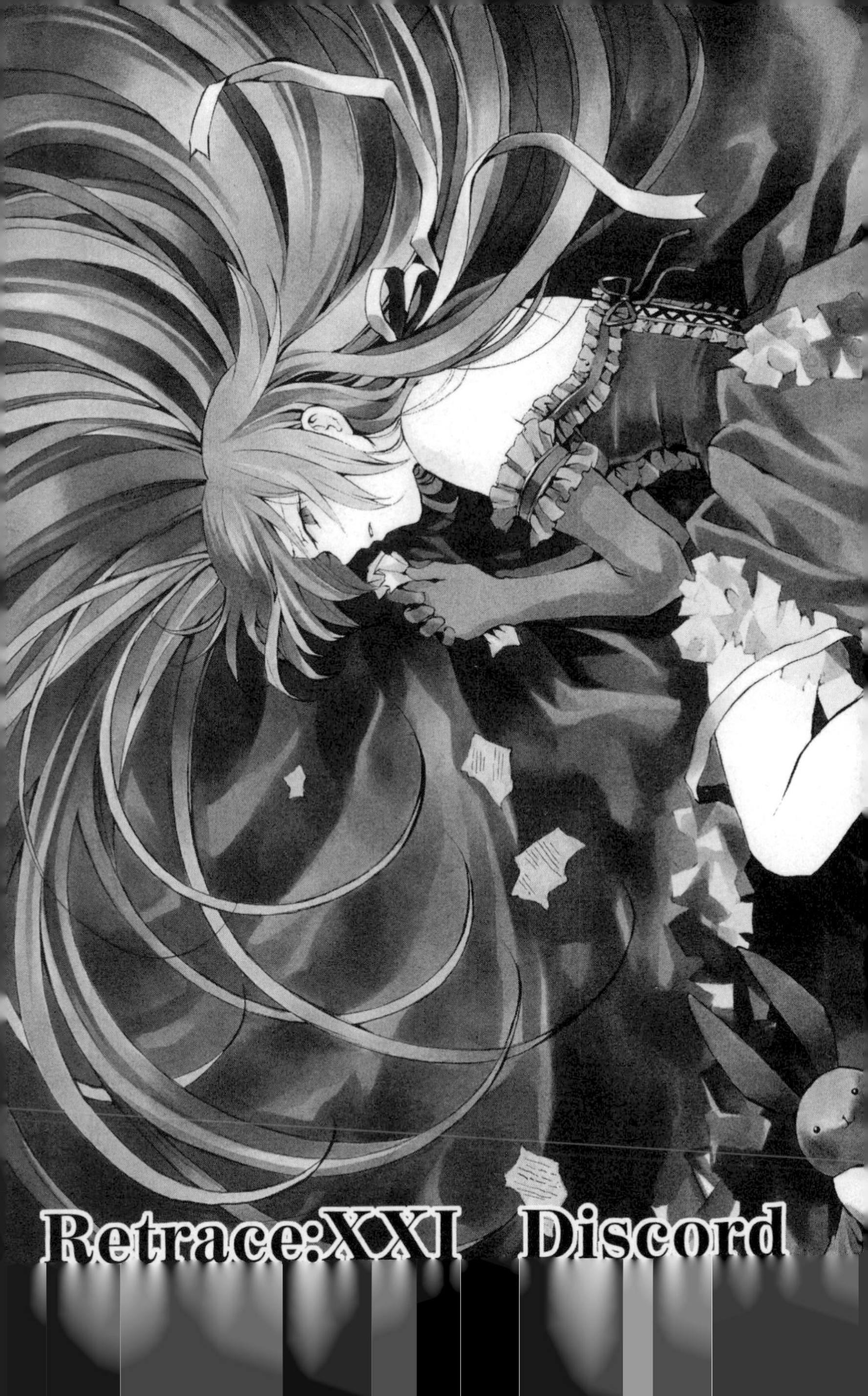

Retrace:XXI Discord

Bonus: Ten Years of Mister Hatter and Master Gilbert, Part Two

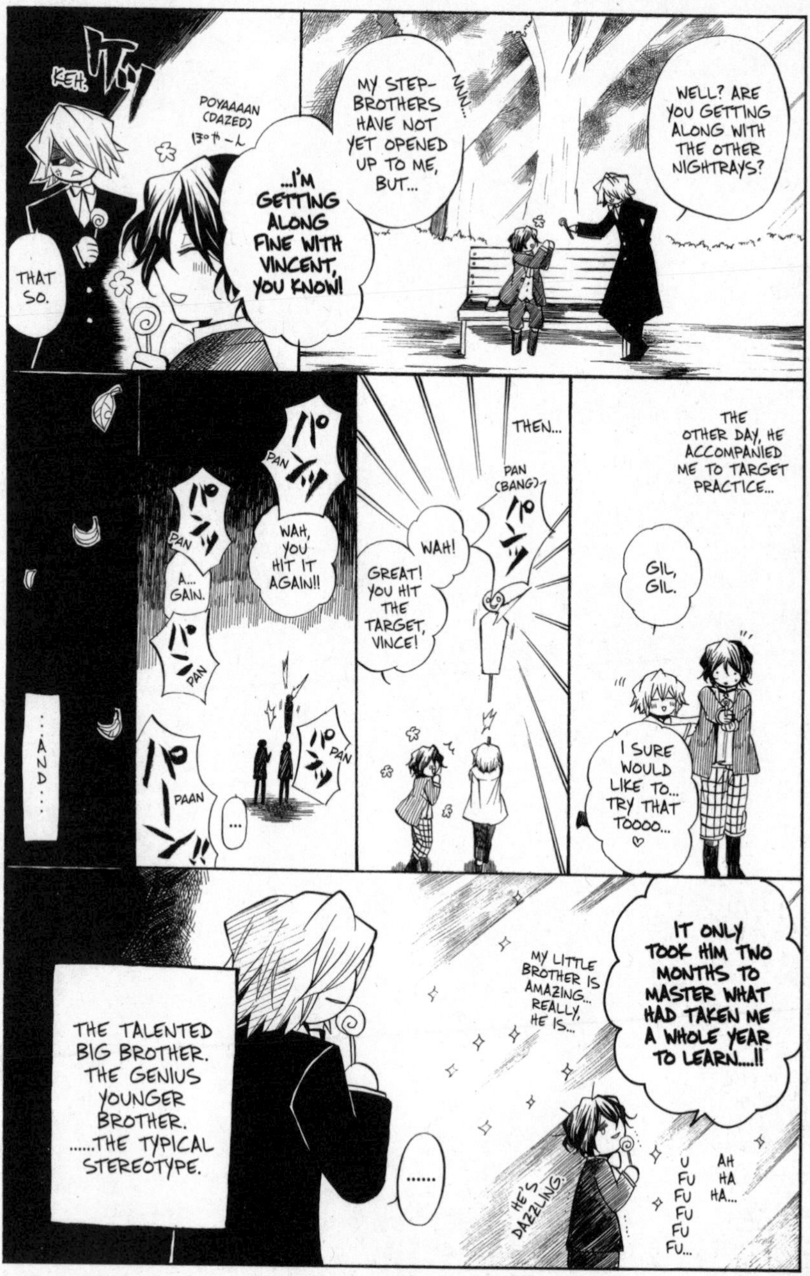
WELL? ARE YOU GETTING ALONG WITH THE OTHER NIGHTRAYS?
NNN...
MY STEP-BROTHERS HAVE NOT YET OPENED UP TO ME, BUT...
...I'M GETTING ALONG FINE WITH VINCENT, YOU KNOW!
POYAAAAN (DAZED)
ぽやーん
KEH.
ケッ
THAT SO.
THE OTHER DAY, HE ACCOMPANIED ME TO TARGET PRACTICE...
GIL, GIL.
I SURE WOULD LIKE TO... TRY THAT TOOOO... ♡
THEN...
PAN (BANG)
WAH!
GREAT! YOU HIT THE TARGET, VINCE!
PAN
WAH, YOU HIT IT AGAIN!!
PAN
A... GAIN.
PAN
PAN
PAAN
...
...AND...
IT ONLY TOOK HIM TWO MONTHS TO MASTER WHAT HAD TAKEN ME A WHOLE YEAR TO LEARN...!!
MY LITTLE BROTHER IS AMAZING... REALLY, HE IS...
AH HA HA...
U FU FU FU FU FU...
HE'S DAZZLING.
......
THE TALENTED BIG BROTHER. THE GENIUS YOUNGER BROTHER. ......THE TYPICAL STEREOTYPE.

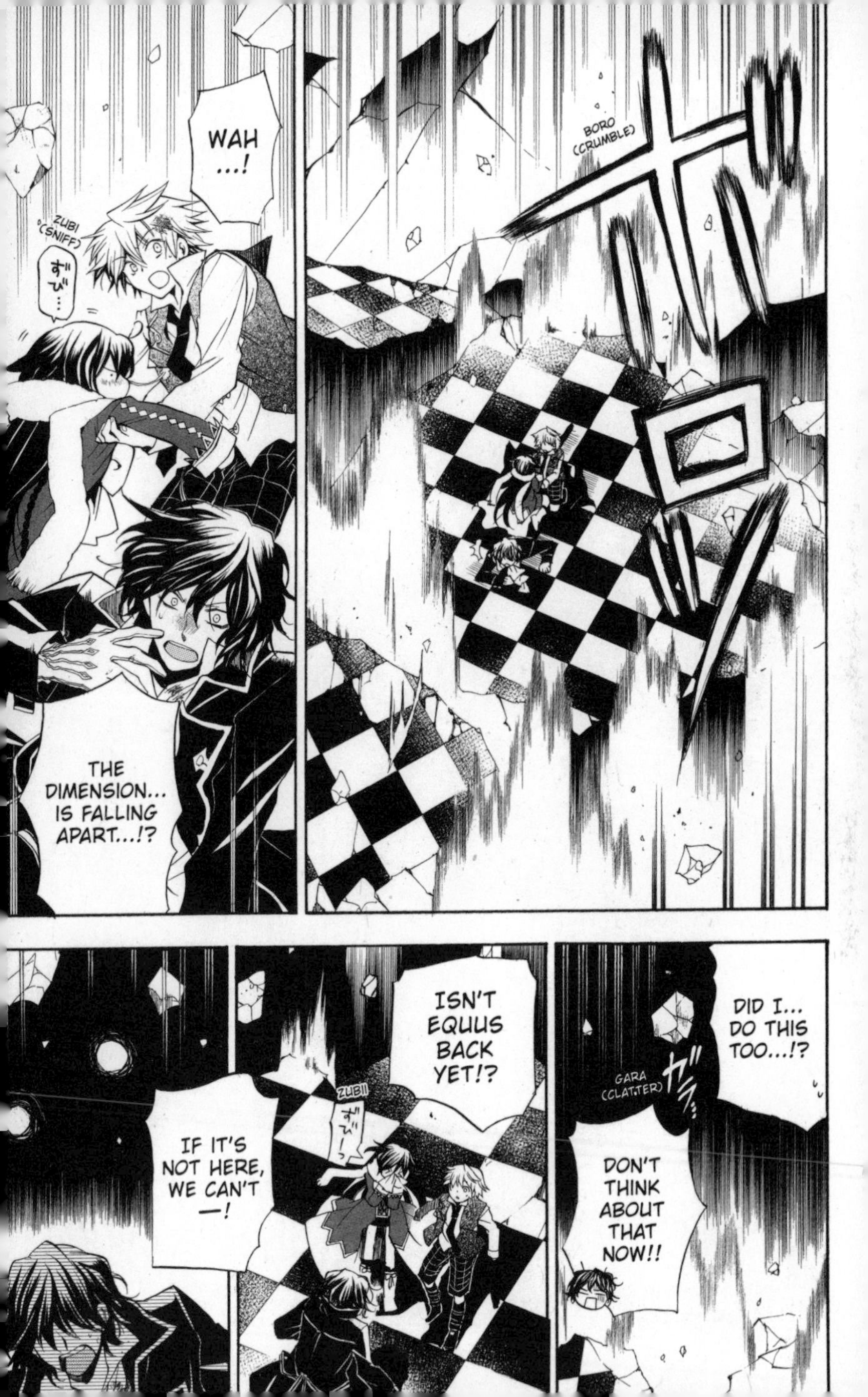
BORO (CRUMBLE)
WAH ...!
ZUBI (SNIFF)
ずび…
THE DIMENSION... IS FALLING APART...!?
DID I... DO THIS TOO...!?
GARA (CLATTER)
DON'T THINK ABOUT THAT NOW!!
ISN'T EQUUS BACK YET!?
ZUBII
ずびーっ
IF IT'S NOT HERE, WE CAN'T—!

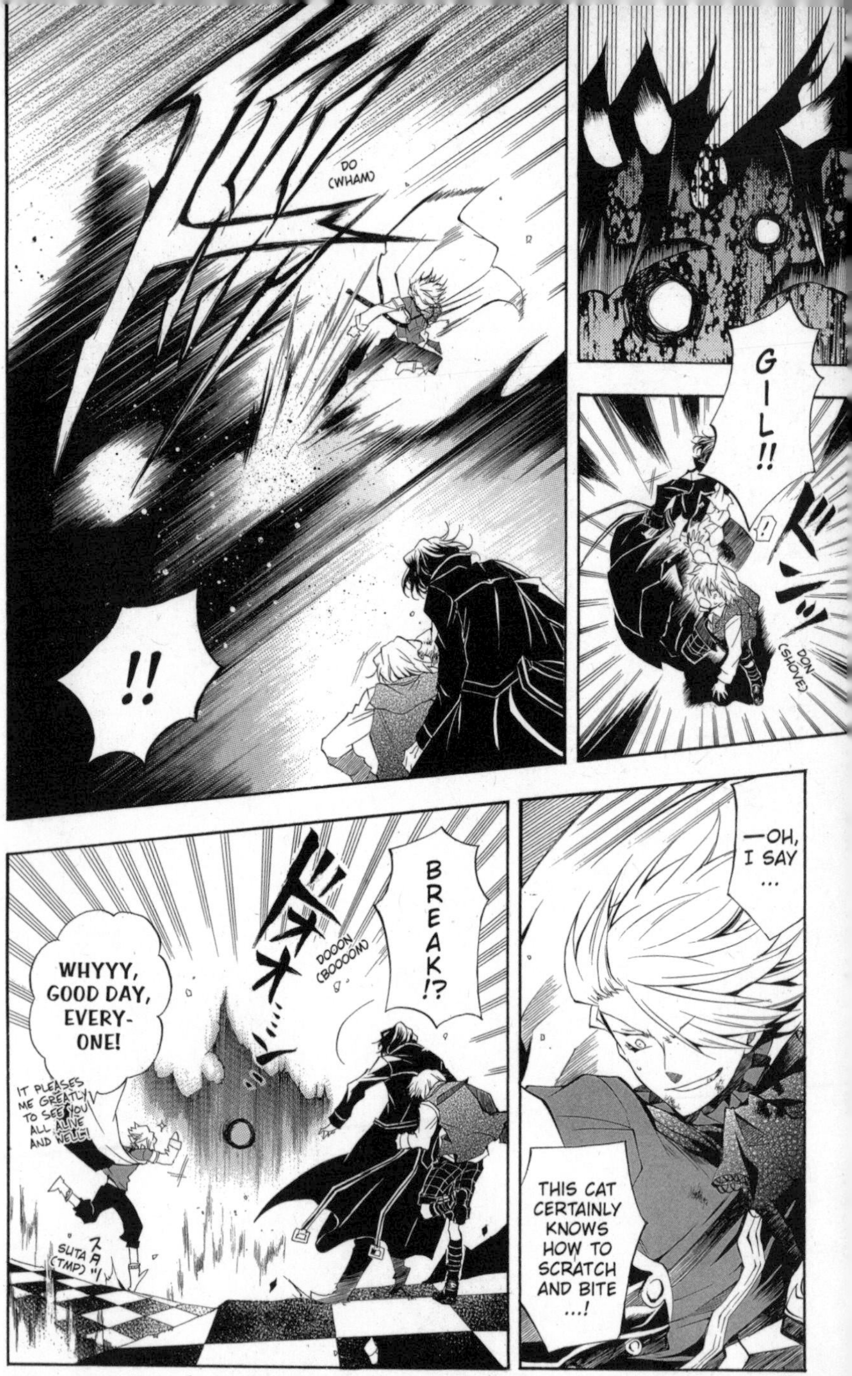

GIL!!
DON (SHOVE)
DO (WHAM)
!!
—OH, I SAY ...
THIS CAT CERTAINLY KNOWS HOW TO SCRATCH AND BITE ...!
BREAK!?
DOOON (BOOOOM)
WHYYY, GOOD DAY, EVERY-ONE!
IT PLEASES ME GREATLY TO SEE YOU ALL ALIVE AND WELL!
SUTA (TMP)

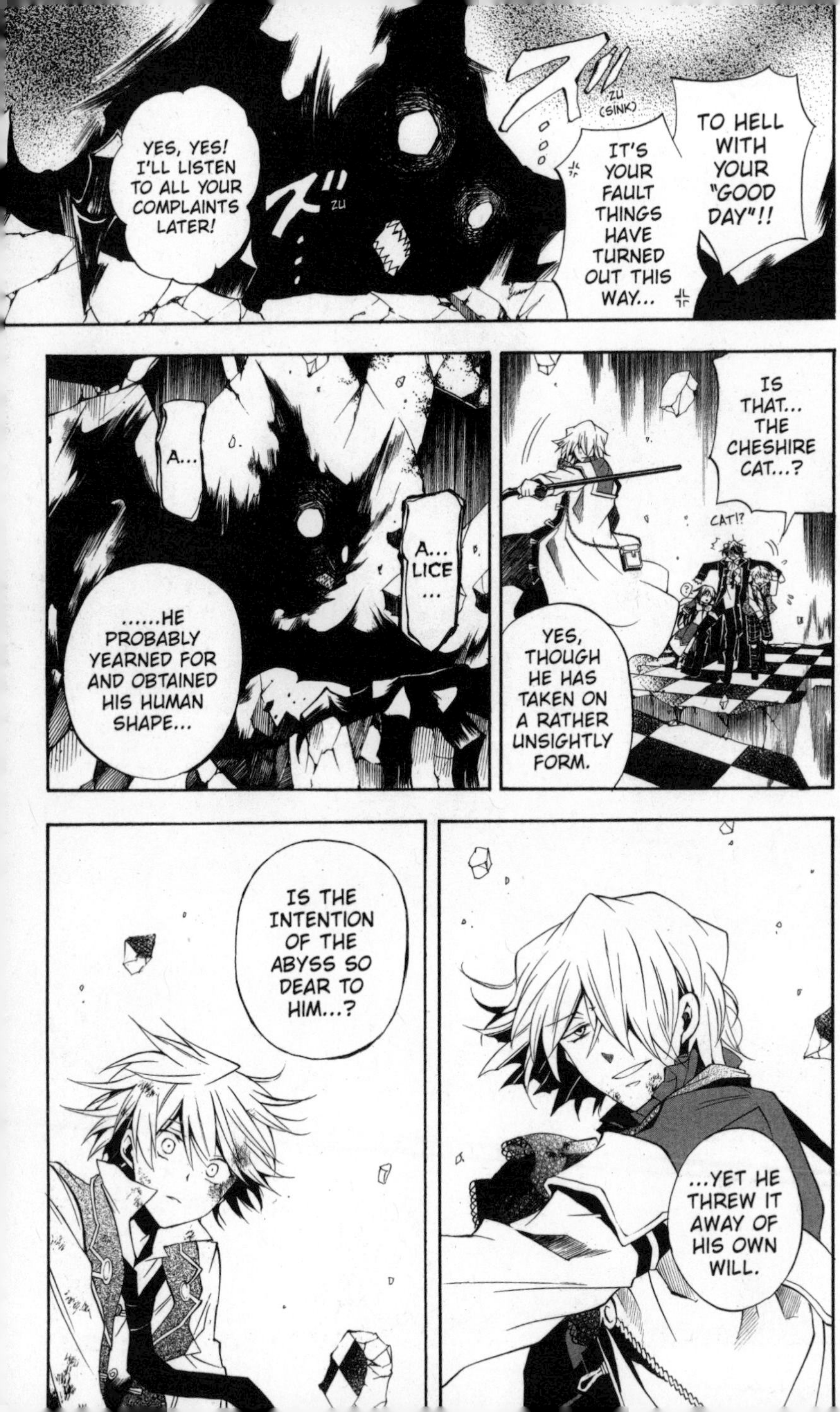
TO HELL WITH YOUR "GOOD DAY"!!
IT'S YOUR FAULT THINGS HAVE TURNED OUT THIS WAY...
ZU (SINK)
ZU
YES, YES! I'LL LISTEN TO ALL YOUR COMPLAINTS LATER!
IS THAT... THE CHESHIRE CAT...?
CAT!?
YES, THOUGH HE HAS TAKEN ON A RATHER UNSIGHTLY FORM.
A... LICE ...
A...
......HE PROBABLY YEARNED FOR AND OBTAINED HIS HUMAN SHAPE...
...YET HE THREW IT AWAY OF HIS OWN WILL.
IS THE INTENTION OF THE ABYSS SO DEAR TO HIM...?

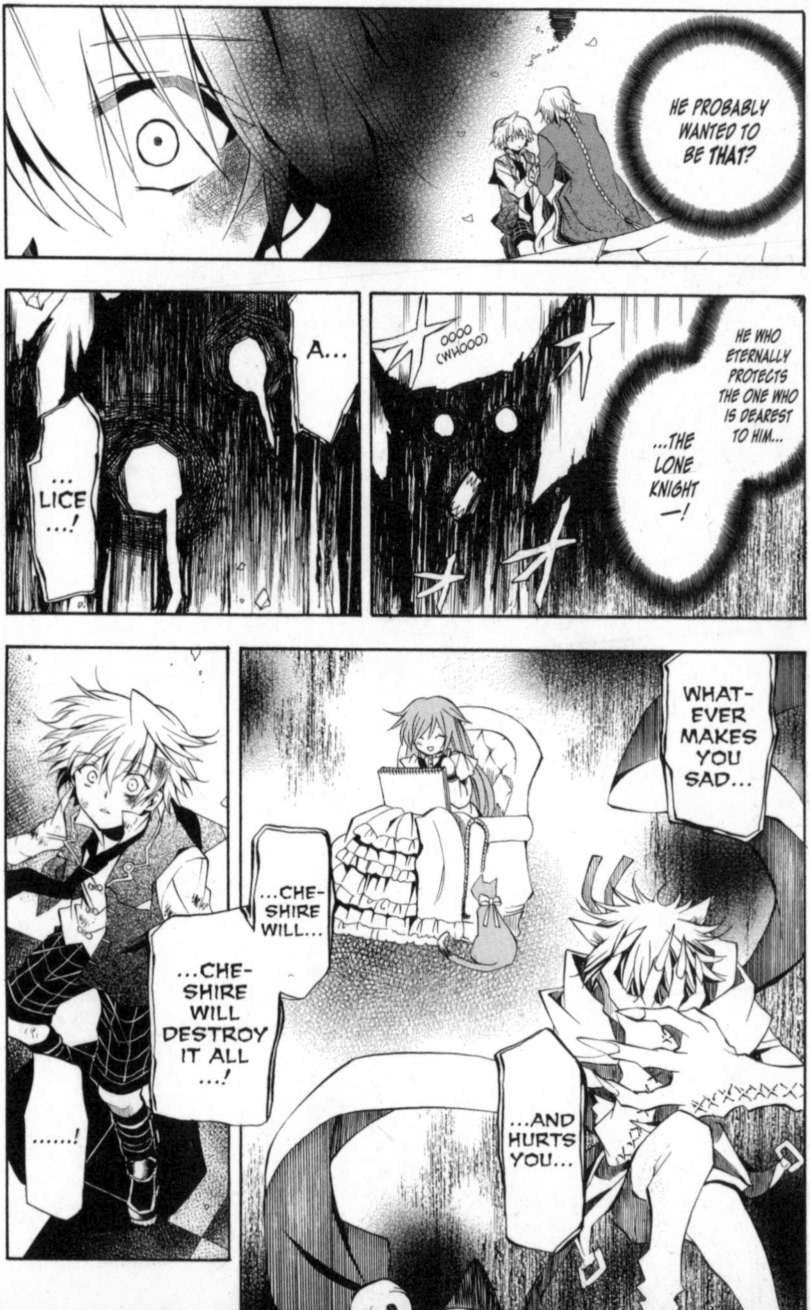
HE PROBABLY WANTED TO BE THAT?
HE WHO ETERNALLY PROTECTS THE ONE WHO IS DEAREST TO HIM...
...THE LONE KNIGHT —!
OOOO (WHOOO)
A...
...LICE...!
WHAT-EVER MAKES YOU SAD...
...AND HURTS YOU...
...CHESHIRE WILL...
...CHE-SHIRE WILL DESTROY IT ALL...!
......!

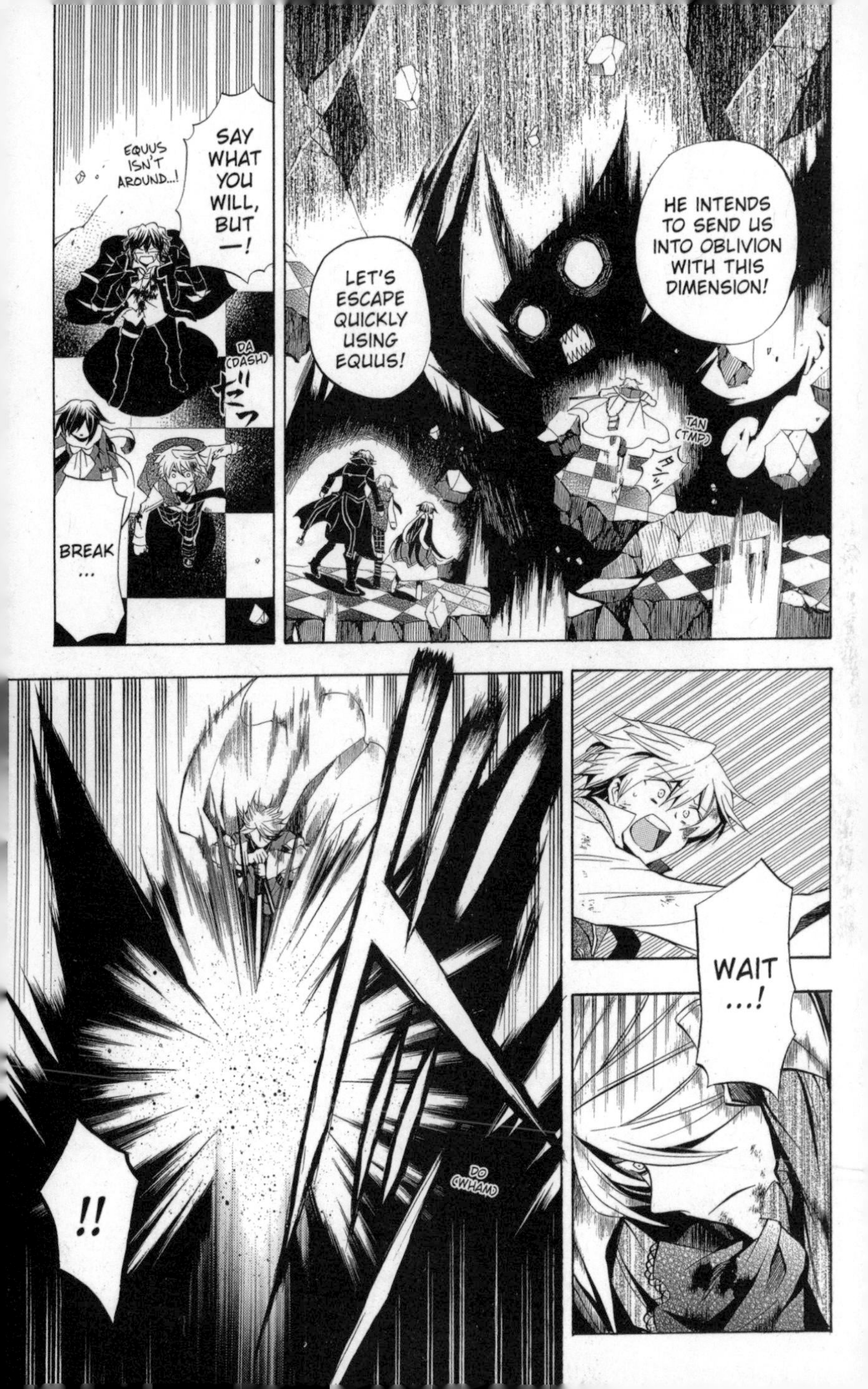
HE INTENDS TO SEND US INTO OBLIVION WITH THIS DIMENSION!
LET'S ESCAPE QUICKLY USING EQUUS!
TAN (TMP)
SAY WHAT YOU WILL, BUT—!
EQUUS ISN'T AROUND...!
DA (DASH)
だっ
BREAK ...
WAIT ...!
DO (WHAM)
!!

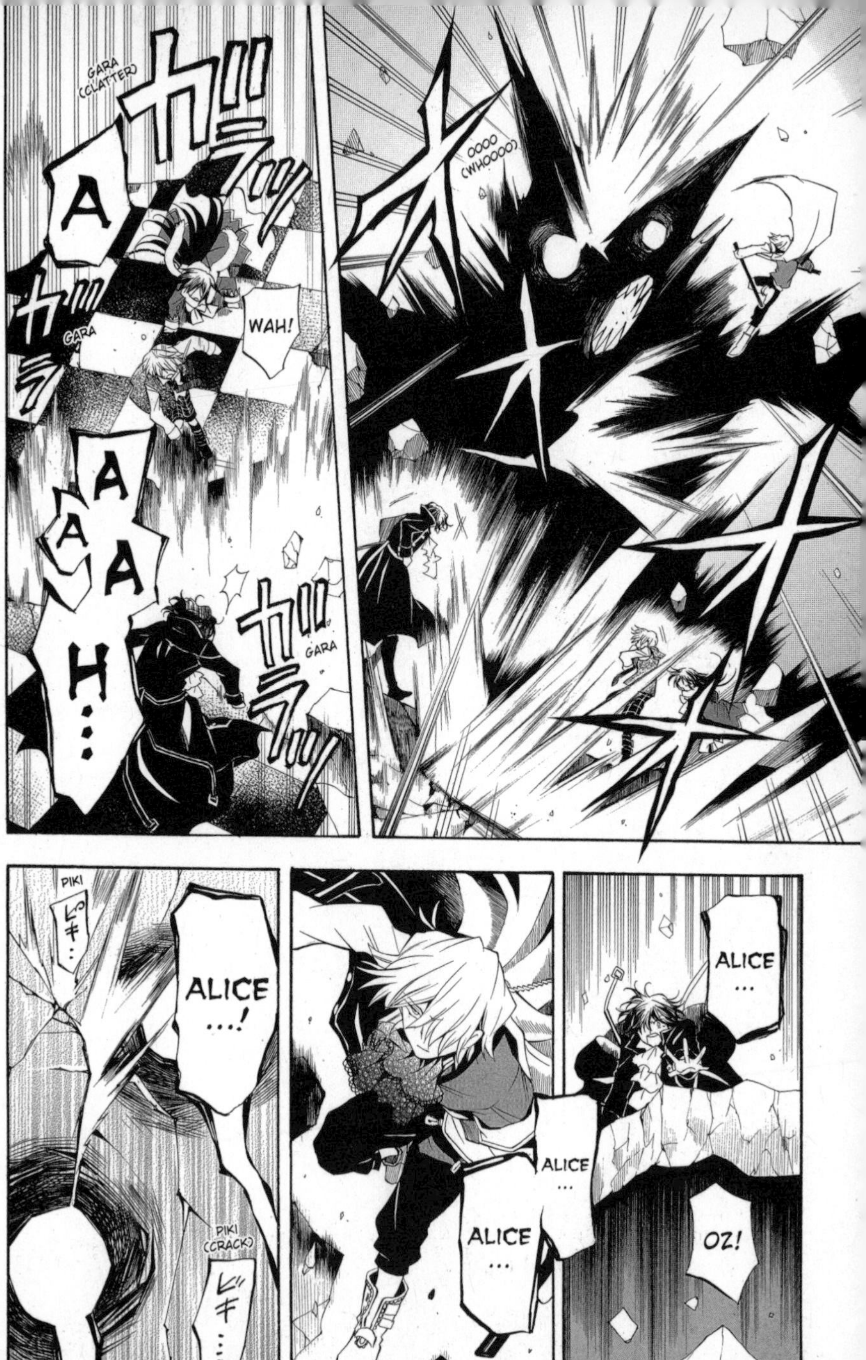

OOOO (WHOOOO)
GARA (CLATTER)
A
WAH!
GARA
AAAH...
GARA
ALICE...
OZ!
ALICE...
ALICE...
PIKI
ALICE...!
PIKI (CRACK)

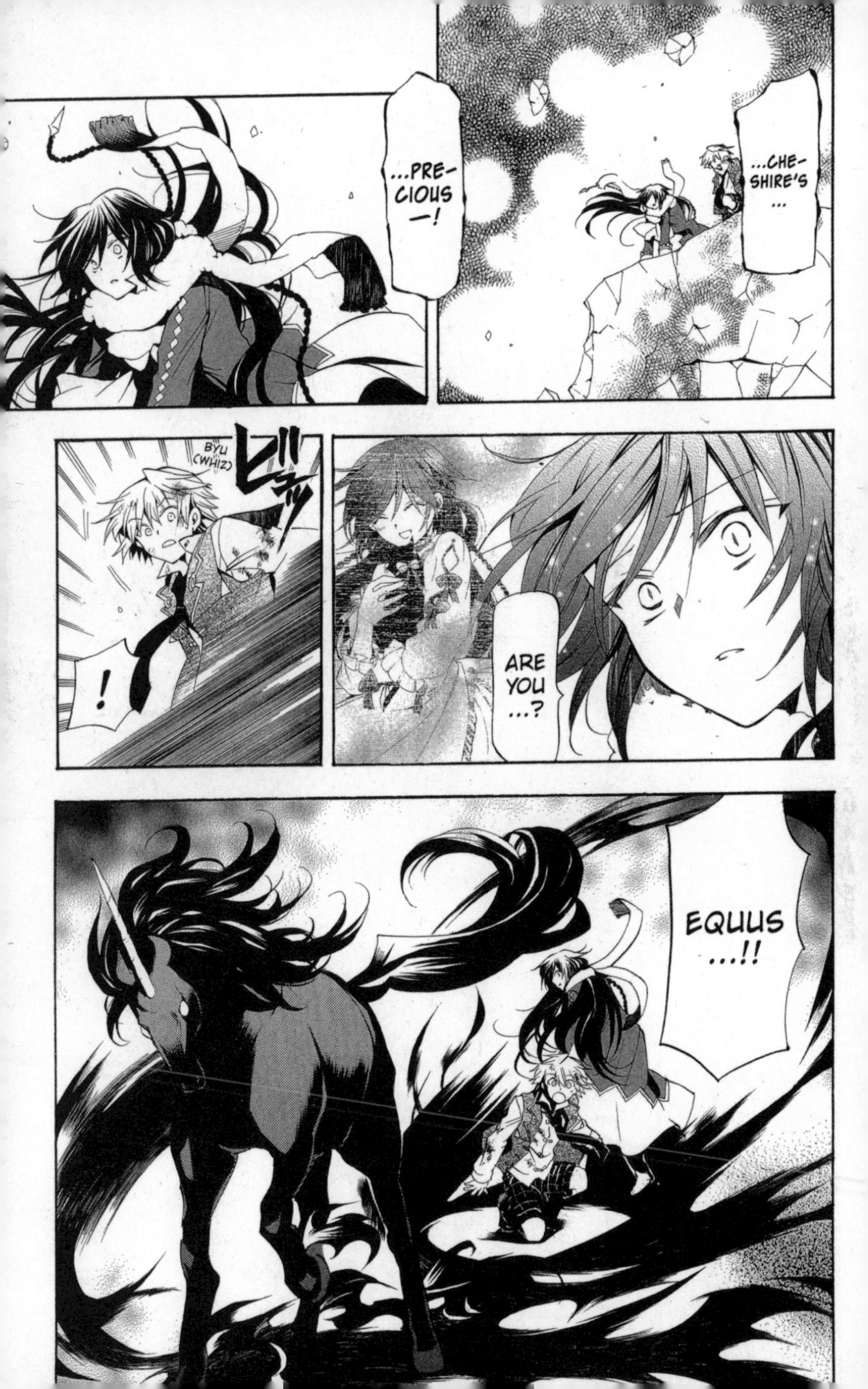
...CHE-SHIRE'S ...
...PRE-CIOUS—!
ARE YOU ...?
BYU (WHIZ)
!
EQUUS ...!!

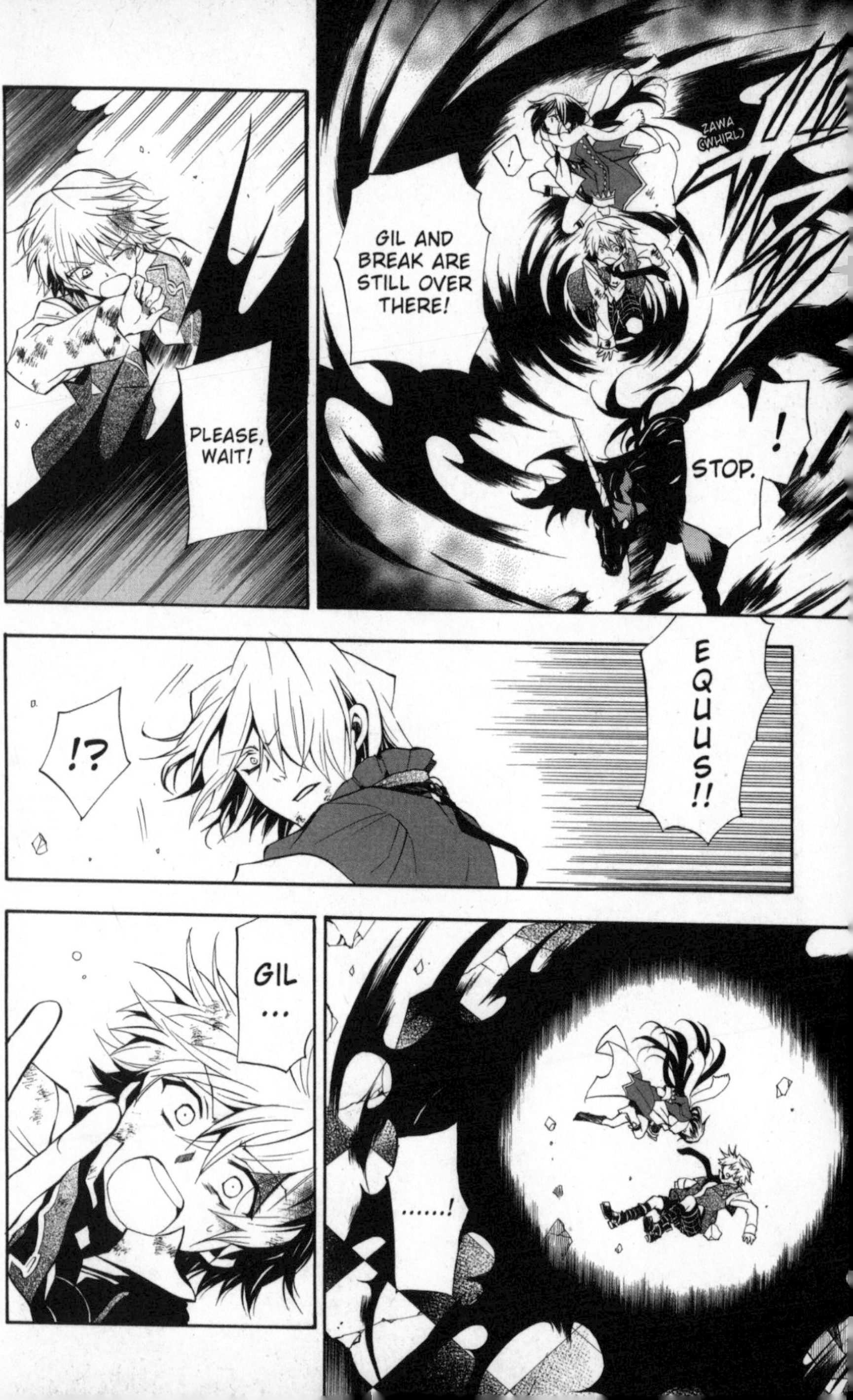
ZAWA (WHIRL)
!
GIL AND BREAK ARE STILL OVER THERE!
!
STOP.
PLEASE, WAIT!
EQUUS!!
!?
......!
GIL ...

BREAK
—!!

...NO...
(ZA)
(ZA)
(ZA)
(SWSH)

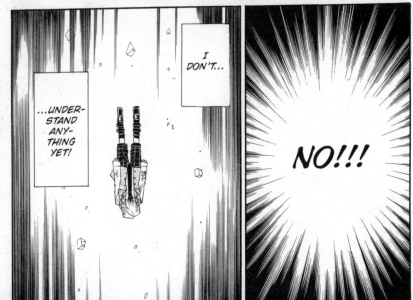

...UNDER-STAND ANY-THING YET!

I DON'T...

NO!!!

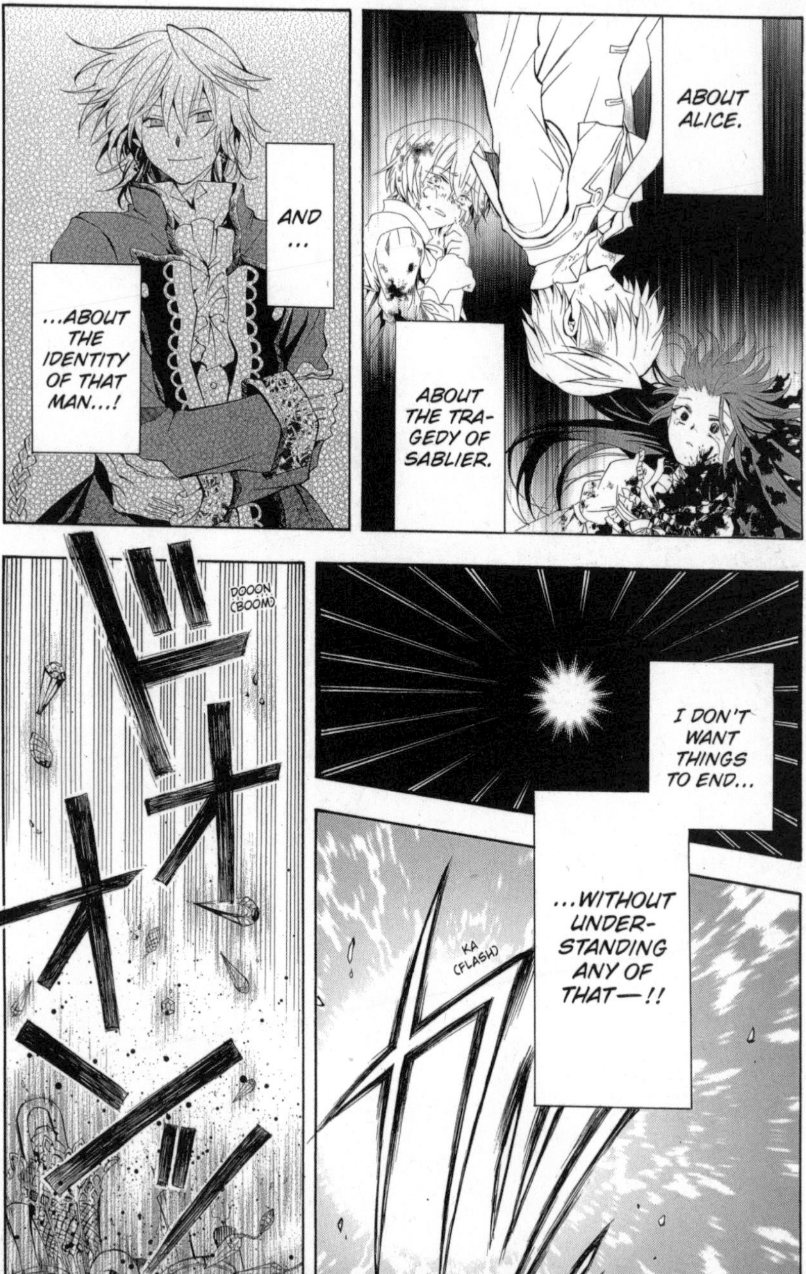
ABOUT ALICE.
ABOUT THE TRAGEDY OF SABLIER.
AND ...
...ABOUT THE IDENTITY OF THAT MAN...!
I DON'T WANT THINGS TO END...
...WITHOUT UNDERSTANDING ANY OF THAT—!!
KA (FLASH)
DOOON (BOOM)
ドオン

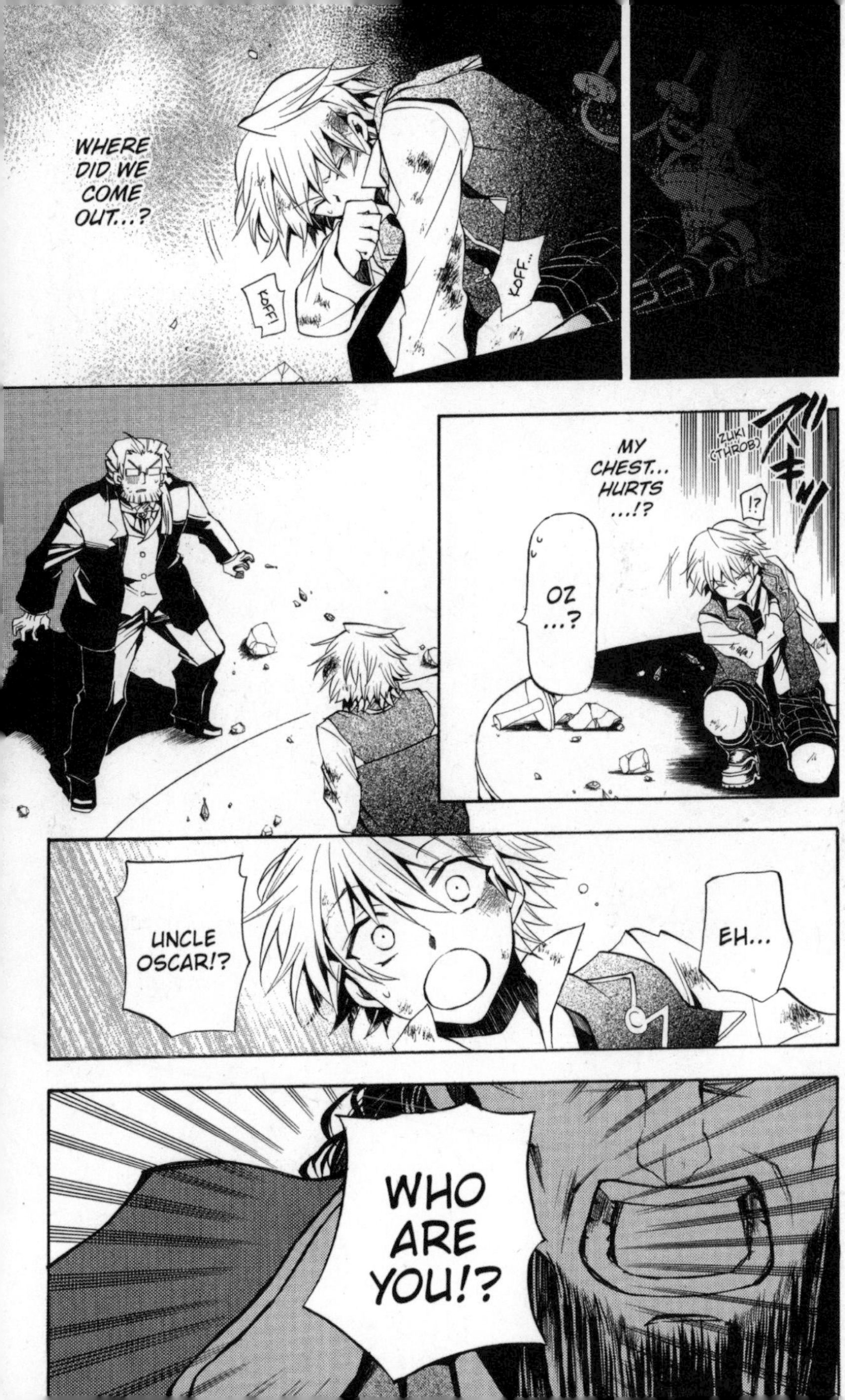
KOFF...
KOFF!
WHERE DID WE COME OUT...?
ズキッ
ZUKI (THROB)
MY CHEST... HURTS ...!?
!?
OZ ...?
EH...
UNCLE OSCAR!?
WHO ARE YOU!?

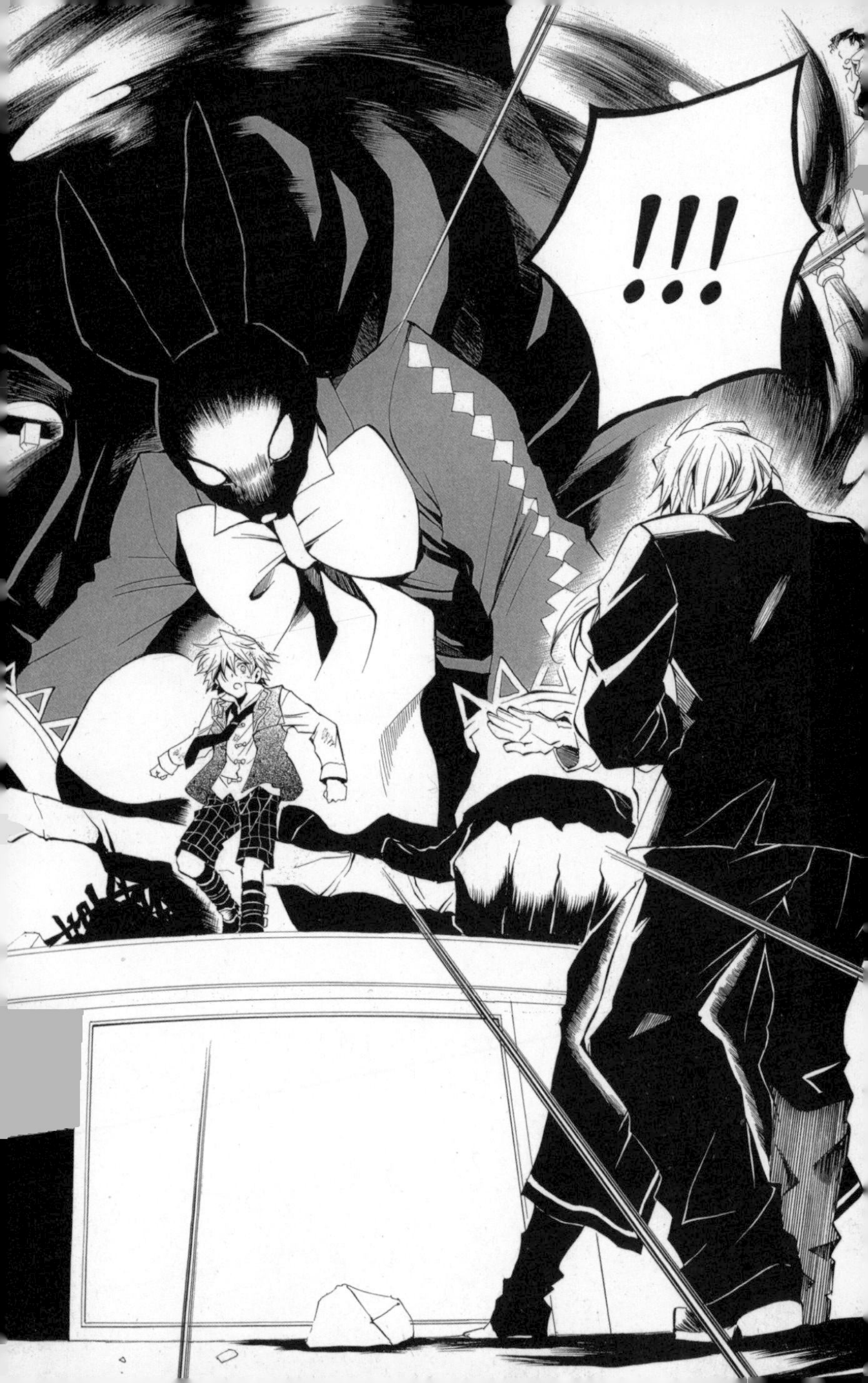
!!!

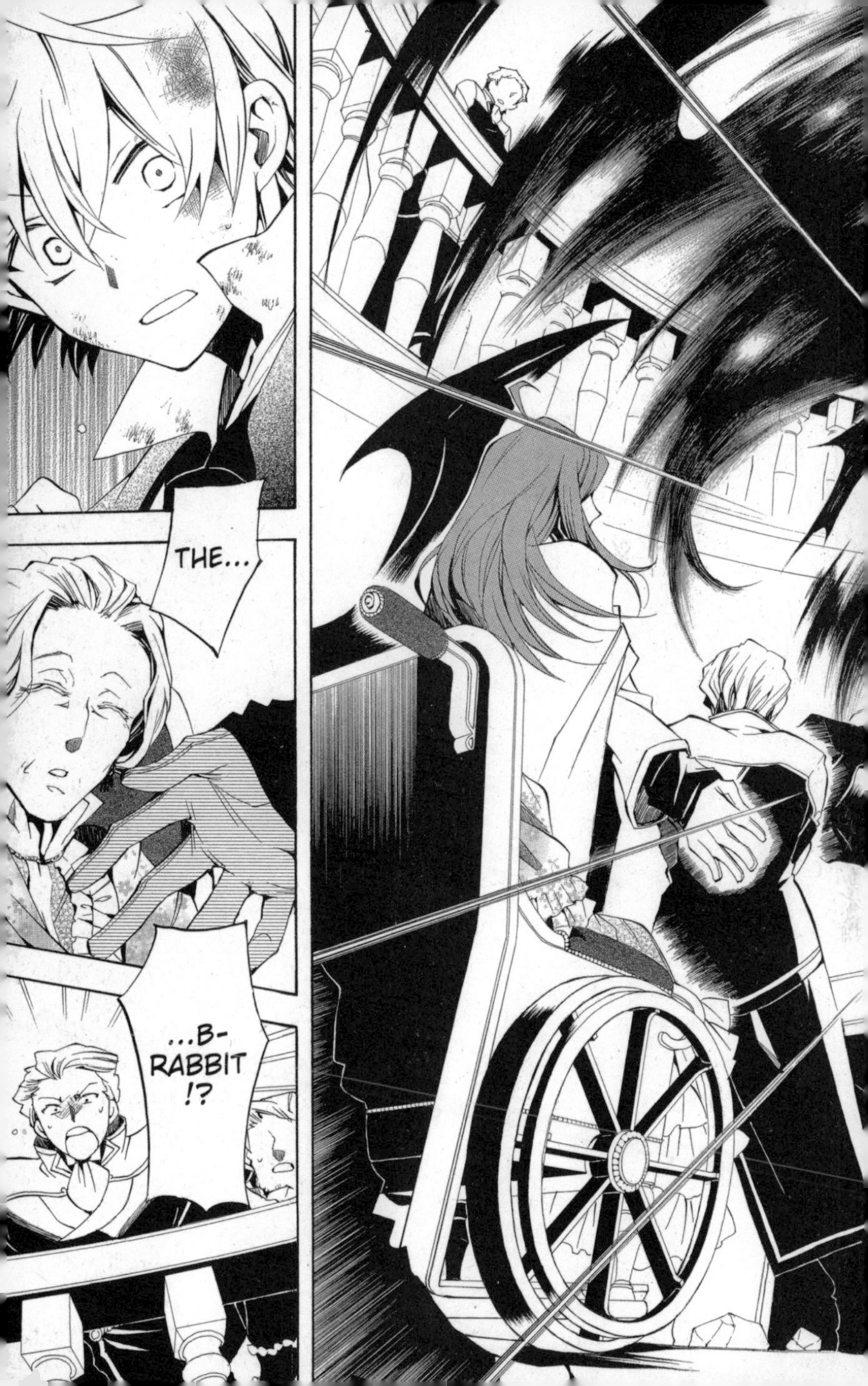
THE...
...B-RABBIT!?

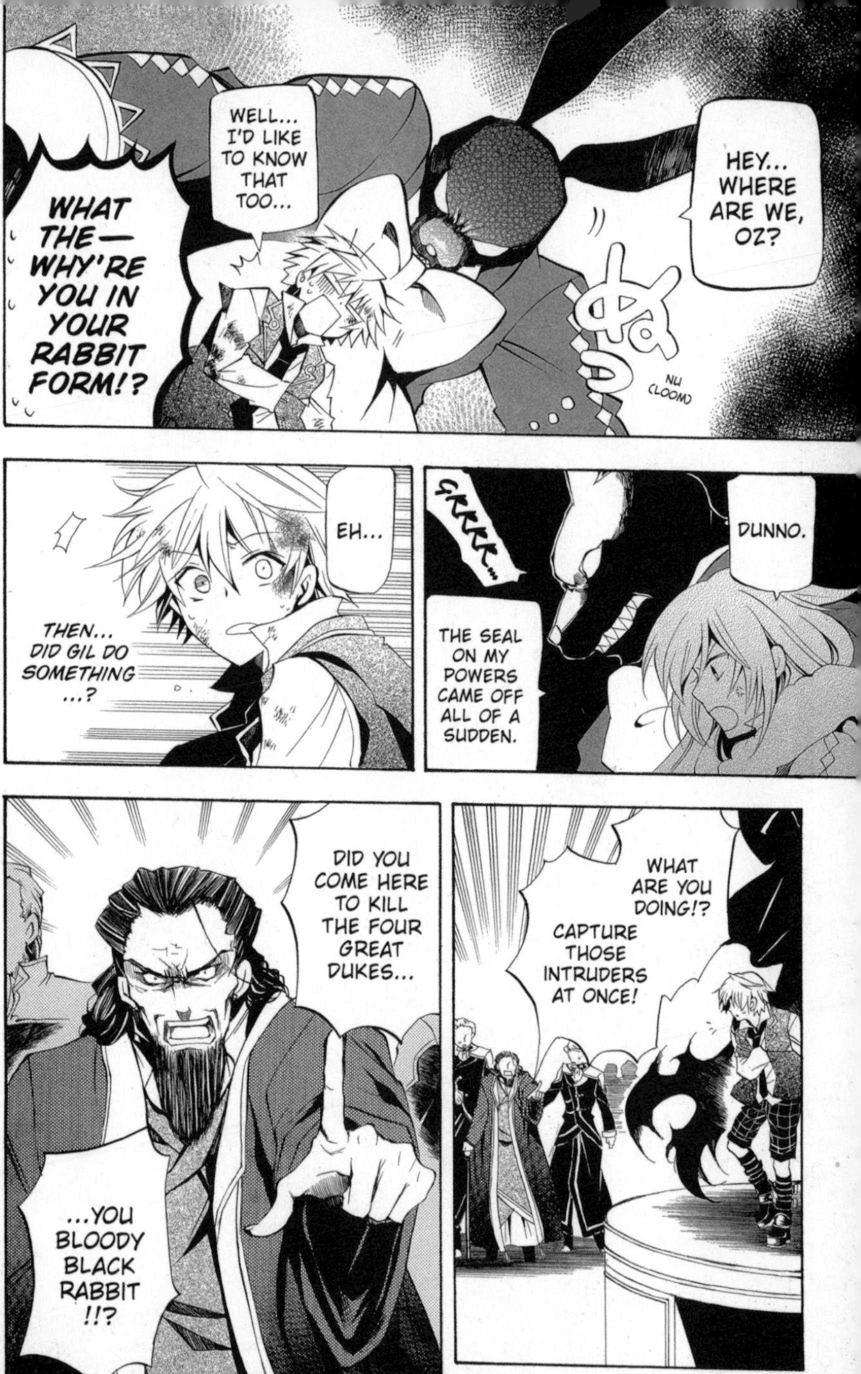
HEY... WHERE ARE WE, OZ?
ぬ
NU (LOOM)
WELL... I'D LIKE TO KNOW THAT TOO...
WHAT THE— WHY'RE YOU IN YOUR RABBIT FORM!?
DUNNO.
GRRRR...
THE SEAL ON MY POWERS CAME OFF ALL OF A SUDDEN.
EH...
THEN... DID GIL DO SOMETHING...?
WHAT ARE YOU DOING!?
CAPTURE THOSE INTRUDERS AT ONCE!
DID YOU COME HERE TO KILL THE FOUR GREAT DUKES...
...YOU BLOODY BLACK RABBIT!!?

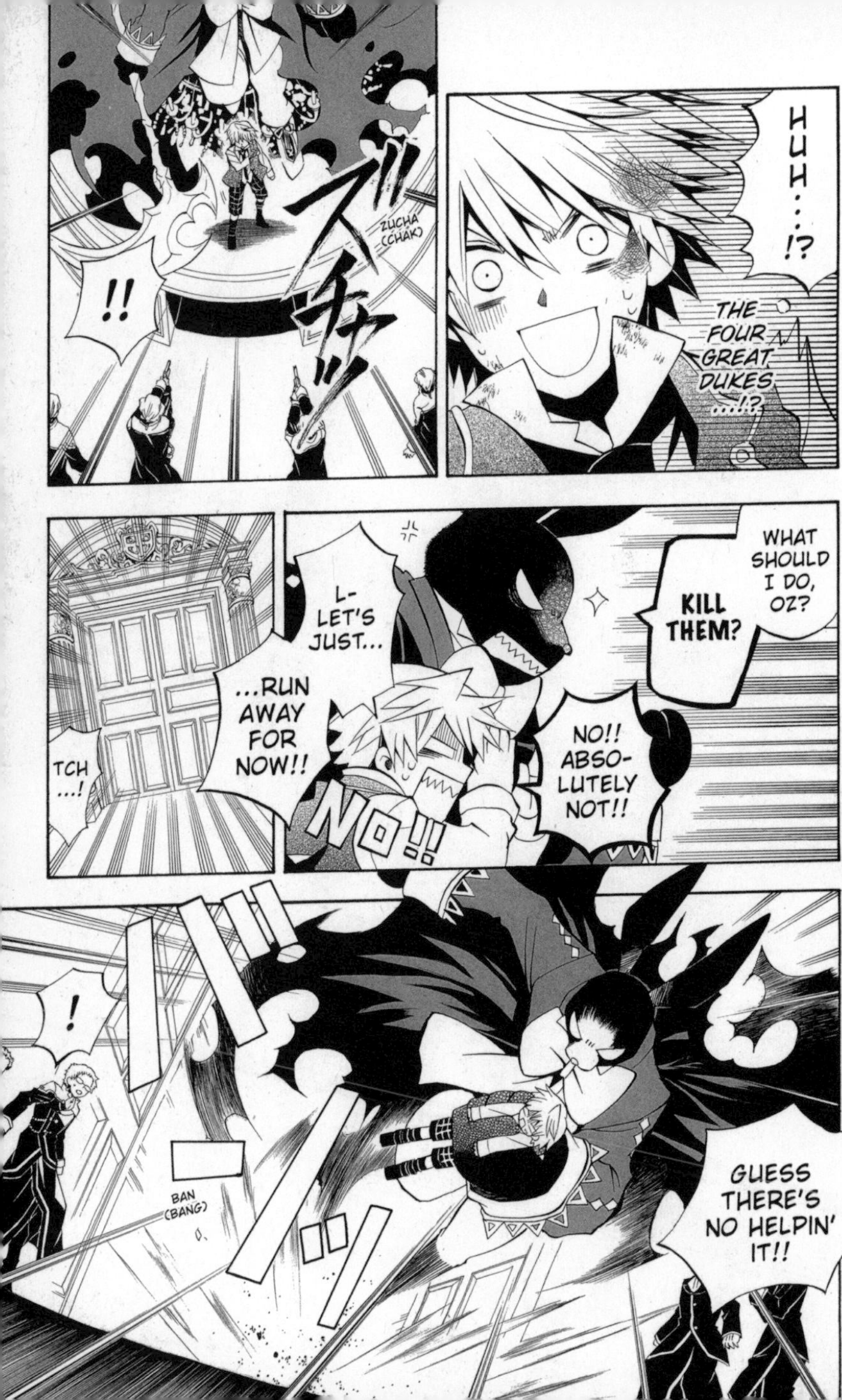
HUH...!?
THE FOUR GREAT DUKES ...!?
ZUCHA (CHAK)
!!
WHAT SHOULD I DO, OZ?
KILL THEM?
NO!! ABSOLUTELY NOT!!
NO!!
L- LET'S JUST...
...RUN AWAY FOR NOW!!
TCH ...!
GUESS THERE'S NO HELPIN' IT!!
!
BAN (BANG)

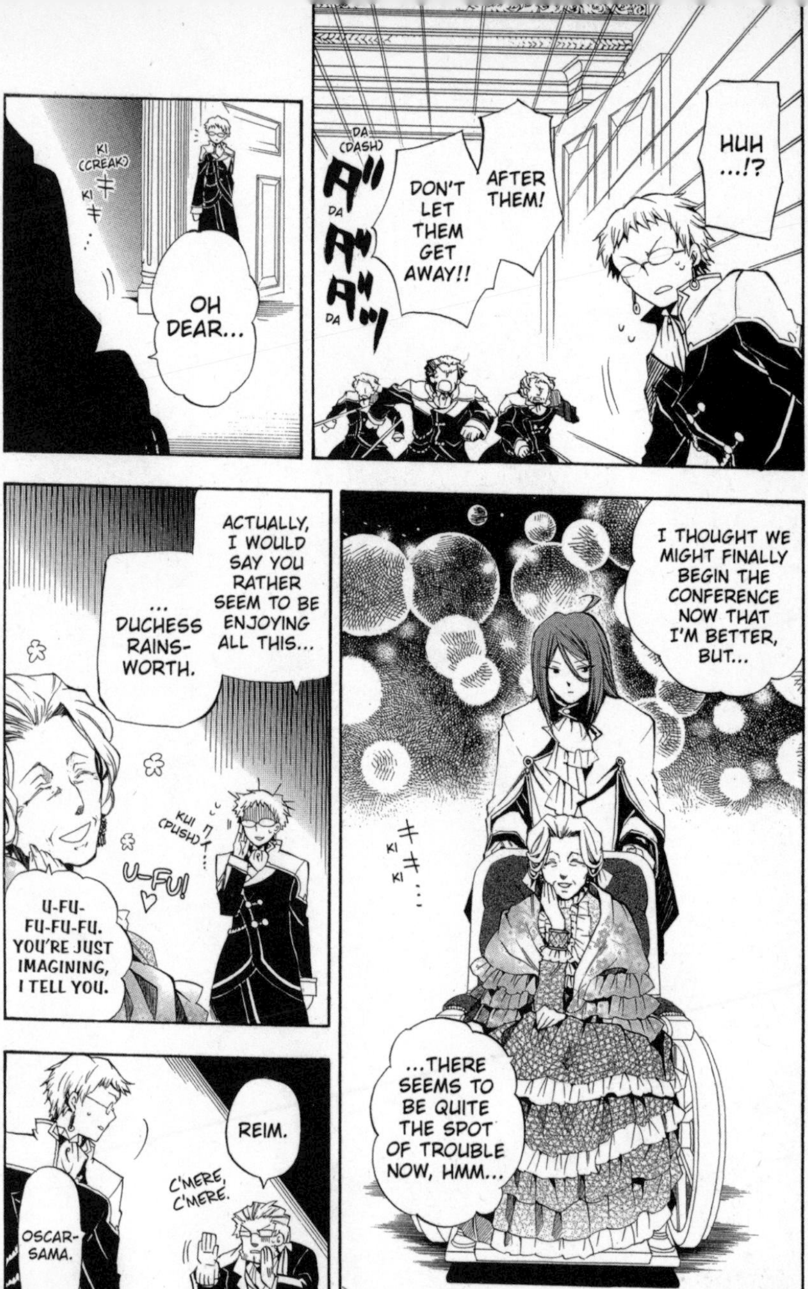
HUH ...!?
AFTER THEM!
DON'T LET THEM GET AWAY!!
DA (DASH)
DA
DA
KI (CREAK)
KI
OH DEAR...
I THOUGHT WE MIGHT FINALLY BEGIN THE CONFERENCE NOW THAT I'M BETTER, BUT...
KI
KI
...THERE SEEMS TO BE QUITE THE SPOT OF TROUBLE NOW, HMM...
ACTUALLY, I WOULD SAY YOU RATHER SEEM TO BE ENJOYING ALL THIS...
... DUCHESS RAINS-WORTH.
KUI (PUSH)
U-FU!
U-FU-FU-FU-FU. YOU'RE JUST IMAGINING, I TELL YOU.
REIM.
C'MERE, C'MERE.
OSCAR-SAMA.

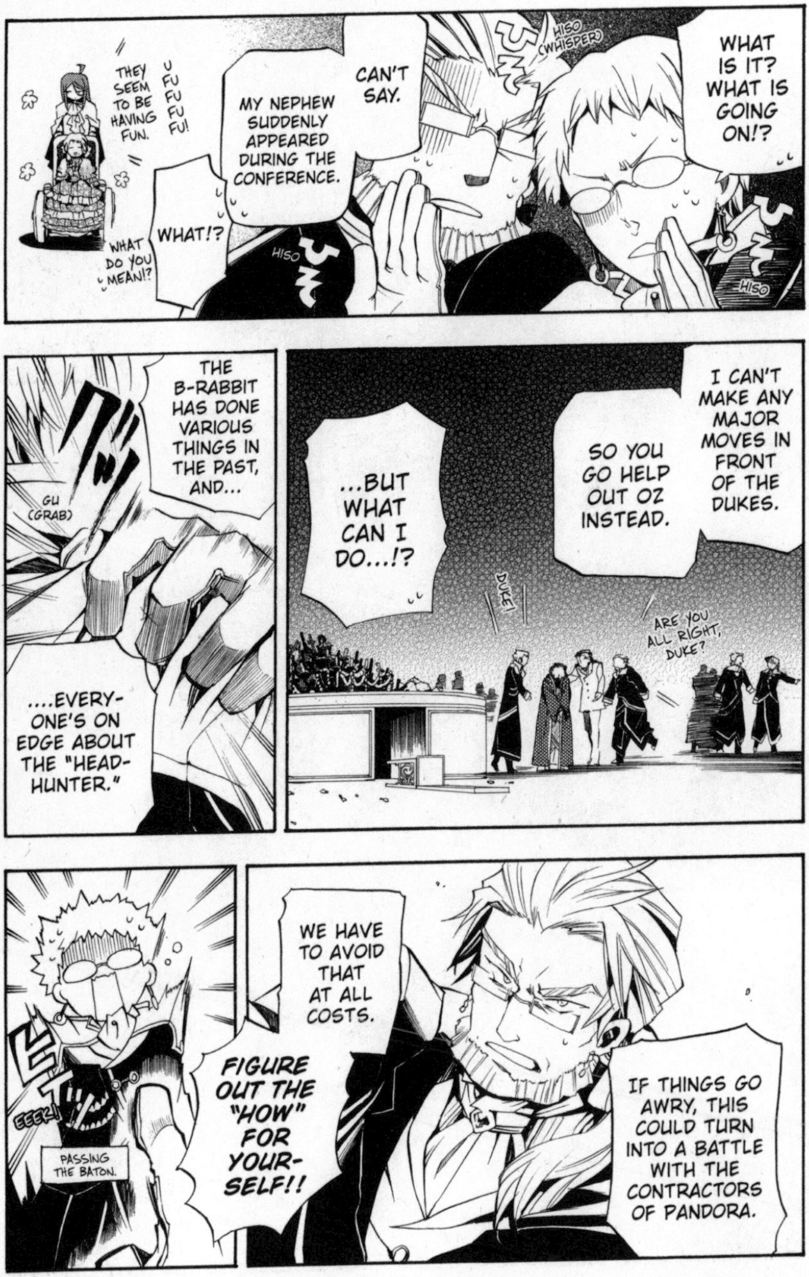
WHAT IS IT? WHAT IS GOING ON!?
HISO (WHISPER)
CAN'T SAY.
MY NEPHEW SUDDENLY APPEARED DURING THE CONFERENCE.
THEY SEEM TO BE HAVING FUN.
U FU FU FU FU!
WHAT!?
WHAT DO YOU MEAN!?
HISO
HISO
I CAN'T MAKE ANY MAJOR MOVES IN FRONT OF THE DUKES.
SO YOU GO HELP OUT OZ INSTEAD.
...BUT WHAT CAN I DO...!?
ARE YOU ALL RIGHT, DUKE?
DUKE!
THE B-RABBIT HAS DONE VARIOUS THINGS IN THE PAST, AND...
GU (GRAB)
....EVERY-ONE'S ON EDGE ABOUT THE "HEAD-HUNTER."
IF THINGS GO AWRY, THIS COULD TURN INTO A BATTLE WITH THE CONTRACTORS OF PANDORA.
WE HAVE TO AVOID THAT AT ALL COSTS.
FIGURE OUT THE "HOW" FOR YOUR-SELF!!
EEEK!
PASSING THE BATON.

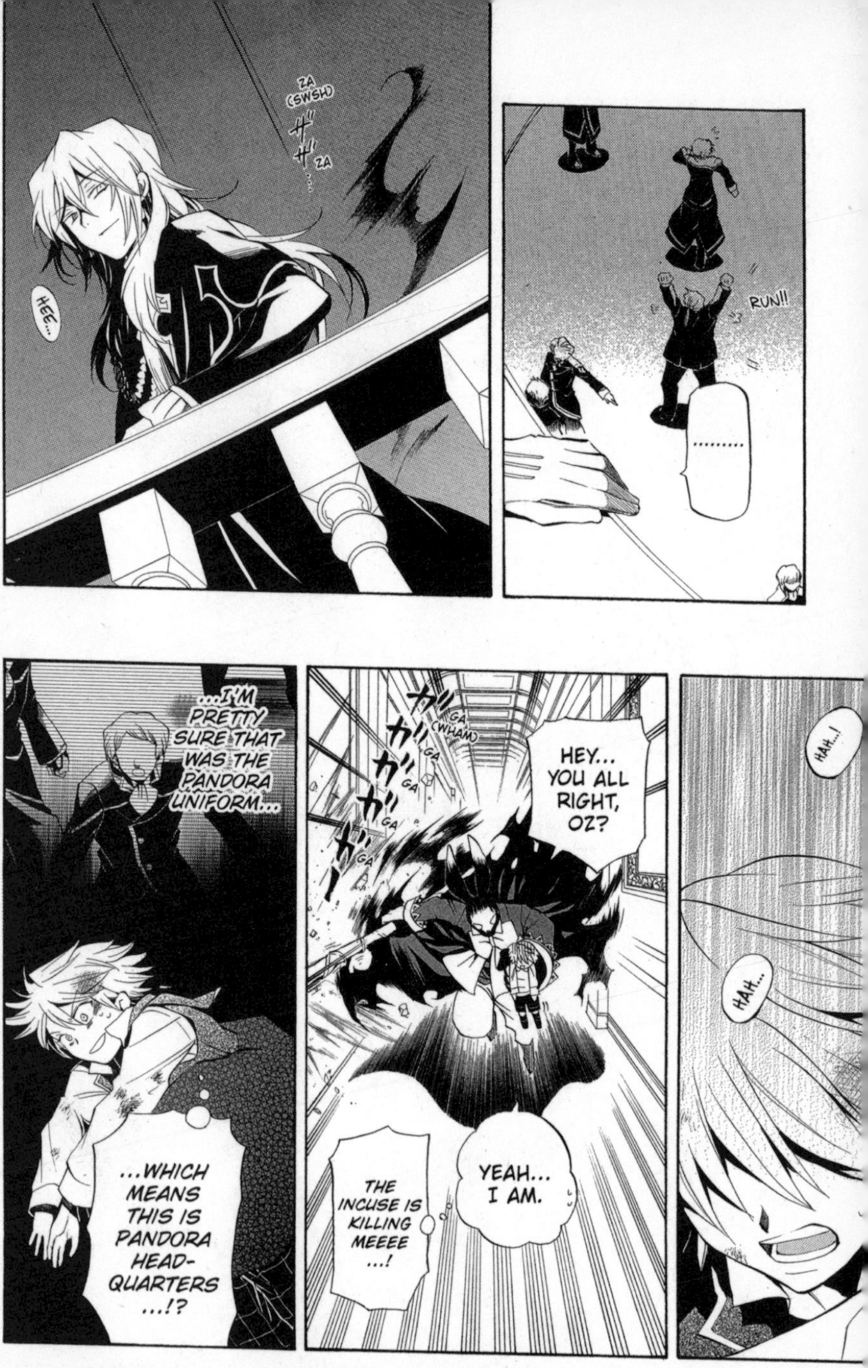
RUN!!
....
ZA (SWSH)
ZA...
HEE...
HAH...!
HAH...
GA (WHAM)
GA
GA
GA
GA
HEY... YOU ALL RIGHT, OZ?
YEAH... I AM.
THE INCUSE IS KILLING MEEEE...!
...I'M PRETTY SURE THAT WAS THE PANDORA UNIFORM...
...WHICH MEANS THIS IS PANDORA HEAD-QUARTERS...!?

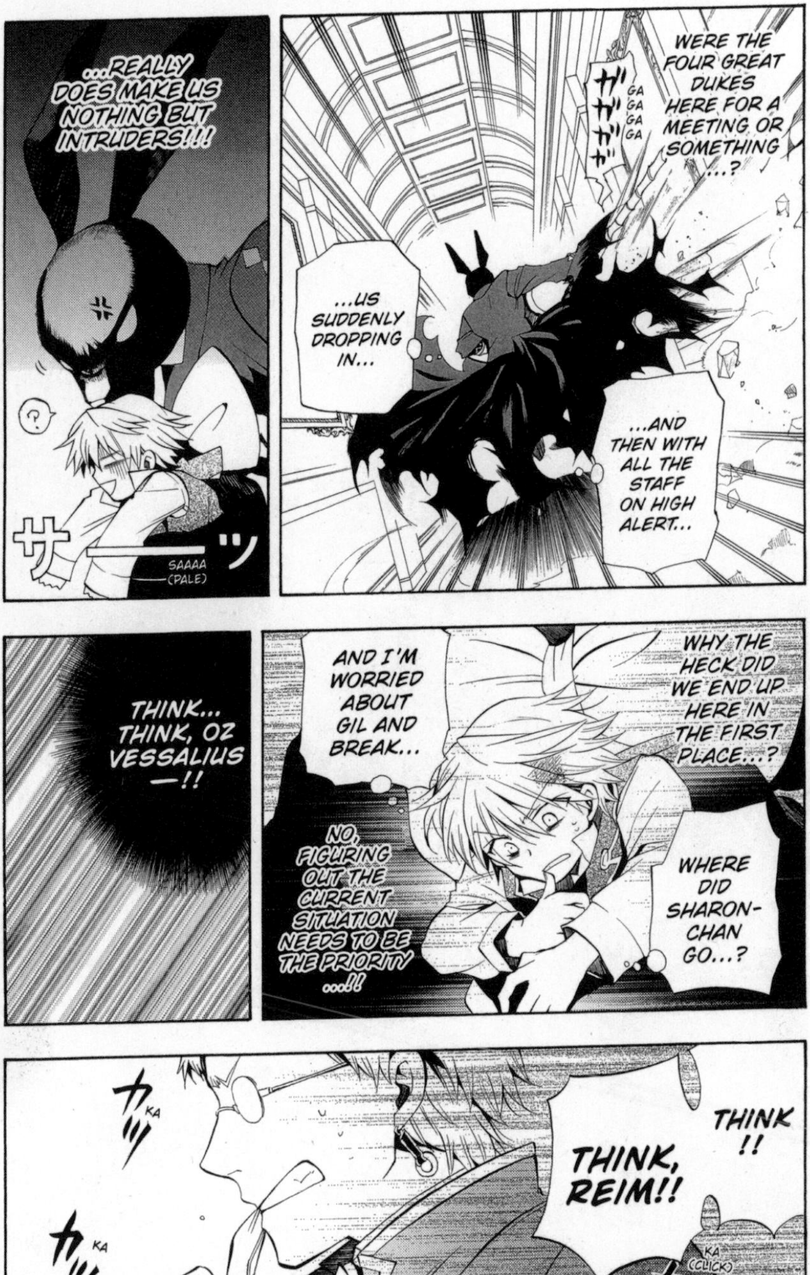

WERE THE FOUR GREAT DUKES HERE FOR A MEETING OR SOMETHING ...?
ガガガガ
GA GA GA GA
...US SUDDENLY DROPPING IN...
...AND THEN WITH ALL THE STAFF ON HIGH ALERT...
...REALLY DOES MAKE US NOTHING BUT INTRUDERS!!!
サーーッ
SAAAA (PALE)
WHY THE HECK DID WE END UP HERE IN THE FIRST PLACE...?
AND I'M WORRIED ABOUT GIL AND BREAK...
WHERE DID SHARON-CHAN GO...?
NO, FIGURING OUT THE CURRENT SITUATION NEEDS TO BE THE PRIORITY ...!!
THINK... THINK, OZ VESSALIUS —!!
THINK !!
THINK, REIM!!
カッ
KA (CLICK)
カッ
KA
カッ
KA

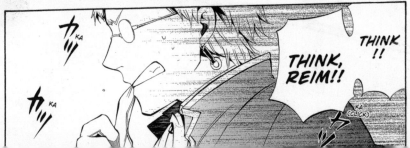

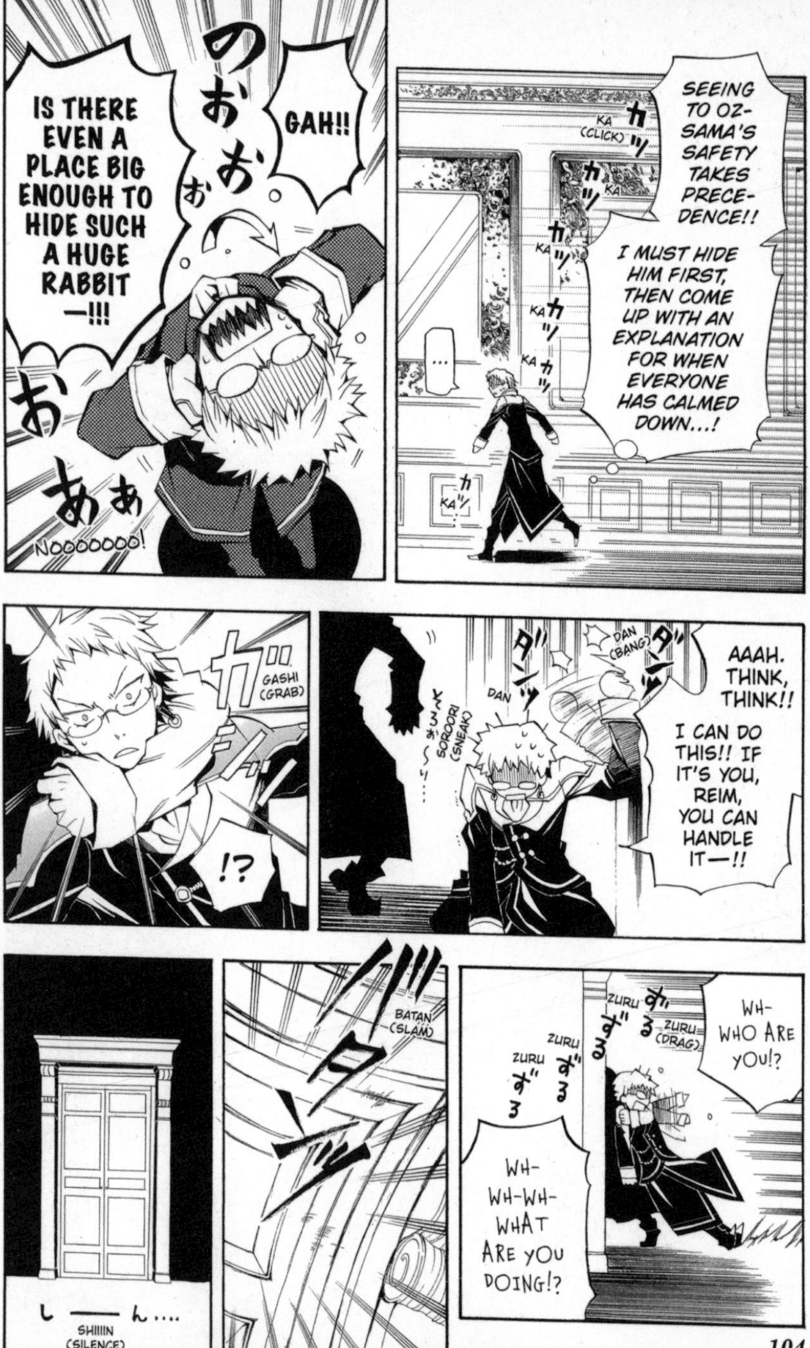
SEEING TO OZ-SAMA'S SAFETY TAKES PRECEDENCE!!
I MUST HIDE HIM FIRST, THEN COME UP WITH AN EXPLANATION FOR WHEN EVERYONE HAS CALMED DOWN...!
カッ KA (CLICK)
カッ KA
カッ KA
カッ KA
カッ KA
...
カッ KA
GAH!!
IS THERE EVEN A PLACE BIG ENOUGH TO HIDE SUCH A HUGE RABBIT—!!!
のおおお
おああ
NOOOOOOO!
AAAH. THINK, THINK!!
I CAN DO THIS!! IF IT'S YOU, REIM, YOU CAN HANDLE IT—!!
ダン DAN (BANG)
ダンッ DAN
そろ～り SOROORI (SNEAK)
ガッ GASHI (GRAB)
!?
WH-WHO ARE YOU!?
ずる ZURU
ずる ZURU (DRAG)
ずる ZURU
ずる ZURU
WH-WH-WH-WHAT ARE YOU DOING!?
バタン BATAN (SLAM)
し——ん.... SHIIIIN (SILENCE)

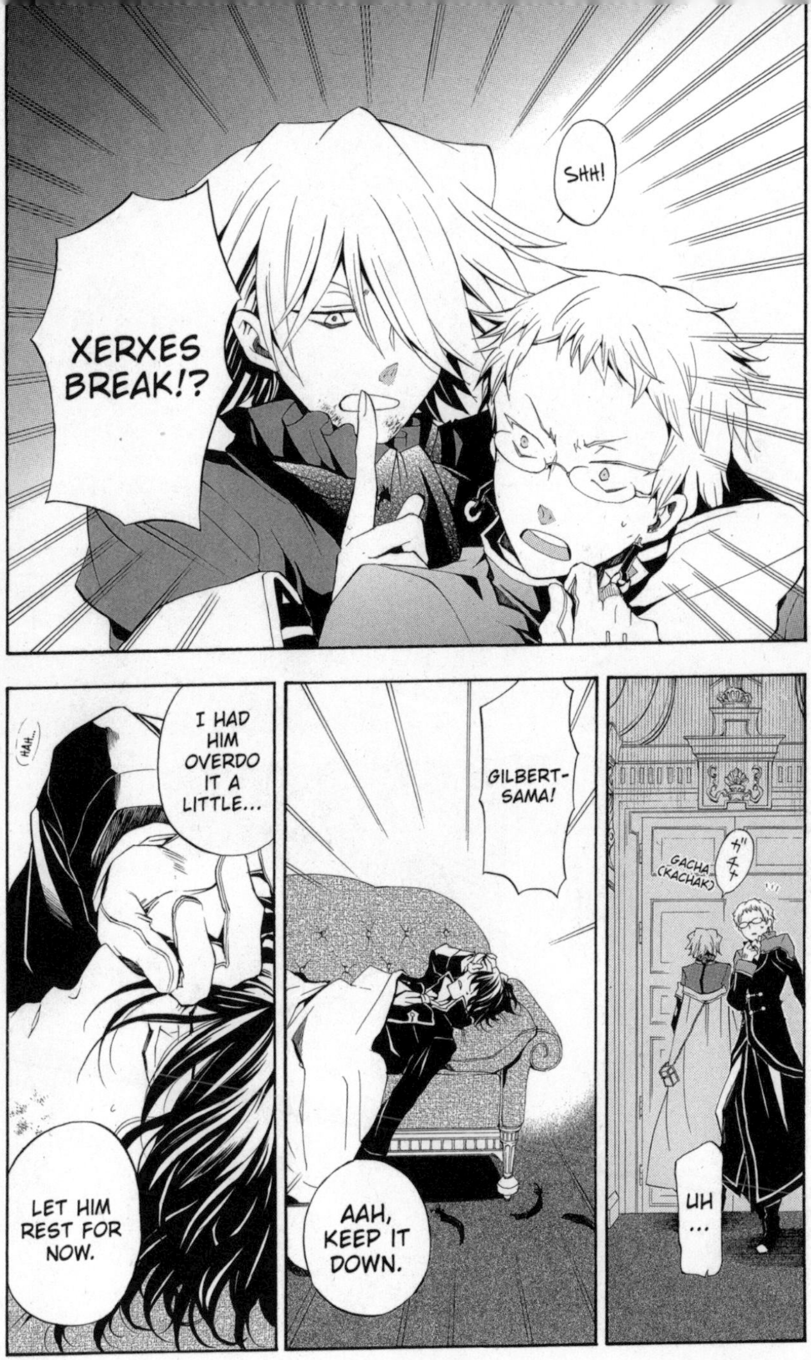
SHH!
XERXES BREAK!?
ガチャ
GACHA (KACHAK)
UH ...
GILBERT-SAMA!
AAH, KEEP IT DOWN.
HAH...
I HAD HIM OVERDO IT A LITTLE...
LET HIM REST FOR NOW.

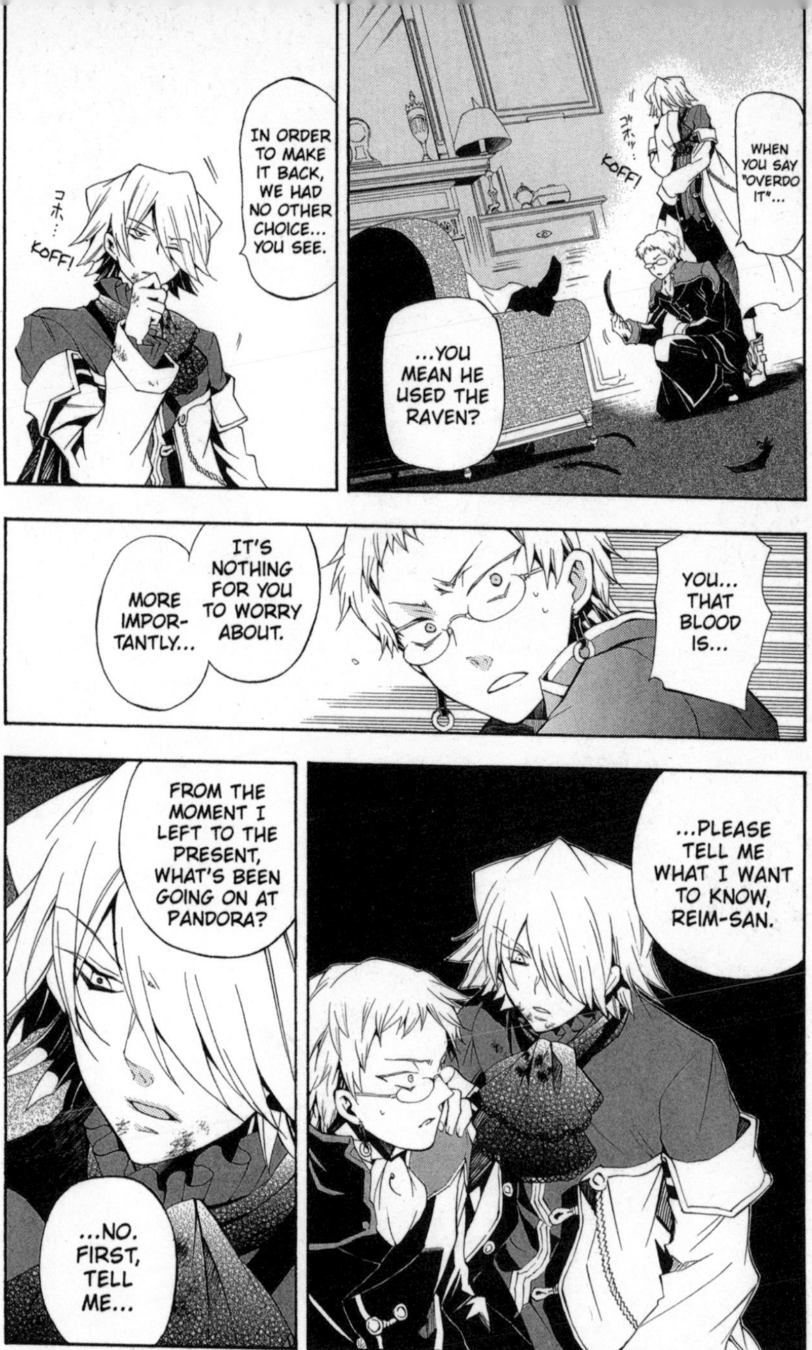
WHEN YOU SAY "OVERDO IT"...
ゴホッ
KOFF!
...YOU MEAN HE USED THE RAVEN?
IN ORDER TO MAKE IT BACK, WE HAD NO OTHER CHOICE... YOU SEE.
コホ…
KOFF!
YOU... THAT BLOOD IS...
IT'S NOTHING FOR YOU TO WORRY ABOUT.
MORE IMPORTANTLY...
...PLEASE TELL ME WHAT I WANT TO KNOW, REIM-SAN.
FROM THE MOMENT I LEFT TO THE PRESENT, WHAT'S BEEN GOING ON AT PANDORA?
...NO. FIRST, TELL ME...

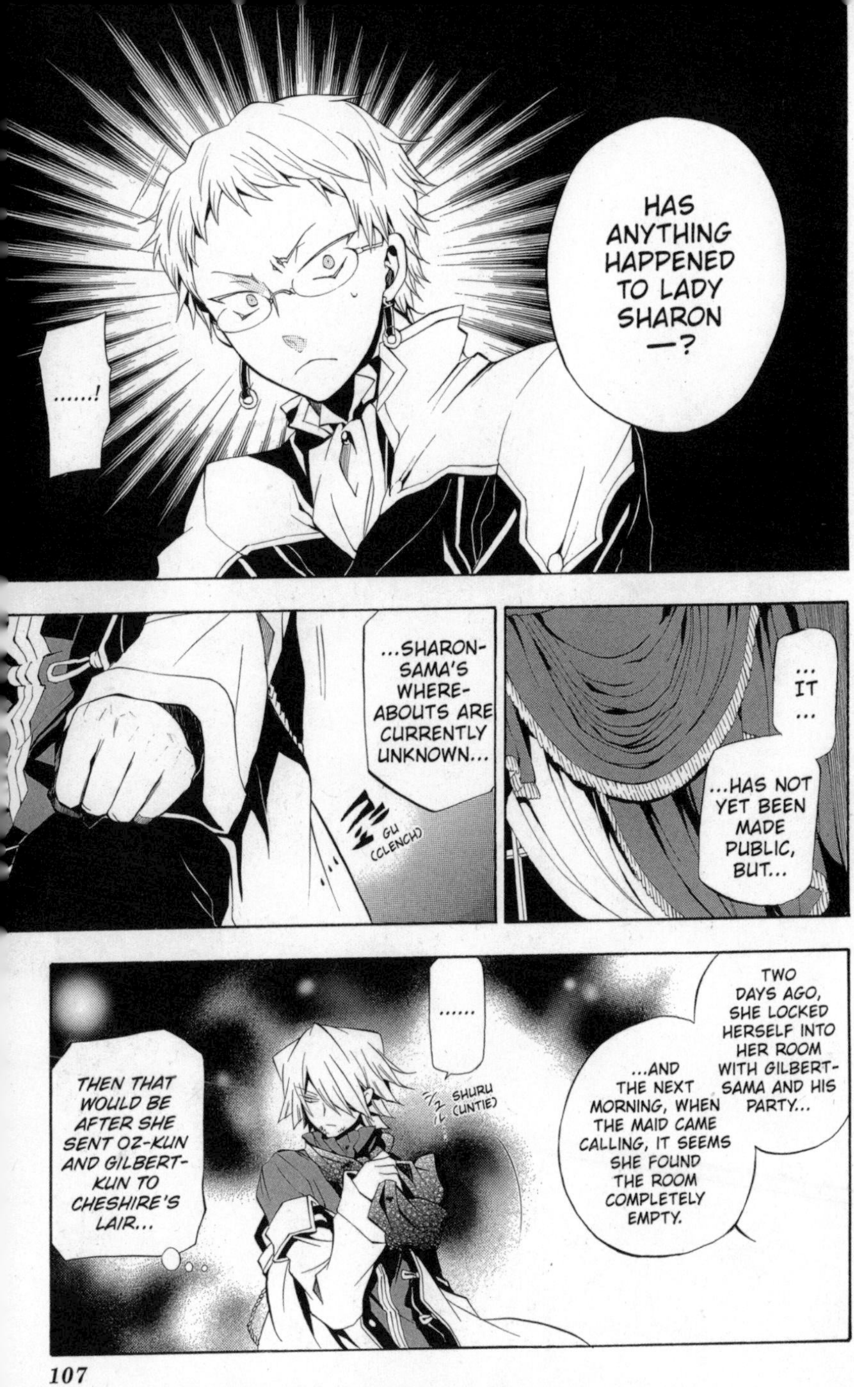
HAS ANYTHING HAPPENED TO LADY SHARON —?
......!
... IT ...
...HAS NOT YET BEEN MADE PUBLIC, BUT...
...SHARON-SAMA'S WHERE-ABOUTS ARE CURRENTLY UNKNOWN...
GU (CLENCH)
TWO DAYS AGO, SHE LOCKED HERSELF INTO HER ROOM WITH GILBERT-SAMA AND HIS PARTY...
...AND THE NEXT MORNING, WHEN THE MAID CAME CALLING, IT SEEMS SHE FOUND THE ROOM COMPLETELY EMPTY.
......
SHURU (UNTIE)
THEN THAT WOULD BE AFTER SHE SENT OZ-KUN AND GILBERT-KUN TO CHESHIRE'S LAIR...

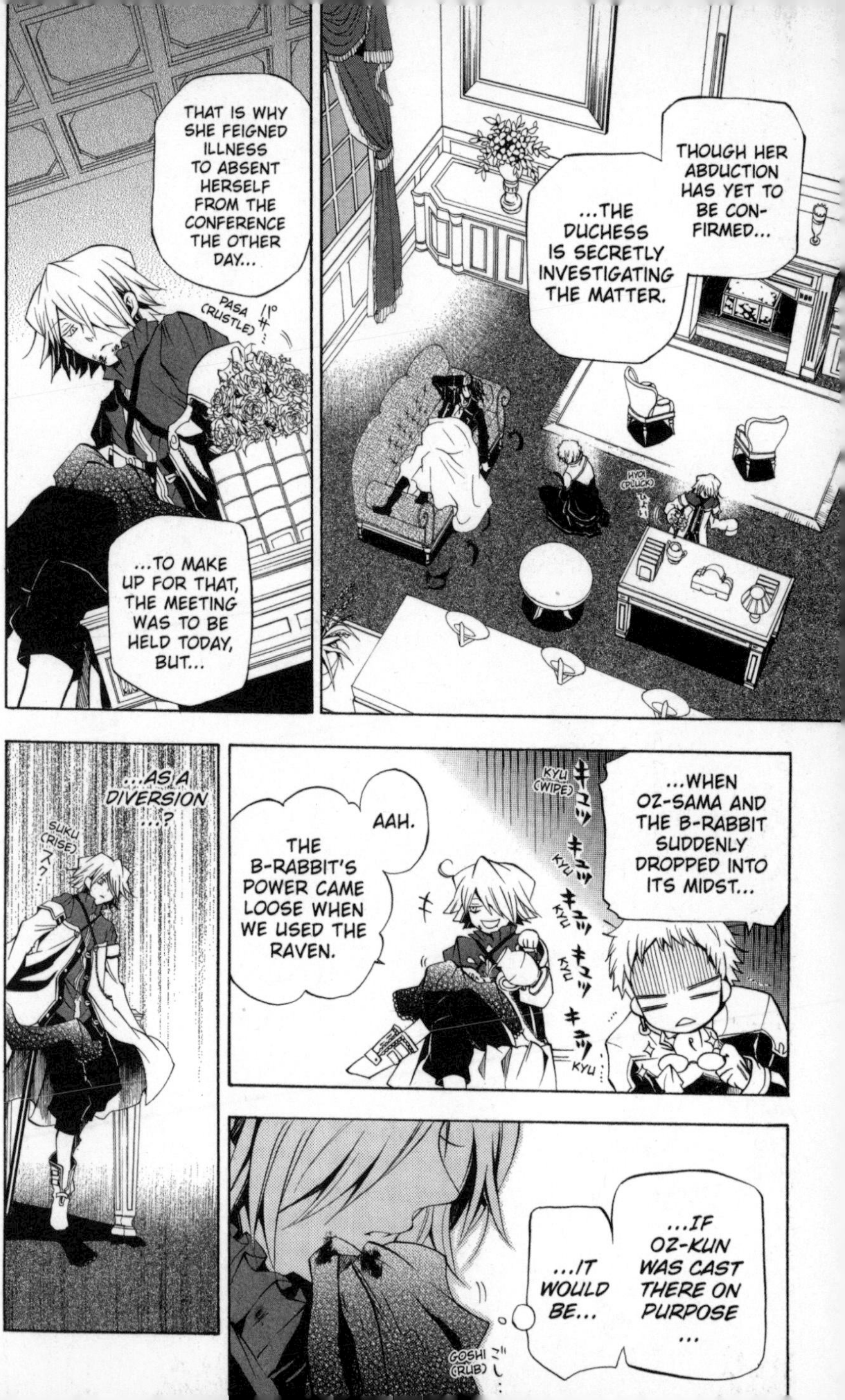
THOUGH HER ABDUCTION HAS YET TO BE CON-FIRMED...
...THE DUCHESS IS SECRETLY INVESTIGATING THE MATTER.
HYOI (PLUCK)
THAT IS WHY SHE FEIGNED ILLNESS TO ABSENT HERSELF FROM THE CONFERENCE THE OTHER DAY...
PASA (RUSTLE)
...TO MAKE UP FOR THAT, THE MEETING WAS TO BE HELD TODAY, BUT...
...WHEN OZ-SAMA AND THE B-RABBIT SUDDENLY DROPPED INTO ITS MIDST...
KYU (WIPE)
KYU
KYU
KYU
KYU...
AAH.
THE B-RABBIT'S POWER CAME LOOSE WHEN WE USED THE RAVEN.
...IF OZ-KUN WAS CAST THERE ON PURPOSE...
...IT WOULD BE...
GOSHI (RUB)
...AS A DIVERSION...?
SUKU (RISE)

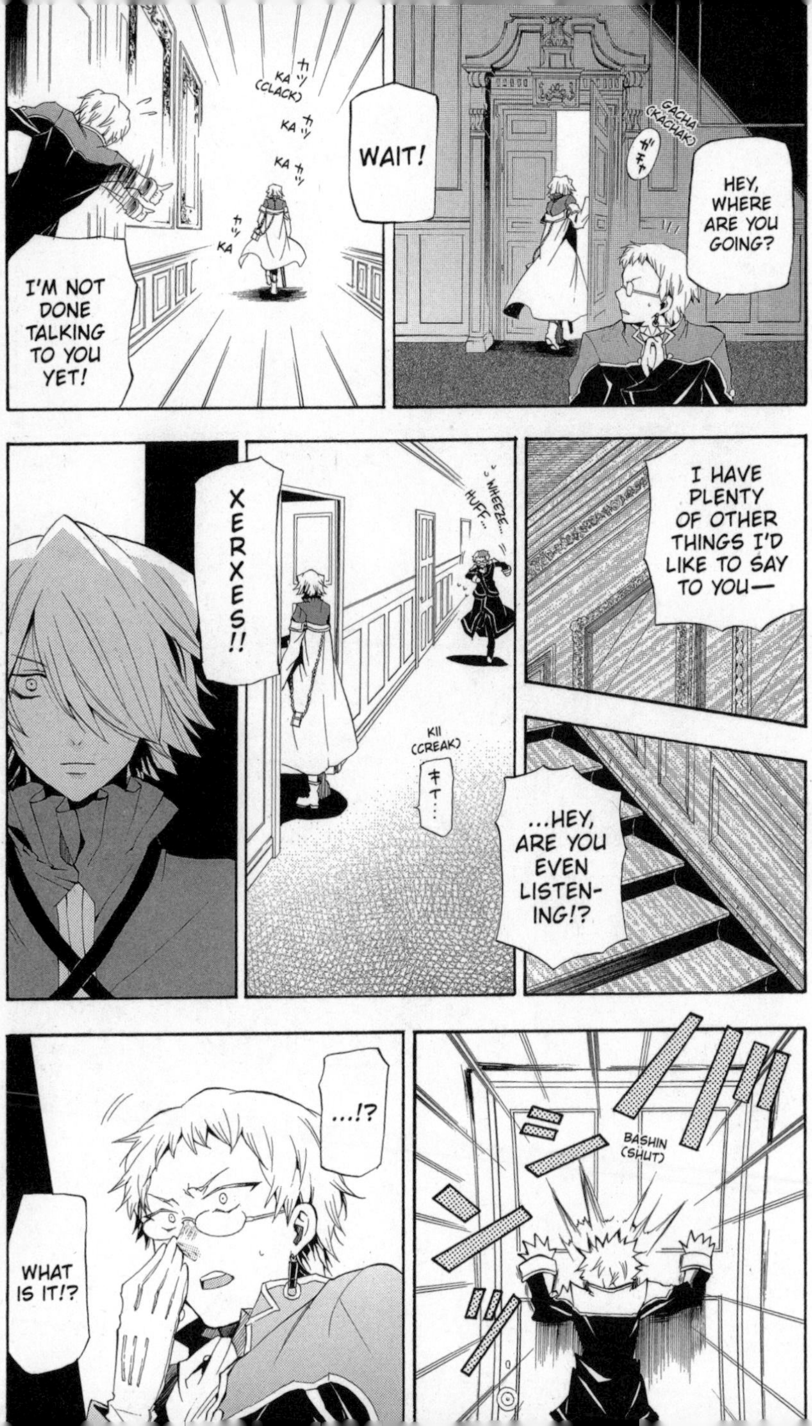
GACHA (KACHAK)
ガチャ
HEY, WHERE ARE YOU GOING?
KA (CLACK)
KA
KA
KA
WAIT!
I'M NOT DONE TALKING TO YOU YET!
I HAVE PLENTY OF OTHER THINGS I'D LIKE TO SAY TO YOU—
...HEY, ARE YOU EVEN LISTENING!?
WHEEZE... HUFF...
KII (CREAK)
キイ…
XERXES!!
BASHIN (SHUT)
...!?
WHAT IS IT!?

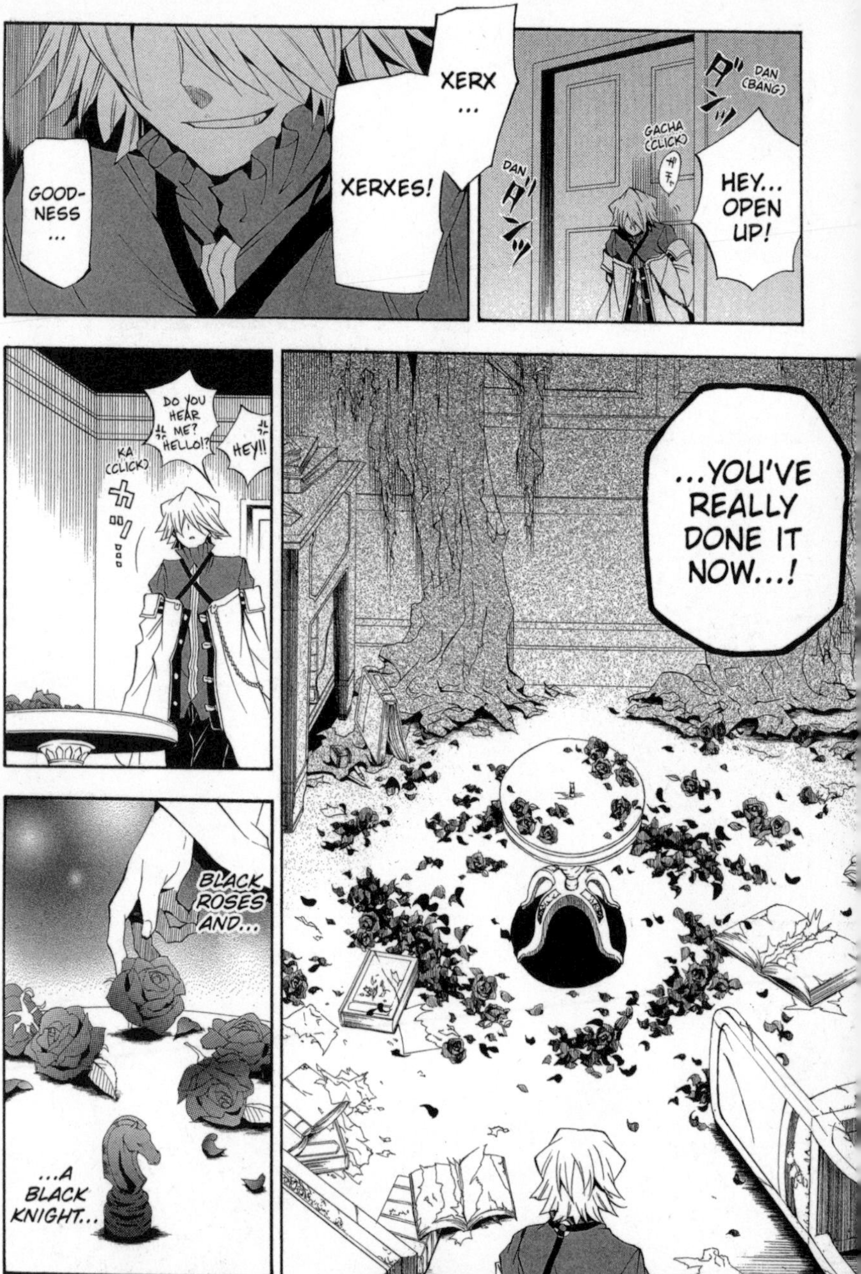
DAN (BANG)
GACHA (CLICK)
DAN
HEY... OPEN UP!
XERX ...
XERXES!
GOODNESS ...
...YOU'VE REALLY DONE IT NOW...!
DO YOU HEAR ME? HELLO!?
HEY!!
KA (CLICK)
BLACK ROSES AND...
...A BLACK KNIGHT...

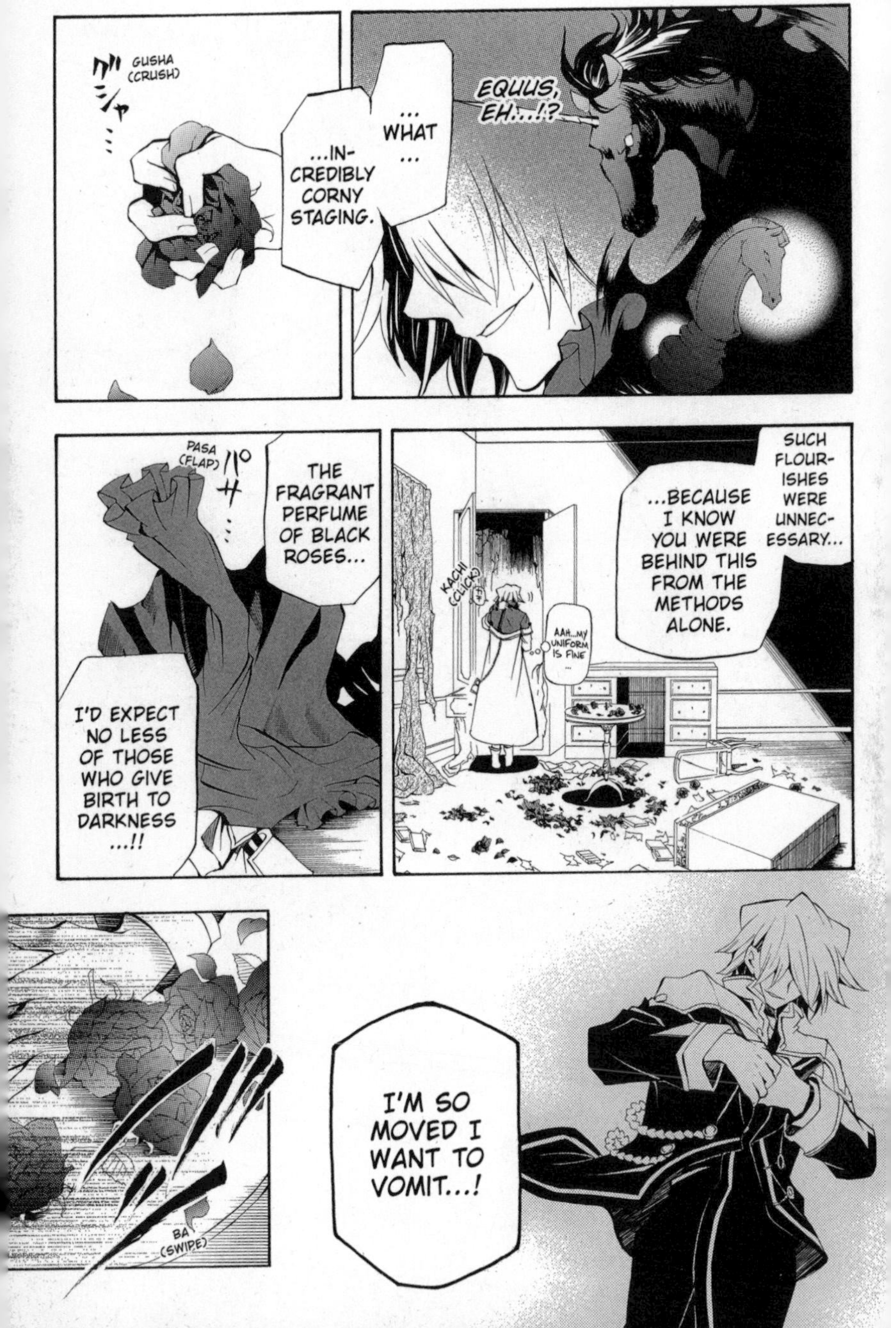
EQUUS, EH...!?
... WHAT ...
...IN-CREDIBLY CORNY STAGING.
グシャ
GUSHA (CRUSH)
SUCH FLOURISHES WERE UNNECESSARY...
...BECAUSE I KNOW YOU WERE BEHIND THIS FROM THE METHODS ALONE.
KACHI (CLICK)
AAH...MY UNIFORM IS FINE ...
パサ
PASA (FLAP)
THE FRAGRANT PERFUME OF BLACK ROSES...
I'D EXPECT NO LESS OF THOSE WHO GIVE BIRTH TO DARKNESS ...!!
I'M SO MOVED I WANT TO VOMIT...!
BA (SWIPE)

YOU NIGHTRAY SEWER RAT...!

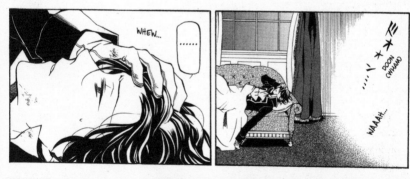

WHEW...

......

NAAAH...

WE HAVE TO... SEAL THE B-RABBIT'S POWERS QUICKLY...

WHERE'S OZ...

...OZ...

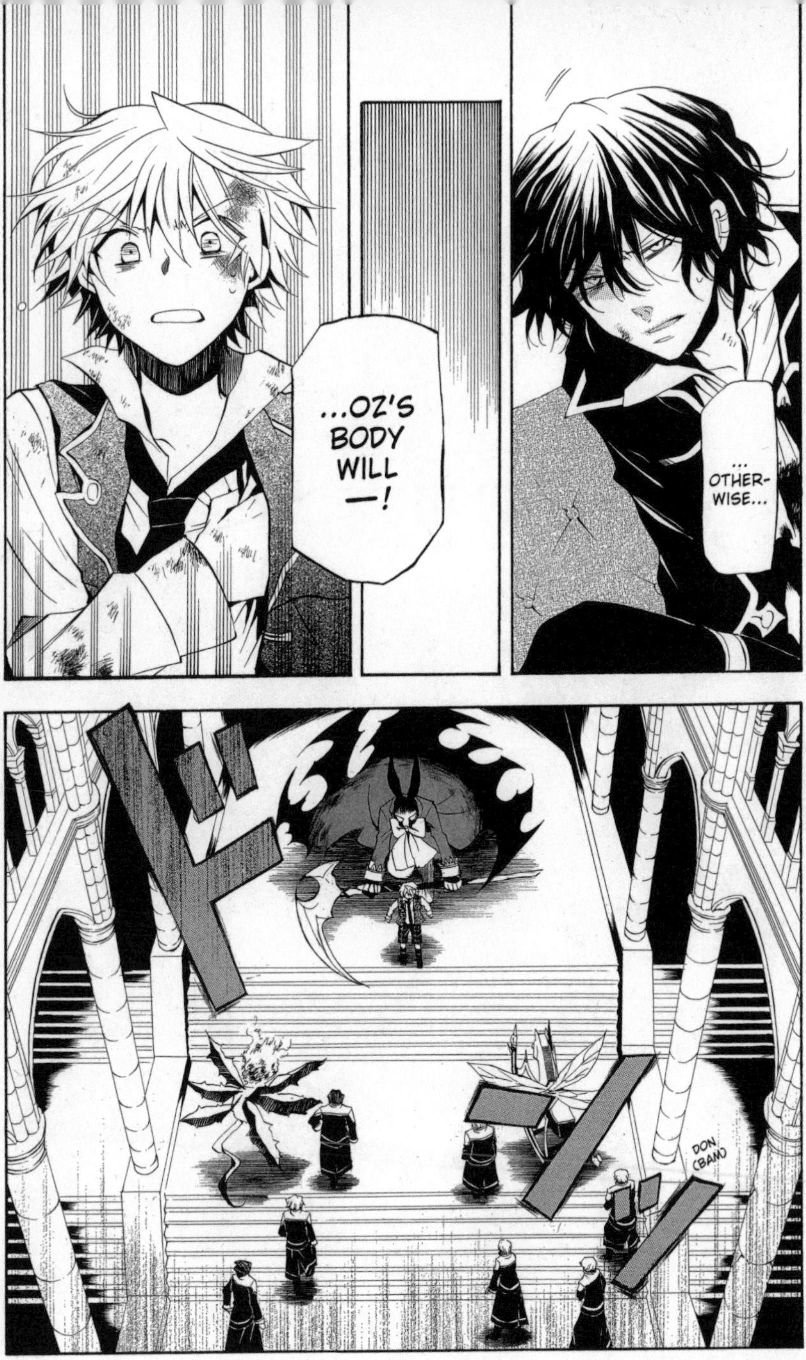
... OTHER-WISE...
...OZ'S BODY WILL —!
DON (BAN)

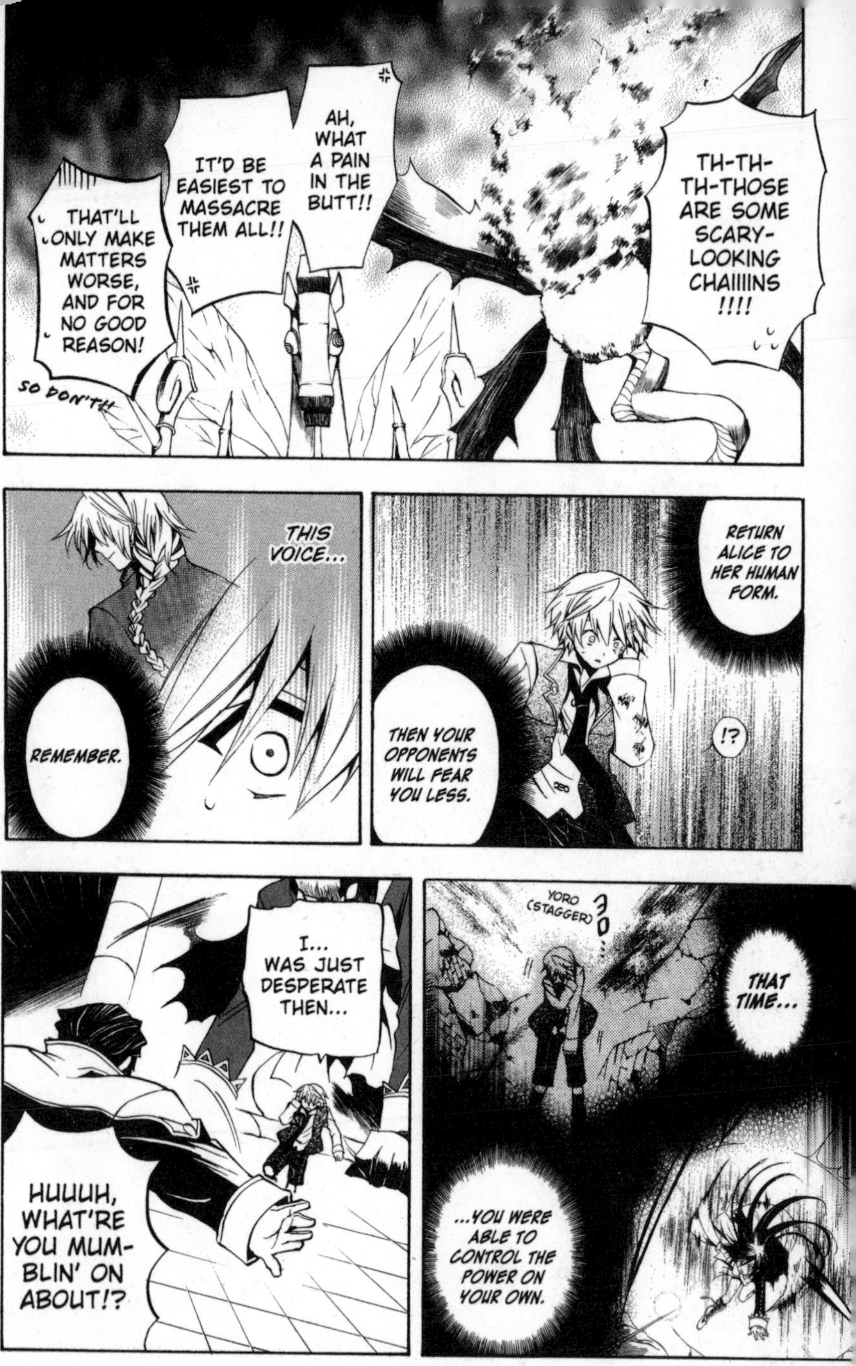

TH-TH-TH-THOSE ARE SOME SCARY-LOOKING CHAIIIINS!!!!
AH, WHAT A PAIN IN THE BUTT!!
IT'D BE EASIEST TO MASSACRE THEM ALL!!
THAT'LL ONLY MAKE MATTERS WORSE, AND FOR NO GOOD REASON!
SO DON'T!!
RETURN ALICE TO HER HUMAN FORM.
!?
THEN YOUR OPPONENTS WILL FEAR YOU LESS.
THIS VOICE...
REMEMBER.
YORO (STAGGER)
THAT TIME...
...YOU WERE ABLE TO CONTROL THE POWER ON YOUR OWN.
I... WAS JUST DESPERATE THEN...
HUUUH, WHAT'RE YOU MUMBLIN' ON ABOUT!?

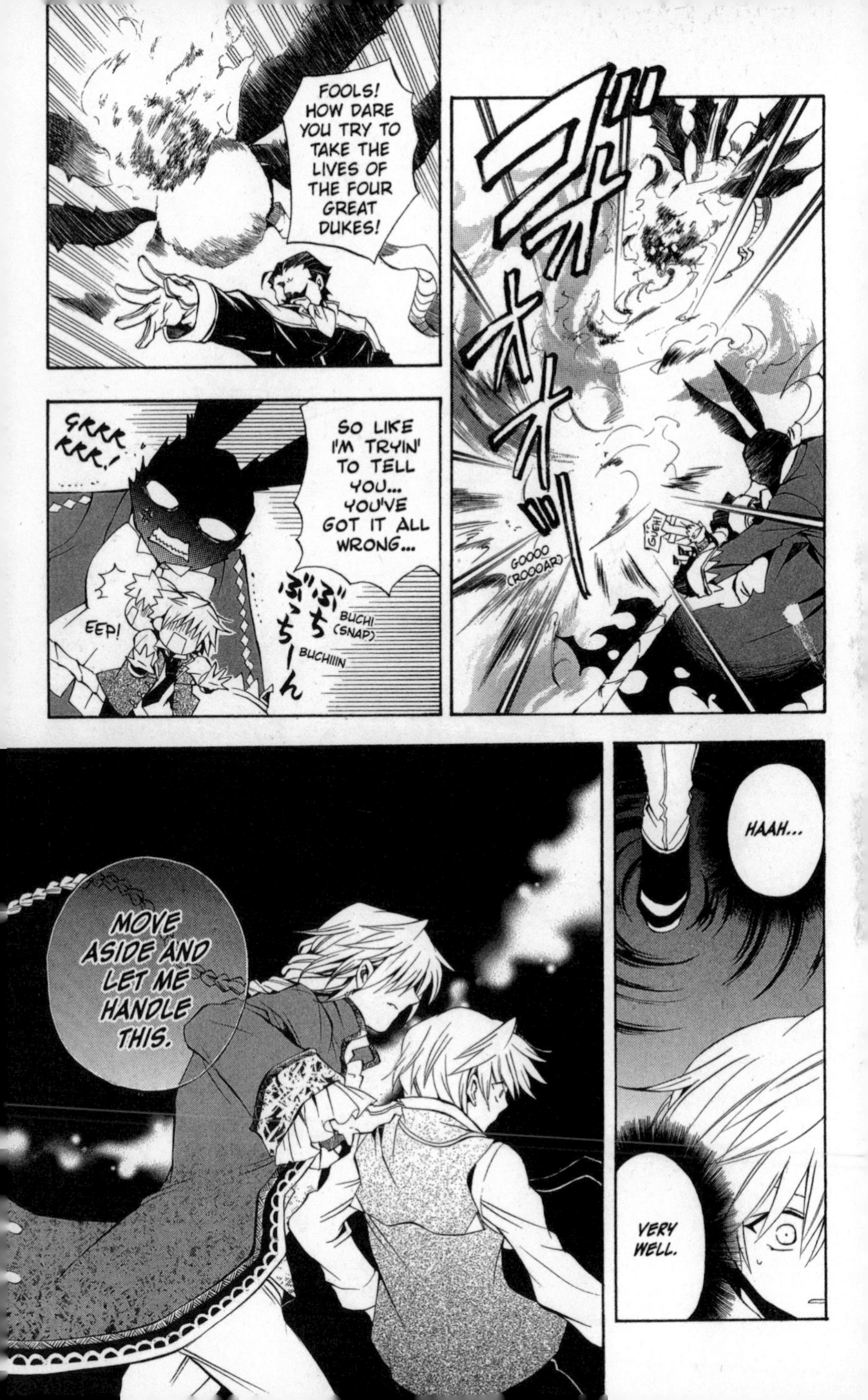
ゴォオオオッ
GUEH!
GOOOO (ROOOAR)
FOOLS! HOW DARE YOU TRY TO TAKE THE LIVES OF THE FOUR GREAT DUKES!
GRRRRRR!
SO LIKE I'M TRYIN' TO TELL YOU... YOU'VE GOT IT ALL WRONG...
ぶち
BUCHI (SNAP)
ぶっちーん
BUCHIIIN
EEP!
HAAH...
VERY WELL.
MOVE ASIDE AND LET ME HANDLE THIS.

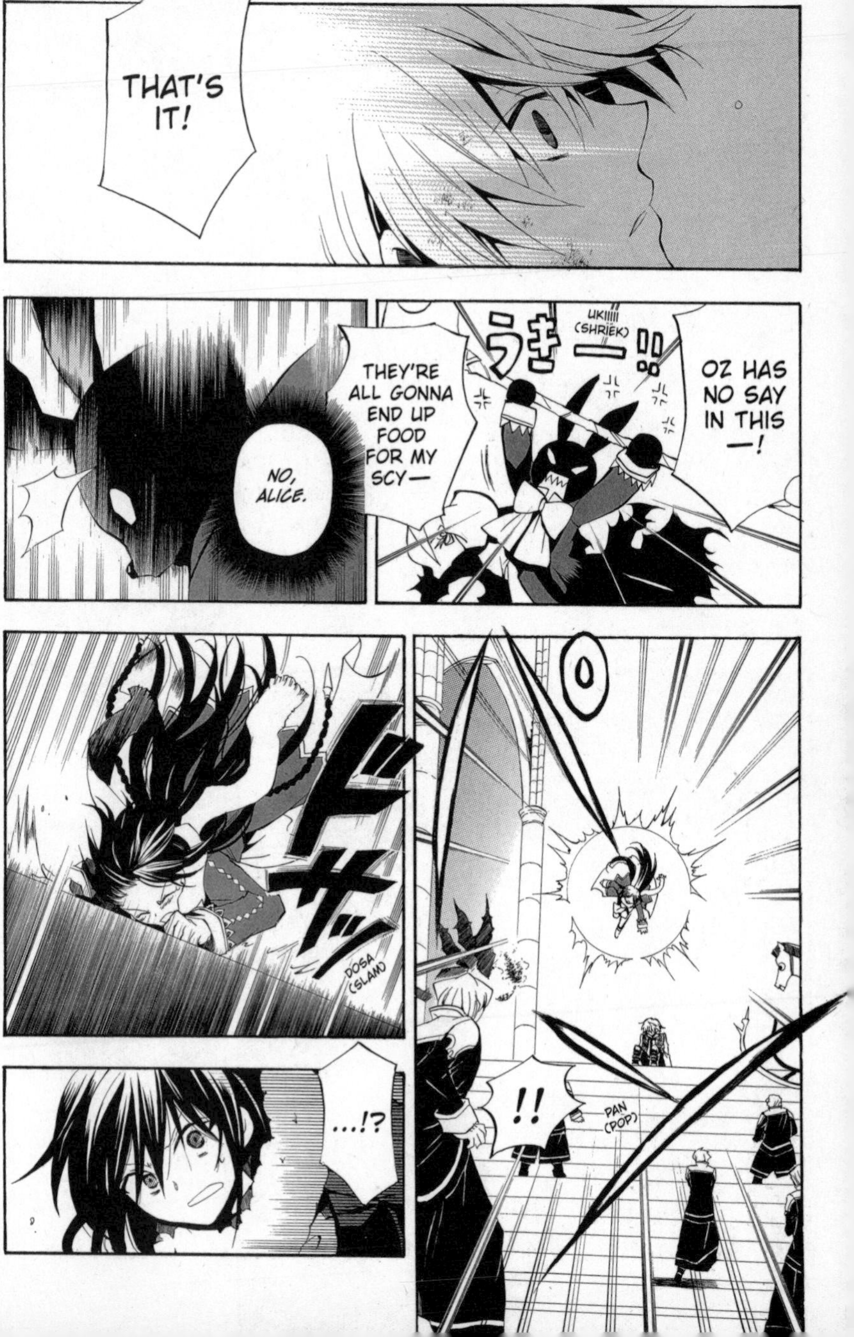
THAT'S IT!
UKI!!!!! (SHRIEK)
OZ HAS NO SAY IN THIS—!
THEY'RE ALL GONNA END UP FOOD FOR MY SCY—
NO, ALICE.
!!
PAN (POP)
DOSA (SLAM)
...!?

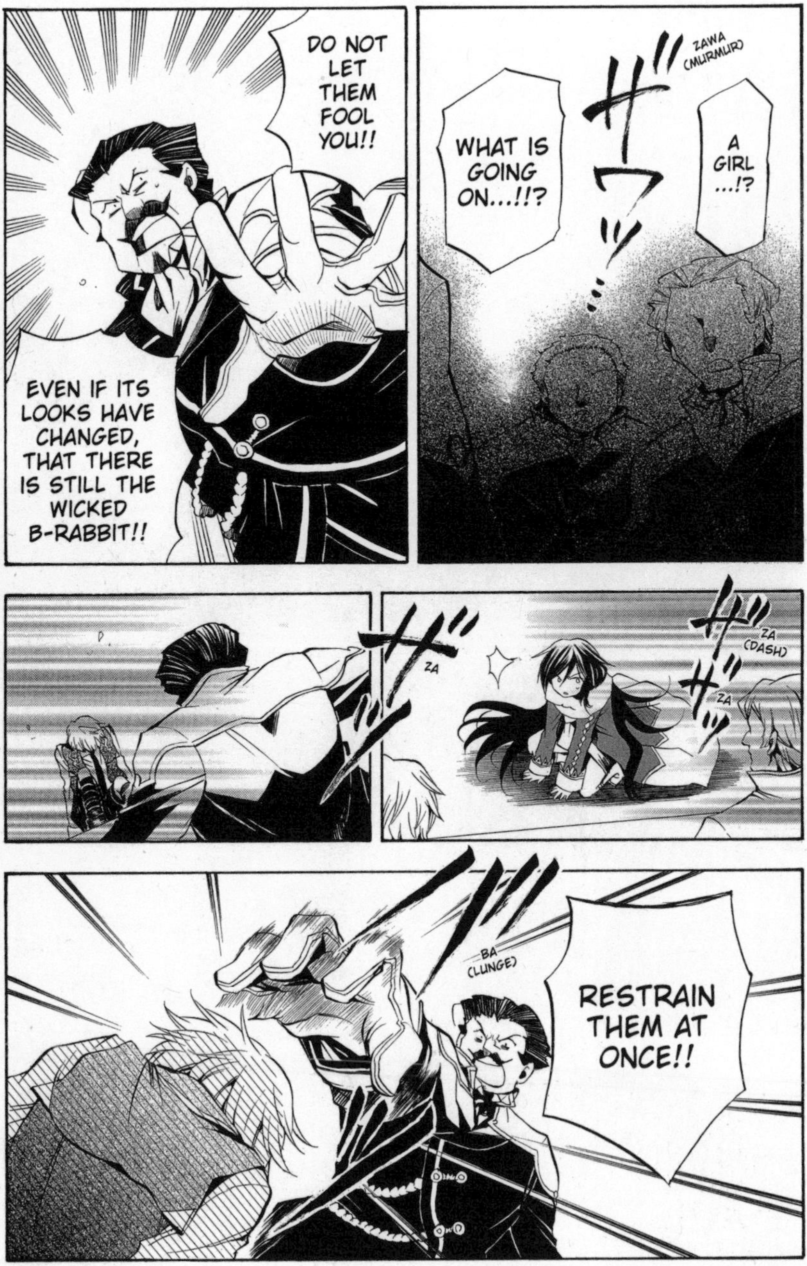
ZAWA (MURMUR)
A GIRL ...!?
WHAT IS GOING ON...!!?
DO NOT LET THEM FOOL YOU!!
EVEN IF ITS LOOKS HAVE CHANGED, THAT THERE IS STILL THE WICKED B-RABBIT!!
ZA (DASH)
ZA
ZA
BA (LUNGE)
RESTRAIN THEM AT ONCE!!

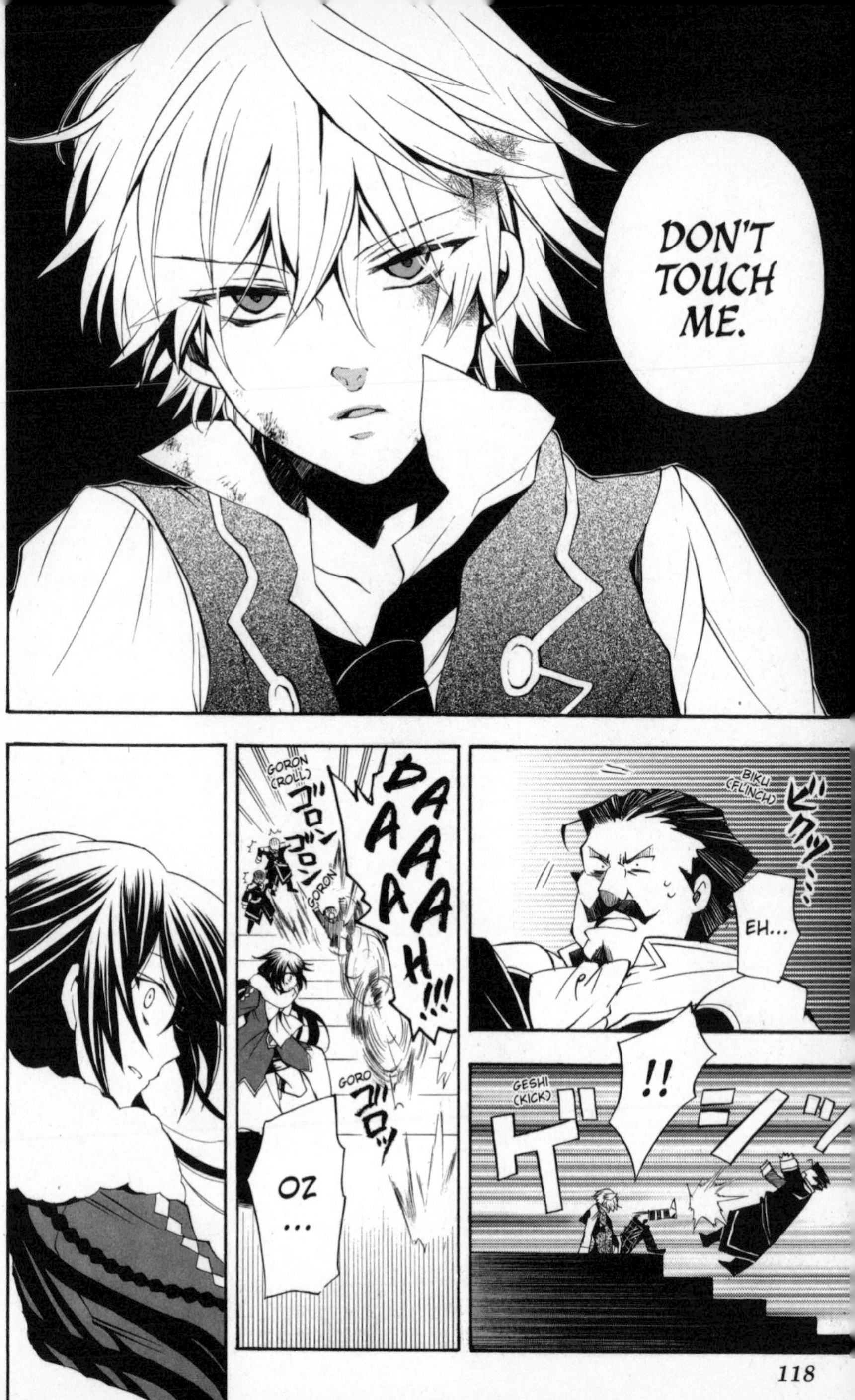
DON'T TOUCH ME.
BIKU (FLINCH)
ビクッ…
EH...
!!
GESHI (KICK)
DAAAAAH!!!
GORON (ROLL)
ゴロン ゴロン
GORON
GORO
ゴロッ
OZ ...

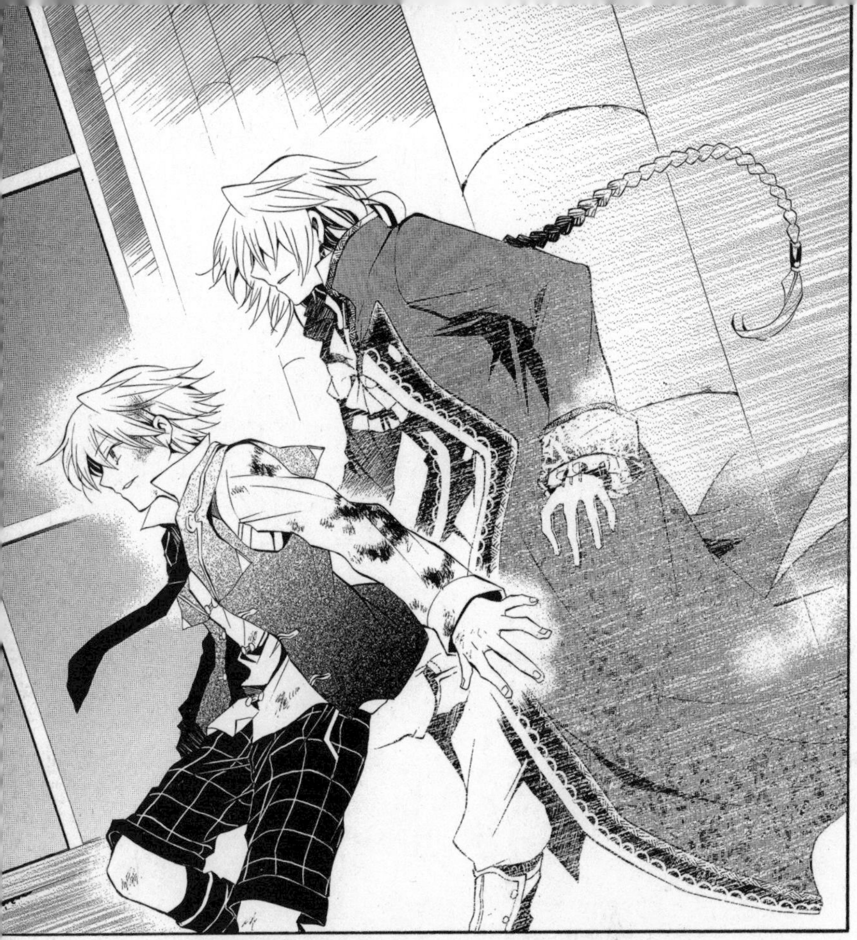

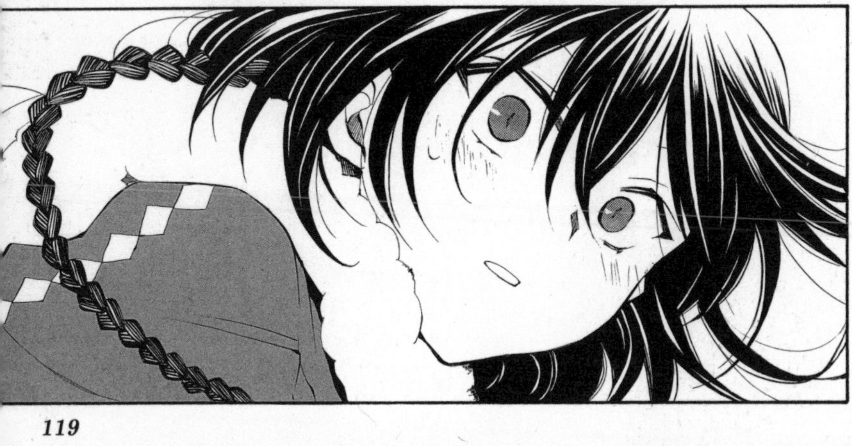

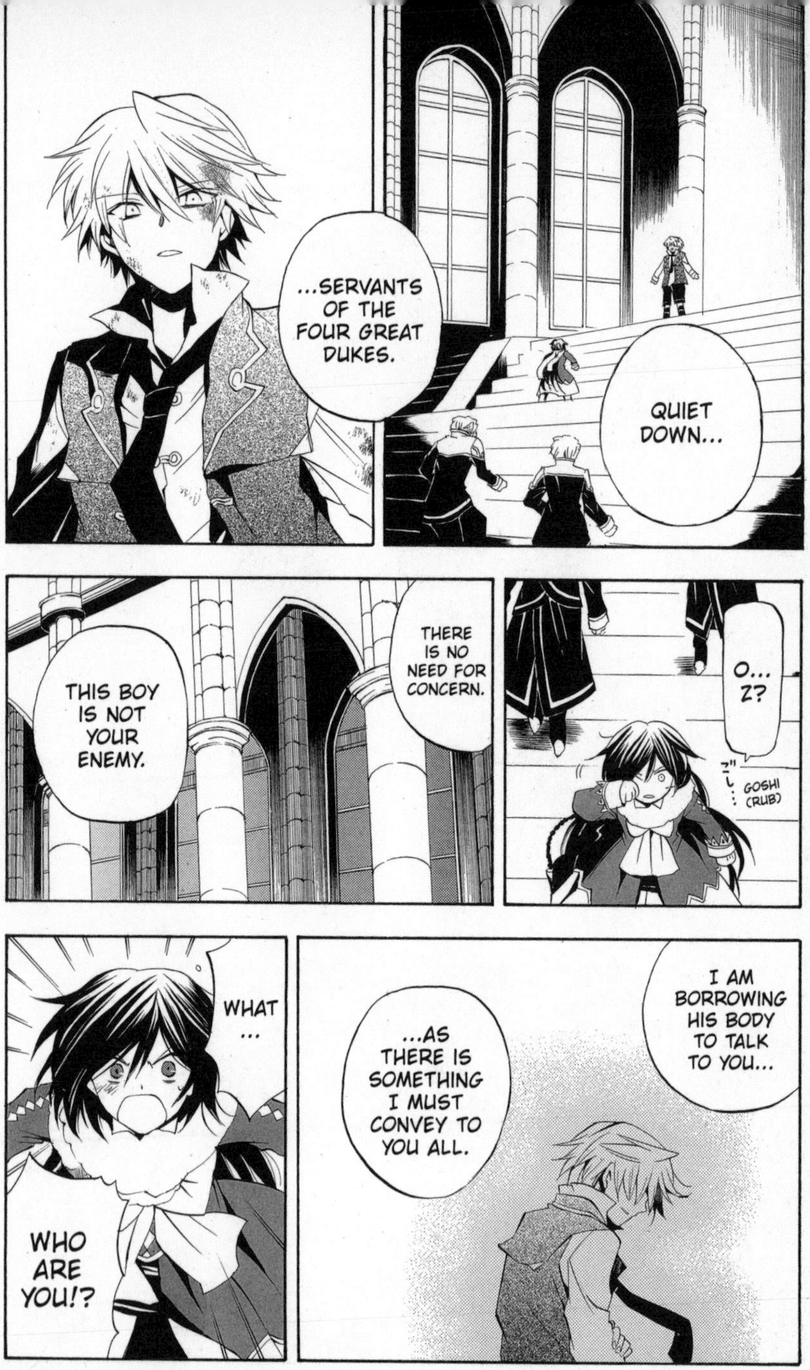
QUIET DOWN...
...SERVANTS OF THE FOUR GREAT DUKES.
O... Z?
ごし…
GOSHI (RUB)
THERE IS NO NEED FOR CONCERN.
THIS BOY IS NOT YOUR ENEMY.
I AM BORROWING HIS BODY TO TALK TO YOU...
...AS THERE IS SOMETHING I MUST CONVEY TO YOU ALL.
WHAT ...
WHO ARE YOU!?

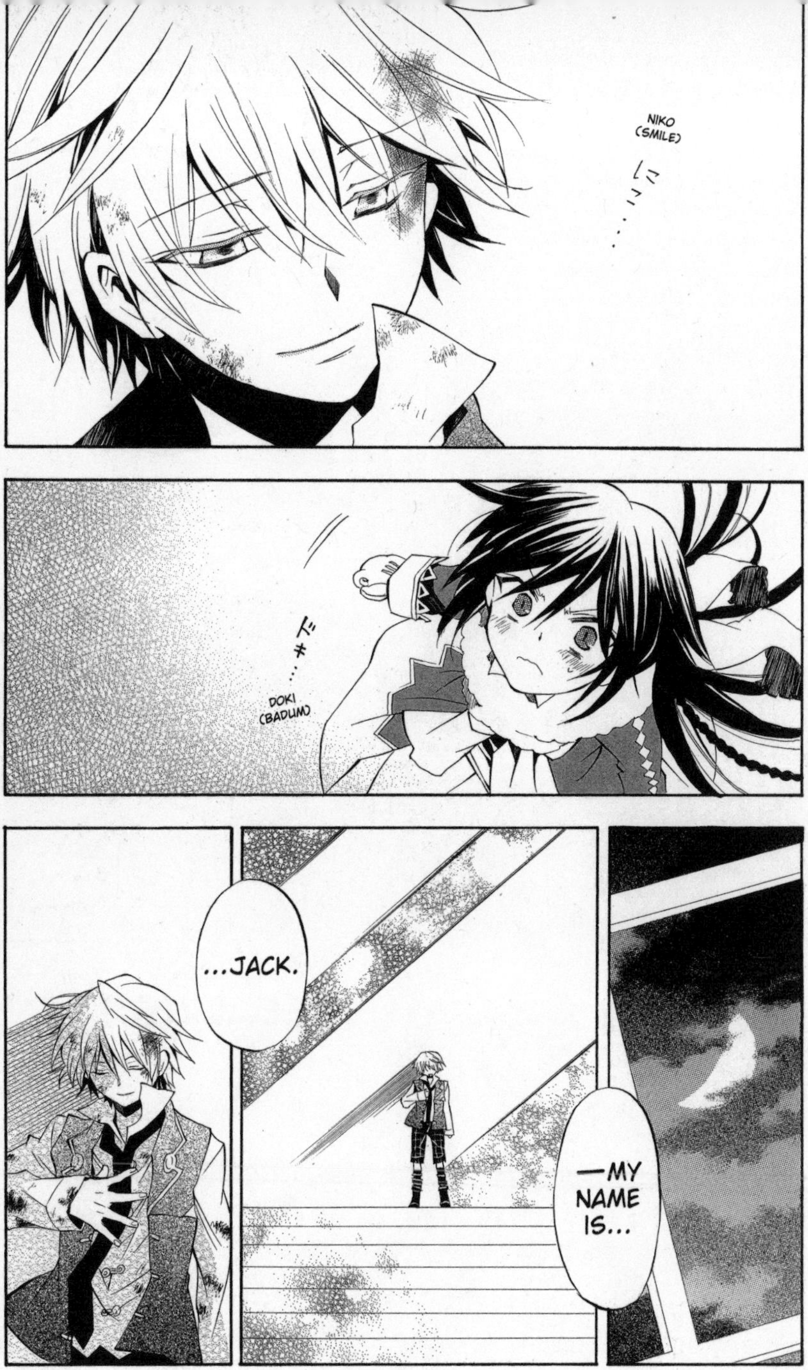
にこ…
NIKO (SMILE)
ドキ…
DOKI (BADUM)
—MY NAME IS...
...JACK.

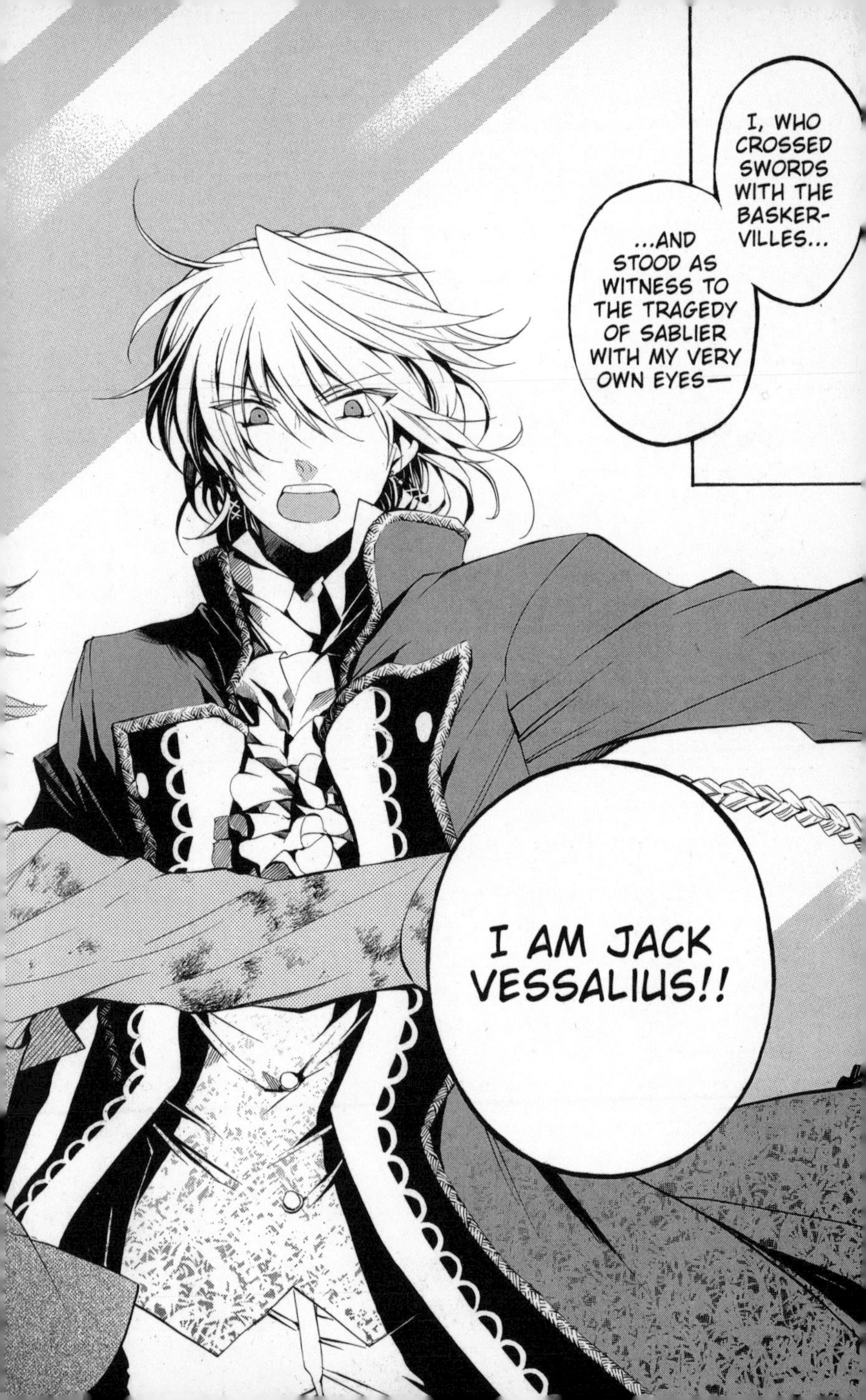
I, WHO CROSSED SWORDS WITH THE BASKER-VILLES...
...AND STOOD AS WITNESS TO THE TRAGEDY OF SABLIER WITH MY VERY OWN EYES—
I AM JACK VESSALIUS!!

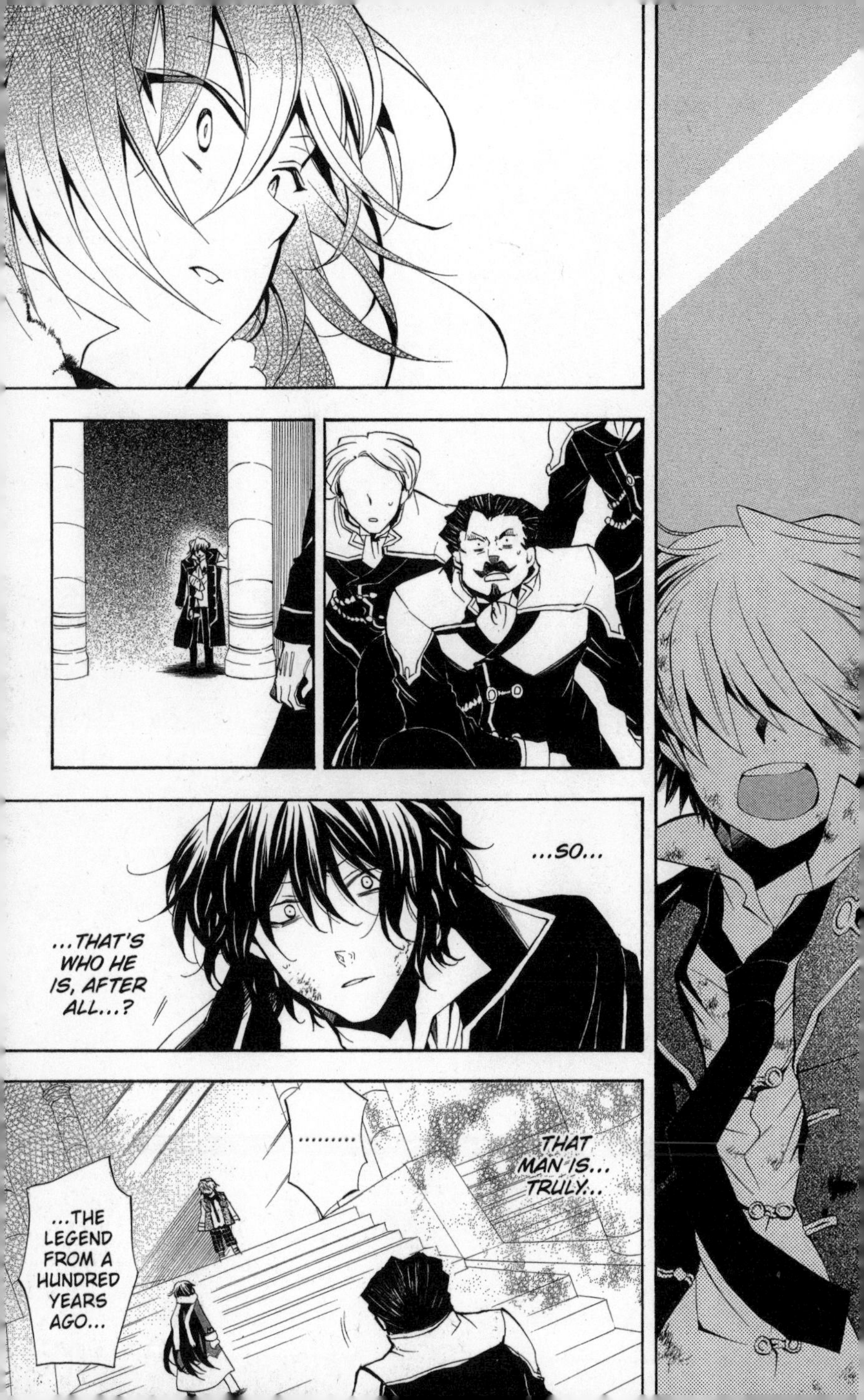

...SO...
...THAT'S WHO HE IS, AFTER ALL...?
THAT MAN IS... TRULY...
....
...THE LEGEND FROM A HUNDRED YEARS AGO...

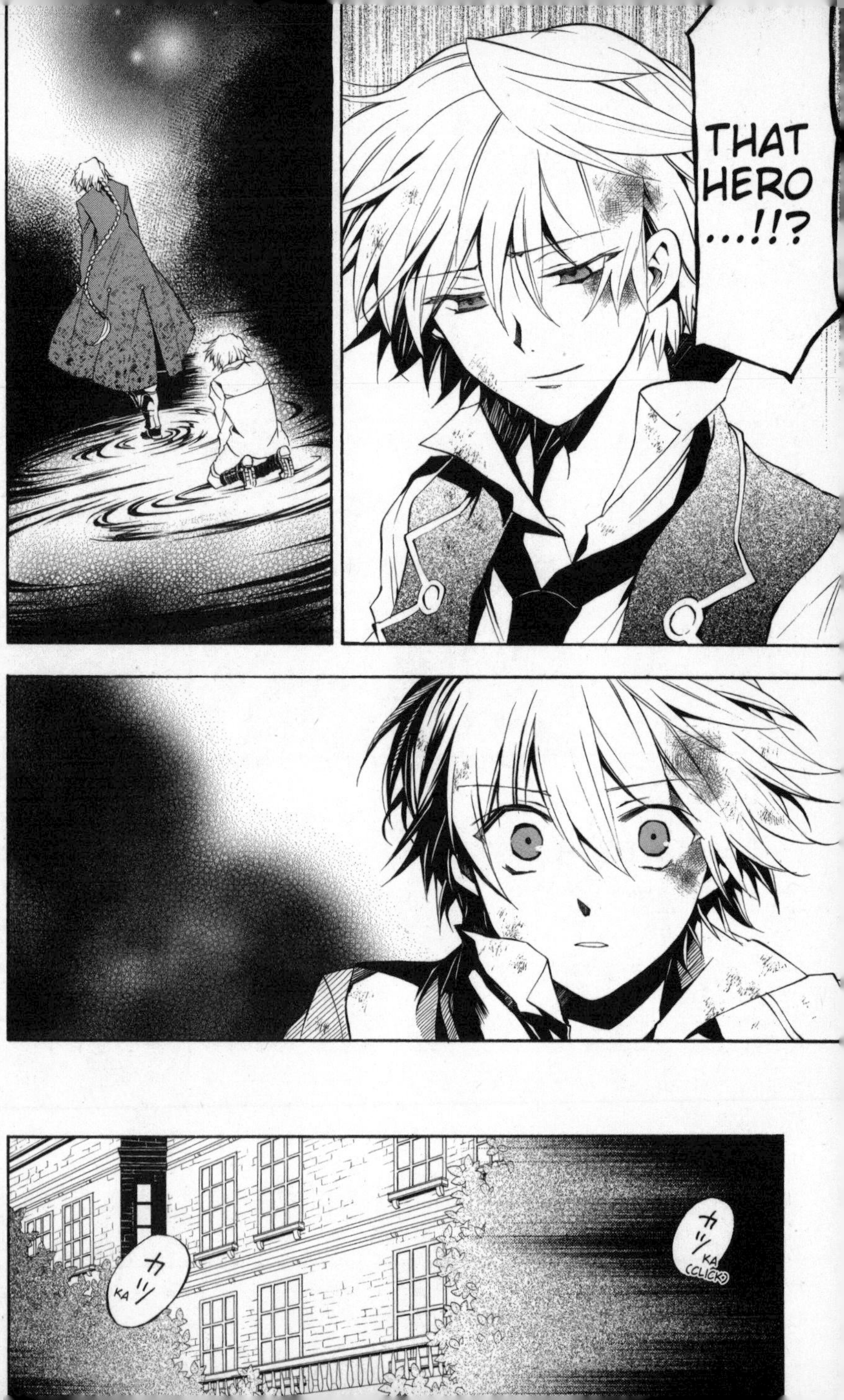
THAT HERO ...!!?
カッ KA (CLICK)
カッ KA

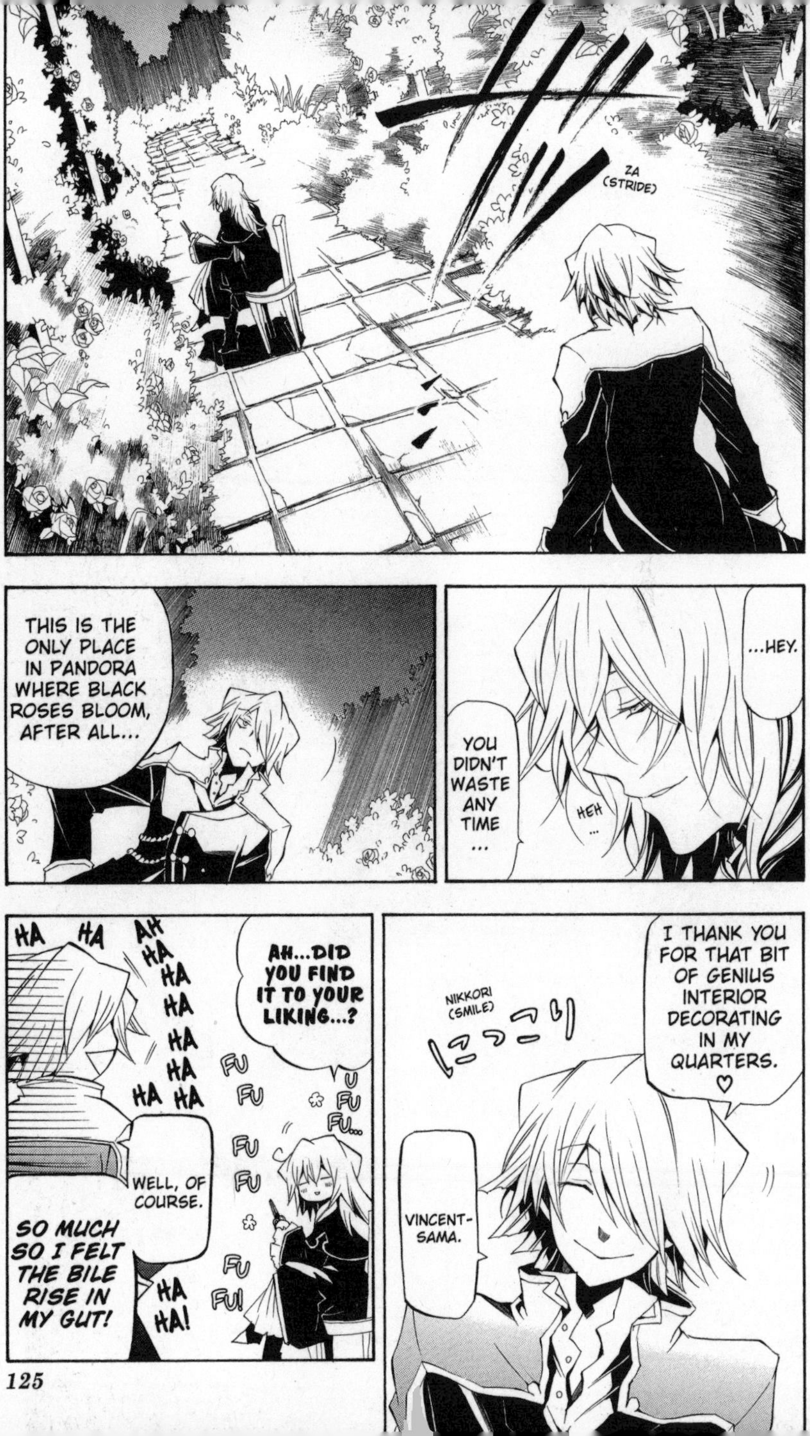
ZA (STRIDE)
...HEY.
YOU DIDN'T WASTE ANY TIME...
HEH...
THIS IS THE ONLY PLACE IN PANDORA WHERE BLACK ROSES BLOOM, AFTER ALL...
I THANK YOU FOR THAT BIT OF GENIUS INTERIOR DECORATING IN MY QUARTERS. ♡
NIKKORI (SMILE)
VINCENT-SAMA.
AH...DID YOU FIND IT TO YOUR LIKING...?
UFU FU...
FU FU FU FU
FU FU!
HA HA AH HA HA HA HA HA HA HA HA
WELL, OF COURSE.
SO MUCH SO I FELT THE BILE RISE IN MY GUT!
HA HA!

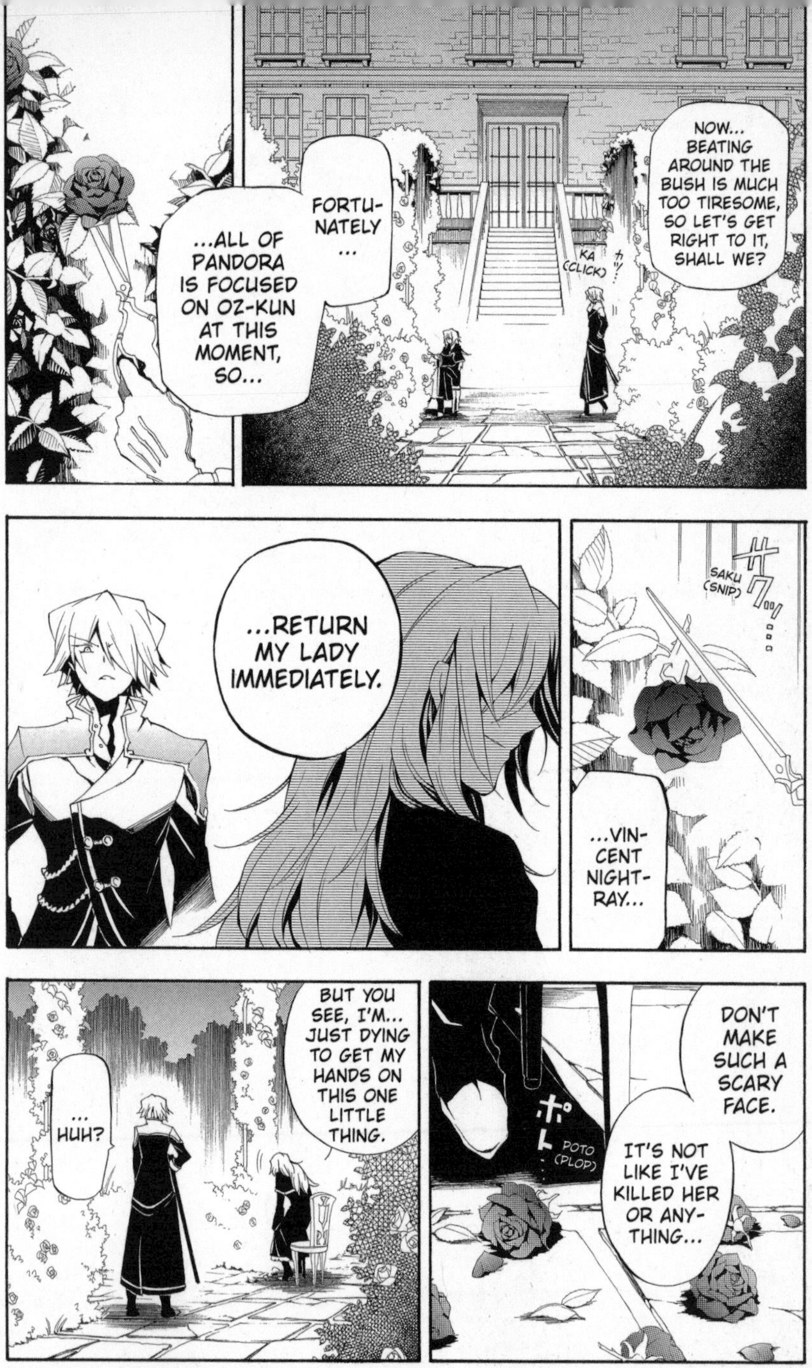
NOW... BEATING AROUND THE BUSH IS MUCH TOO TIRESOME, SO LET'S GET RIGHT TO IT, SHALL WE?
KA (CLICK)
FORTU-NATELY ...
...ALL OF PANDORA IS FOCUSED ON OZ-KUN AT THIS MOMENT, SO...
SAKU (SNIP)
...VIN-CENT NIGHT-RAY...
...RETURN MY LADY IMMEDIATELY.
DON'T MAKE SUCH A SCARY FACE.
POTO (PLOP)
IT'S NOT LIKE I'VE KILLED HER OR ANY-THING...
BUT YOU SEE, I'M... JUST DYING TO GET MY HANDS ON THIS ONE LITTLE THING.
... HUH?

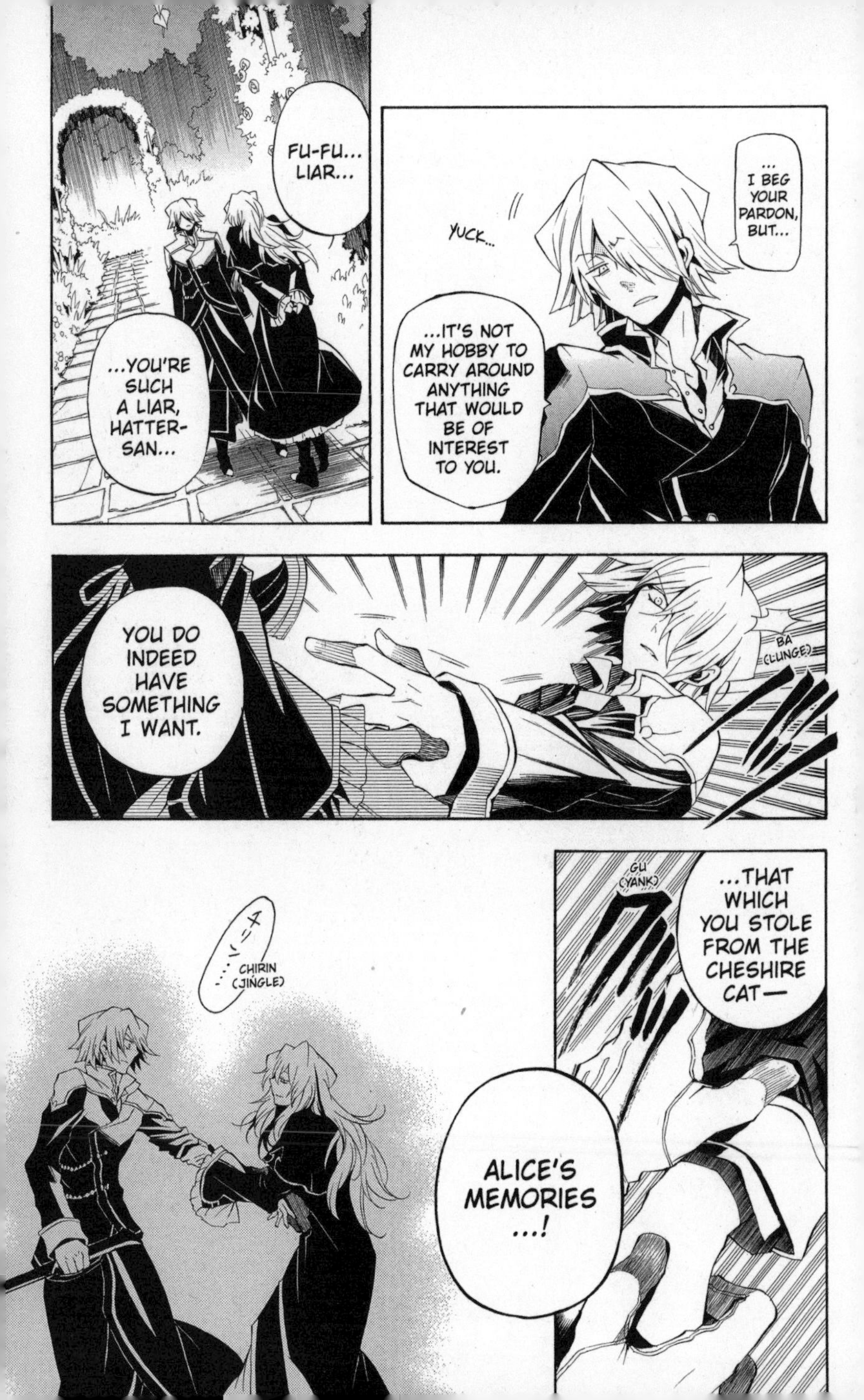
... I BEG YOUR PARDON, BUT...
YUCK...
...IT'S NOT MY HOBBY TO CARRY AROUND ANYTHING THAT WOULD BE OF INTEREST TO YOU.
FU-FU... LIAR...
...YOU'RE SUCH A LIAR, HATTER-SAN...
BA (LUNGE)
YOU DO INDEED HAVE SOMETHING I WANT.
GU (YANK)
...THAT WHICH YOU STOLE FROM THE CHESHIRE CAT—
ALICE'S MEMORIES ...!
CHIRIN (JINGLE)

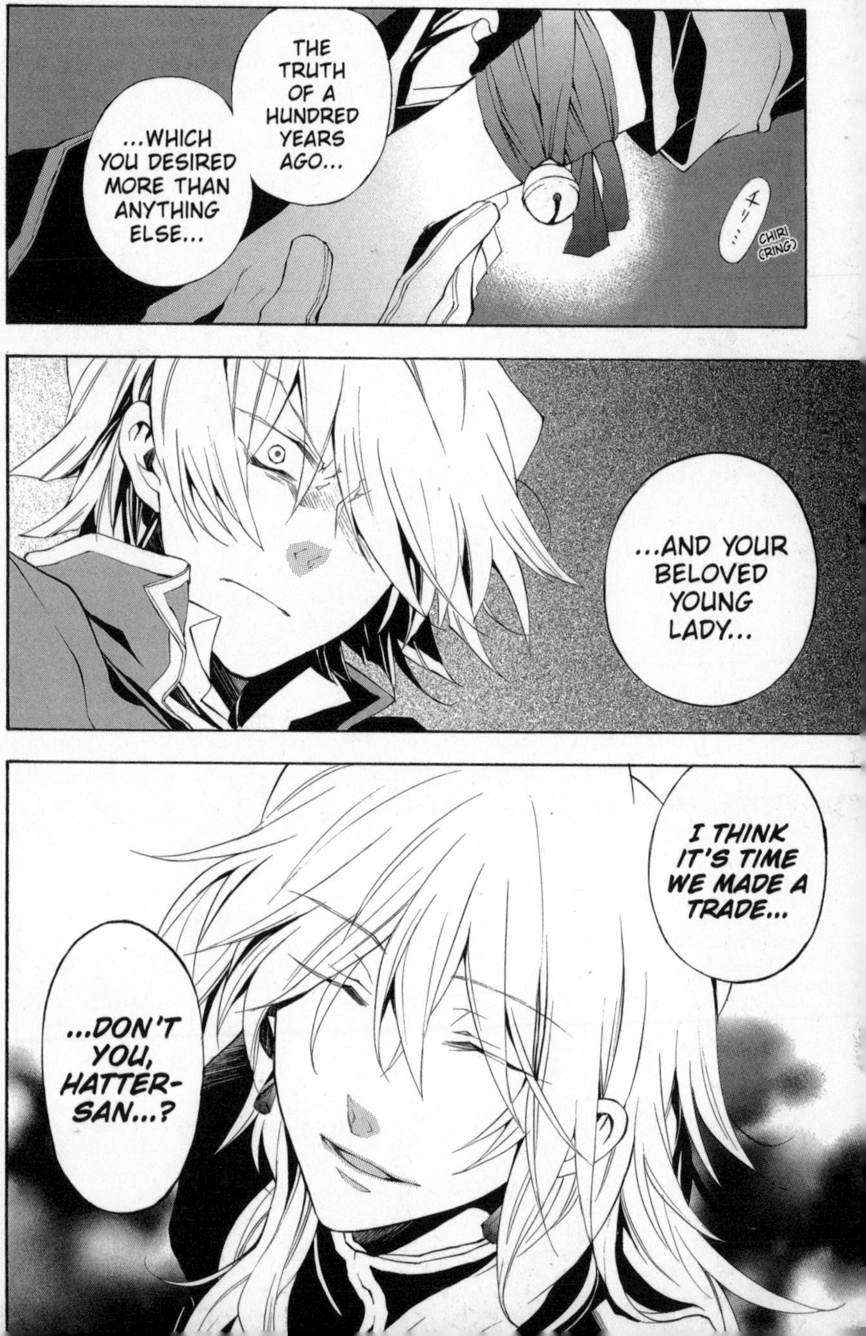
THE TRUTH OF A HUNDRED YEARS AGO...
CHIRI (RING)
...WHICH YOU DESIRED MORE THAN ANYTHING ELSE...
...AND YOUR BELOVED YOUNG LADY...
I THINK IT'S TIME WE MADE A TRADE...
...DON'T YOU, HATTER-SAN...?

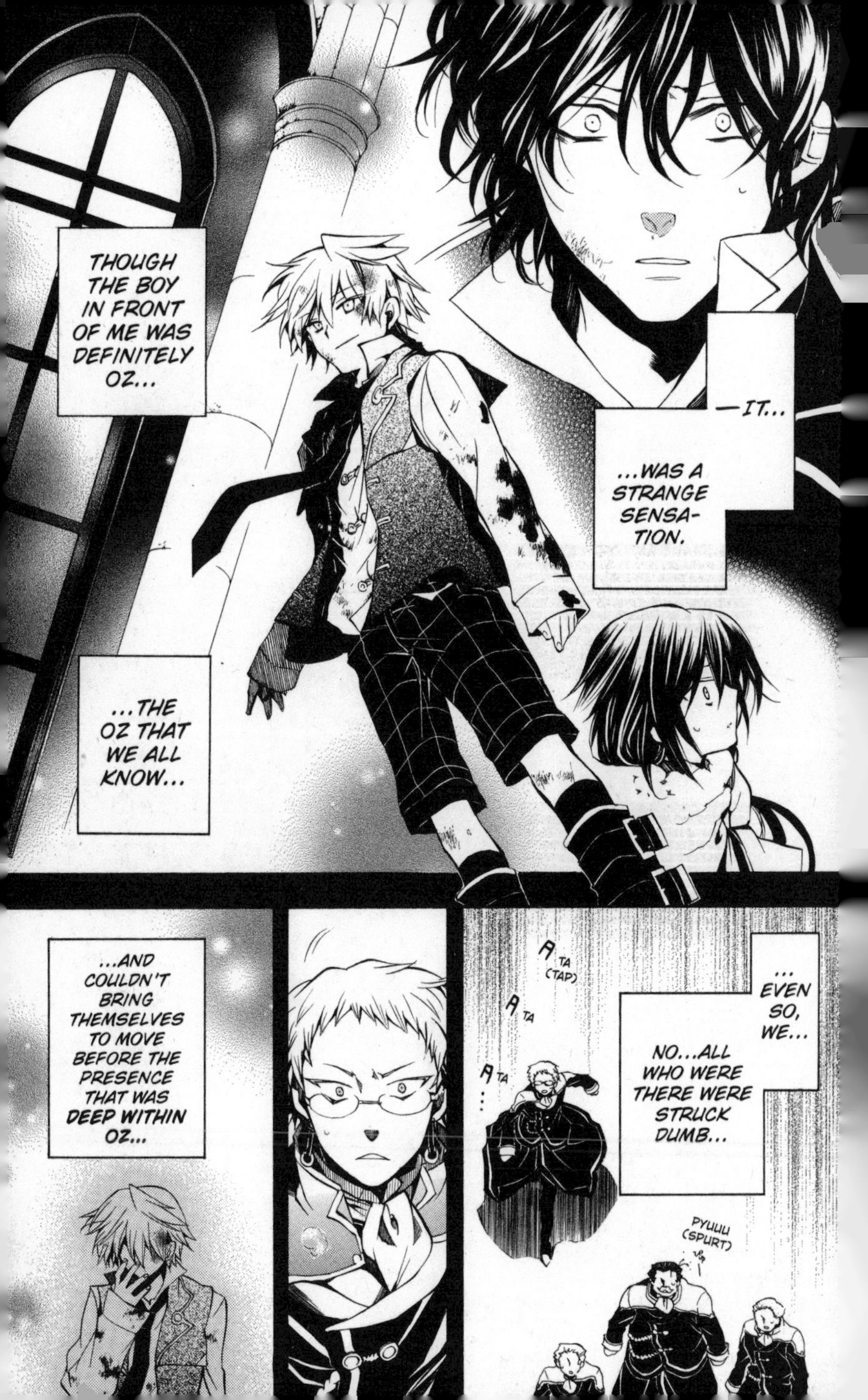
THOUGH THE BOY IN FRONT OF ME WAS DEFINITELY OZ...
...THE OZ THAT WE ALL KNOW...
—IT...
...WAS A STRANGE SENSATION.
...EVEN SO, WE...
NO...ALL WHO WERE THERE WERE STRUCK DUMB...
TA (TAP)
TA
TA
PYUUU (SPURT)
...AND COULDN'T BRING THEMSELVES TO MOVE BEFORE THE PRESENCE THAT WAS DEEP WITHIN OZ...

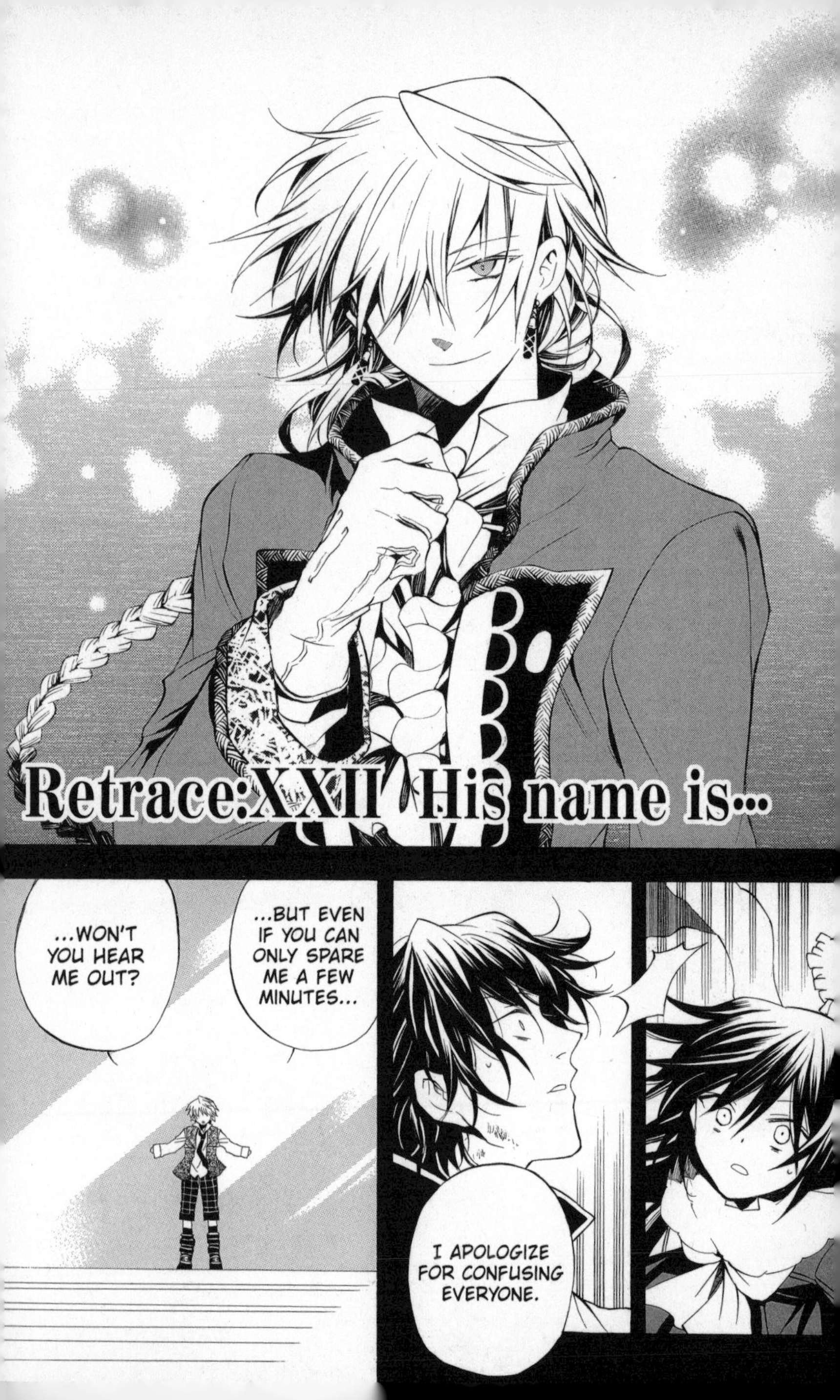
Retrace:XXII His name is...
I APOLOGIZE FOR CONFUSING EVERYONE.
...BUT EVEN IF YOU CAN ONLY SPARE ME A FEW MINUTES...
...WON'T YOU HEAR ME OUT?

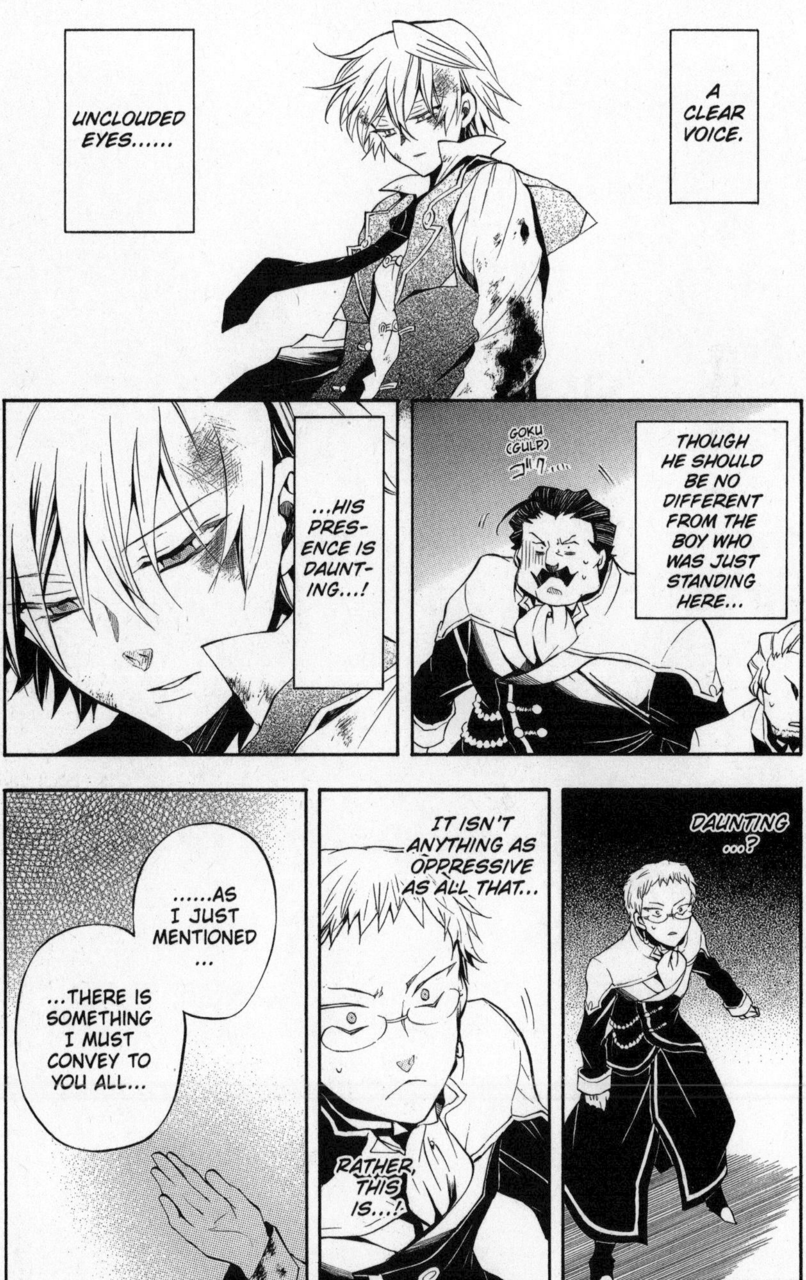
A CLEAR VOICE.
UNCLOUDED EYES......
GOKU (GULP)
THOUGH HE SHOULD BE NO DIFFERENT FROM THE BOY WHO WAS JUST STANDING HERE...
...HIS PRESENCE IS DAUNTING...!
DAUNTING ...?
IT ISN'T ANYTHING AS OPPRESSIVE AS ALL THAT...
RATHER, THIS IS...!
......AS I JUST MENTIONED ...
...THERE IS SOMETHING I MUST CONVEY TO YOU ALL...

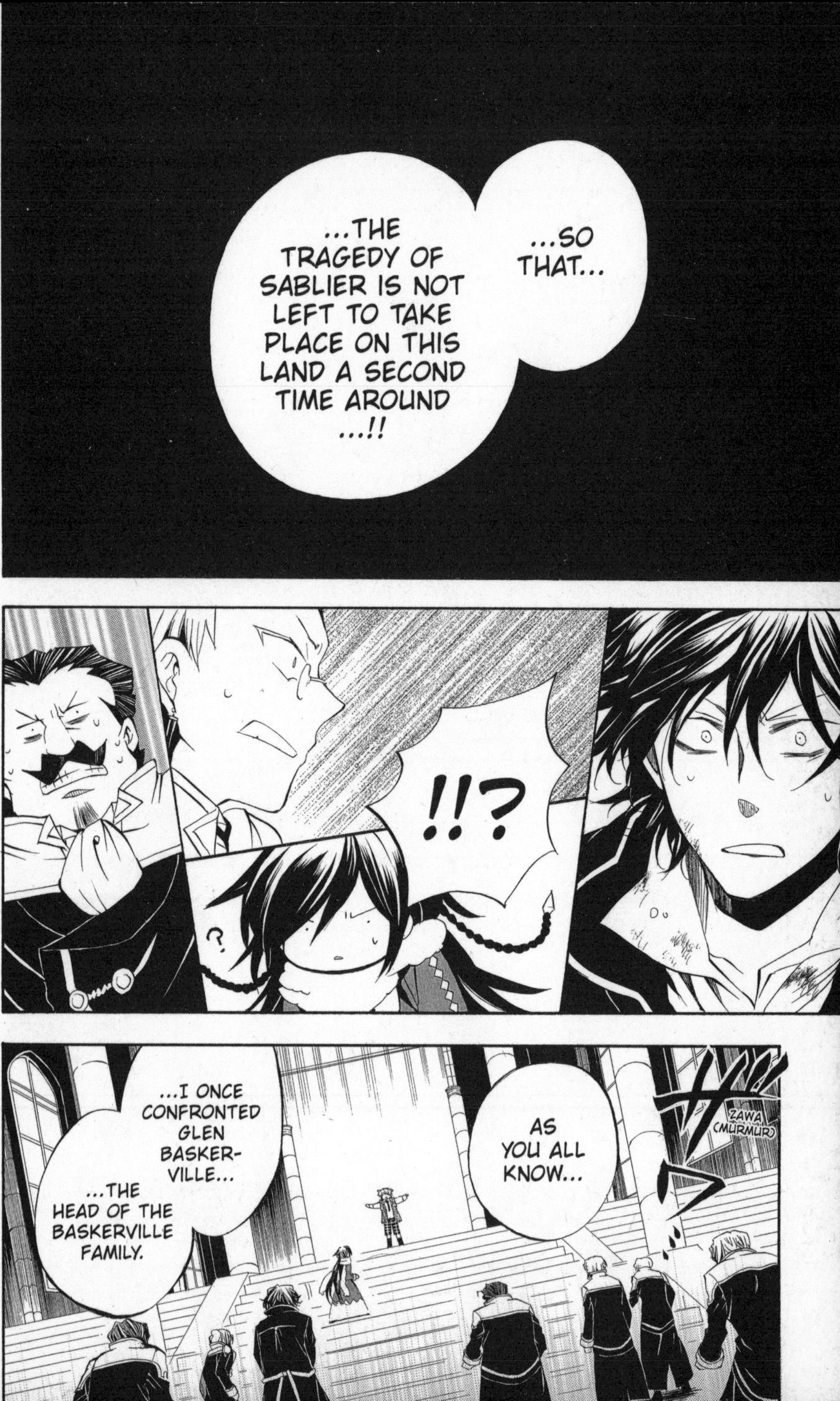
...SO THAT...
...THE TRAGEDY OF SABLIER IS NOT LEFT TO TAKE PLACE ON THIS LAND A SECOND TIME AROUND ...!!
!!?
?
ZAWA (MURMUR)
AS YOU ALL KNOW...
...I ONCE CONFRONTED GLEN BASKER-VILLE...
...THE HEAD OF THE BASKERVILLE FAMILY.

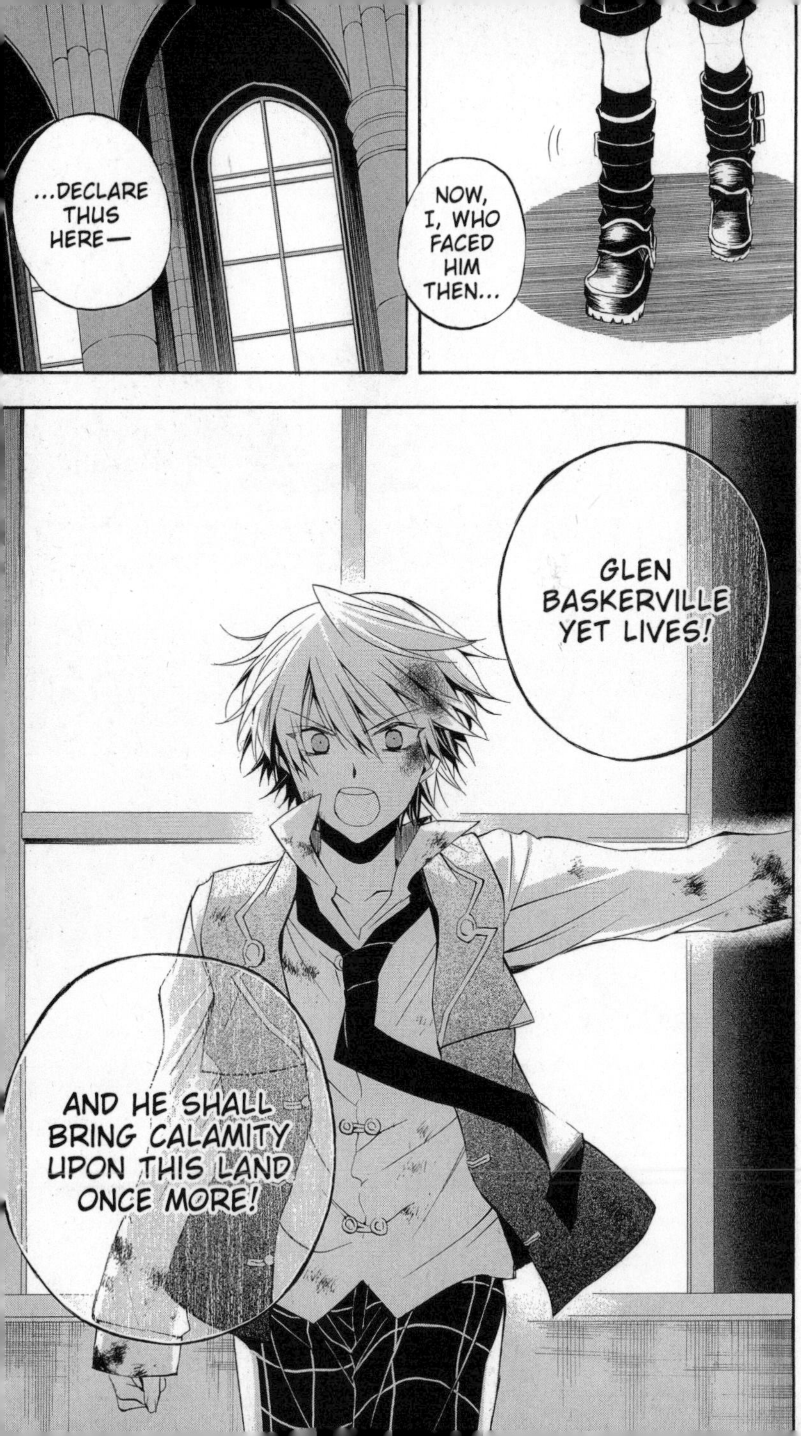
NOW, I, WHO FACED HIM THEN...
...DECLARE THUS HERE—
GLEN BASKERVILLE YET LIVES!
AND HE SHALL BRING CALAMITY UPON THIS LAND ONCE MORE!

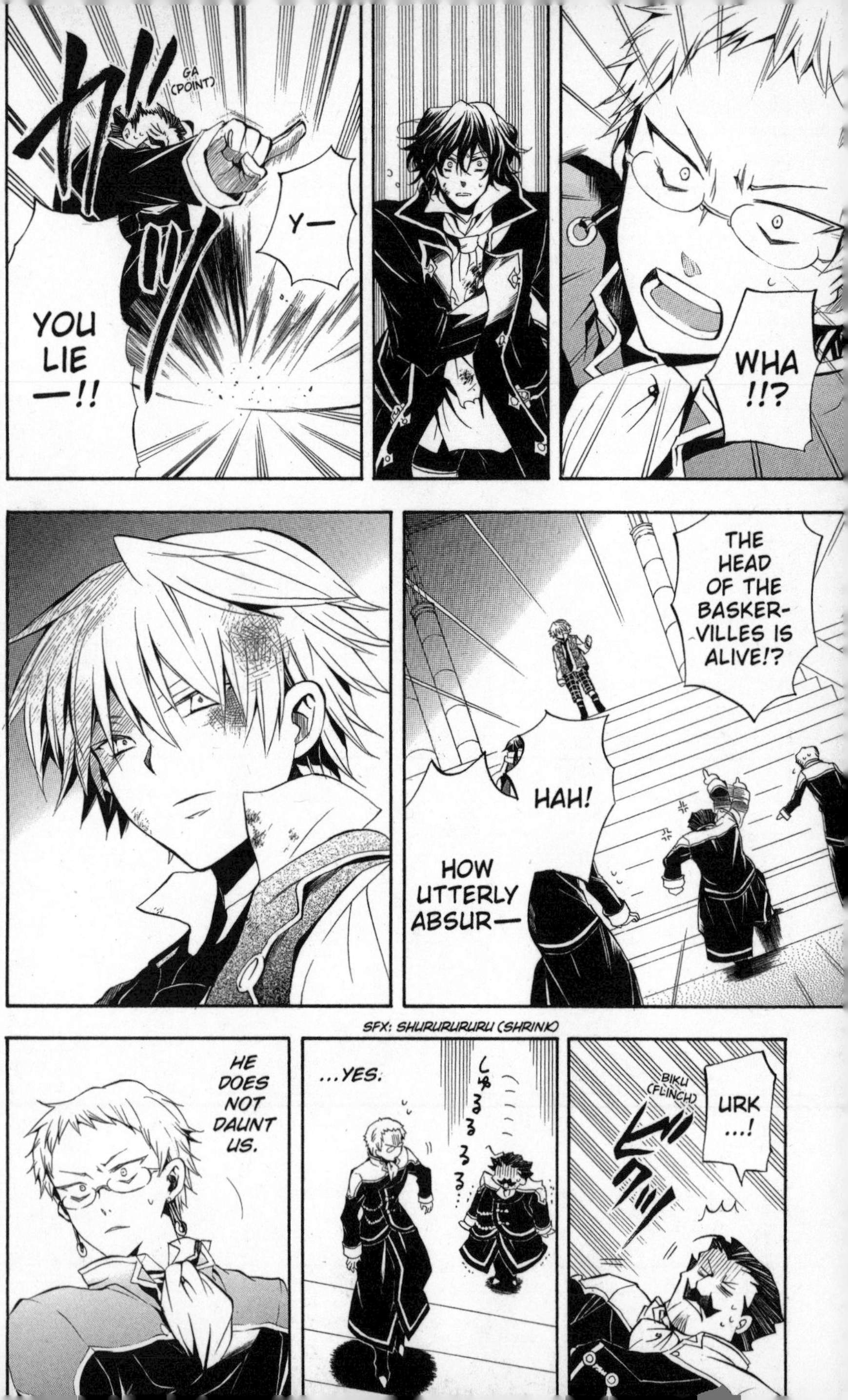
WHA!!?
GA (POINT)
Y—
YOU LIE—!!
THE HEAD OF THE BASKER-VILLES IS ALIVE!?
HAH!
HOW UTTERLY ABSUR—
SFX: SHURURURURU (SHRINK)
BIKU (FLINCH)
URK ...!
...YES.
HE DOES NOT DAUNT US.

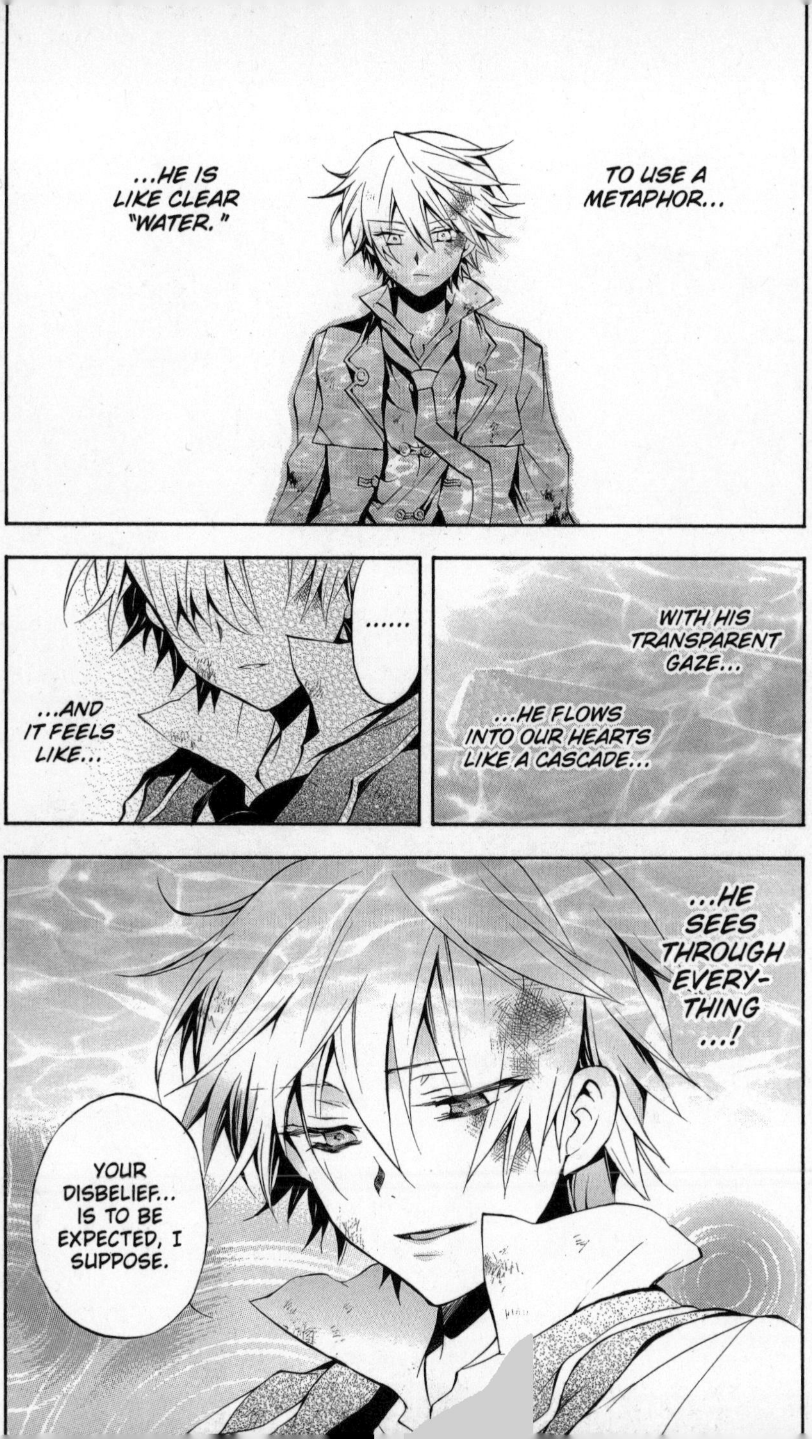
TO USE A METAPHOR...
...HE IS LIKE CLEAR "WATER."
WITH HIS TRANSPARENT GAZE...
...HE FLOWS INTO OUR HEARTS LIKE A CASCADE...
......
...AND IT FEELS LIKE...
...HE SEES THROUGH EVERY-THING...!
YOUR DISBELIEF... IS TO BE EXPECTED, I SUPPOSE.

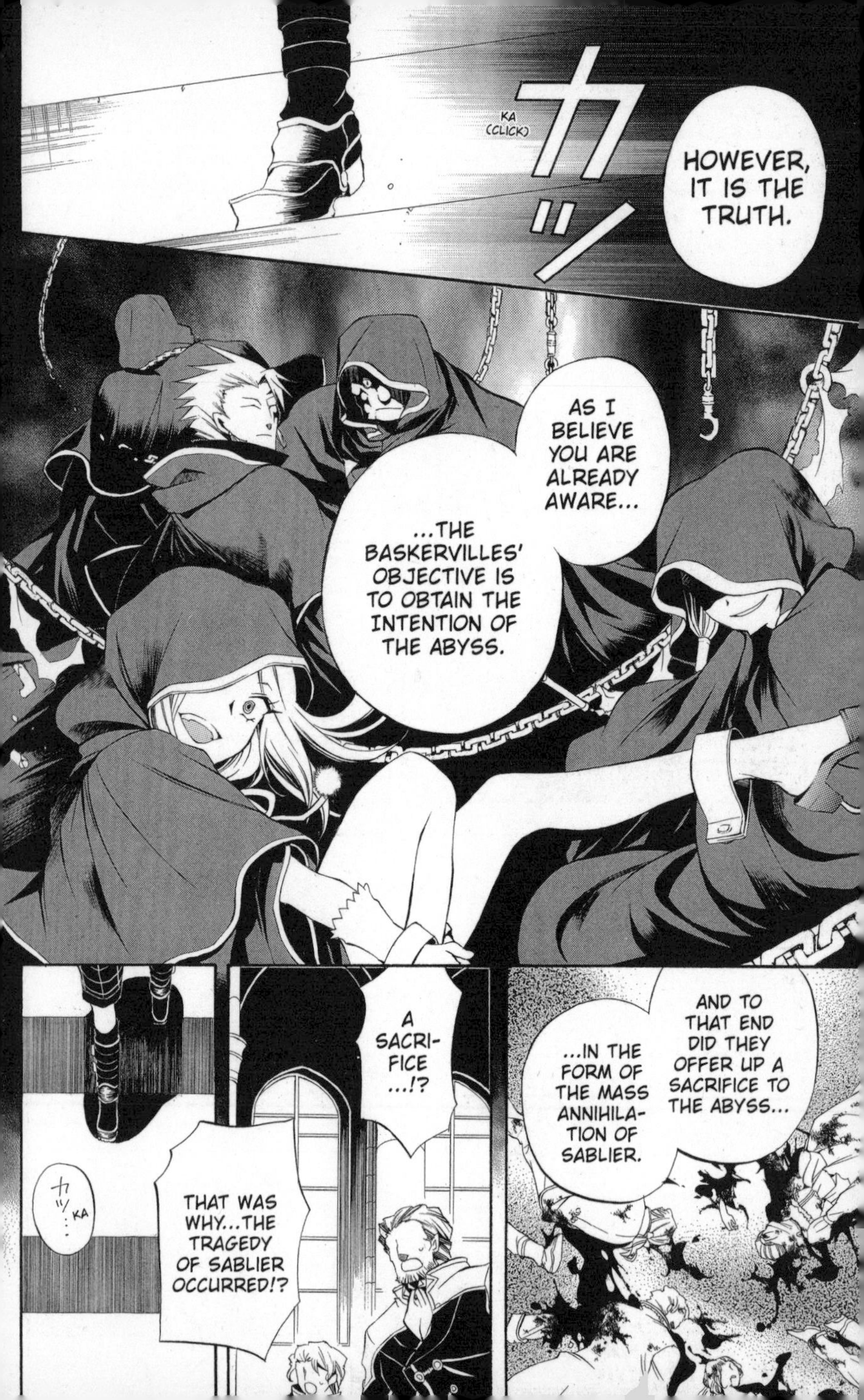
カッ
KA (CLICK)
HOWEVER, IT IS THE TRUTH.
AS I BELIEVE YOU ARE ALREADY AWARE...
...THE BASKERVILLES' OBJECTIVE IS TO OBTAIN THE INTENTION OF THE ABYSS.
AND TO THAT END DID THEY OFFER UP A SACRIFICE TO THE ABYSS...
...IN THE FORM OF THE MASS ANNIHILA-TION OF SABLIER.
A SACRI-FICE ...!?
THAT WAS WHY...THE TRAGEDY OF SABLIER OCCURRED!?
カッ... KA

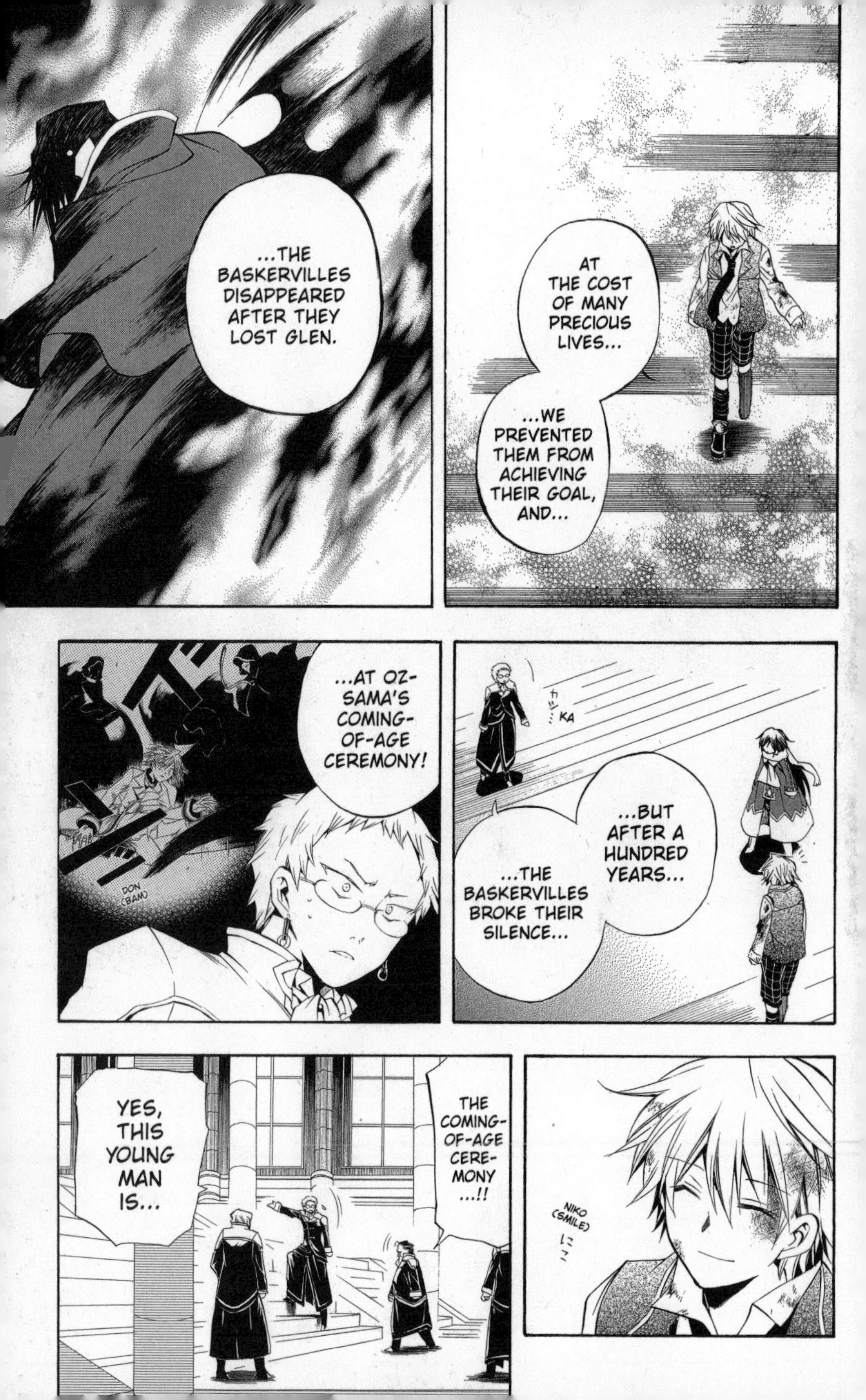
AT THE COST OF MANY PRECIOUS LIVES...
...WE PREVENTED THEM FROM ACHIEVING THEIR GOAL, AND...
...THE BASKERVILLES DISAPPEARED AFTER THEY LOST GLEN.
KA
...BUT AFTER A HUNDRED YEARS...
...THE BASKERVILLES BROKE THEIR SILENCE...
...AT OZ-SAMA'S COMING-OF-AGE CEREMONY!
DON (BAM)
NIKO (SMILE)
にこ
THE COMING-OF-AGE CERE-MONY ...!!
YES, THIS YOUNG MAN IS...

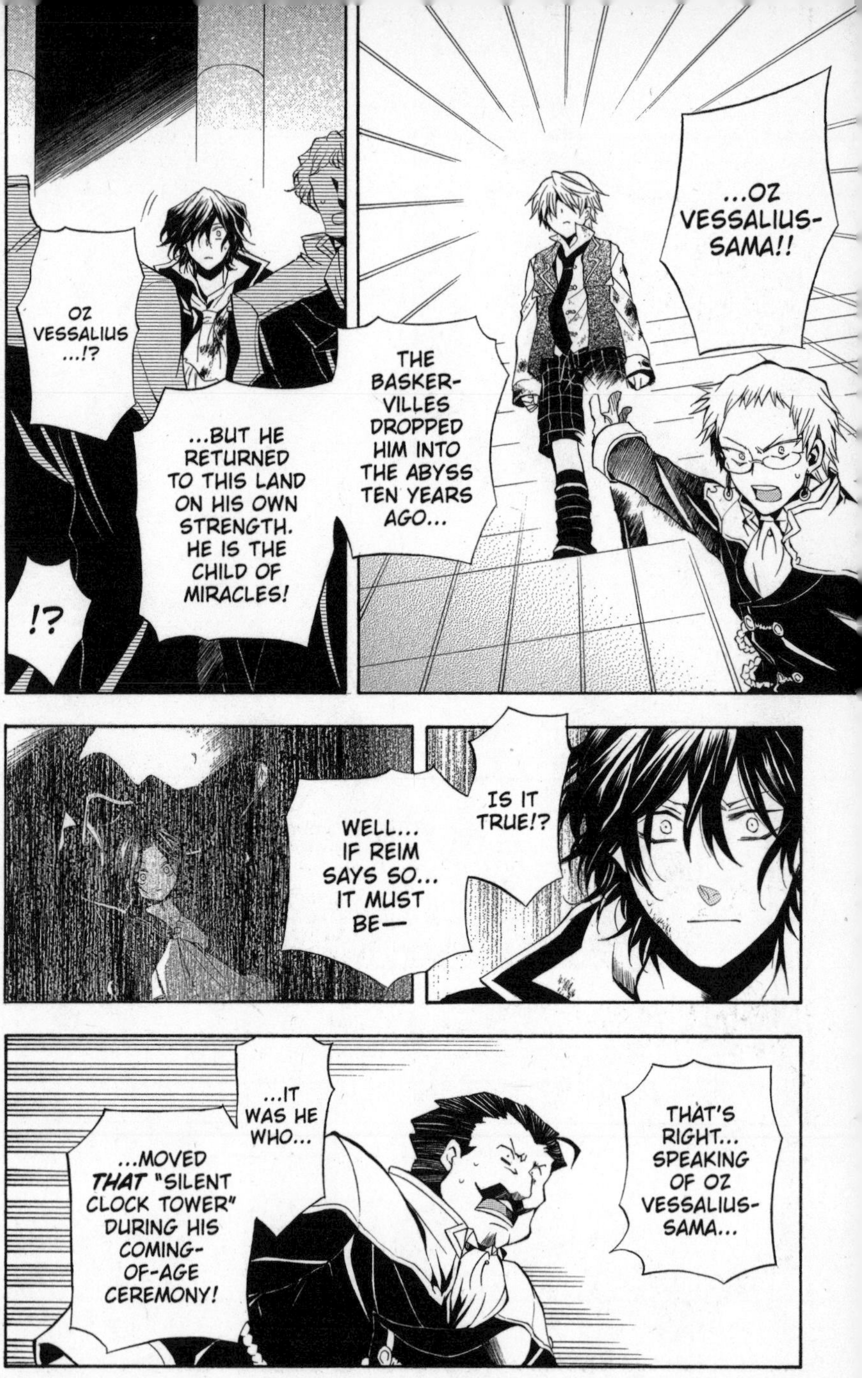
...OZ VESSALIUS-SAMA!!
THE BASKER-VILLES DROPPED HIM INTO THE ABYSS TEN YEARS AGO...
...BUT HE RETURNED TO THIS LAND ON HIS OWN STRENGTH. HE IS THE CHILD OF MIRACLES!
OZ VESSALIUS ...!?
!?
IS IT TRUE!?
WELL... IF REIM SAYS SO... IT MUST BE—
THAT'S RIGHT... SPEAKING OF OZ VESSALIUS-SAMA...
...IT WAS HE WHO...
...MOVED *THAT* "SILENT CLOCK TOWER" DURING HIS COMING-OF-AGE CEREMONY!

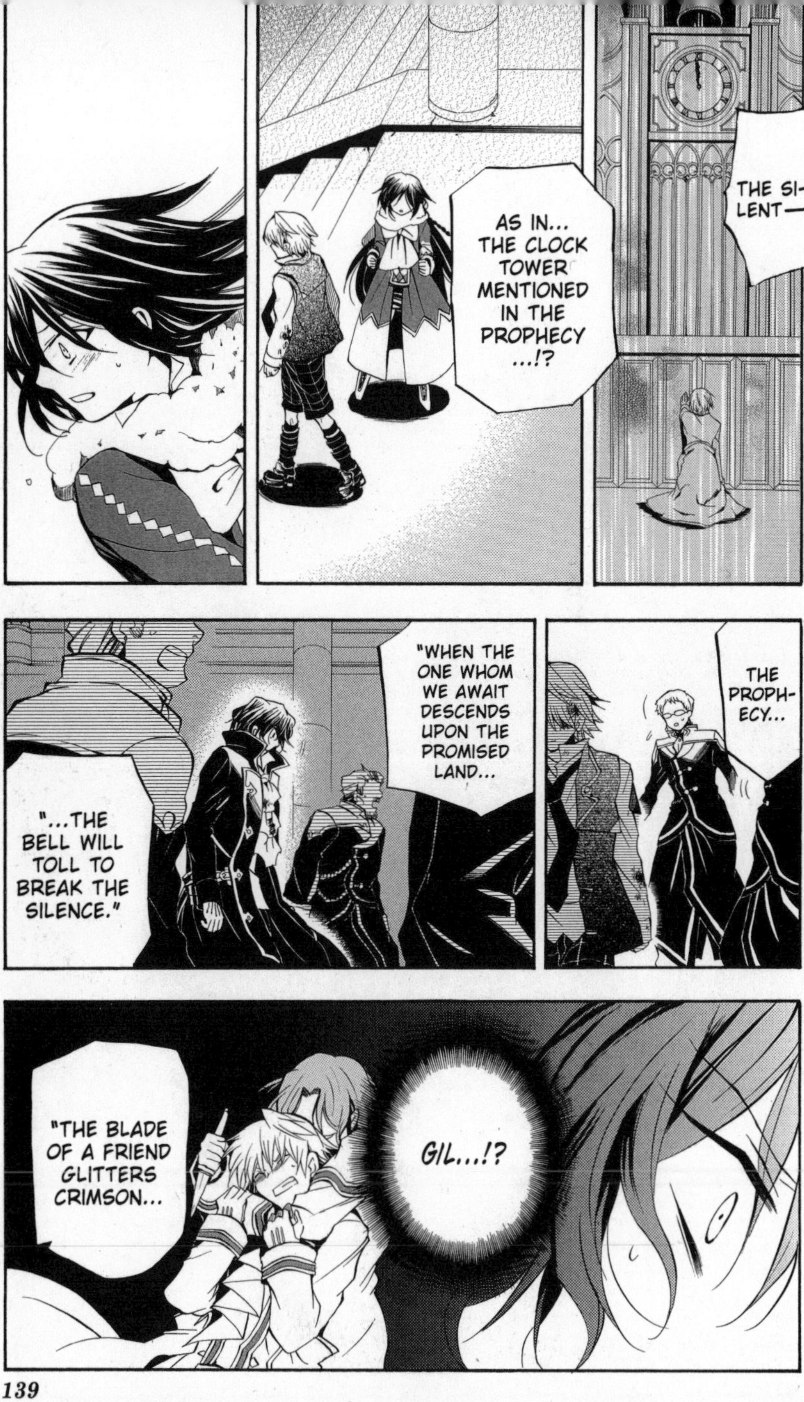
THE SI-LENT—
AS IN... THE CLOCK TOWER MENTIONED IN THE PROPHECY ...!?
THE PROPH-ECY...
"WHEN THE ONE WHOM WE AWAIT DESCENDS UPON THE PROMISED LAND...
"...THE BELL WILL TOLL TO BREAK THE SILENCE."
GIL...!?
"THE BLADE OF A FRIEND GLITTERS CRIMSON...

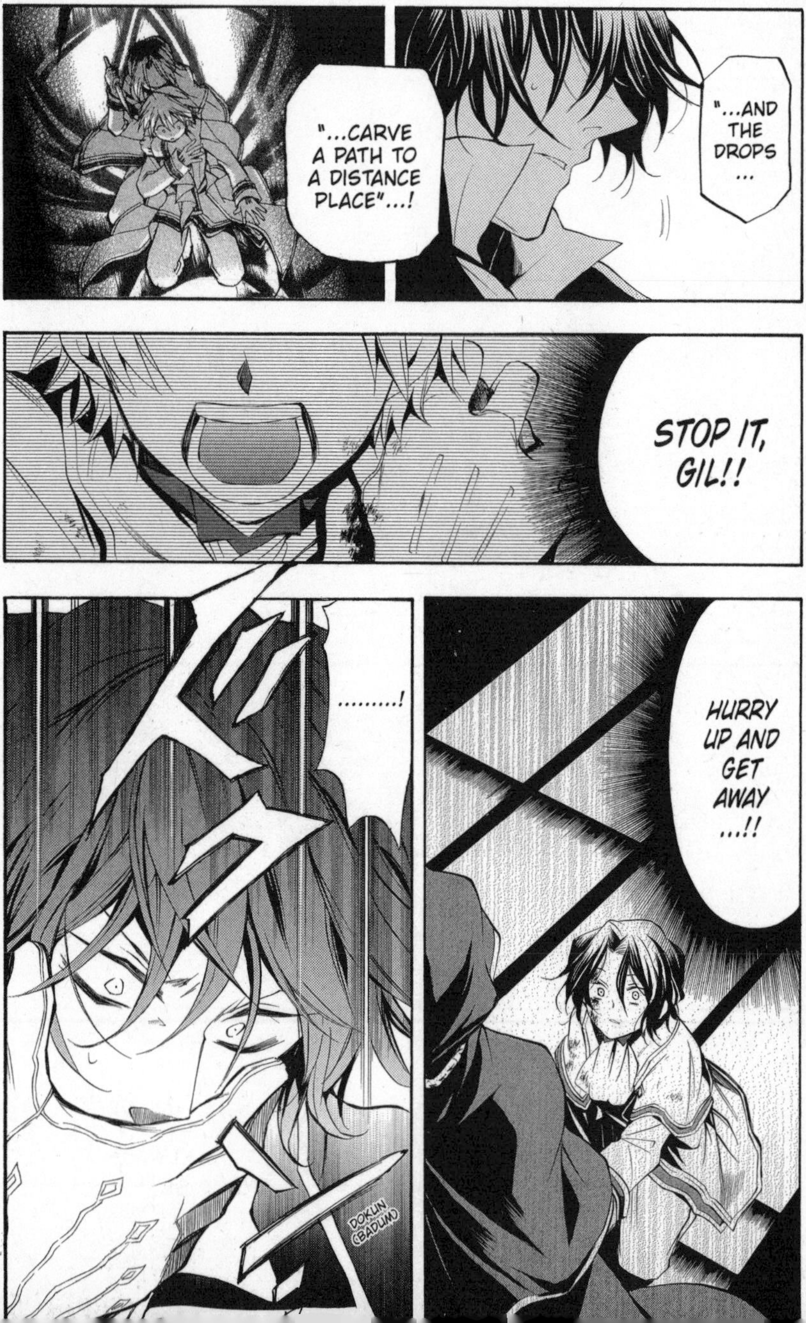
"...AND THE DROPS ...
"...CARVE A PATH TO A DISTANCE PLACE"...!
STOP IT, GIL!!
HURRY UP AND GET AWAY ...!!
.........!
DOKUN (BADUM)

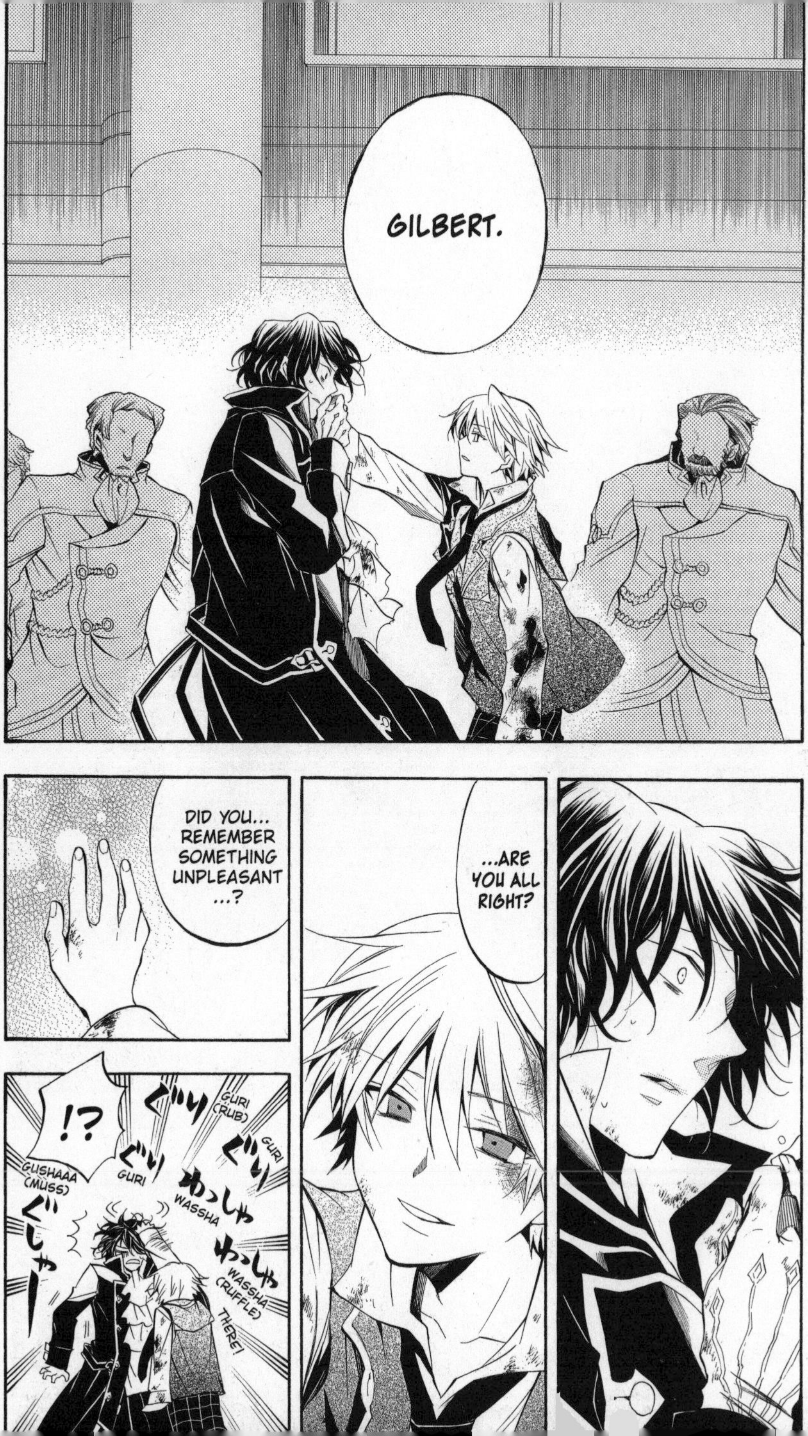
GILBERT.
...ARE YOU ALL RIGHT?
DID YOU... REMEMBER SOMETHING UNPLEASANT ...?
!?
GURI (RUB)
GURI
GURI
WASSHA
WASSHA (RUFFLE)
GUSHAAA (MUSS)
THERE!

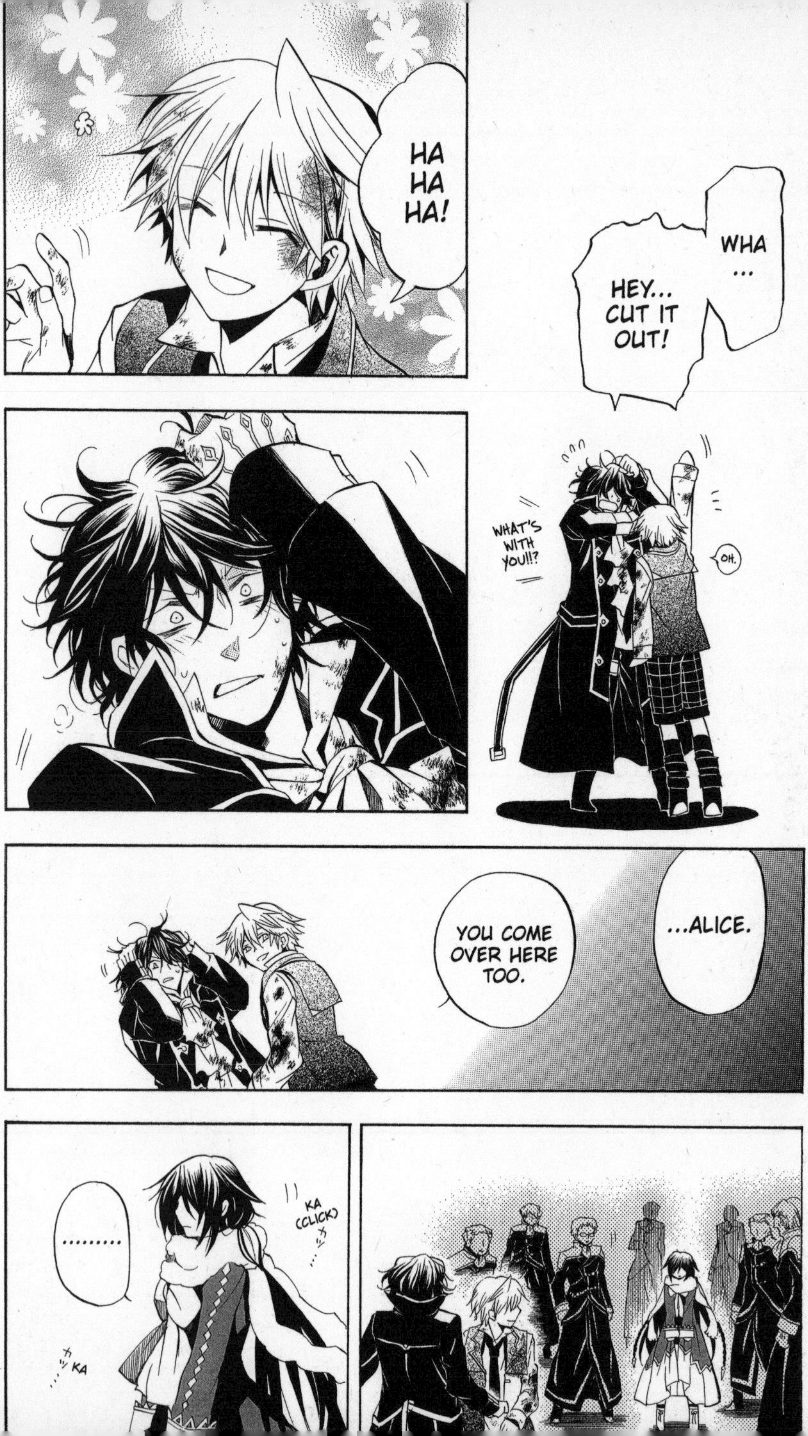
WHA... HEY... CUT IT OUT!
WHAT'S WITH YOU!!?
OH.
HA HA HA!
...ALICE.
YOU COME OVER HERE TOO.
....
KA (CLICK)
KA

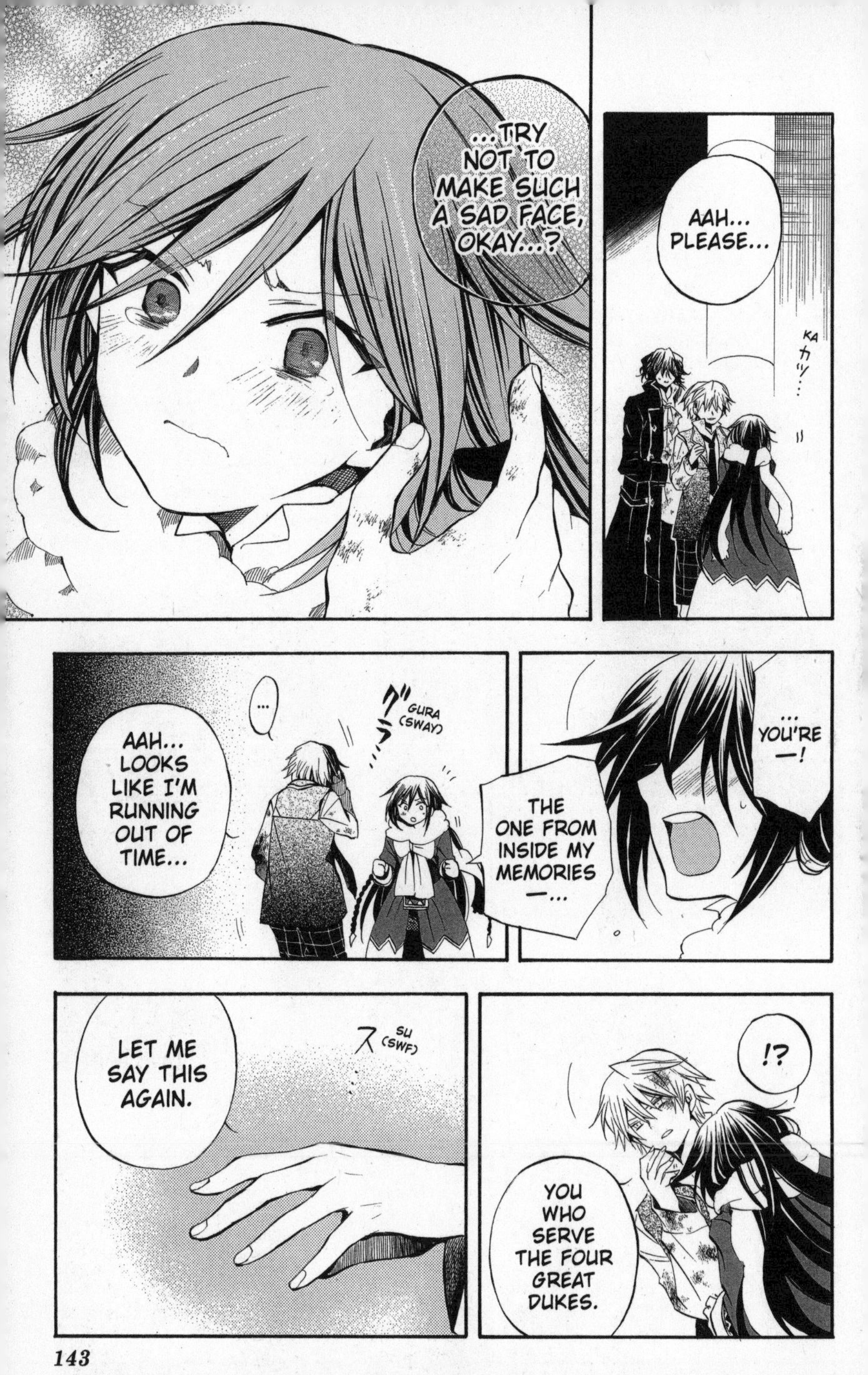
AAH... PLEASE...
KA カッ...
...TRY NOT TO MAKE SUCH A SAD FACE, OKAY...?
...YOU'RE—!
THE ONE FROM INSIDE MY MEMORIES—...
GURA グラ (SWAY)
...
AAH... LOOKS LIKE I'M RUNNING OUT OF TIME...
!?
YOU WHO SERVE THE FOUR GREAT DUKES.
SU ス (SWF)
LET ME SAY THIS AGAIN.

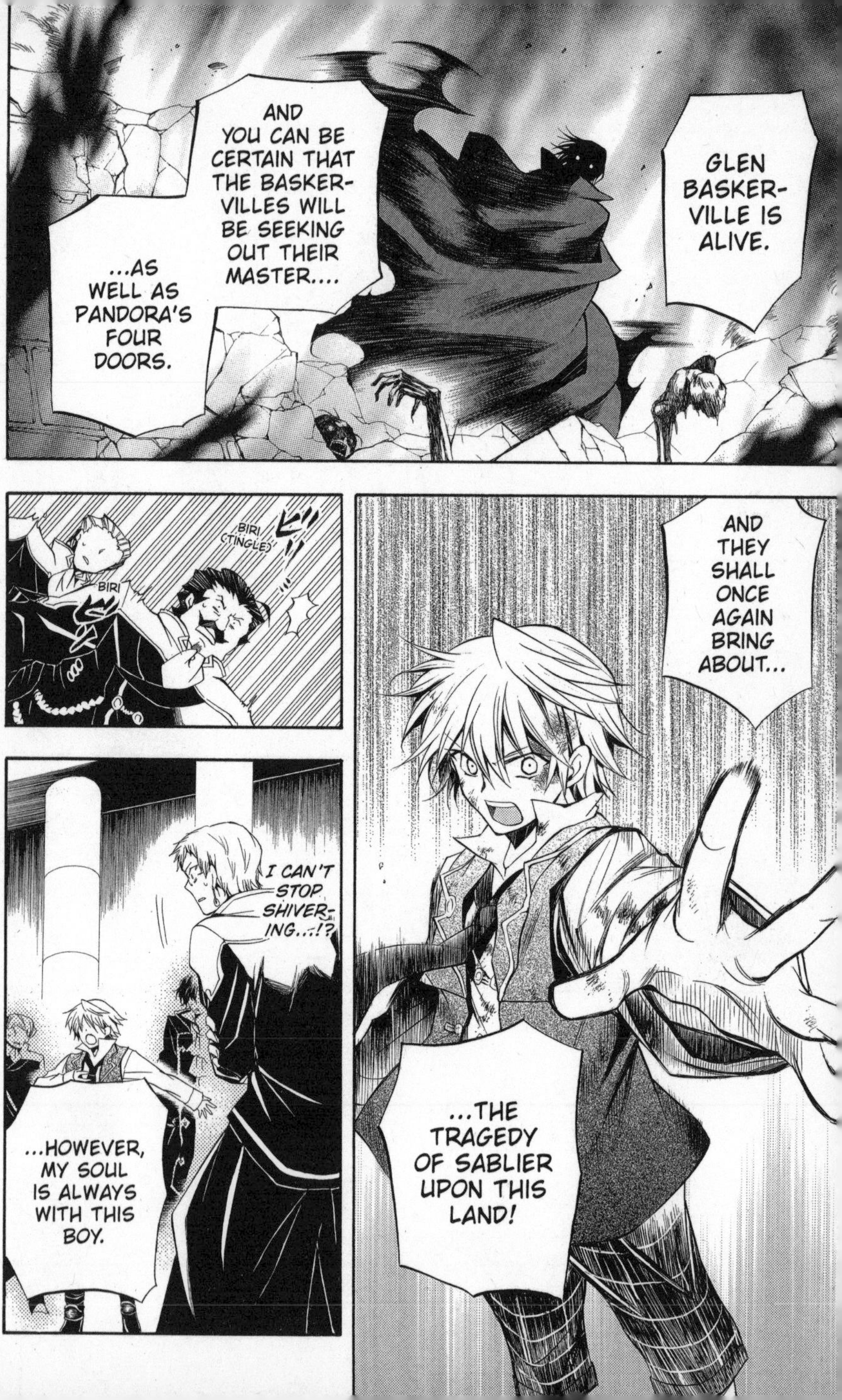
GLEN BASKERVILLE IS ALIVE.
AND YOU CAN BE CERTAIN THAT THE BASKERVILLES WILL BE SEEKING OUT THEIR MASTER....
...AS WELL AS PANDORA'S FOUR DOORS.
AND THEY SHALL ONCE AGAIN BRING ABOUT...
...THE TRAGEDY OF SABLIER UPON THIS LAND!
BIRI (TINGLE)
BIRI
I CAN'T STOP SHIVERING...!?
...HOWEVER, MY SOUL IS ALWAYS WITH THIS BOY.

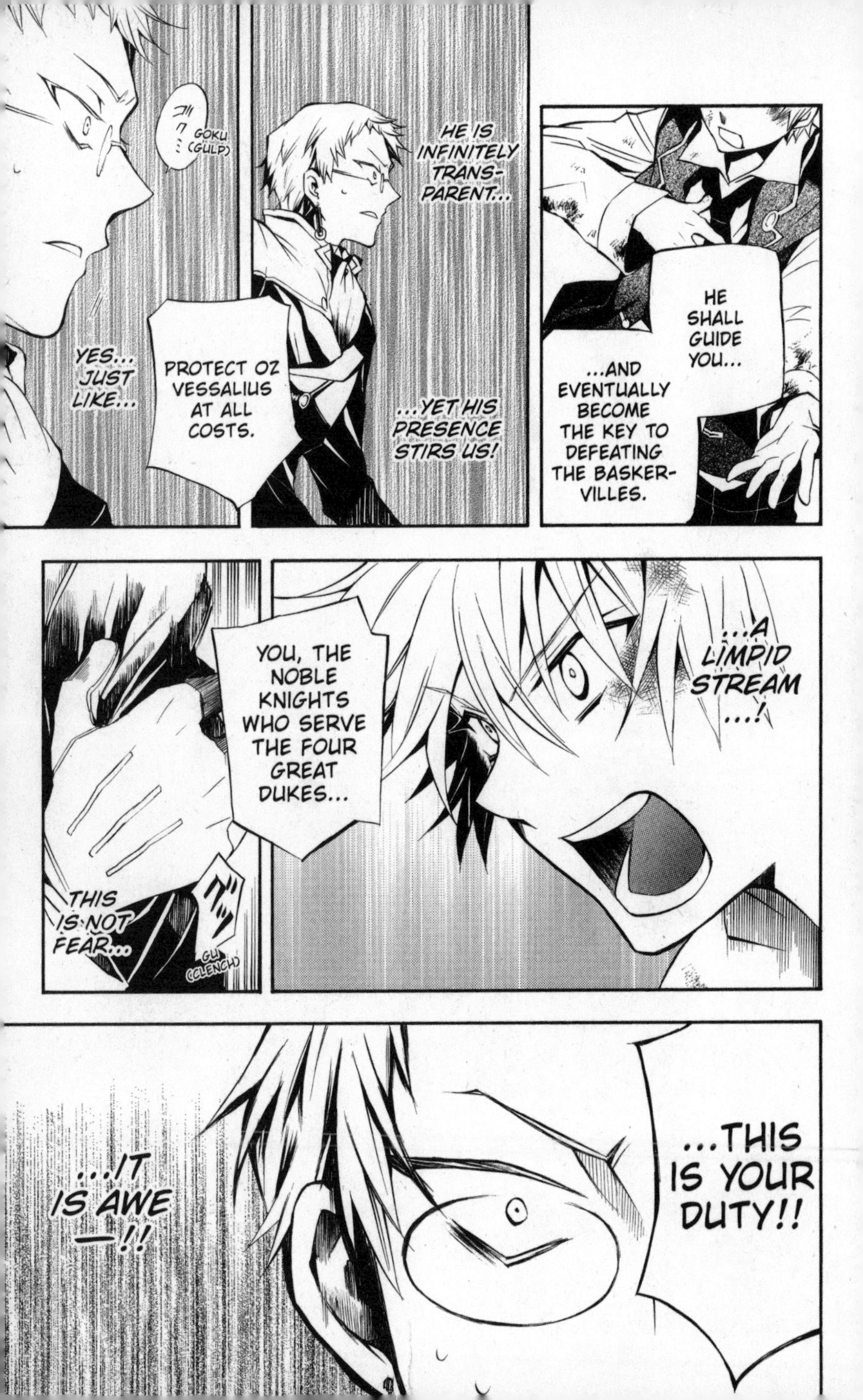
HE SHALL GUIDE YOU...
...AND EVENTUALLY BECOME THE KEY TO DEFEATING THE BASKER-VILLES.
HE IS INFINITELY TRANS-PARENT...
...YET HIS PRESENCE STIRS US!
PROTECT OZ VESSALIUS AT ALL COSTS.
ゴクッ GOKU (GULP)
YES... JUST LIKE...
...A LIMPID STREAM ...!
YOU, THE NOBLE KNIGHTS WHO SERVE THE FOUR GREAT DUKES...
THIS IS NOT FEAR...
グッ GU (CLENCH)
...THIS IS YOUR DUTY!!
...IT IS AWE—!!

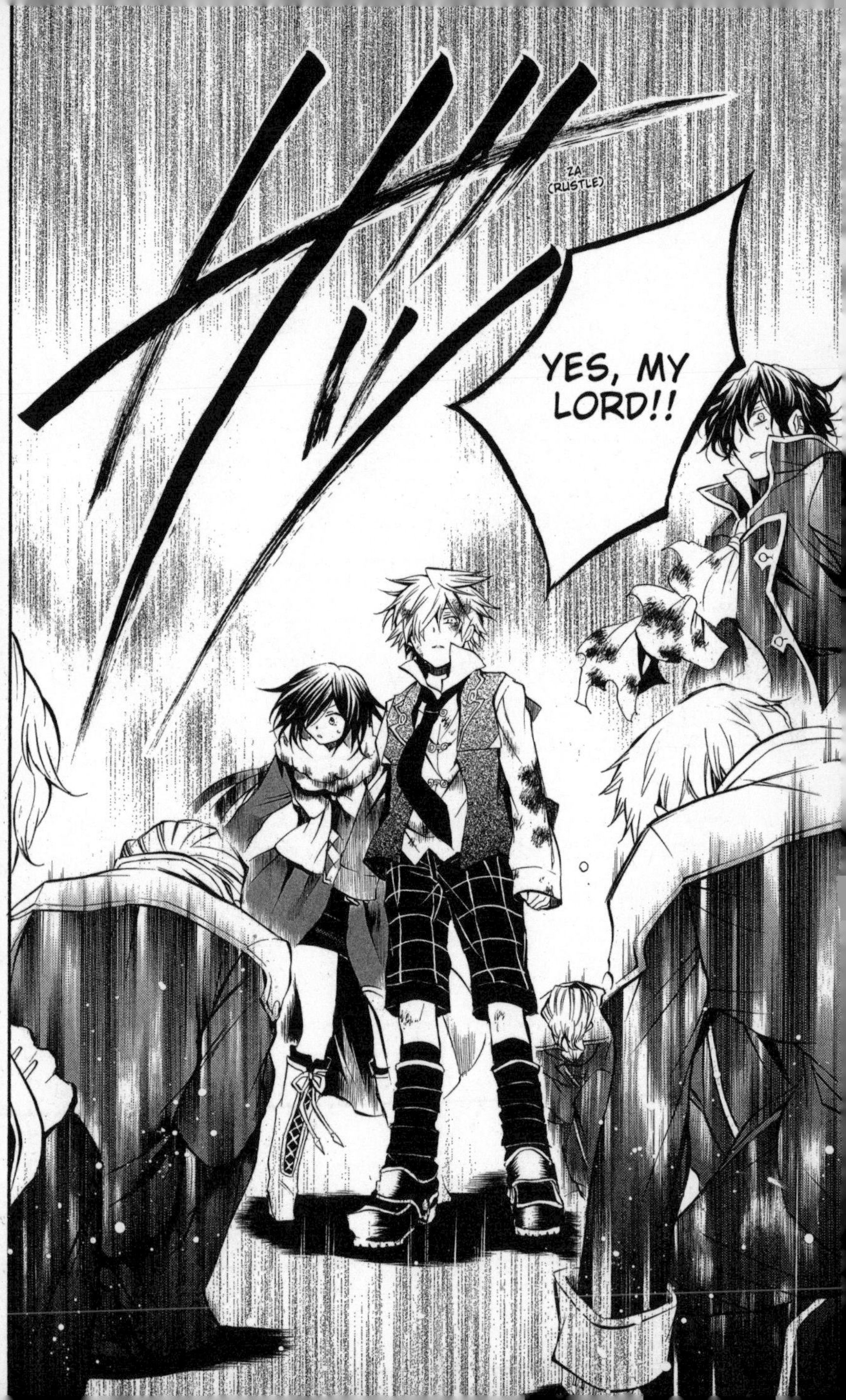
ZA (RUSTLE)
YES, MY LORD!!

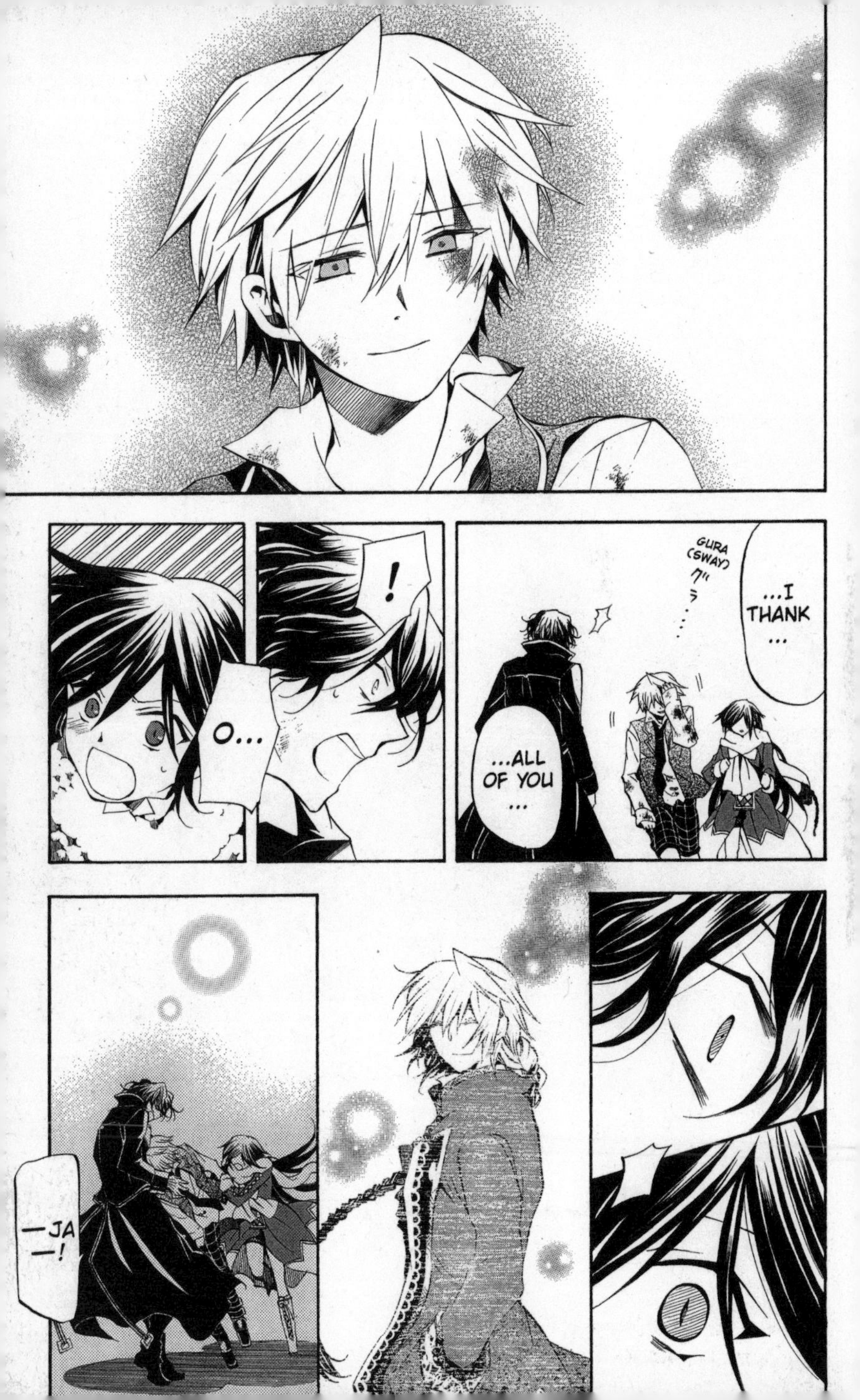
...I THANK ...
GURA (SWAY)
...ALL OF YOU ...
!
O...
—JA—!

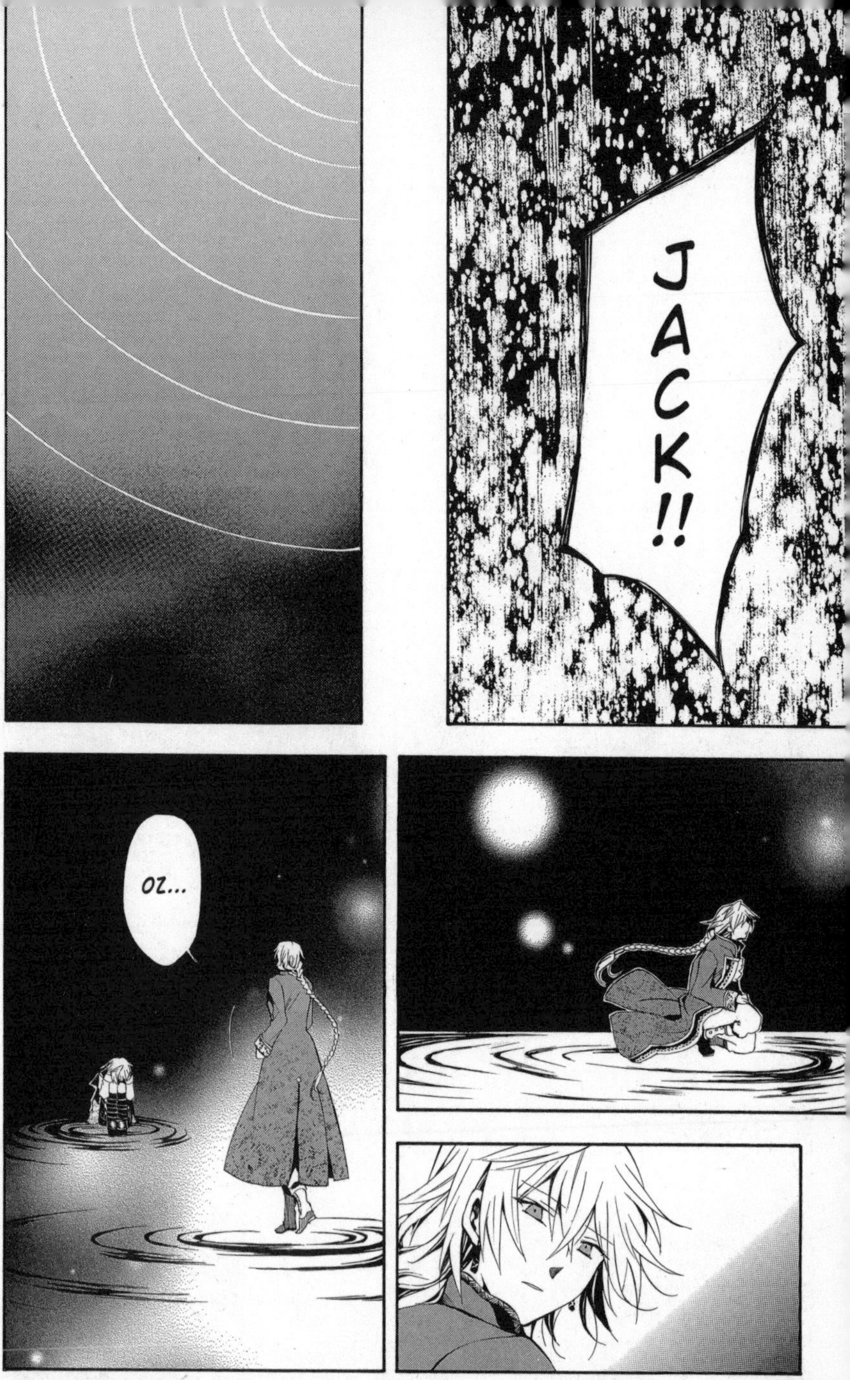
JACK!!
OZ...

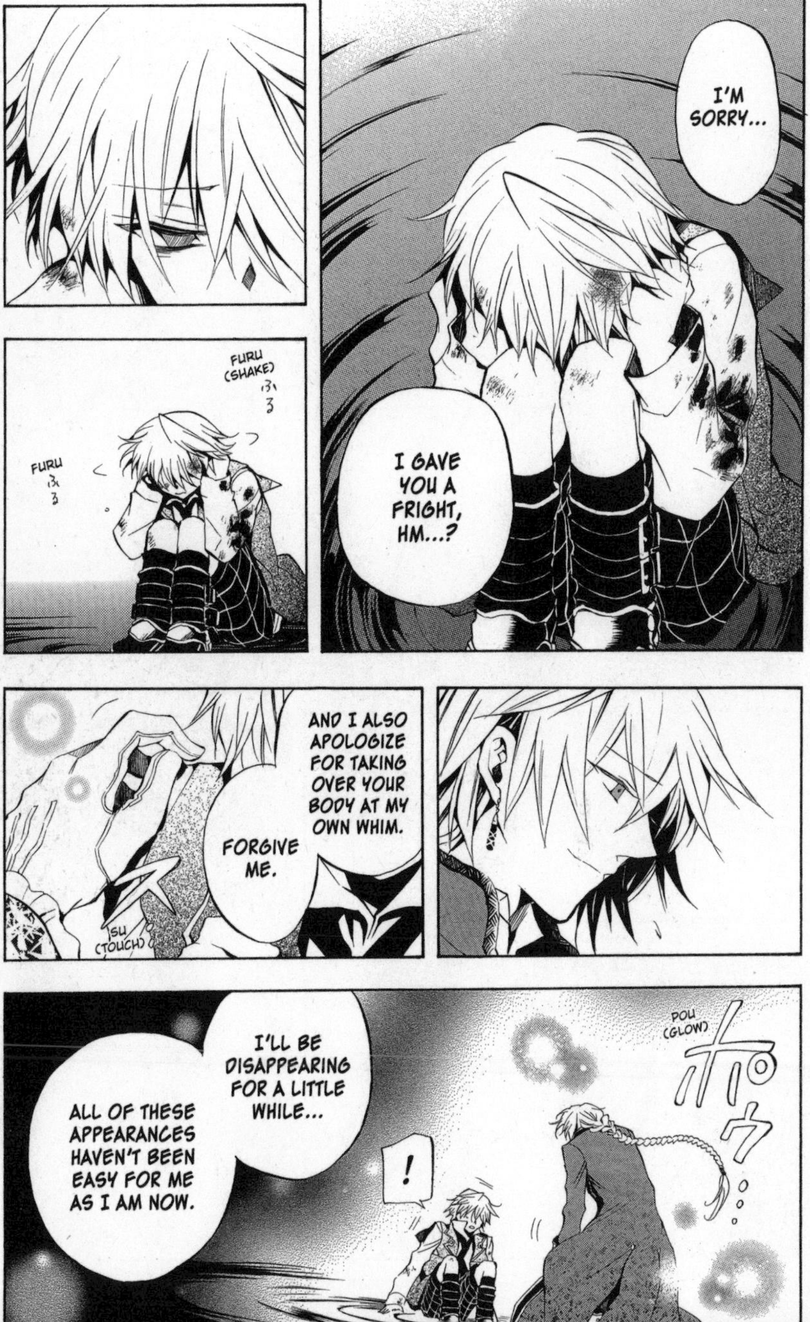
I'M SORRY...
I GAVE YOU A FRIGHT, HM...?
FURU (SHAKE) ふる
FURU ふる
AND I ALSO APOLOGIZE FOR TAKING OVER YOUR BODY AT MY OWN WHIM.
FORGIVE ME.
SU (TOUCH)
POU (GLOW) ポウ
I'LL BE DISAPPEARING FOR A LITTLE WHILE...
!
ALL OF THESE APPEARANCES HAVEN'T BEEN EASY FOR ME AS I AM NOW.

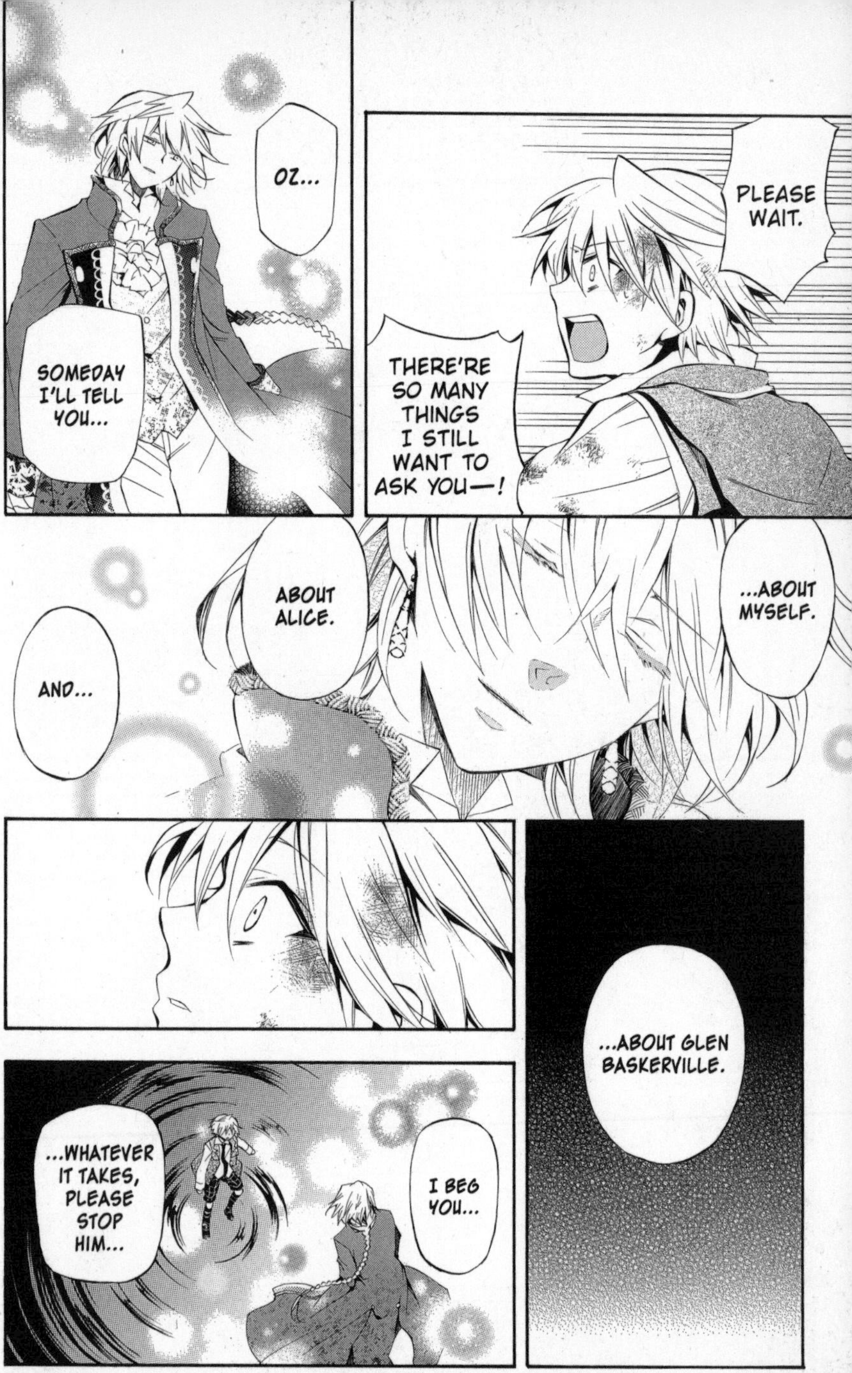
PLEASE WAIT.
THERE'RE SO MANY THINGS I STILL WANT TO ASK YOU—!
OZ...
SOMEDAY I'LL TELL YOU...
...ABOUT MYSELF.
ABOUT ALICE.
AND...
...ABOUT GLEN BASKERVILLE.
I BEG YOU...
...WHATEVER IT TAKES, PLEASE STOP HIM...

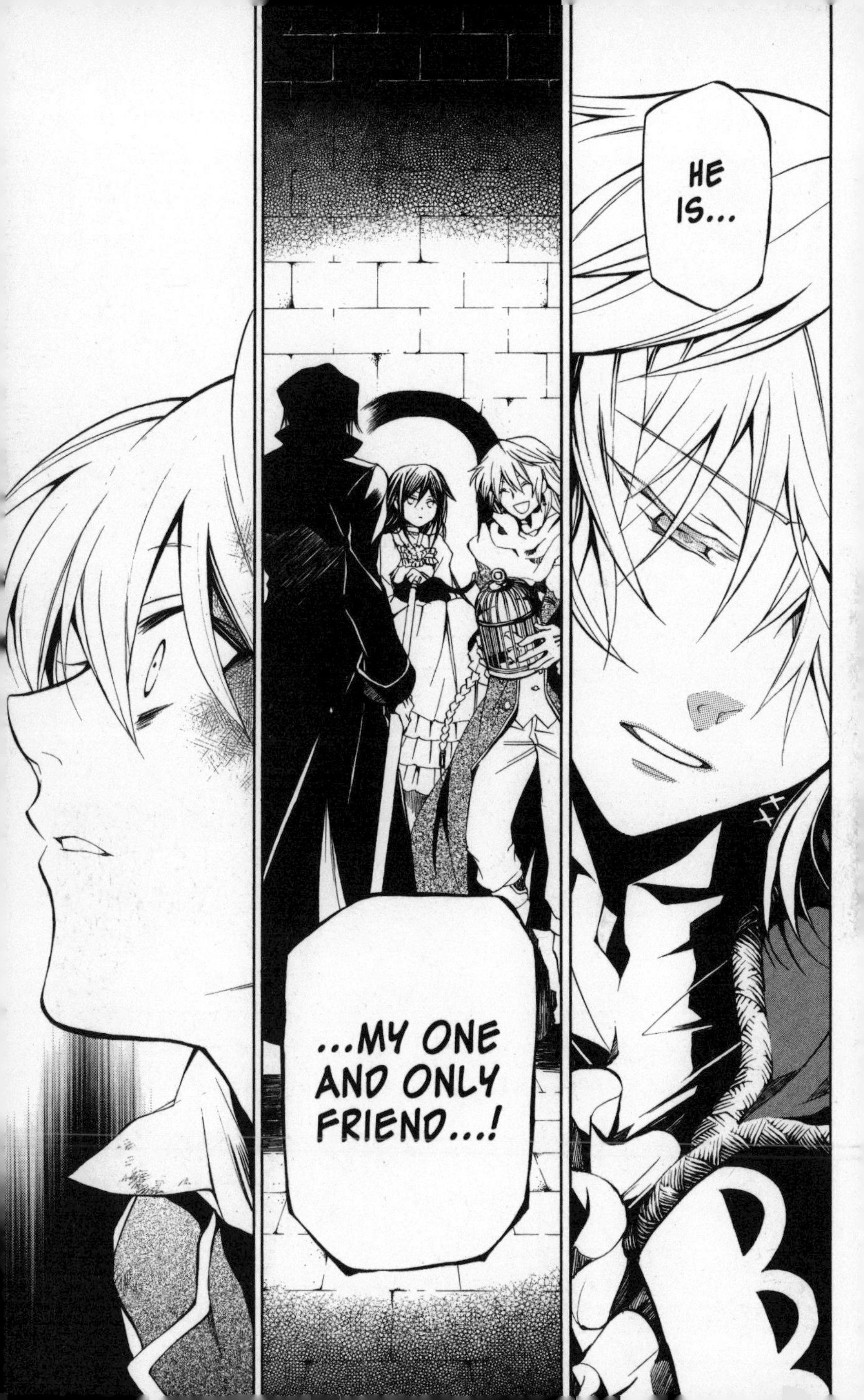
HE IS...
...MY ONE AND ONLY FRIEND...!

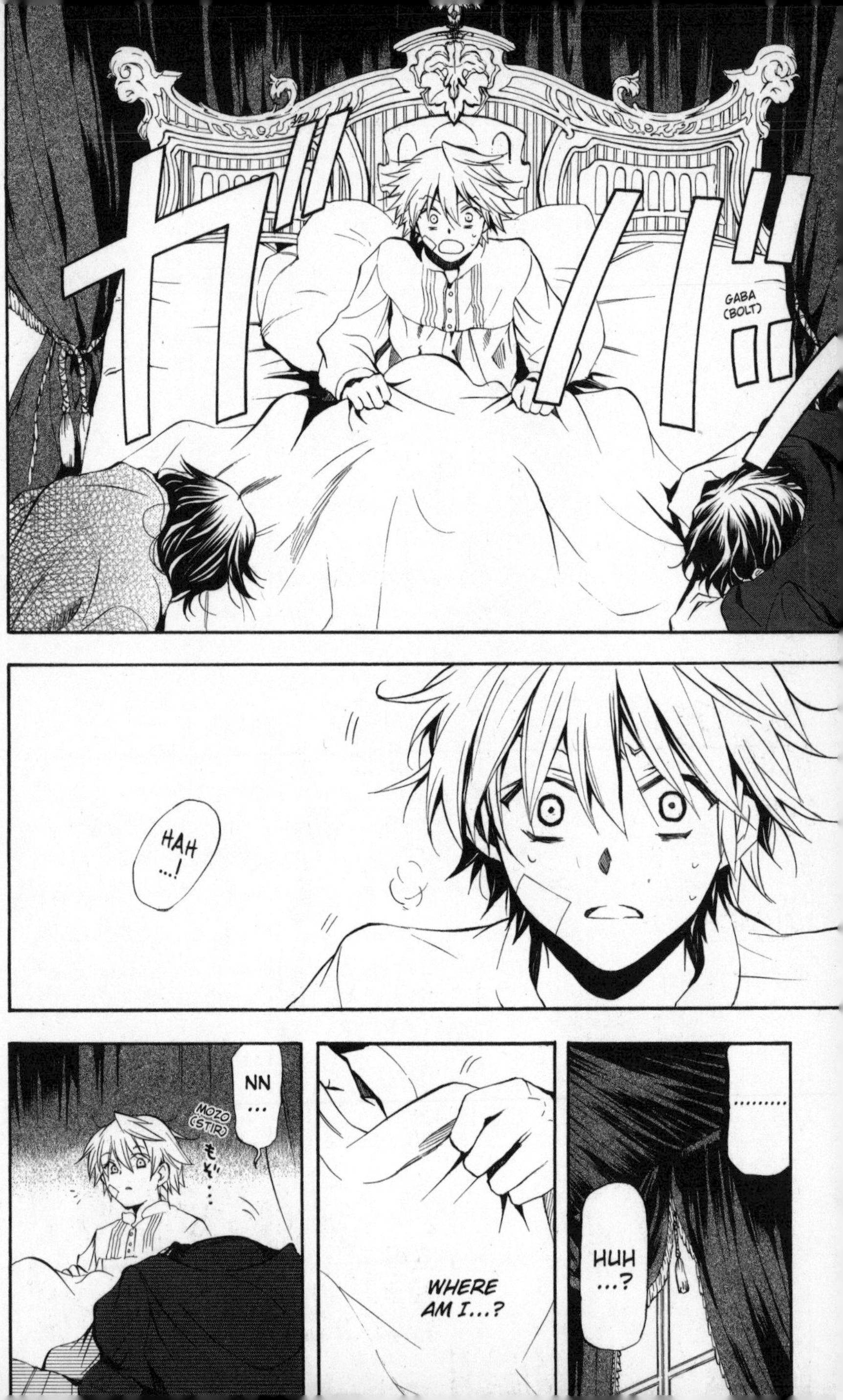
ガバッ
GABA (BOLT)
HAH ...!
....
HUH ...?
WHERE AM I...?
NN ...
MOZO (STIR)
もぞ...

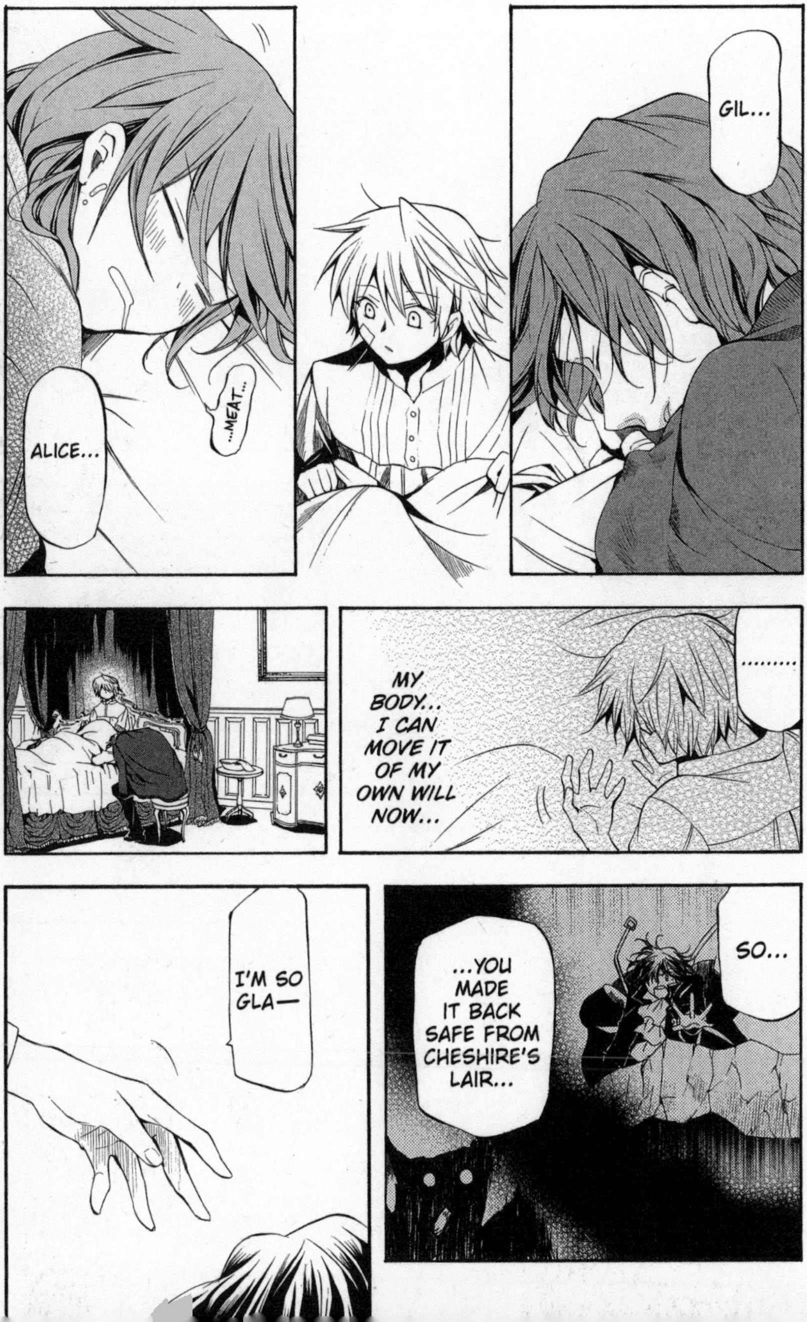
GIL...
...MEAT...
ALICE...
....
MY BODY... I CAN MOVE IT OF MY OWN WILL NOW...
SO...
...YOU MADE IT BACK SAFE FROM CHESHIRE'S LAIR...
I'M SO GLA—

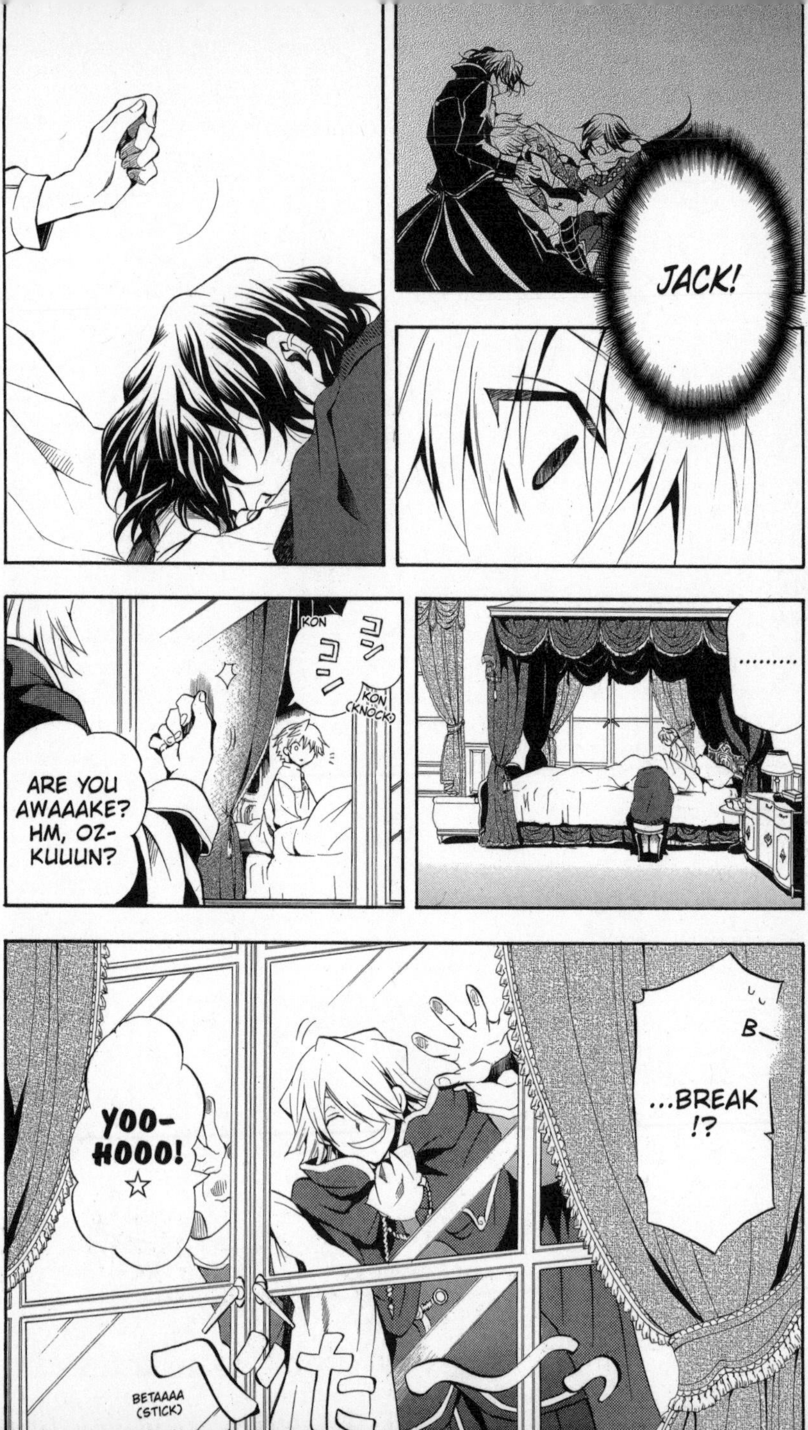
JACK!
....
KON
コン
コン
KON (KNOCK)
ARE YOU AWAAAKE? HM, OZ-KUUUN?
B—
...BREAK!?
YOO-HOOO! ☆
べた〜
BETAAAA (STICK)

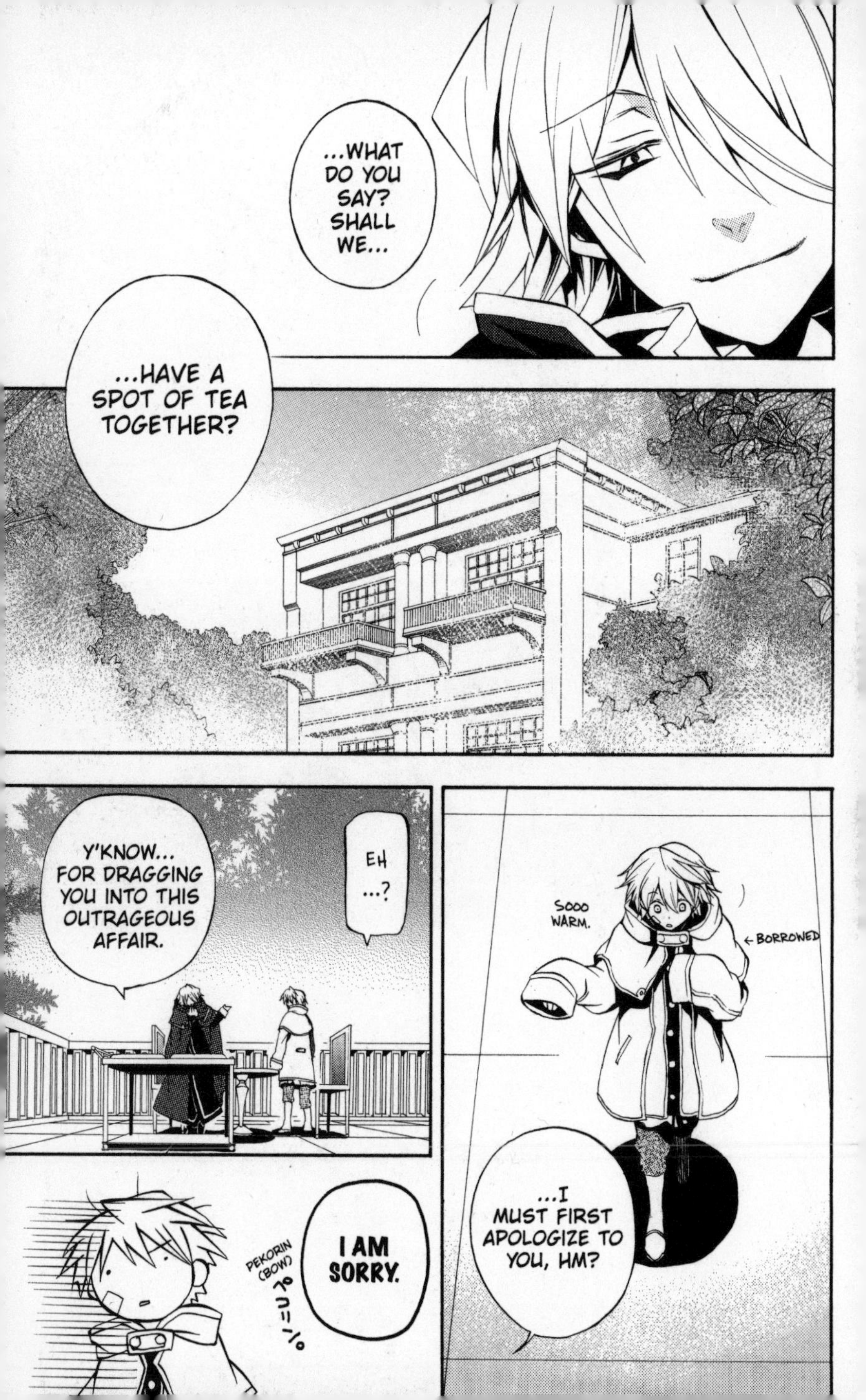
...WHAT DO YOU SAY? SHALL WE...
...HAVE A SPOT OF TEA TOGETHER?
SOOO WARM.
← BORROWED
...I MUST FIRST APOLOGIZE TO YOU, HM?
Y'KNOW... FOR DRAGGING YOU INTO THIS OUTRAGEOUS AFFAIR.
EH ...?
I AM SORRY.
PEKORIN (BOW)

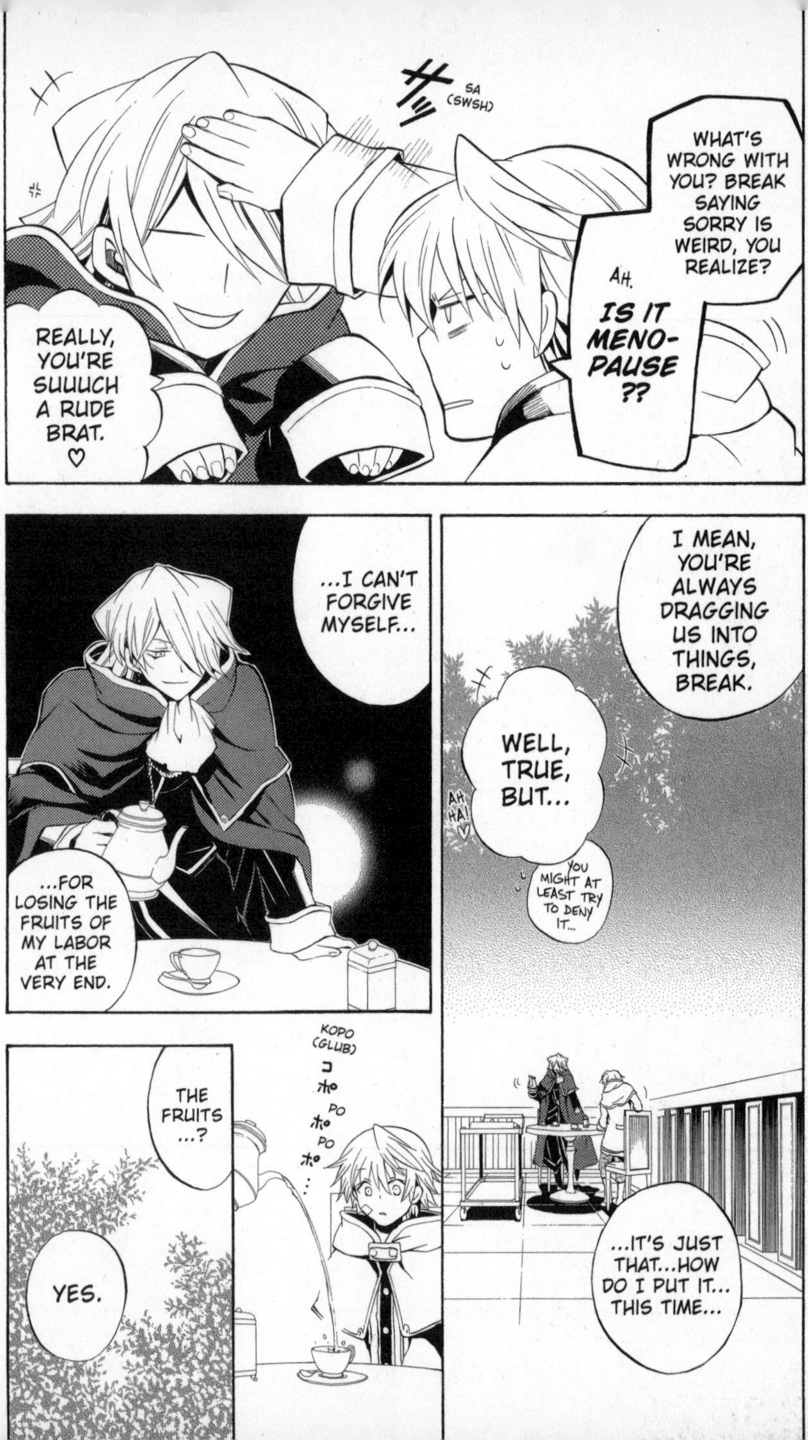
WHAT'S WRONG WITH YOU? BREAK SAYING SORRY IS WEIRD, YOU REALIZE?
SA (SWSH)
AH.
IS IT MENOPAUSE??
REALLY, YOU'RE SUUUCH A RUDE BRAT. ♡
I MEAN, YOU'RE ALWAYS DRAGGING US INTO THINGS, BREAK.
WELL, TRUE, BUT...
AH HA! ♡
YOU MIGHT AT LEAST TRY TO DENY IT...
...IT'S JUST THAT...HOW DO I PUT IT... THIS TIME...
...I CAN'T FORGIVE MYSELF...
...FOR LOSING THE FRUITS OF MY LABOR AT THE VERY END.
KOPO (GLUB)
PO PO
THE FRUITS ...?
YES.

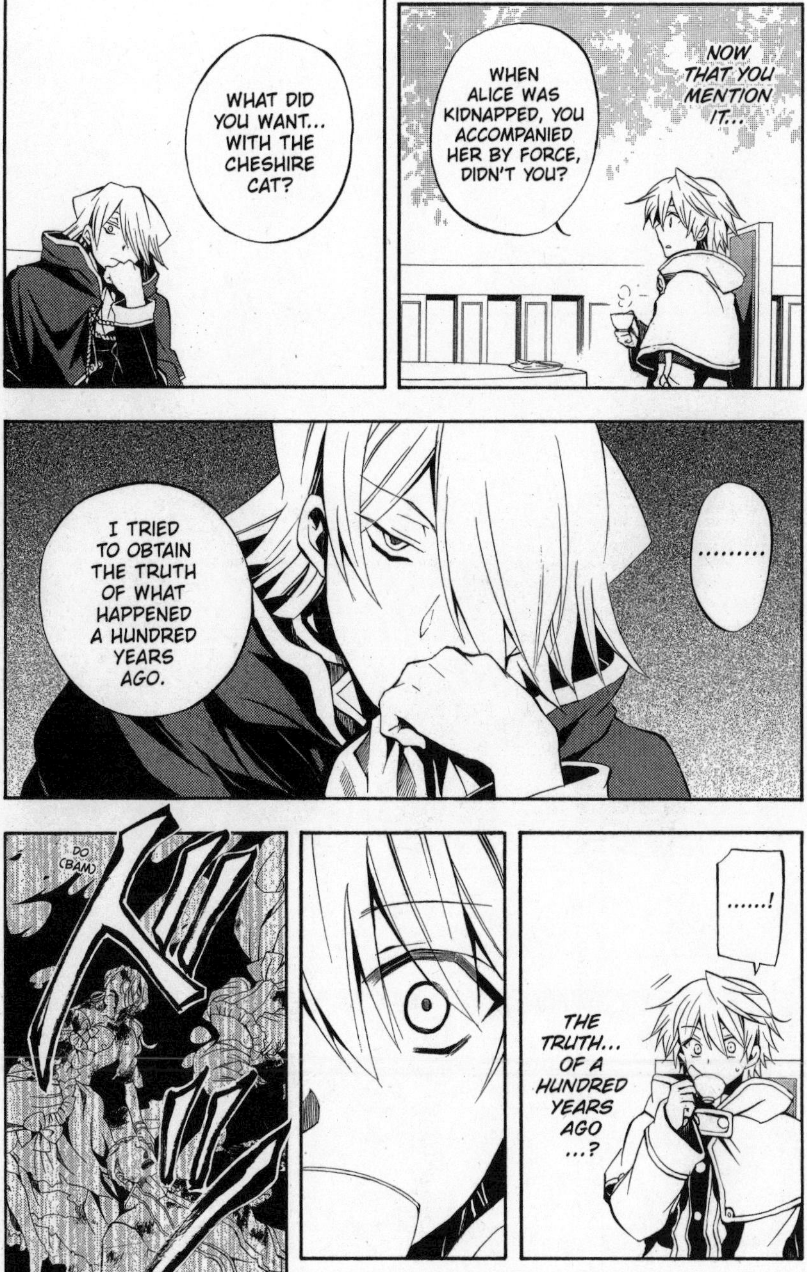
NOW THAT YOU MENTION IT...
WHEN ALICE WAS KIDNAPPED, YOU ACCOMPANIED HER BY FORCE, DIDN'T YOU?
WHAT DID YOU WANT... WITH THE CHESHIRE CAT?
....
I TRIED TO OBTAIN THE TRUTH OF WHAT HAPPENED A HUNDRED YEARS AGO.
......!
THE TRUTH... OF A HUNDRED YEARS AGO ...?
DO (BAM)

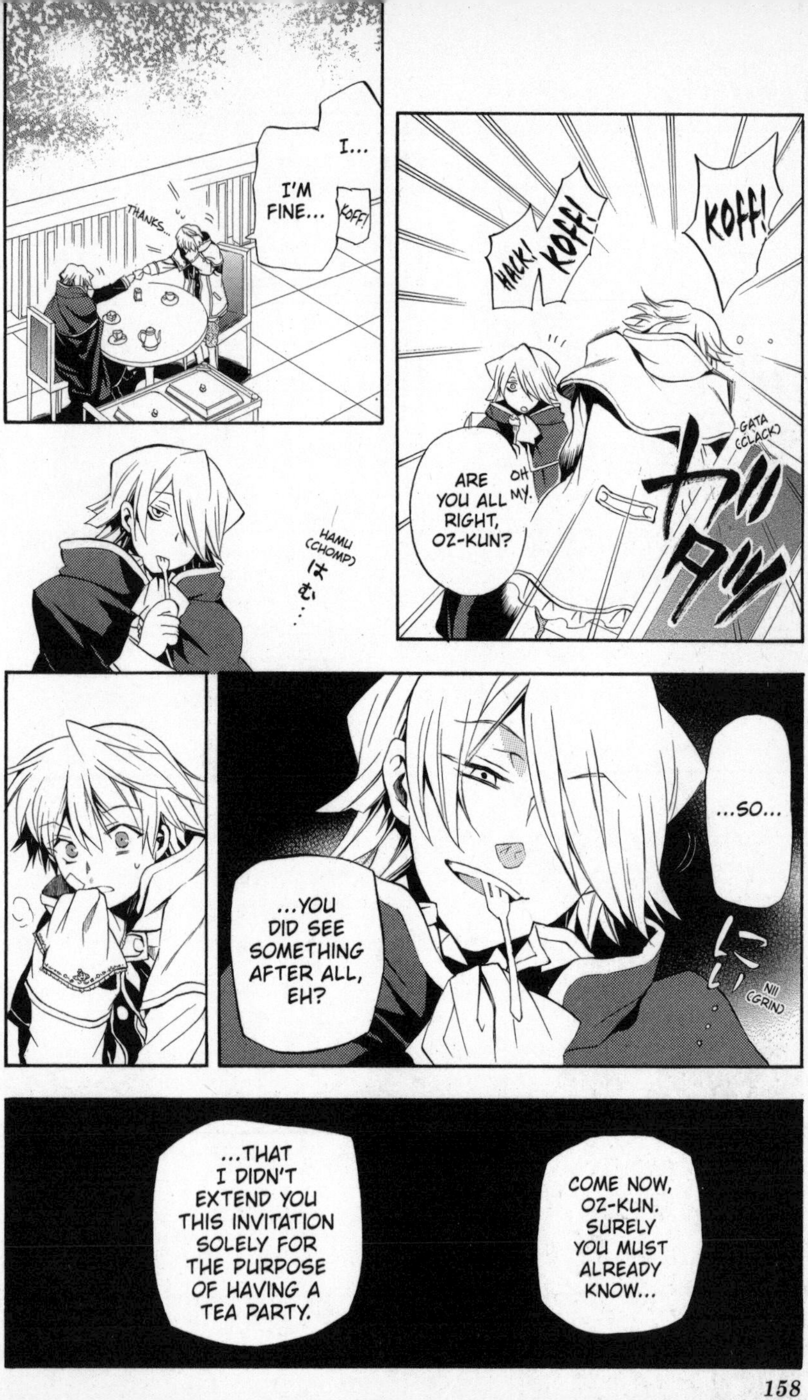
KOFF!
HACK! KOFF!
GATA (CLACK)
OH MY.
ARE YOU ALL RIGHT, OZ-KUN?
I...
I'M FINE...
KOFF!
THANKS...
HAMU (CHOMP)
はむ…
...SO...
NII (GRIN)
...YOU DID SEE SOMETHING AFTER ALL, EH?
COME NOW, OZ-KUN. SURELY YOU MUST ALREADY KNOW...
...THAT I DIDN'T EXTEND YOU THIS INVITATION SOLELY FOR THE PURPOSE OF HAVING A TEA PARTY.

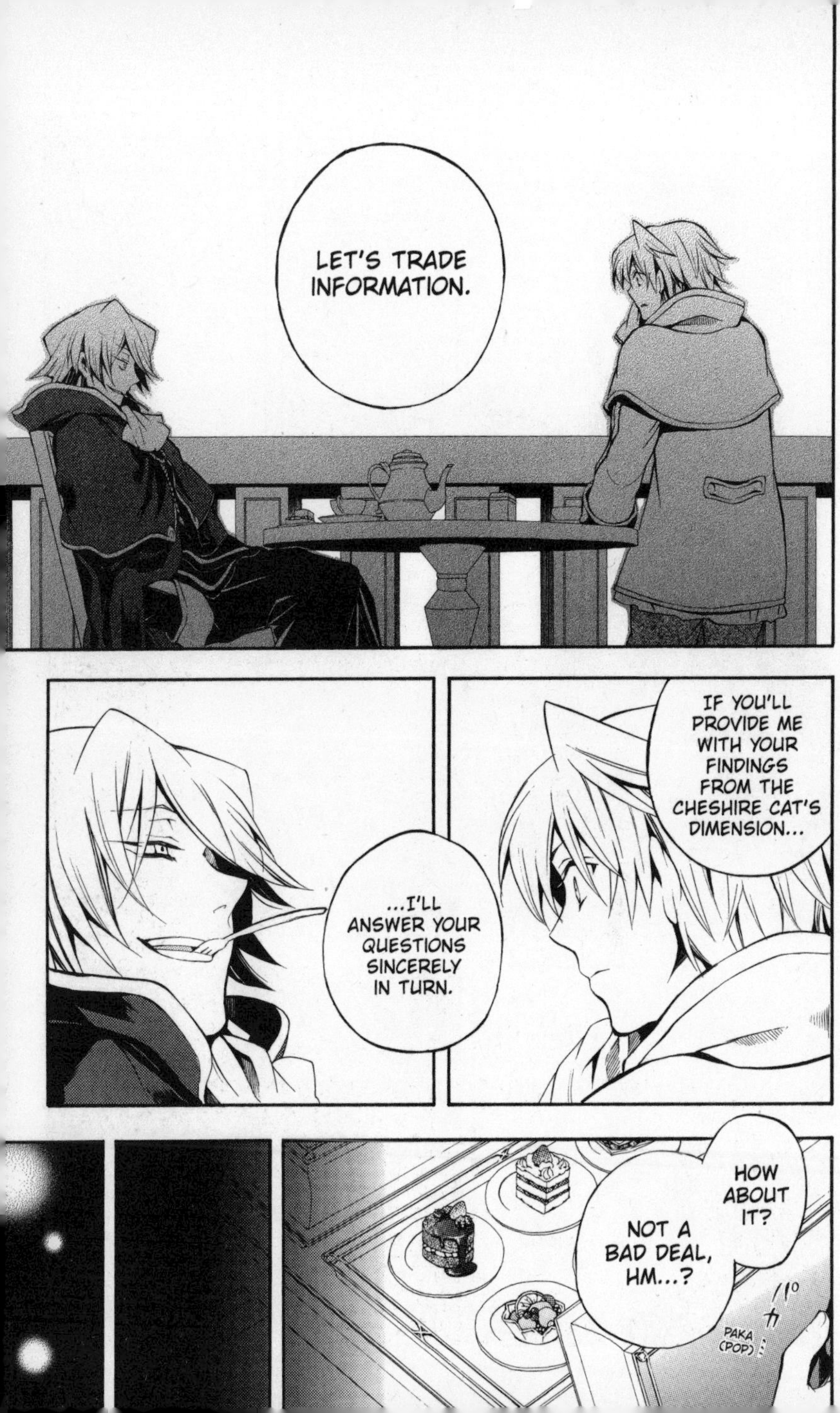
LET'S TRADE INFORMATION.
IF YOU'LL PROVIDE ME WITH YOUR FINDINGS FROM THE CHESHIRE CAT'S DIMENSION...
...I'LL ANSWER YOUR QUESTIONS SINCERELY IN TURN.
HOW ABOUT IT?
NOT A BAD DEAL, HM...?
パカ
PAKA (POP)

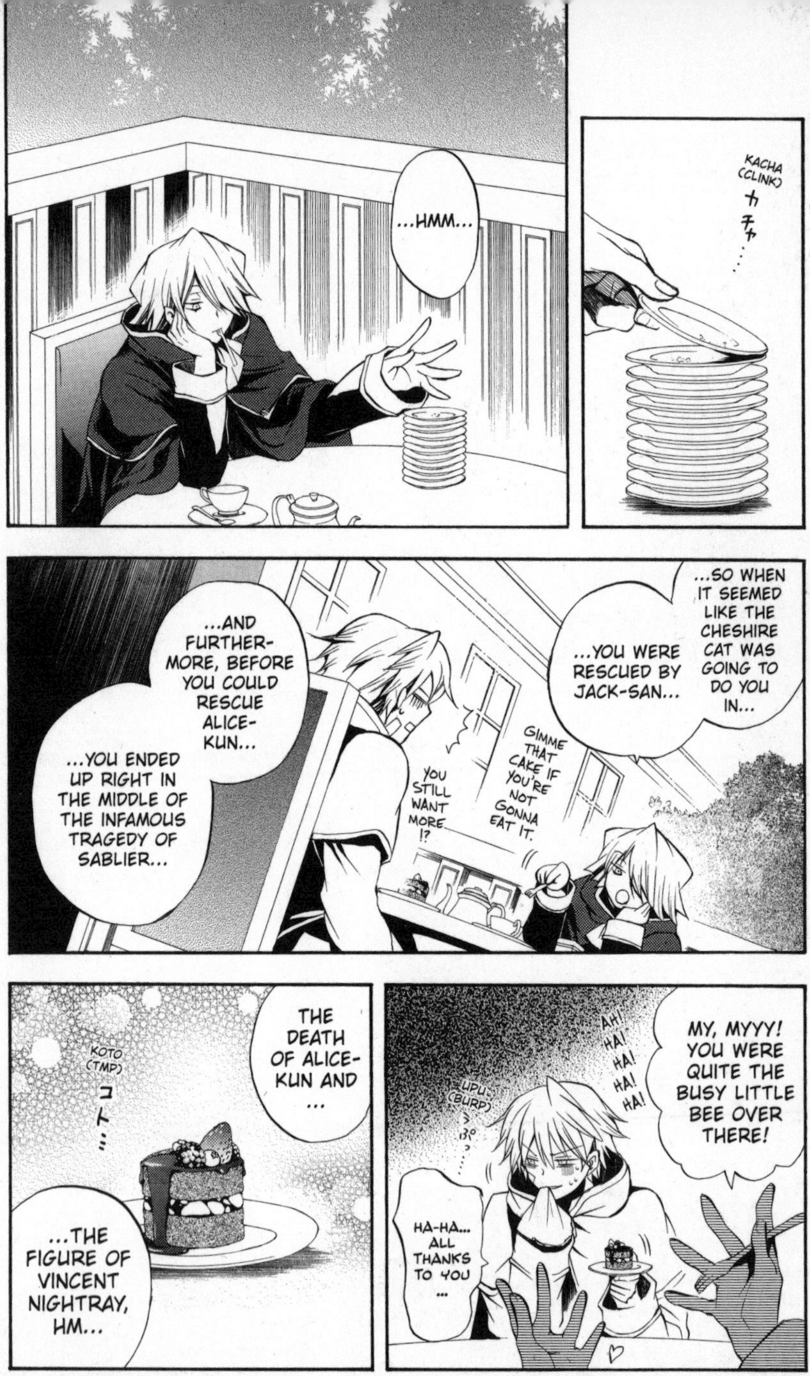
KACHA (CLINK)
カチャ…
...HMM...
...SO WHEN IT SEEMED LIKE THE CHESHIRE CAT WAS GOING TO DO YOU IN...
...YOU WERE RESCUED BY JACK-SAN...
GIMME THAT CAKE IF YOU'RE NOT GONNA EAT IT.
YOU STILL WANT MORE!?
...AND FURTHERMORE, BEFORE YOU COULD RESCUE ALICE-KUN...
...YOU ENDED UP RIGHT IN THE MIDDLE OF THE INFAMOUS TRAGEDY OF SABLIER...
MY, MYYY! YOU WERE QUITE THE BUSY LITTLE BEE OVER THERE!
AH! HA! HA! HA! HA!
UPU (BURP)
うぷ…
HA-HA... ALL THANKS TO YOU ...
THE DEATH OF ALICE-KUN AND ...
KOTO (TMP)
コト…
...THE FIGURE OF VINCENT NIGHTRAY, HM...

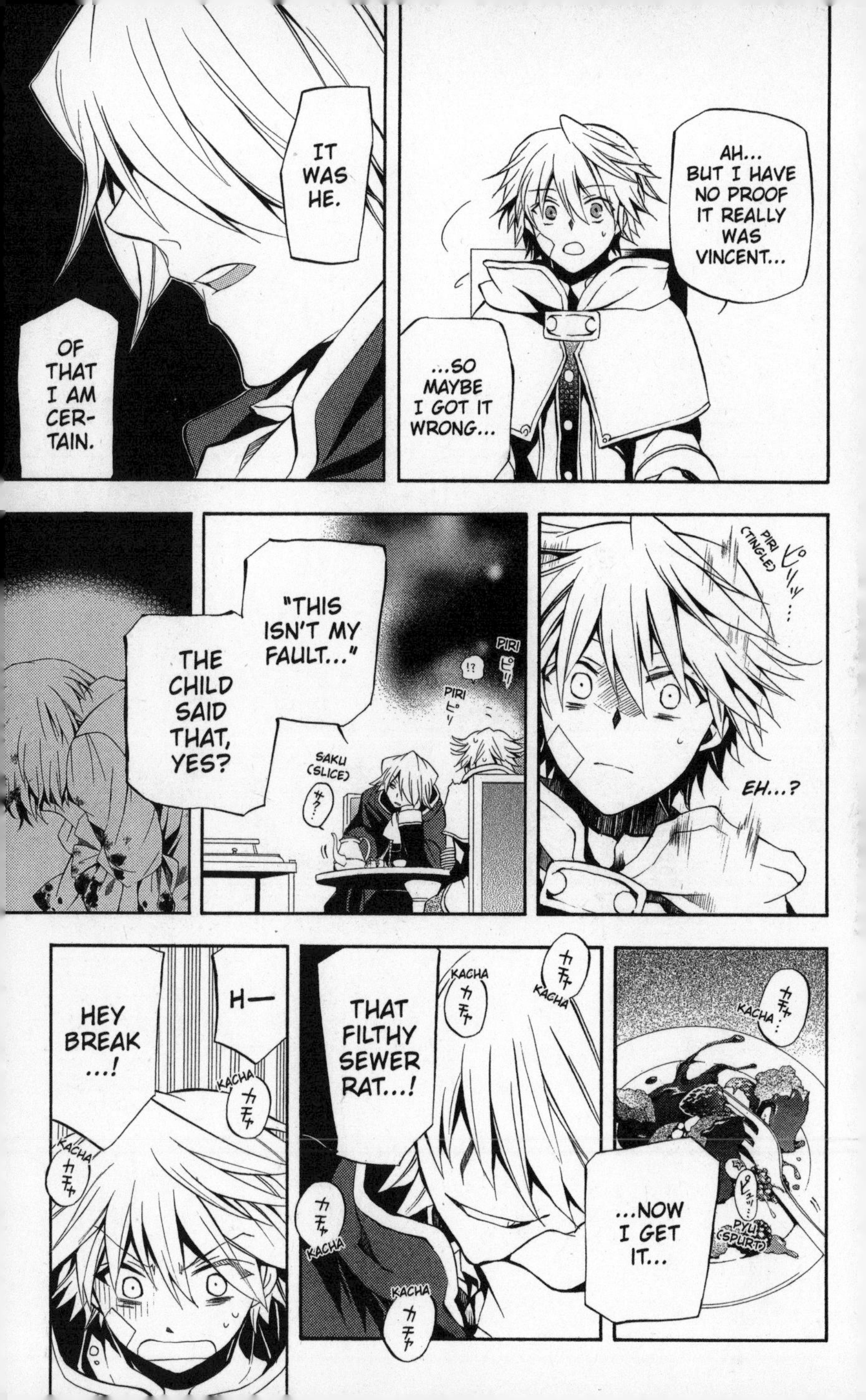
AH... BUT I HAVE NO PROOF IT REALLY WAS VINCENT...
...SO MAYBE I GOT IT WRONG...
IT WAS HE.
OF THAT I AM CER-TAIN.
PIRI (TINGLE)
ピリッ…
EH...?
"THIS ISN'T MY FAULT..."
THE CHILD SAID THAT, YES?
PIRI
ピ
!?
PIRI
ピ
SAKU (SLICE)
サク…
カチャ
KACHA...
...NOW I GET IT...
ピュッ…
PYU (SPURT)
カチャ
KACHA
KACHA
カチャ
THAT FILTHY SEWER RAT...!
カチャ
KACHA
KACHA
カチャ
H—
HEY BREAK...!
KACHA
カチャ
KACHA
カチャ

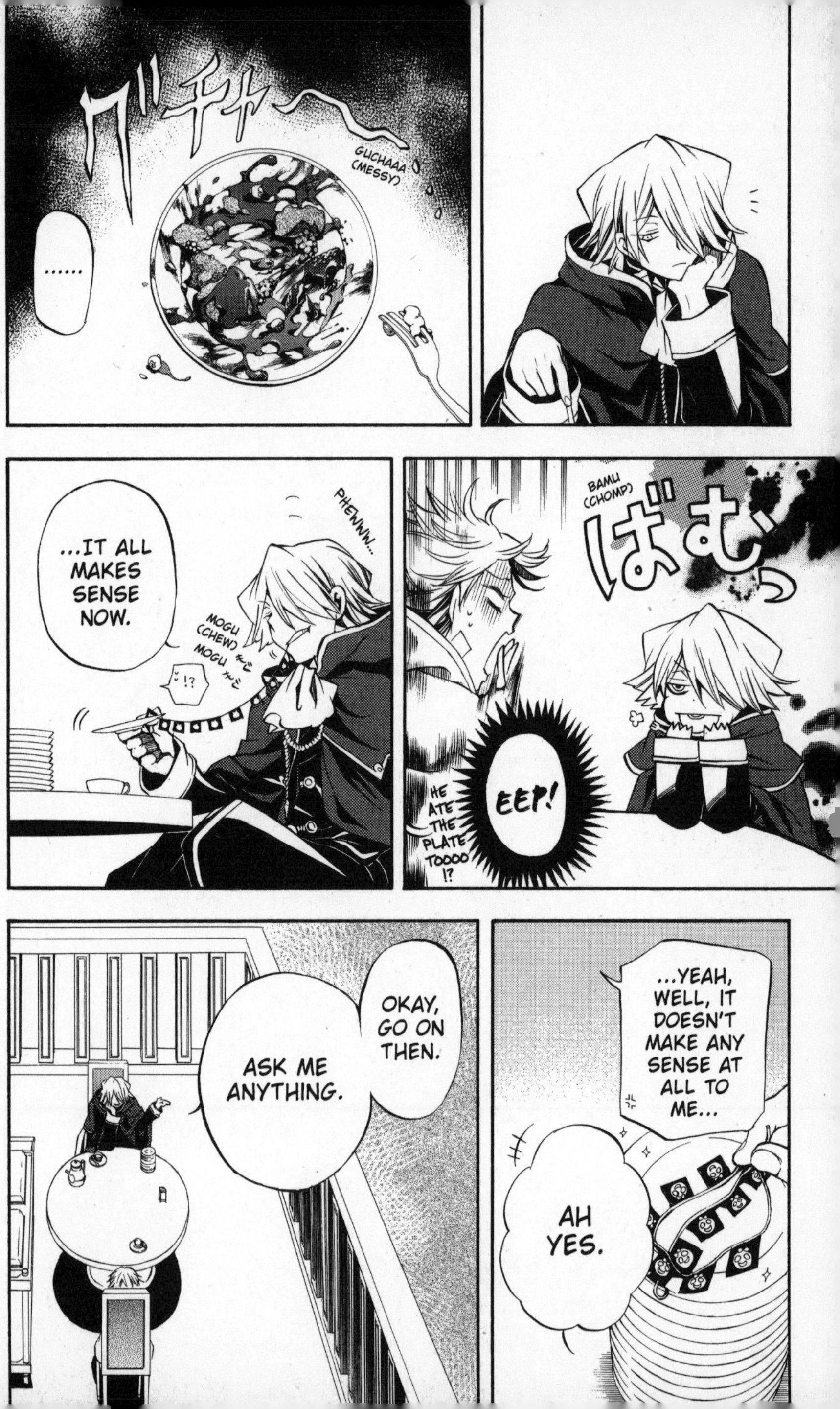
グチャ〜
GUCHAAA (MESSY)
......
BAMU (CHOMP)
ばむっ
EEP!
HE ATE THE PLATE TOOOO !?
PHEWWW...
...IT ALL MAKES SENSE NOW.
MOGU (CHEW) MOGU
もぐ もぐ
!?
...YEAH, WELL, IT DOESN'T MAKE ANY SENSE AT ALL TO ME...
AH YES.
OKAY, GO ON THEN.
ASK ME ANYTHING.

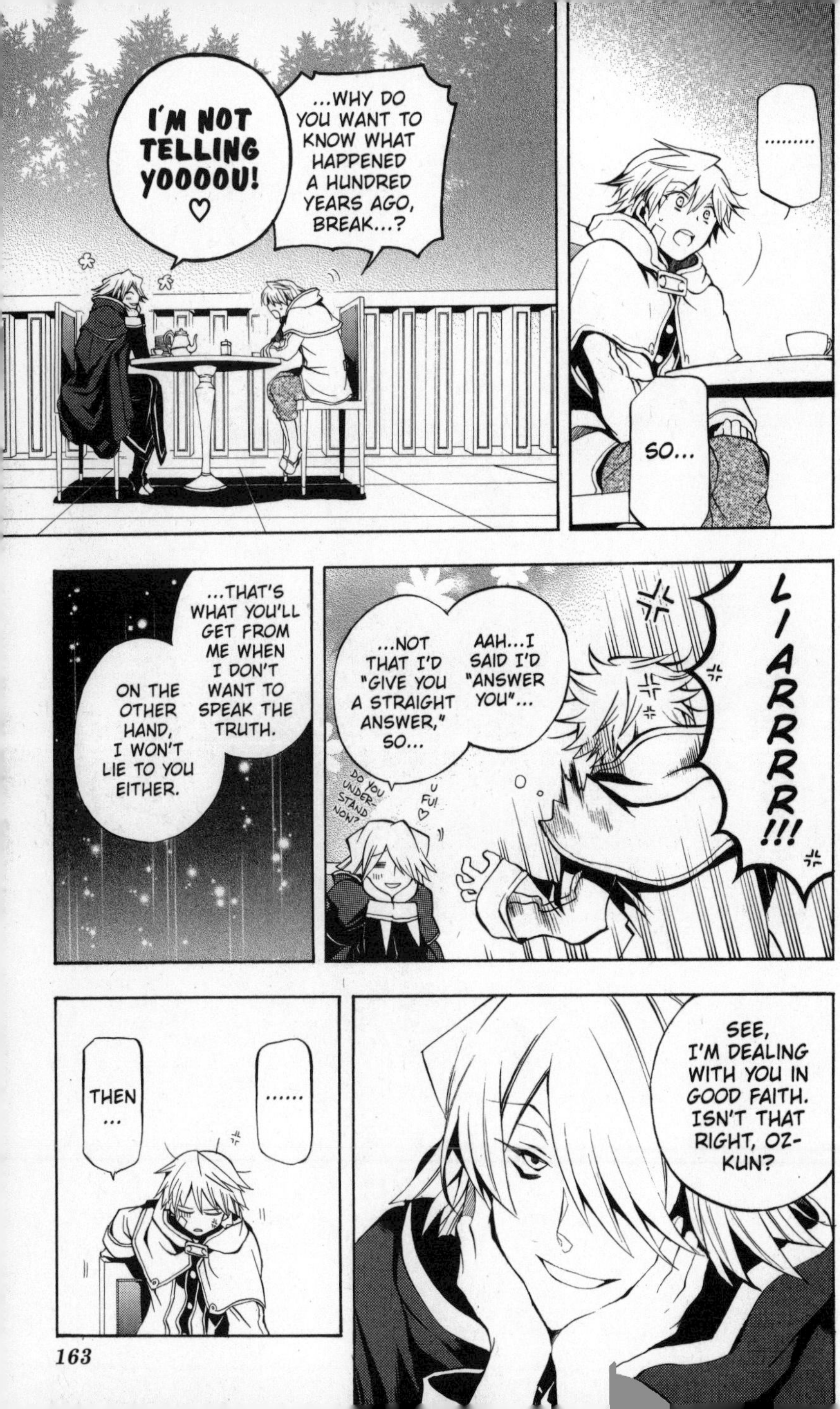
....
SO...
...WHY DO YOU WANT TO KNOW WHAT HAPPENED A HUNDRED YEARS AGO, BREAK...?
I'M NOT TELLING YOOOOU! ♡
LIARRRR!!!
AAH...I SAID I'D "ANSWER YOU"...
...NOT THAT I'D "GIVE YOU A STRAIGHT ANSWER," SO...
DO YOU UNDERSTAND NOW?
U FU ♡
...THAT'S WHAT YOU'LL GET FROM ME WHEN I DON'T WANT TO SPEAK THE TRUTH.
ON THE OTHER HAND, I WON'T LIE TO YOU EITHER.
SEE, I'M DEALING WITH YOU IN GOOD FAITH. ISN'T THAT RIGHT, OZ-KUN?
......
THEN ...

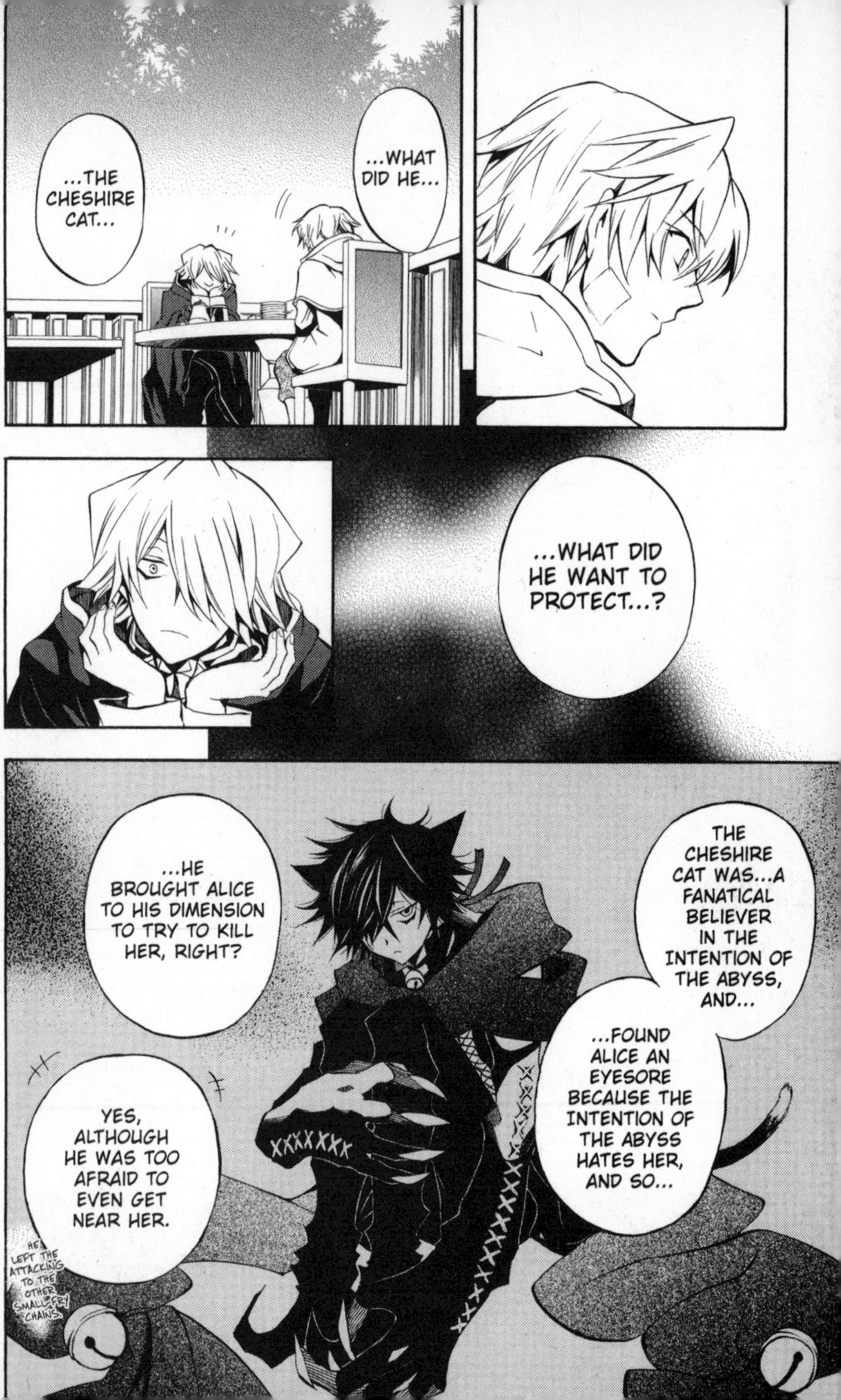
...WHAT DID HE...
...THE CHESHIRE CAT...
...WHAT DID HE WANT TO PROTECT...?
THE CHESHIRE CAT WAS...A FANATICAL BELIEVER IN THE INTENTION OF THE ABYSS, AND...
...FOUND ALICE AN EYESORE BECAUSE THE INTENTION OF THE ABYSS HATES HER, AND SO...
...HE BROUGHT ALICE TO HIS DIMENSION TO TRY TO KILL HER, RIGHT?
YES, ALTHOUGH HE WAS TOO AFRAID TO EVEN GET NEAR HER.
HE LEFT THE ATTACKING TO THE OTHER SMALL-FRY CHAINS.

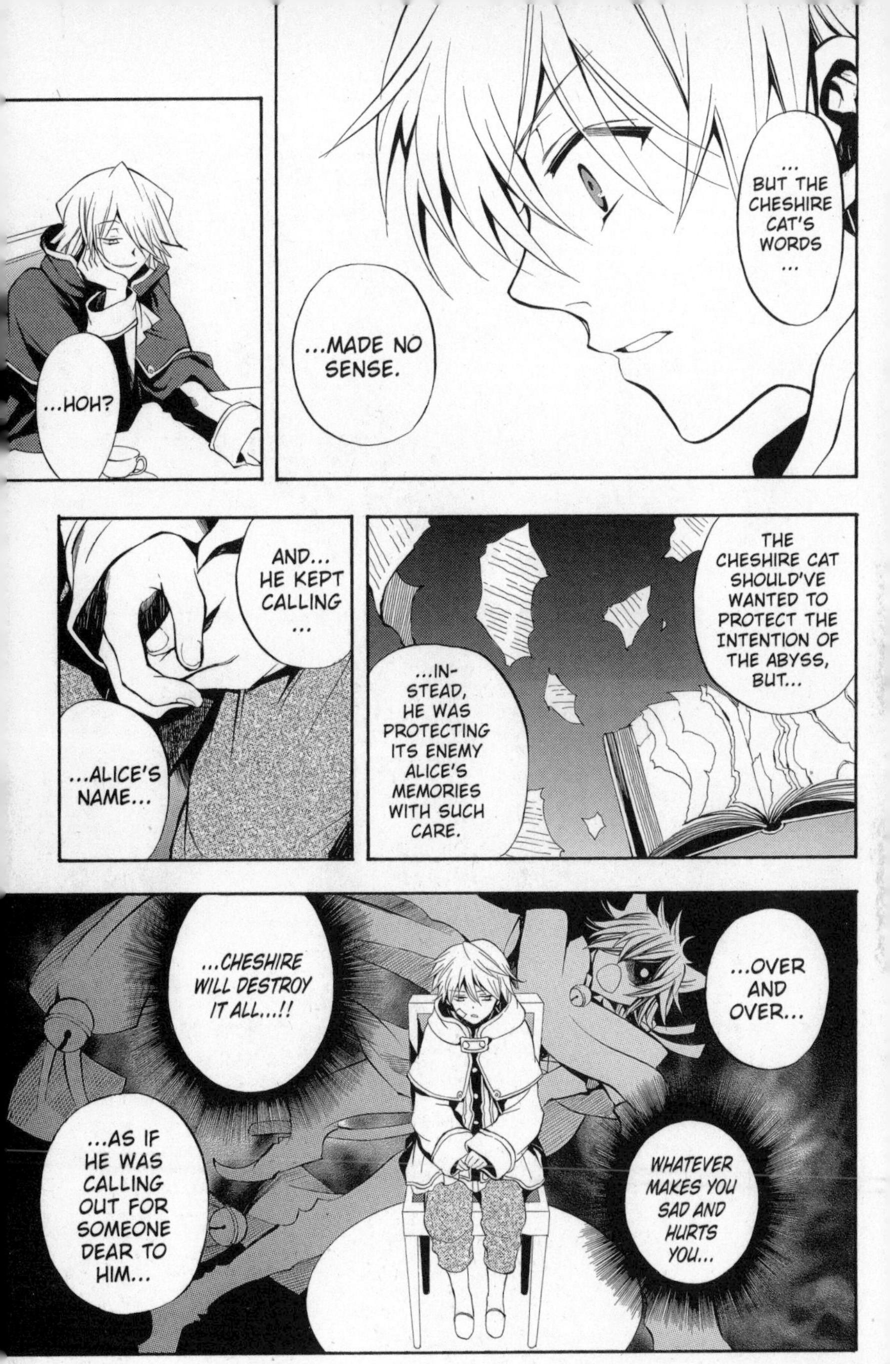
...BUT THE CHESHIRE CAT'S WORDS...
...MADE NO SENSE.
...HOH?
THE CHESHIRE CAT SHOULD'VE WANTED TO PROTECT THE INTENTION OF THE ABYSS, BUT...
...IN-STEAD, HE WAS PROTECTING ITS ENEMY ALICE'S MEMORIES WITH SUCH CARE.
AND... HE KEPT CALLING...
...ALICE'S NAME...
...OVER AND OVER...
...CHESHIRE WILL DESTROY IT ALL...!!
WHATEVER MAKES YOU SAD AND HURTS YOU...
...AS IF HE WAS CALLING OUT FOR SOMEONE DEAR TO HIM...

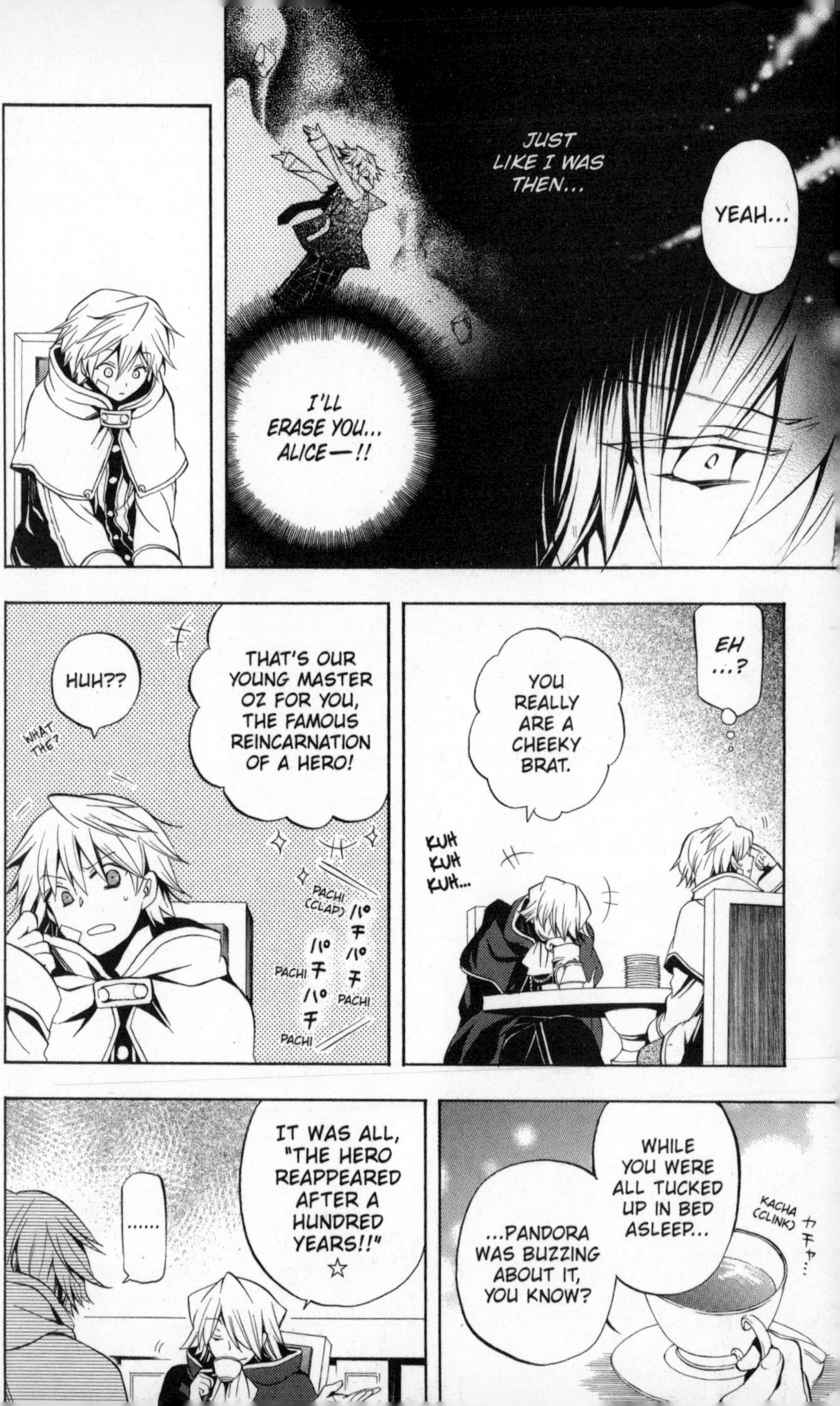
YEAH...
JUST LIKE I WAS THEN...
I'LL ERASE YOU... ALICE—!!
EH ...?
YOU REALLY ARE A CHEEKY BRAT.
KUH KUH KUH...
THAT'S OUR YOUNG MASTER OZ FOR YOU, THE FAMOUS REINCARNATION OF A HERO!
HUH??
WHAT THE?
PACHI (CLAP)
パチパチパチパチ
PACHI
PACHI
PACHI
WHILE YOU WERE ALL TUCKED UP IN BED ASLEEP...
...PANDORA WAS BUZZING ABOUT IT, YOU KNOW?
KACHA (CLINK)
カチャ...
IT WAS ALL, "THE HERO REAPPEARED AFTER A HUNDRED YEARS!!" ☆
......

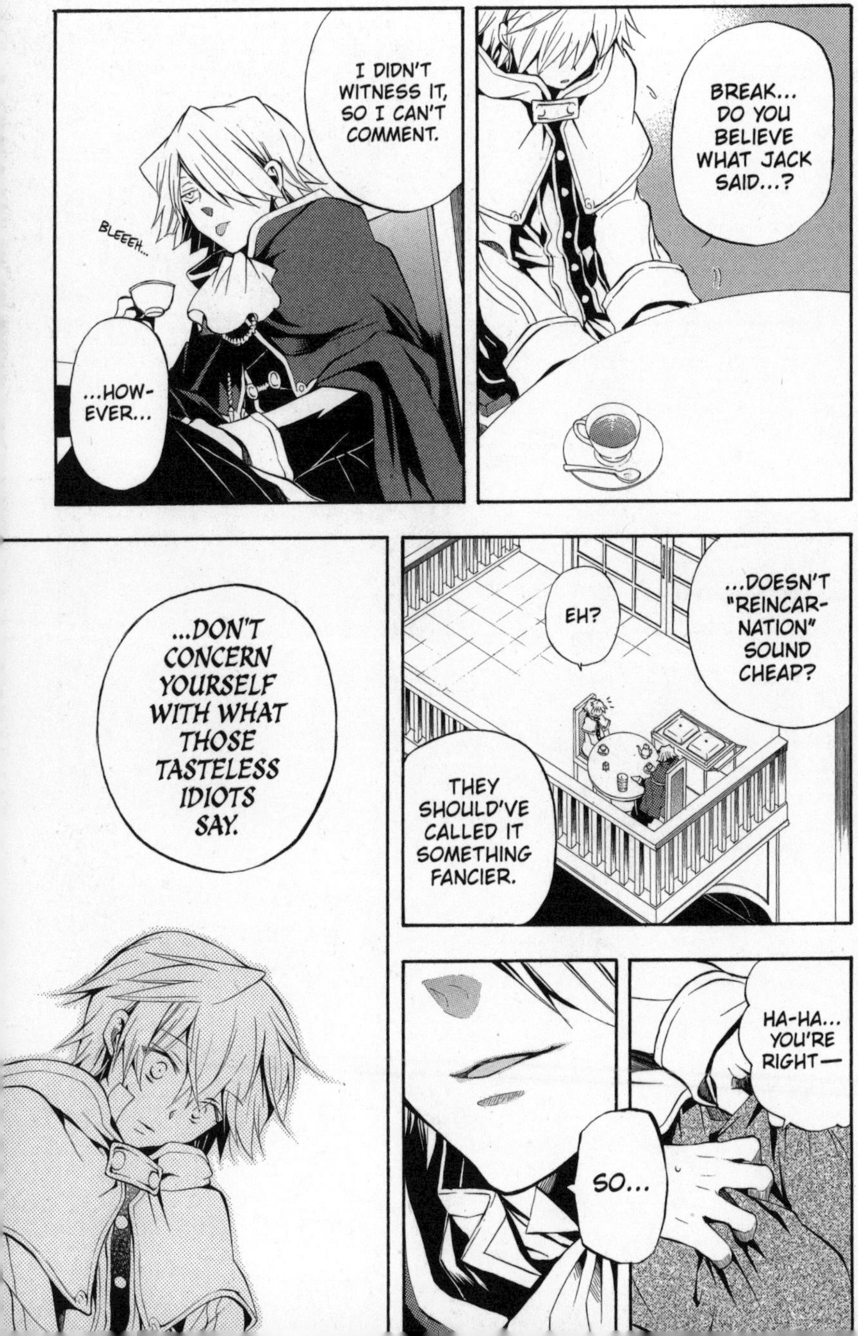
BREAK... DO YOU BELIEVE WHAT JACK SAID...?
I DIDN'T WITNESS IT, SO I CAN'T COMMENT.
BLEEEH...
...HOW-EVER...
...DOESN'T "REINCAR-NATION" SOUND CHEAP?
EH?
THEY SHOULD'VE CALLED IT SOMETHING FANCIER.
HA-HA... YOU'RE RIGHT—
SO...
...DON'T CONCERN YOURSELF WITH WHAT THOSE TASTELESS IDIOTS SAY.

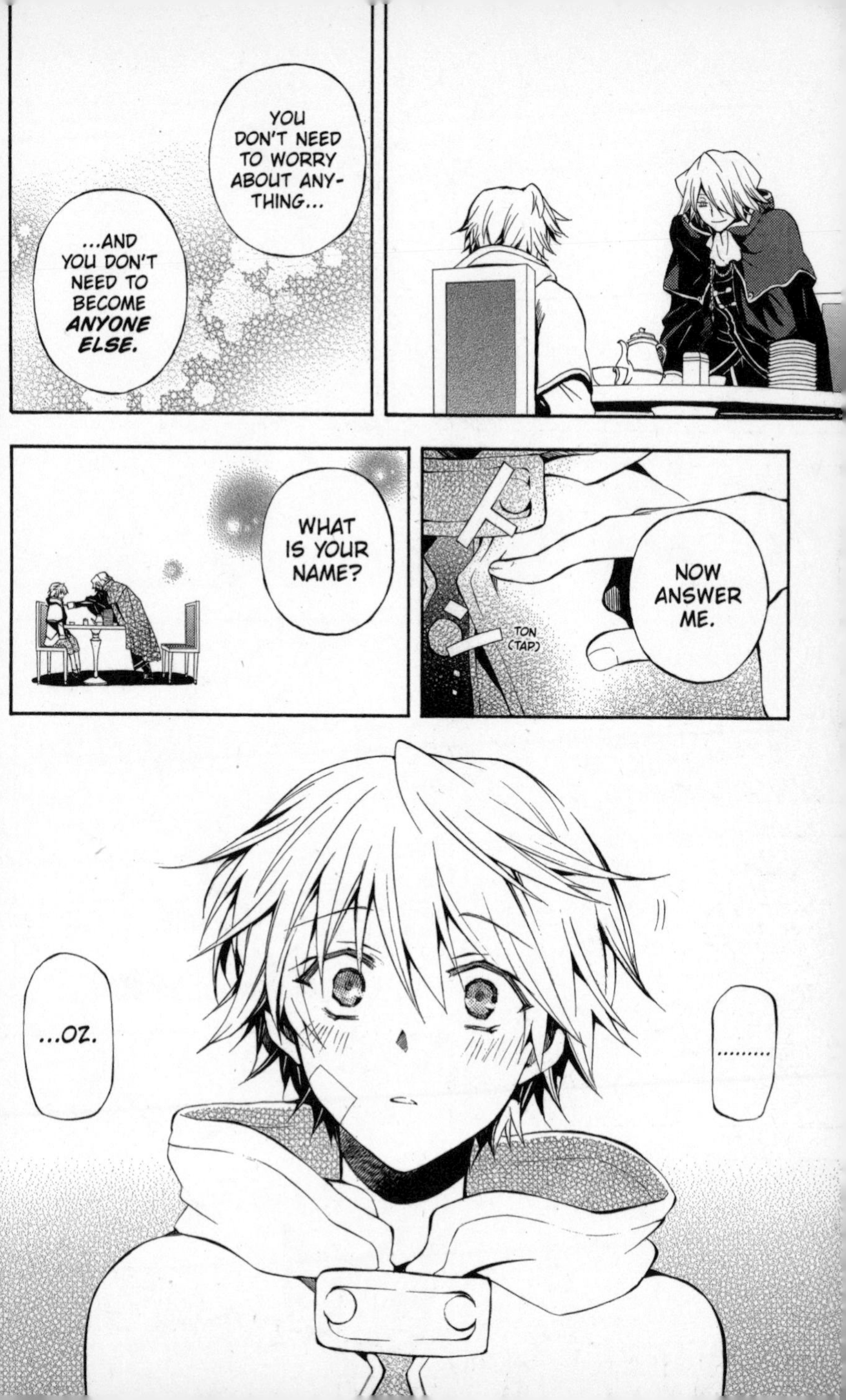
YOU DON'T NEED TO WORRY ABOUT ANY-THING...
...AND YOU DON'T NEED TO BECOME ANYONE ELSE.
NOW ANSWER ME.
TON (TAP)
WHAT IS YOUR NAME?
....
...OZ.

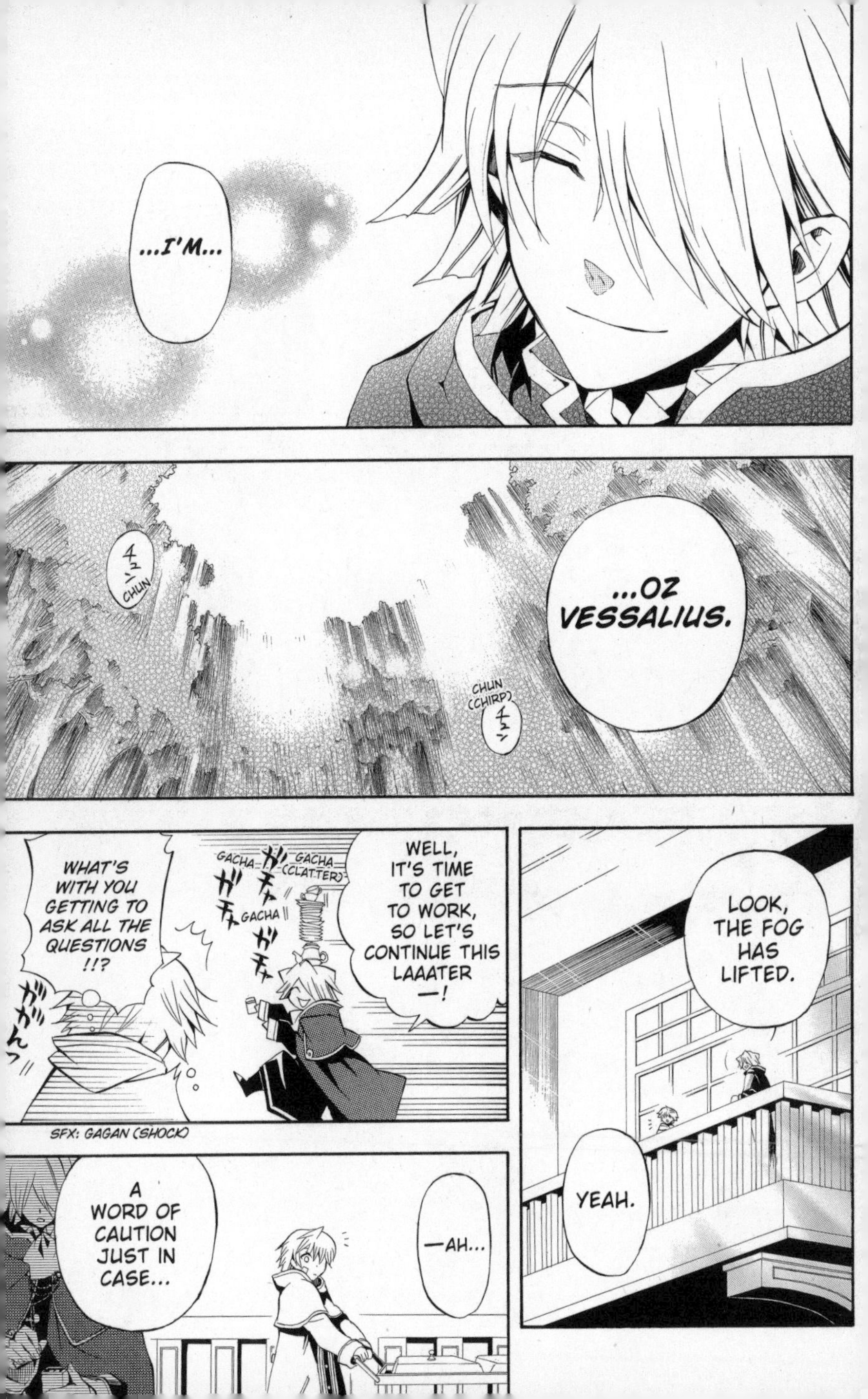
...I'M...
CHUN
CHUN (CHIRP)
...OZ VESSALIUS.
LOOK, THE FOG HAS LIFTED.
YEAH.
GACHA GACHA (CLATTER) GACHA
WELL, IT'S TIME TO GET TO WORK, SO LET'S CONTINUE THIS LAAATER—!
WHAT'S WITH YOU GETTING TO ASK ALL THE QUESTIONS!!?
SFX: GAGAN (SHOCK)
—AH...
A WORD OF CAUTION JUST IN CASE...

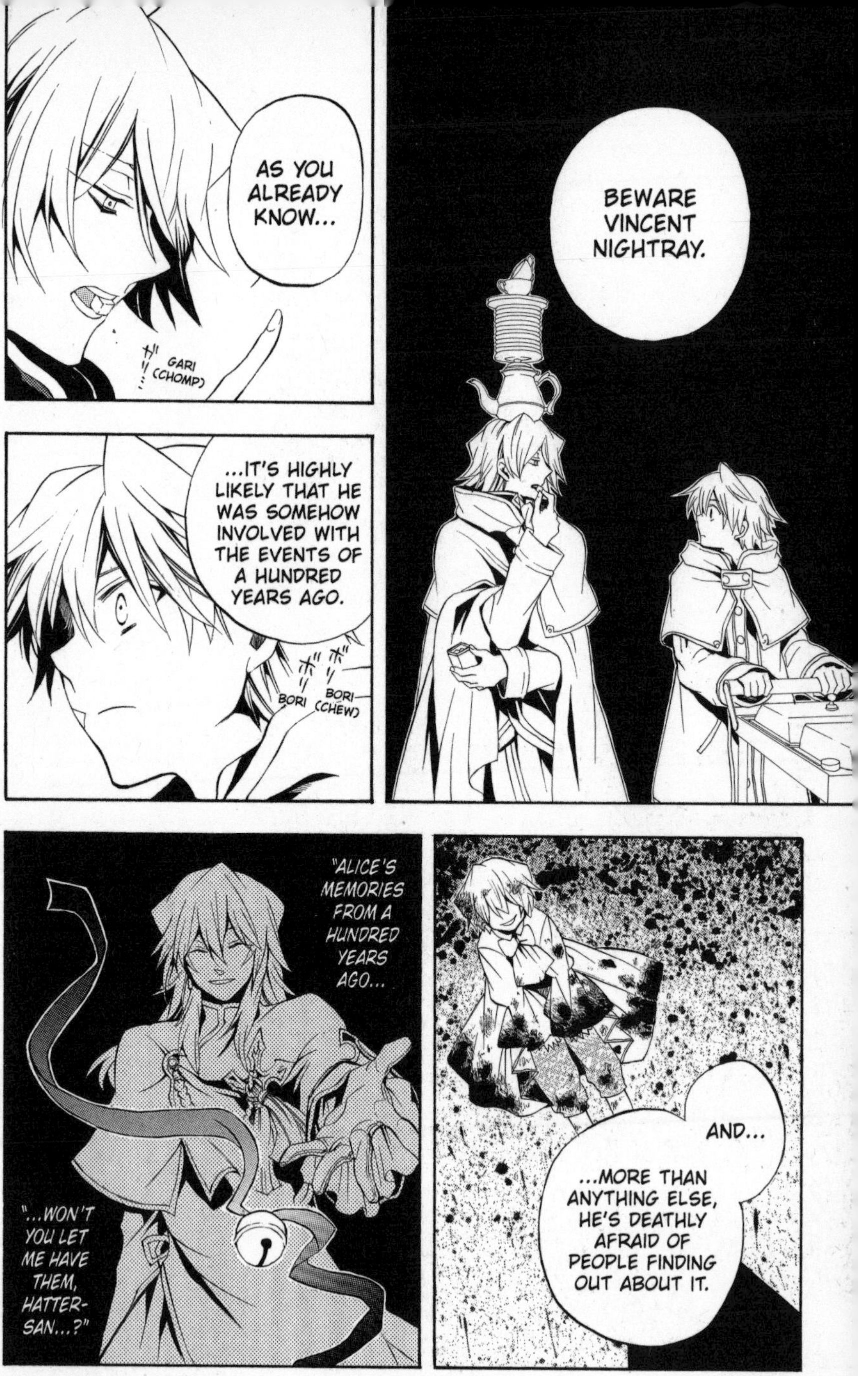
BEWARE VINCENT NIGHTRAY.
AS YOU ALREADY KNOW...
GARI (CHOMP)
...IT'S HIGHLY LIKELY THAT HE WAS SOMEHOW INVOLVED WITH THE EVENTS OF A HUNDRED YEARS AGO.
BORI BORI (CHEW)
AND...
...MORE THAN ANYTHING ELSE, HE'S DEATHLY AFRAID OF PEOPLE FINDING OUT ABOUT IT.
"ALICE'S MEMORIES FROM A HUNDRED YEARS AGO...
"...WON'T YOU LET ME HAVE THEM, HATTER-SAN...?"

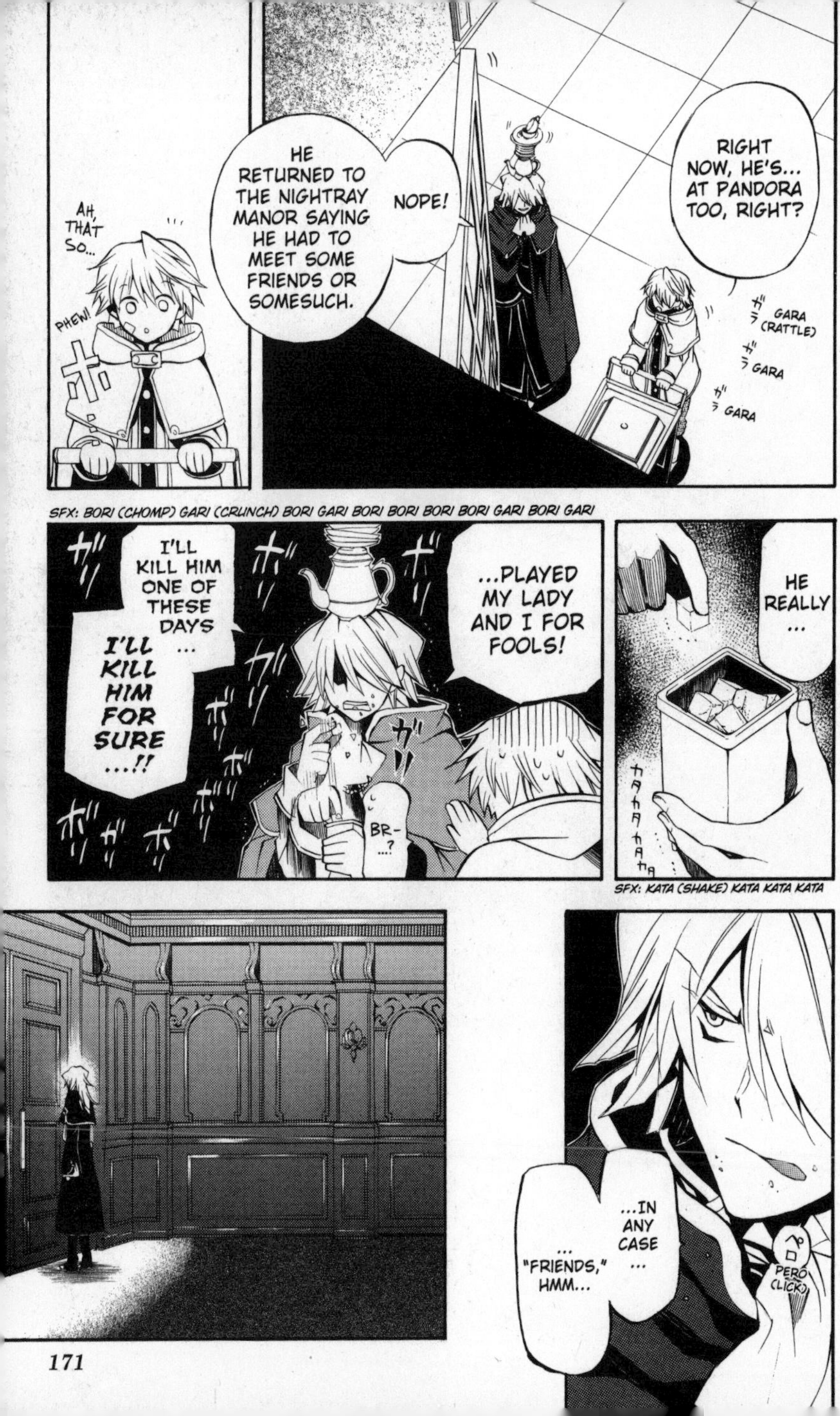
RIGHT NOW, HE'S... AT PANDORA TOO, RIGHT?
NOPE!
HE RETURNED TO THE NIGHTRAY MANOR SAYING HE HAD TO MEET SOME FRIENDS OR SOMESUCH.
GARA (RATTLE)
GARA
GARA
AH, THAT SO...
PHEW!
SFX: BORI (CHOMP) GARI (CRUNCH) BORI GARI BORI BORI BORI BORI GARI BORI GARI
HE REALLY...
SFX: KATA (SHAKE) KATA KATA KATA
...PLAYED MY LADY AND I FOR FOOLS!
I'LL KILL HIM ONE OF THESE DAYS...
I'LL KILL HIM FOR SURE...!!
BR-...?
...IN ANY CASE...
... "FRIENDS," HMM...
PERO (LICK)

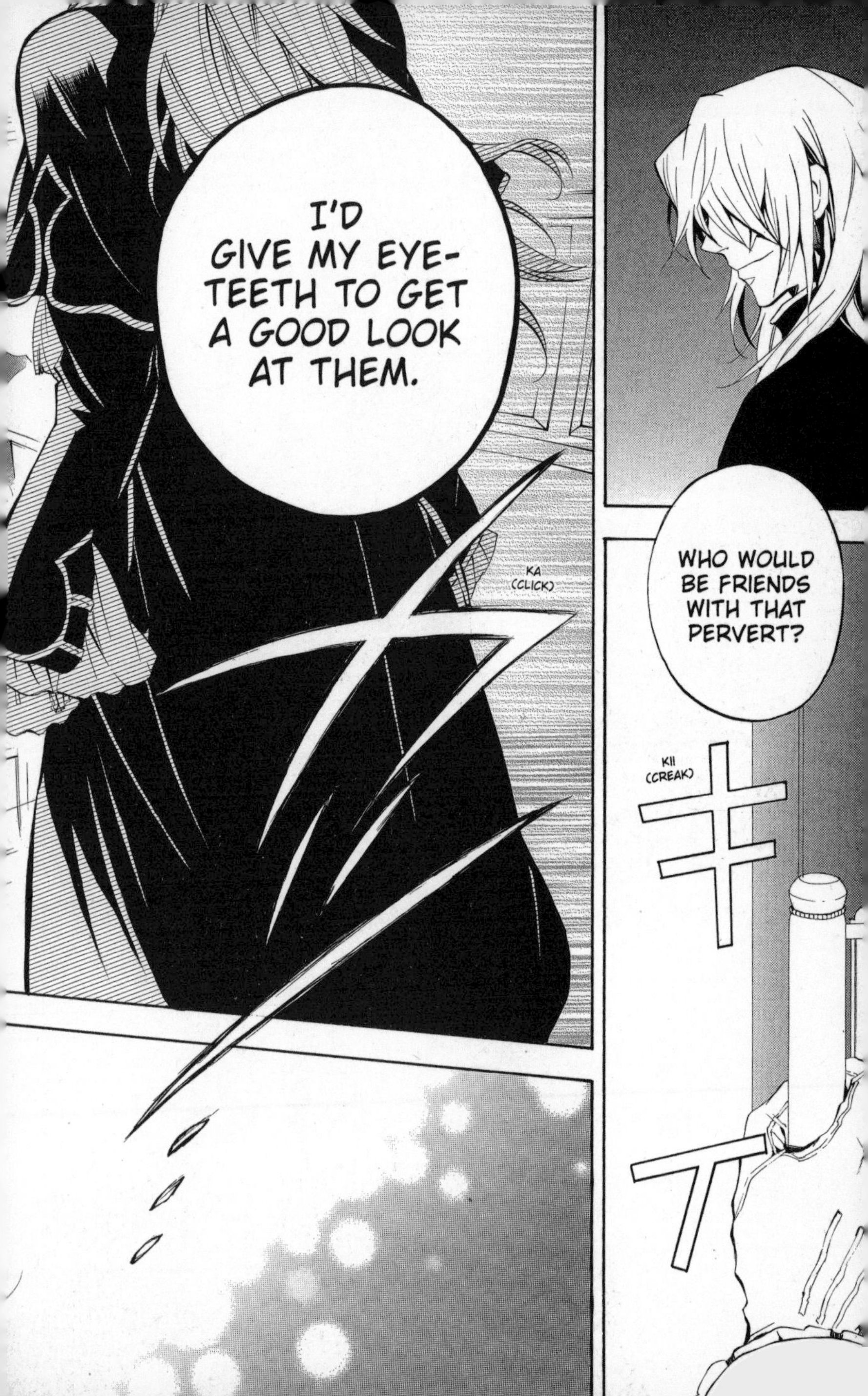
WHO WOULD BE FRIENDS WITH THAT PERVERT?
KII (CREAK)
I'D GIVE MY EYE-TEETH TO GET A GOOD LOOK AT THEM.
KA (CLICK)

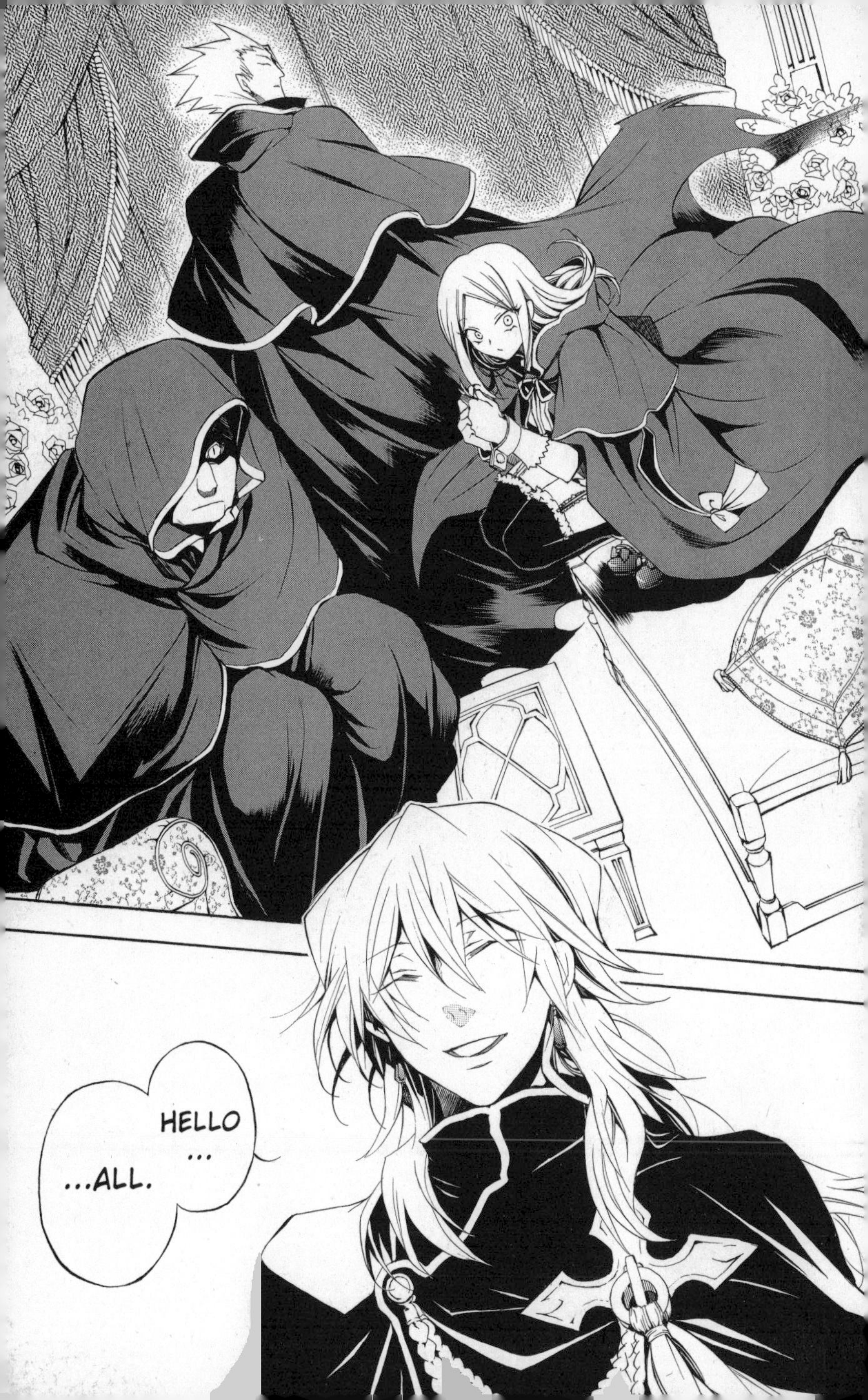
HELLO
...
...ALL.

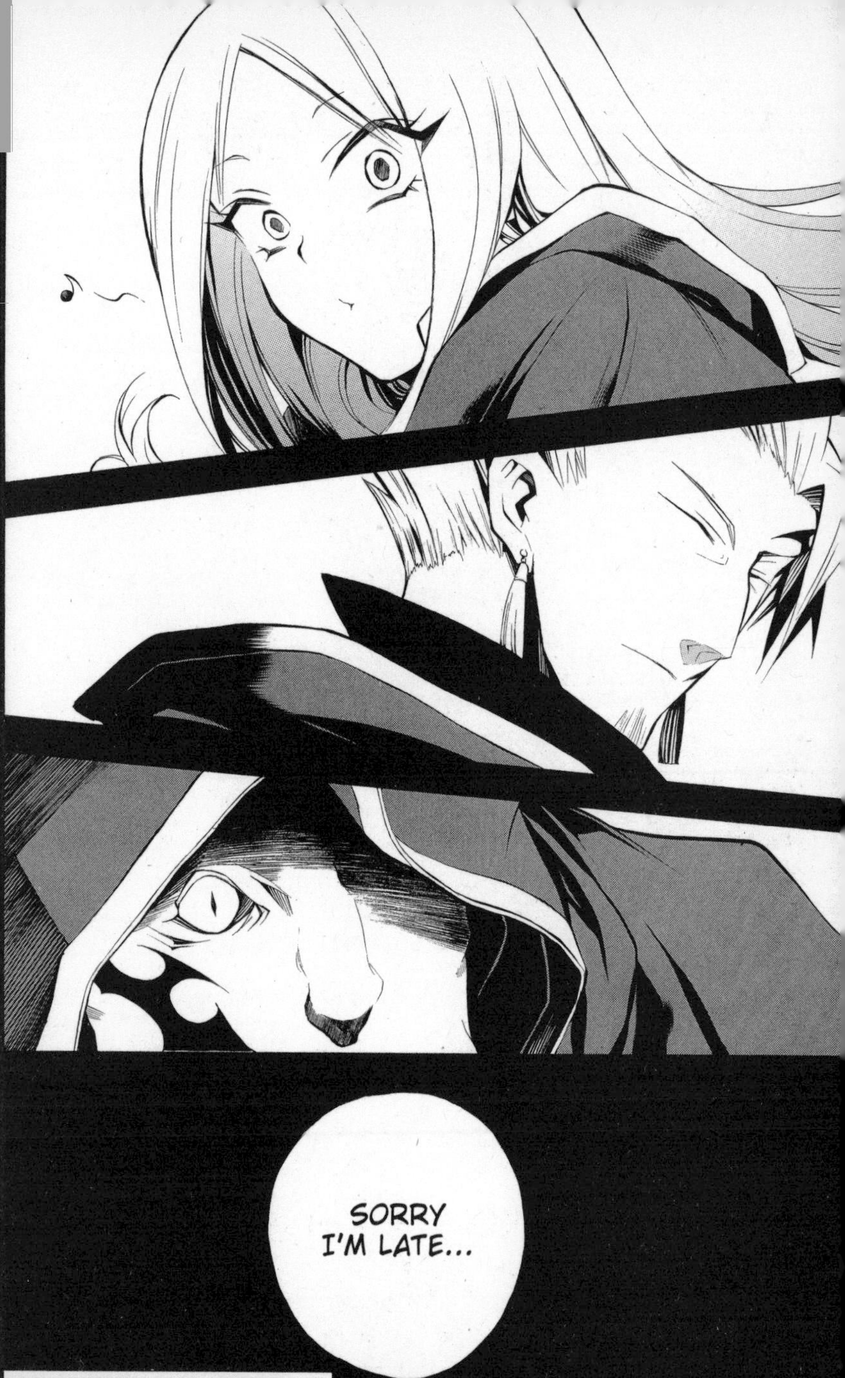
♪ ~
SORRY I'M LATE...
TO BE CONTINUED IN PANDORA HEARTS 6

BONUS: TEN YEARS OF MISTER HATTER AND MASTER GILBERT, PART THREE

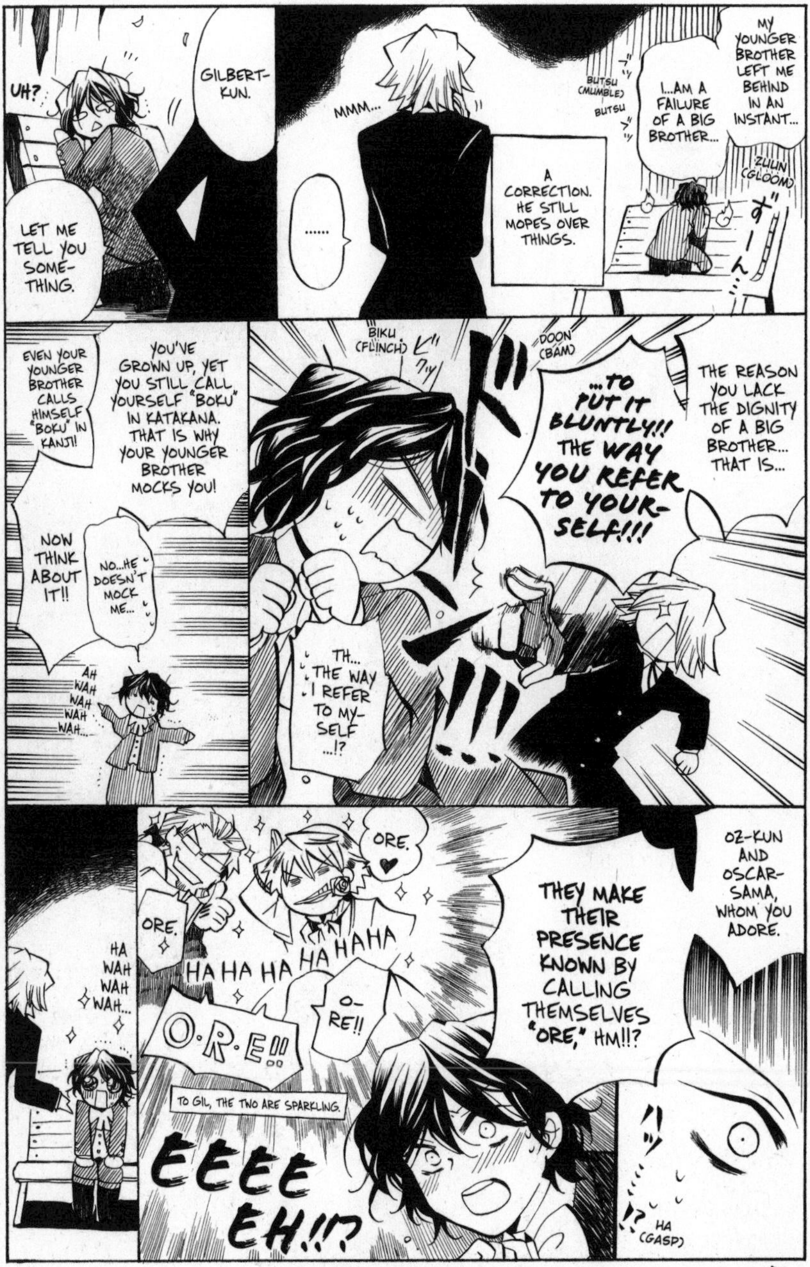
MY YOUNGER BROTHER LEFT ME BEHIND IN AN INSTANT...
I...AM A FAILURE OF A BIG BROTHER...
BUTSU (MUMBLE) BUTSU
ZUUN (GLOOM)
A CORRECTION. HE STILL MOPES OVER THINGS.
MMM...
......
GILBERT-KUN.
UH?
LET ME TELL YOU SOMETHING.
THE REASON YOU LACK THE DIGNITY OF A BIG BROTHER... THAT IS...
DOON (BAM)
...TO PUT IT BLUNTLY!! THE WAY YOU REFER TO YOURSELF!!!
BIKU (FLINCH)
TH... THE WAY I REFER TO MYSELF ...!?
YOU'VE GROWN UP, YET YOU STILL CALL YOURSELF "BOKU" IN KATAKANA. THAT IS WHY YOUR YOUNGER BROTHER MOCKS YOU!
EVEN YOUR YOUNGER BROTHER CALLS HIMSELF "BOKU" IN KANJI!
NO...HE DOESN'T MOCK ME...
NOW THINK ABOUT IT!!
AH WAH WAH WAH WAH...
OZ-KUN AND OSCAR-SAMA, WHOM YOU ADORE.
HA (GASP)
THEY MAKE THEIR PRESENCE KNOWN BY CALLING THEMSELVES "ORE," HM!!?
ORE.
ORE.
HA HA HA HA HA HA
O-RE!!
O·R·E!!
TO GIL, THE TWO ARE SPARKLING.
EEEEEH!!?
HA WAH WAH WAH...

MANGAKA'S CONFESSION...I'M SORRY, I FORGOT TO DRAW EMILY.

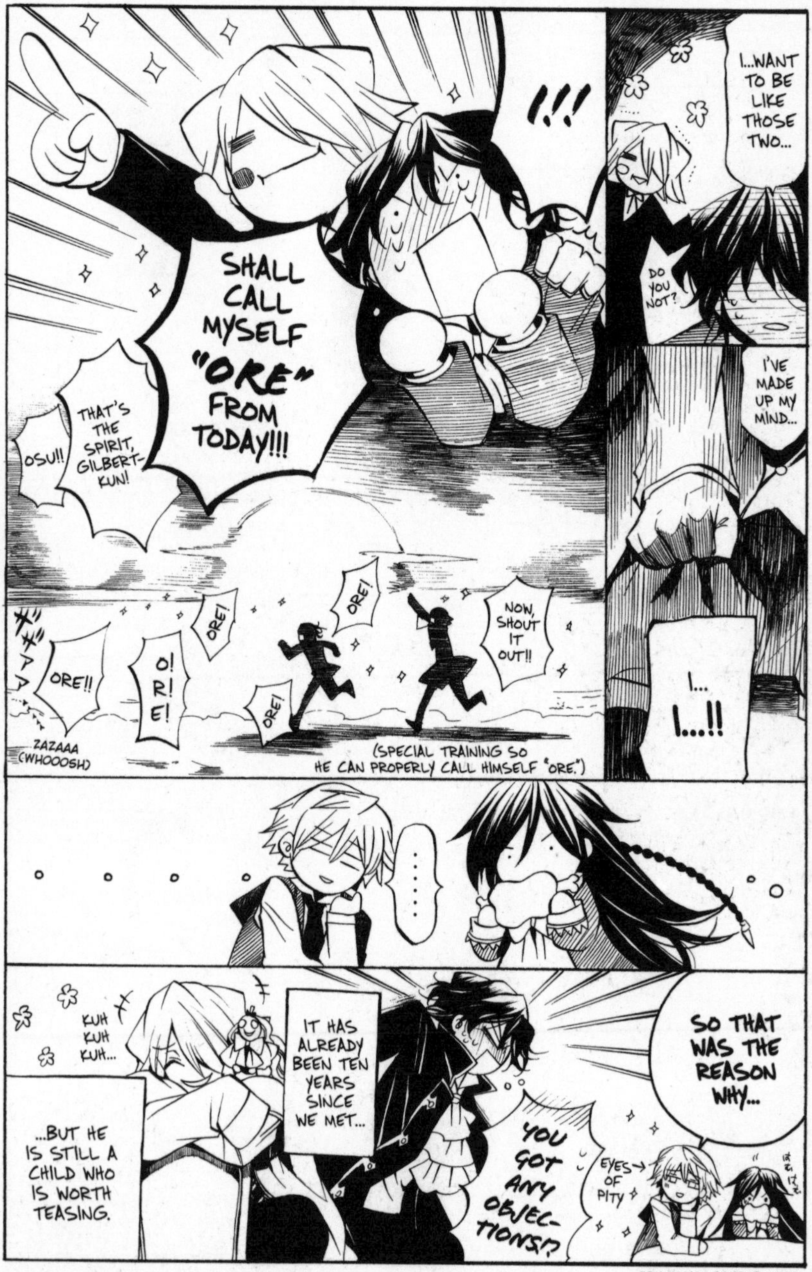
I...WANT TO BE LIKE THOSE TWO...
DO YOU NOT?
I'VE MADE UP MY MIND...
I... I...!!
I.!!
SHALL CALL MYSELF "ORE" FROM TODAY!!!!
THAT'S THE SPIRIT, GILBERT-KUN!
OSU!!
NOW, SHOUT IT OUT!!
ORE!
ORE!
ORE!
O! R! E!
ORE!!
ZAZAAA (WHOOOSH)
(SPECIAL TRAINING SO HE CAN PROPERLY CALL HIMSELF "ORE.")
° ° ° °
......
°
SO THAT WAS THE REASON WHY...
EYES OF PITY
YOU GOT ANY OBJECTIONS!?
IT HAS ALREADY BEEN TEN YEARS SINCE WE MET...
...BUT HE IS STILL A CHILD WHO IS WORTH TEASING.
KUH KUH KUH...

SFX: HAMU (CHEW) HAMU

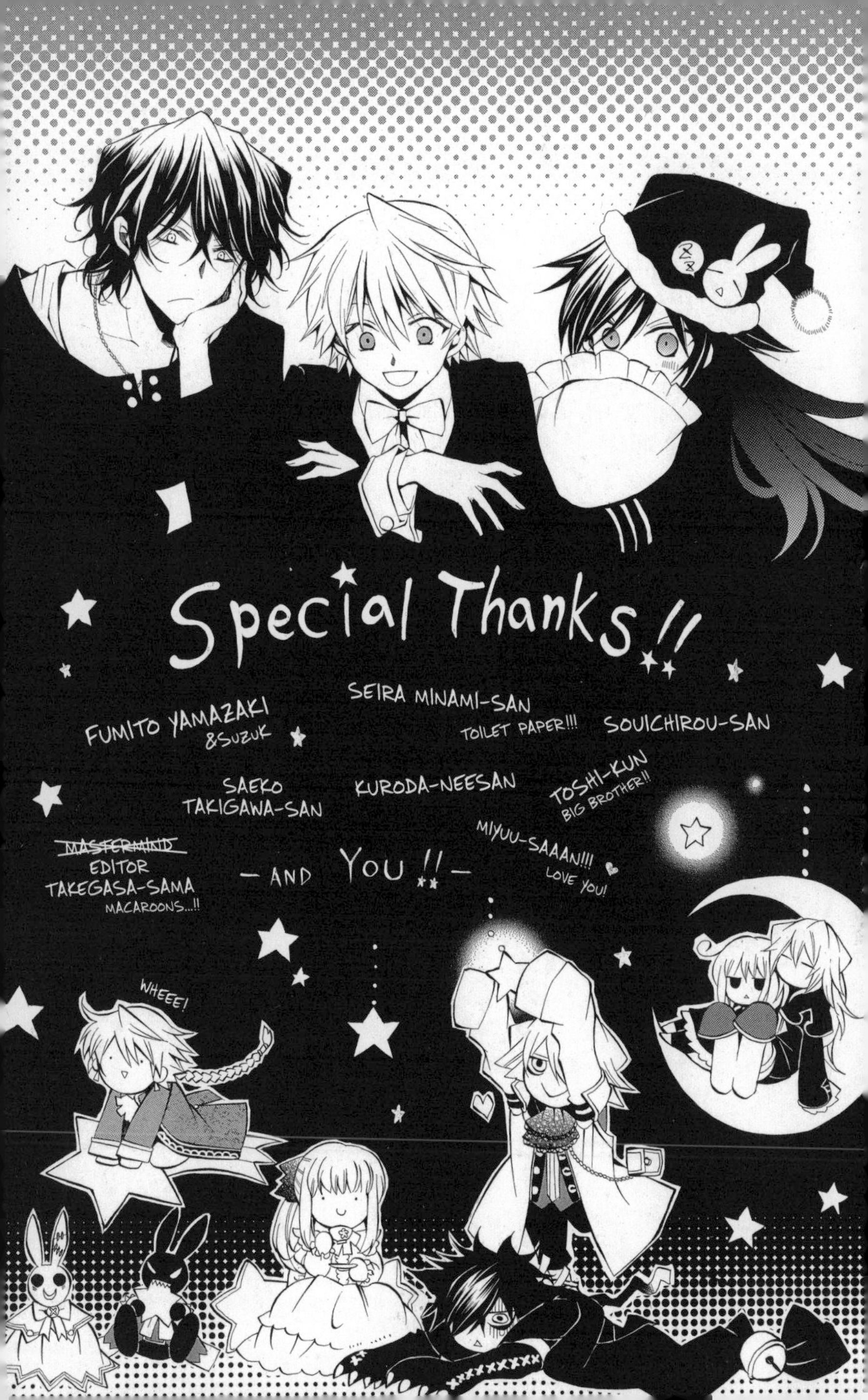

Special Thanks!!
SEIRA MINAMI-SAN
TOILET PAPER!!!
FUMITO YAMAZAKI
&SUZUK
SOUICHIROU-SAN
SAEKO
TAKIGAWA-SAN
KURODA-NEESAN
TOSHI-KUN
BIG BROTHER!!
~~MASTERMIND~~
EDITOR
TAKEGASA-SAMA
MACAROONS...!!
—AND YOU!!—
MIYUU-SAAAN!!!
LOVE YOU!
WHEEE!

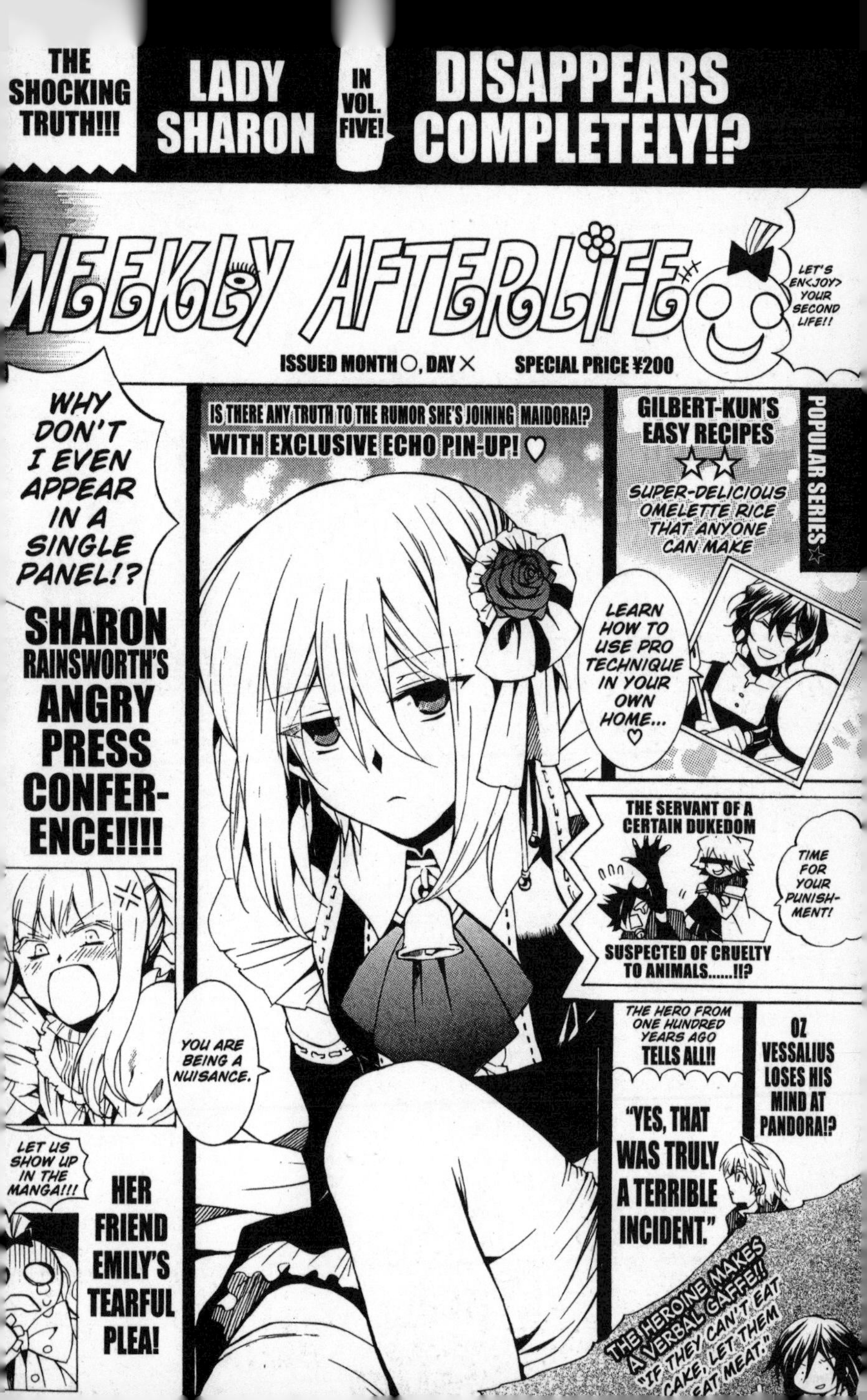

THE SHOCKING TRUTH!!!
LADY SHARON
IN VOL. FIVE!
DISAPPEARS COMPLETELY!?
WEEKLY AFTERLIFE
LET'S EN<JOY> YOUR SECOND LIFE!!
ISSUED MONTH ○, DAY ×
SPECIAL PRICE ¥200
POPULAR SERIES ☆
GILBERT-KUN'S EASY RECIPES ☆☆
SUPER-DELICIOUS OMELETTE RICE THAT ANYONE CAN MAKE
LEARN HOW TO USE PRO TECHNIQUE IN YOUR OWN HOME... ♡
IS THERE ANY TRUTH TO THE RUMOR SHE'S JOINING MAIDORA!?
WITH EXCLUSIVE ECHO PIN-UP! ♡
WHY DON'T I EVEN APPEAR IN A SINGLE PANEL!?
SHARON RAINSWORTH'S ANGRY PRESS CONFERENCE!!!!!
THE SERVANT OF A CERTAIN DUKEDOM
TIME FOR YOUR PUNISHMENT!
SUSPECTED OF CRUELTY TO ANIMALS......!!?
YOU ARE BEING A NUISANCE.
THE HERO FROM ONE HUNDRED YEARS AGO TELLS ALL!!
"YES, THAT WAS TRULY A TERRIBLE INCIDENT."
OZ VESSALIUS LOSES HIS MIND AT PANDORA!?
LET US SHOW UP IN THE MANGA!!!
HER FRIEND EMILY'S TEARFUL PLEA!
THE HEROINE MAKES A VERBAL GAFFE!!
"IF THEY CAN'T EAT CAKE, LET THEM EAT MEAT."

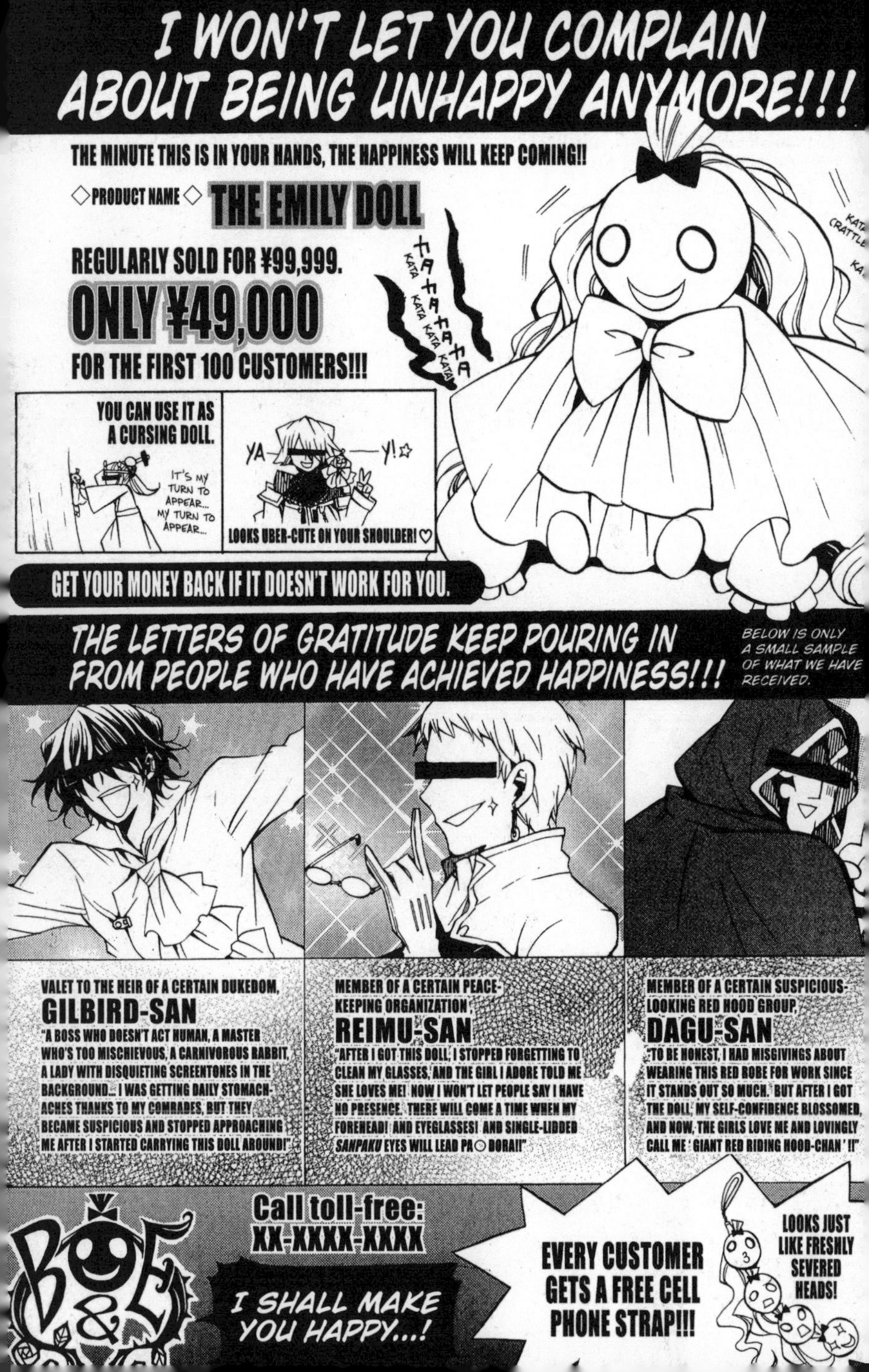
I WON'T LET YOU COMPLAIN ABOUT BEING UNHAPPY ANYMORE!!!
THE MINUTE THIS IS IN YOUR HANDS, THE HAPPINESS WILL KEEP COMING!!
◇PRODUCT NAME◇ THE EMILY DOLL
REGULARLY SOLD FOR ¥99,999.
ONLY ¥49,000
FOR THE FIRST 100 CUSTOMERS!!!
カタカタカタカタ KATA KATA KATA KATA
YOU CAN USE IT AS A CURSING DOLL.
IT'S MY TURN TO APPEAR... MY TURN TO APPEAR...
YA——Y!☆
LOOKS UBER-CUTE ON YOUR SHOULDER! ♡
GET YOUR MONEY BACK IF IT DOESN'T WORK FOR YOU.
THE LETTERS OF GRATITUDE KEEP POURING IN FROM PEOPLE WHO HAVE ACHIEVED HAPPINESS!!!
BELOW IS ONLY A SMALL SAMPLE OF WHAT WE HAVE RECEIVED.
VALET TO THE HEIR OF A CERTAIN DUKEDOM, GILBIRD-SAN
"A BOSS WHO DOESN'T ACT HUMAN, A MASTER WHO'S TOO MISCHIEVOUS, A CARNIVOROUS RABBIT, A LADY WITH DISQUIETING SCREENTONES IN THE BACKGROUND... I WAS GETTING DAILY STOMACH-ACHES THANKS TO MY COMRADES, BUT THEY BECAME SUSPICIOUS AND STOPPED APPROACHING ME AFTER I STARTED CARRYING THIS DOLL AROUND!"
MEMBER OF A CERTAIN PEACE-KEEPING ORGANIZATION, REIMU-SAN
"AFTER I GOT THIS DOLL, I STOPPED FORGETTING TO CLEAN MY GLASSES, AND THE GIRL I ADORE TOLD ME SHE LOVES ME! NOW I WON'T LET PEOPLE SAY I HAVE NO PRESENCE. THERE WILL COME A TIME WHEN MY FOREHEAD! AND EYEGLASSES! AND SINGLE-LIDDED SANPAKU EYES WILL LEAD PA○DORA!!"
MEMBER OF A CERTAIN SUSPICIOUS-LOOKING RED HOOD GROUP, DAGU-SAN
"TO BE HONEST, I HAD MISGIVINGS ABOUT WEARING THIS RED ROBE FOR WORK SINCE IT STANDS OUT SO MUCH. BUT AFTER I GOT THE DOLL, MY SELF-CONFIDENCE BLOSSOMED, AND NOW, THE GIRLS LOVE ME AND LOVINGLY CALL ME 'GIANT RED RIDING HOOD-CHAN'!!"
B&E
Call toll-free: XX-XXXX-XXXX
I SHALL MAKE YOU HAPPY...!
EVERY CUSTOMER GETS A FREE CELL PHONE STRAP!!!
LOOKS JUST LIKE FRESHLY SEVERED HEADS!

COMMON HONORIFICS

no honorific: Indicates familiarity or closeness; if used without permission or reason, addressing someone in this manner would constitute an insult.

-san: The Japanese equivalent of Mr./Mrs./Miss. If a situation calls for politeness, this is the fail-safe honorific.

-sama: Conveys great respect; may also indicate that the social status of the speaker is lower than that of the addressee.

-kun: Used most often when referring to boys (though it can be applied to girls as well), this indicates affection or familiarity. Occasionally used by older men among their peers, but it may also be used by anyone referring to a person of lower standing.

-chan: An affectionate honorific indicating familiarity used mostly in reference to girls; also used in reference to cute persons or animals of either gender.

boku vs. *ore* — page 175-6

These personal pronouns are both commonly used by boys and men; however, the former brings to mind a younger person or someone who is lower in a hierarchy, while the latter speaks to a more confident, assured, possibly even boastful individual. *Boku* coupled with Gil's use of katakana when referring to himself makes him seem childish and weak because hiragana and katakana are learned before kanji, which Vincent uses. Also, *ore* and the Spanish *olé* are homophones in Japanese, which is why Oz has a rose in his teeth!

Osu! — page 176

A greeting used mostly by practitioners of the martial arts.

Let's en<joy> your second life! — page 177

The "en" of "en<joy>" has been replaced by the kanji character for "grudge" (also pronounced "en"), hence the pun.

cursing doll — page 178

Sharon is performing the *ushinokoku-mairi*, where you visit a shrine in the wee hours of the morning to cast a curse on someone. A straw doll, representing a person who you hate, is nailed to a tree.

sanpaku eyes — page 178

Eyes with the whites showing beneath and on both sides of the irises.

PandoraHearts

MOCHIZUKI'S MUSINGS

VOLUME 5

One day, while I was working, I suddenly had the realization that my being able to draw manga for a living was an amazing miracle. My heart filled with gratitude for the many people who support that miracle. So I told my assistants, "Thanks for always helping me," but they brushed it off, saying, "Eh, you're being creepy!" Ha-ha, what a shock!!!!

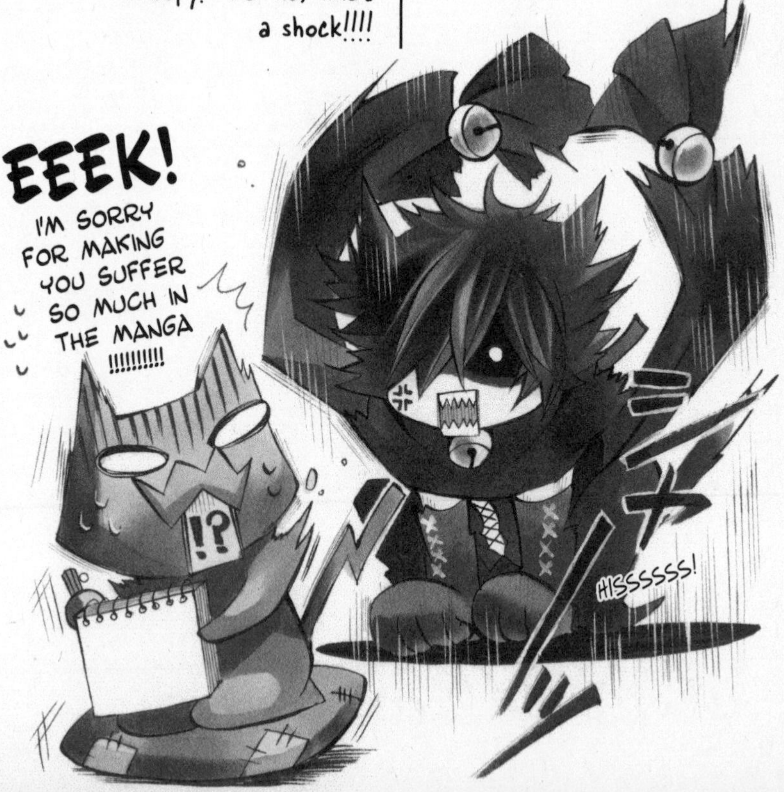
EEEK!
I'M SORRY FOR MAKING YOU SUFFER SO MUCH IN THE MANGA !!!!!!!!!
!?
HISSSSSS!

PandoraHearts

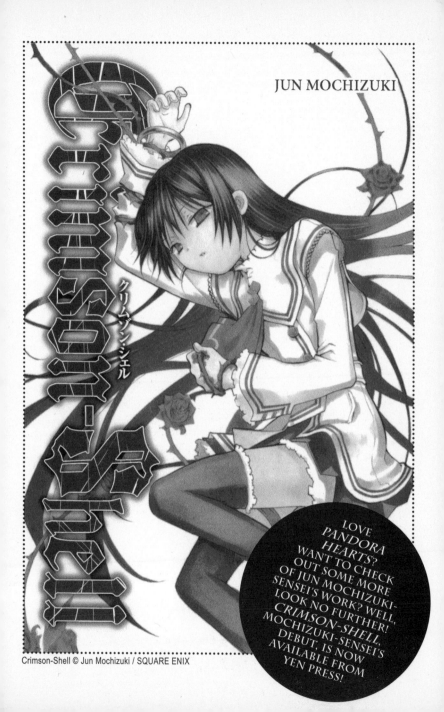

JUN MOCHIZUKI

Crimson-Shell クリムゾン・シェル

LOVE *PANDORA HEARTS*? WANT TO CHECK OUT SOME MORE OF JUN MOCHIZUKI-SENSEI'S WORK? WELL, LOOK NO FURTHER! *CRIMSON-SHELL*, MOCHIZUKI-SENSEI'S DEBUT, IS NOW AVAILABLE FROM YEN PRESS!

PandoraHearts

WANT TO READ
MANGA ON YOUR IPAD?

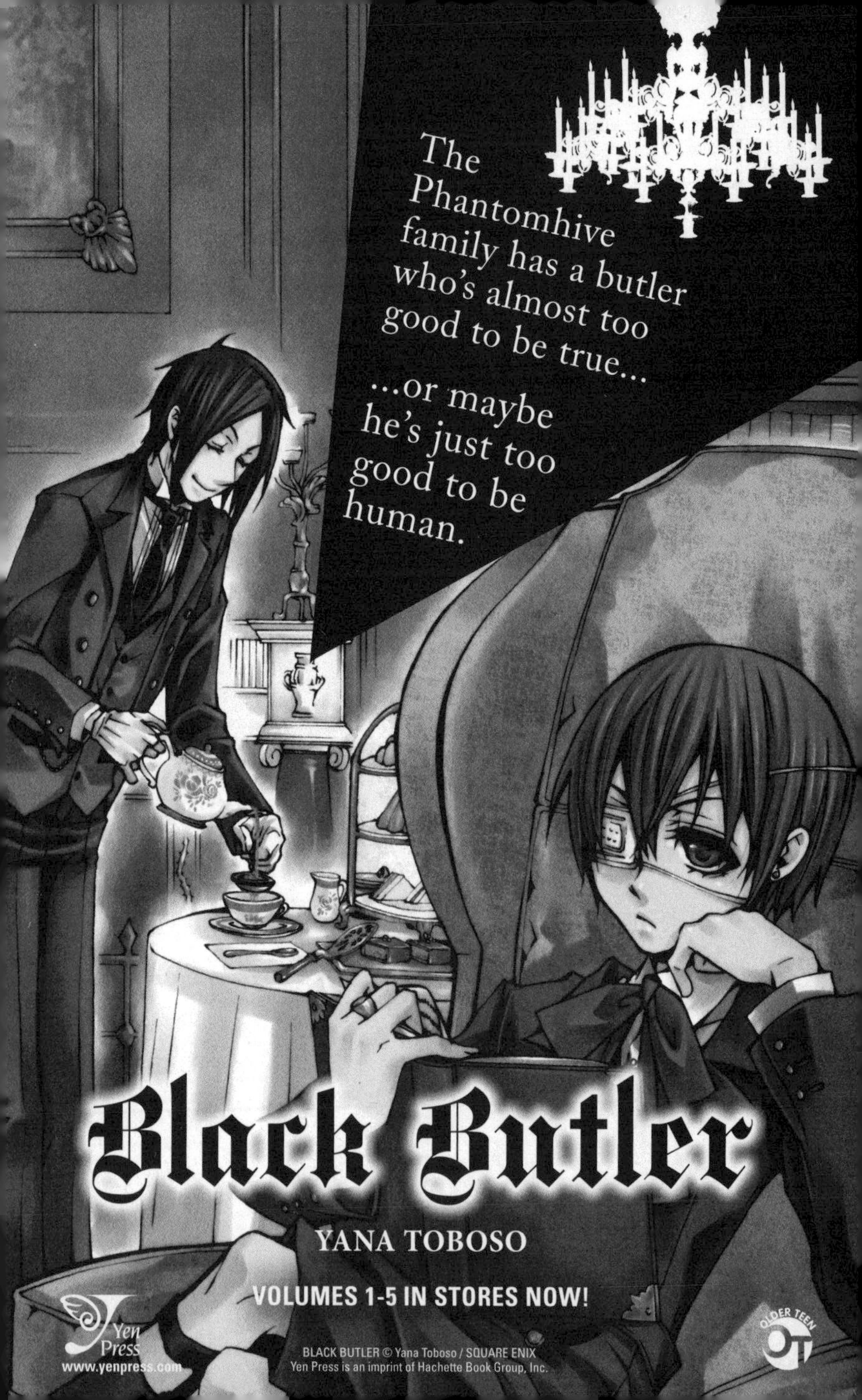
The Phantomhive family has a butler who's almost too good to be true...
...or maybe he's just too good to be human.
Black Butler
YANA TOBOSO
VOLUMES 1-5 IN STORES NOW!
Yen Press
www.yenpress.com
OLDER TEEN
OT
BLACK BUTLER © Yana Toboso / SQUARE ENIX
Yen Press is an imprint of Hachette Book Group, Inc.

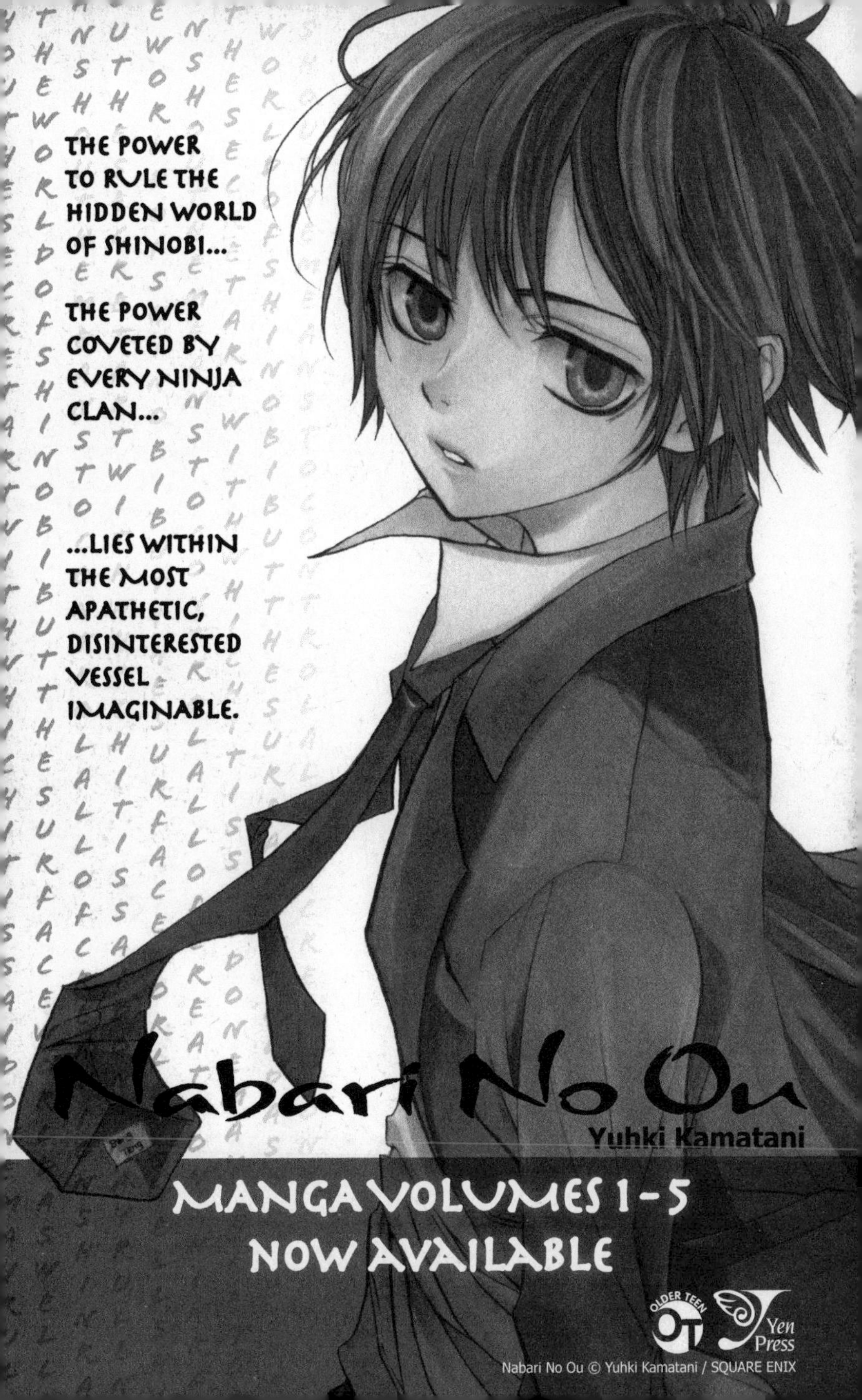
THE POWER TO RULE THE HIDDEN WORLD OF SHINOBI...
THE POWER COVETED BY EVERY NINJA CLAN...
...LIES WITHIN THE MOST APATHETIC, DISINTERESTED VESSEL IMAGINABLE.
Nabari No Ou
Yuhki Kamatani
MANGA VOLUMES 1-5 NOW AVAILABLE
OLDER TEEN OT
Yen Press
Nabari No Ou © Yuhki Kamatani / SQUARE ENIX

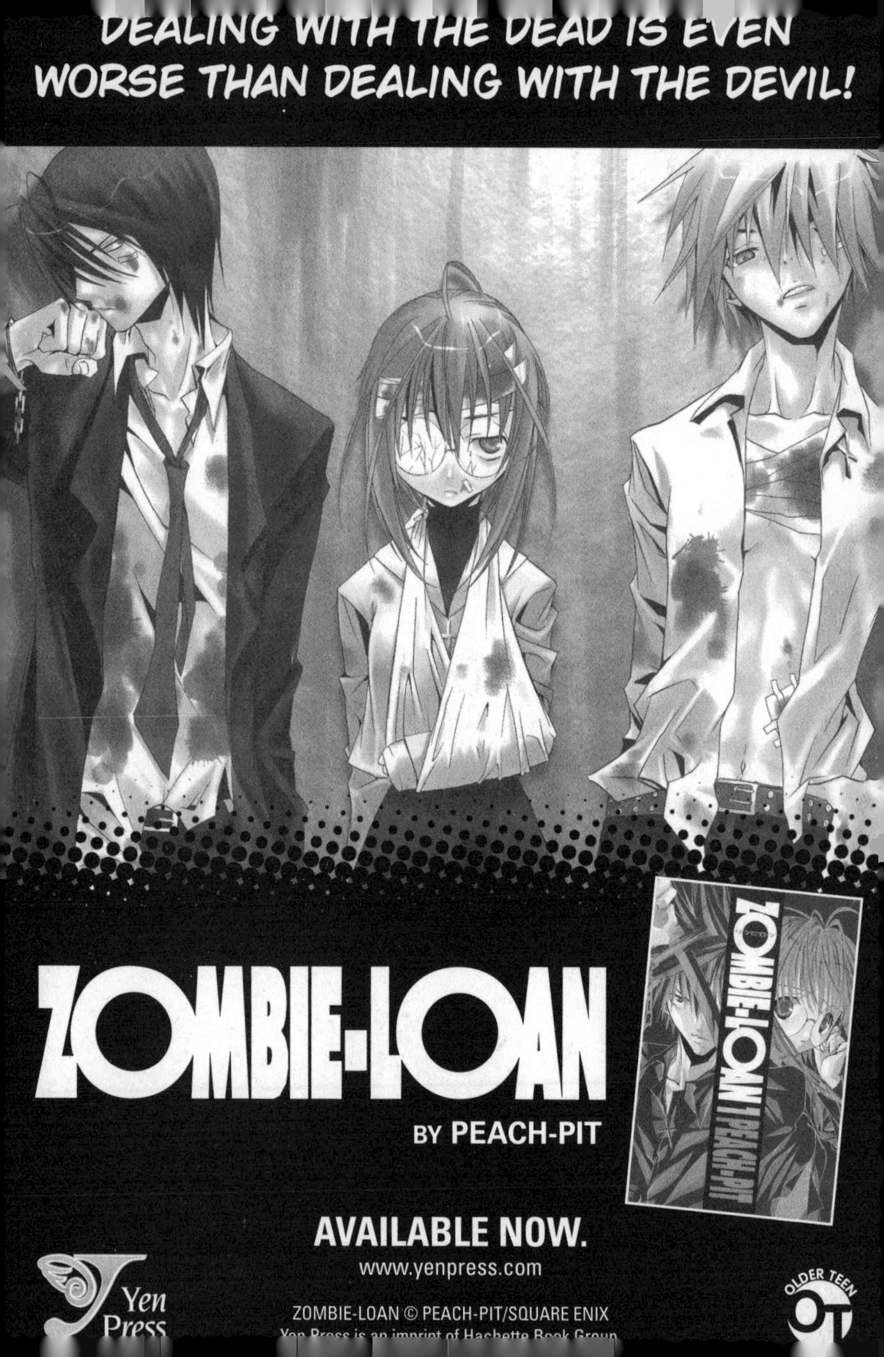
DEALING WITH THE DEAD IS EVEN WORSE THAN DEALING WITH THE DEVIL!
ZOMBIE-LOAN
ZOMBIE-LOAN 1 PEACH-PIT
BY PEACH-PIT
AVAILABLE NOW.
www.yenpress.com
Yen Press
OLDER TEEN OT
ZOMBIE-LOAN © PEACH-PIT/SQUARE ENIX
Yen Press is an imprint of Hachette Book Group

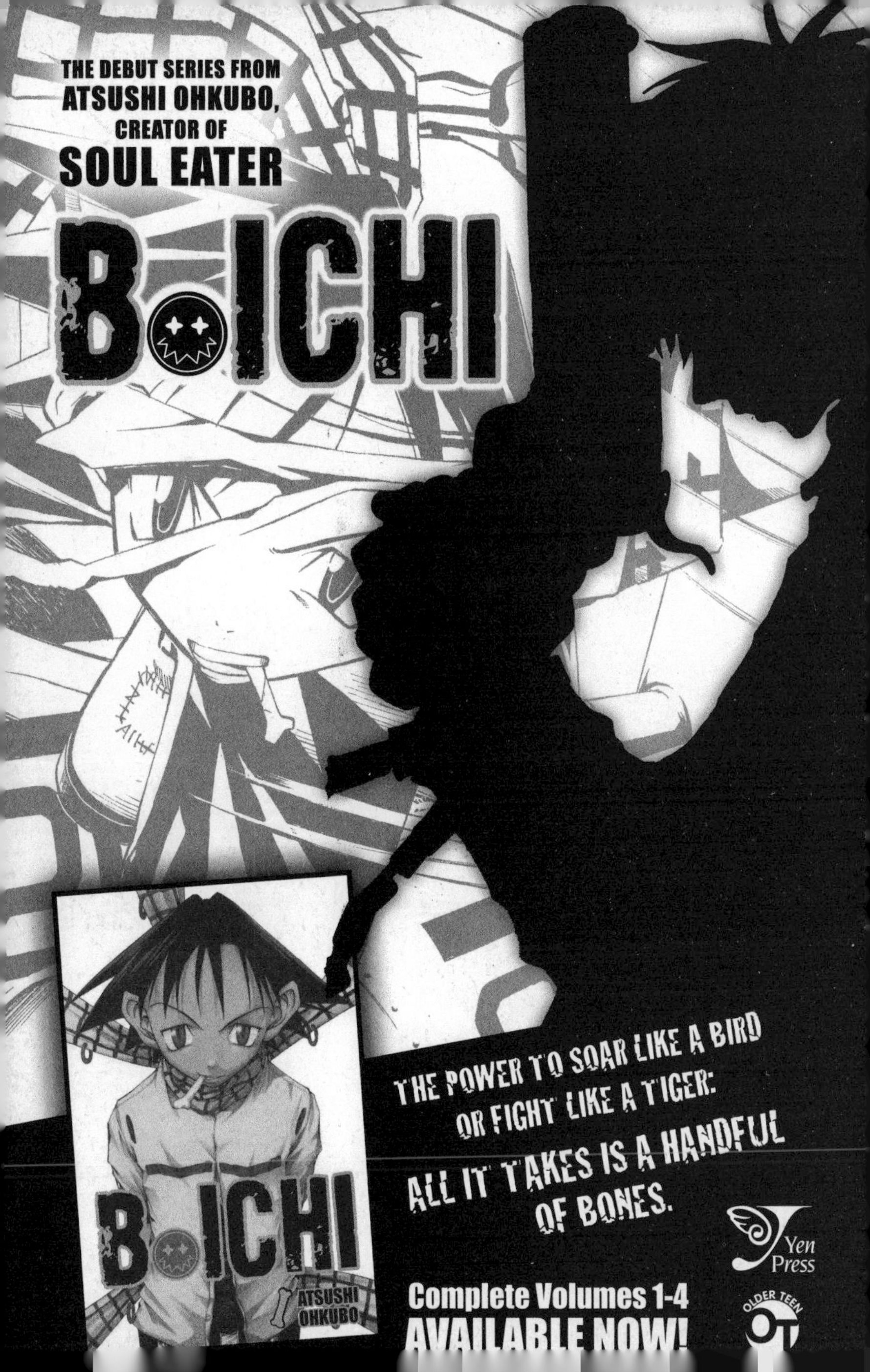
THE DEBUT SERIES FROM ATSUSHI OHKUBO, CREATOR OF SOUL EATER
B ICHI
THE POWER TO SOAR LIKE A BIRD OR FIGHT LIKE A TIGER:
ALL IT TAKES IS A HANDFUL OF BONES.
B ICHI
ATSUSHI OHKUBO
Yen Press
Complete Volumes 1-4
AVAILABLE NOW!
OLDER TEEN
OT

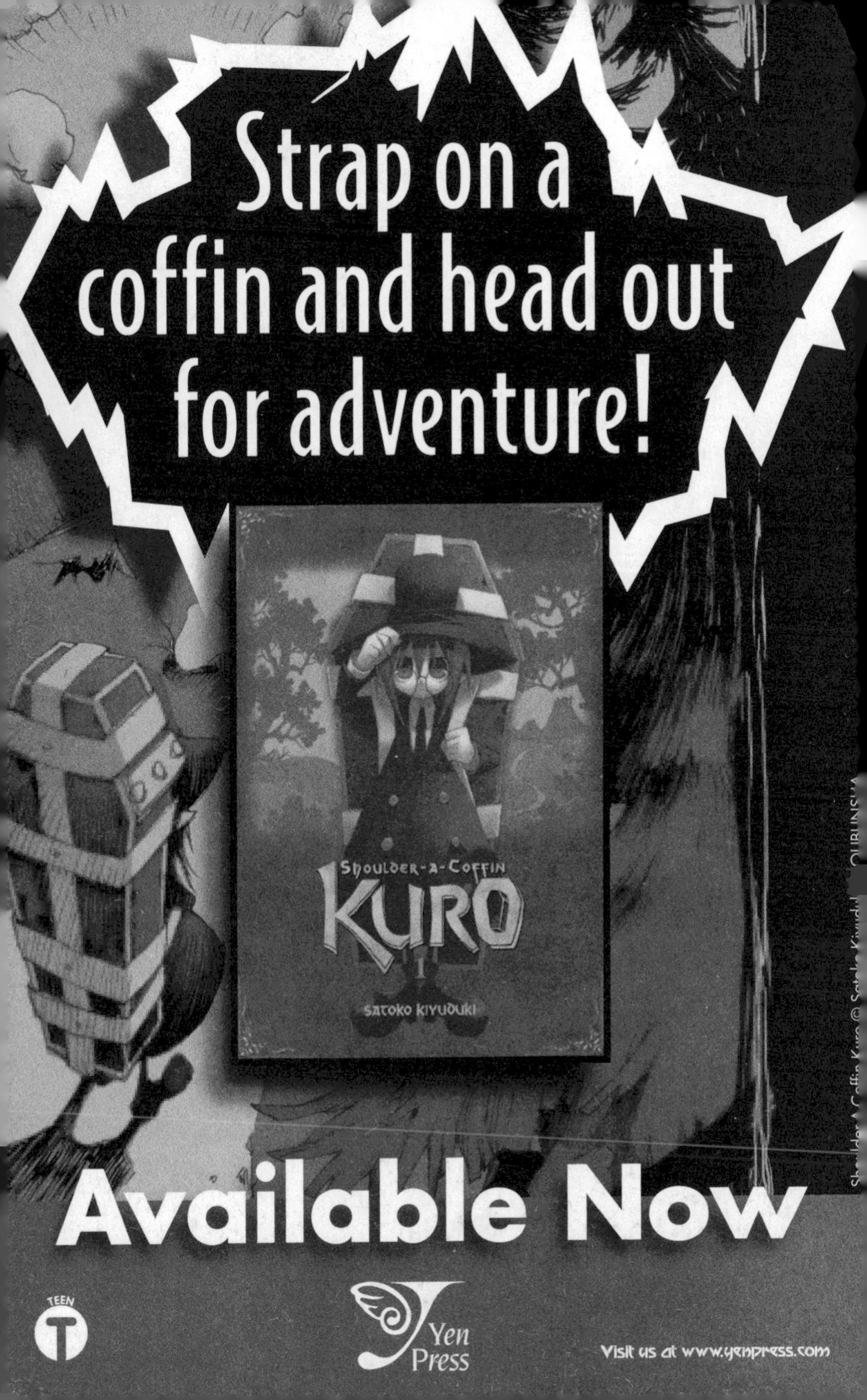
Strap on a coffin and head out for adventure!
SHOULDER-A-COFFIN
KURO
1
SATOKO KIYUDUKI
Available Now
TEEN
T
Yen Press
Visit us at www.yenpress.com

PandoraHearts ❺

JUN MOCHIZUKI

Translation: Tomo Kimura • Lettering: Alexis Eckerman

PandoraHearts Vol. 5 © 2008 Jun Mochizuki / SQUARE ENIX CO., LTD. All rights reserved. First published in Japan in 2008 by SQUARE ENIX CO., LTD. English translation rights arranged with SQUARE ENIX CO., LTD. and Hachette Book Group through Tuttle-Mori Agency, Inc.

Translation © 2011 by SQUARE ENIX CO., LTD.

Yen Press
Hachette Book Group
237 Park Avenue, New York, NY 10017

www.HachetteBookGroup.com
www.YenPress.com

Yen Press is an imprint of Hachette Book Group, Inc. The Yen Press name and logo are trademarks of Hachette Book Group, Inc.

First Yen Press Edition: April 2011

ISBN: 978-0-316-07612-8

10 9 8 7

BVG

Printed in the United States of America